The World Wide Web for Scientists & Engineers

The World Wide Web for Scientists & Engineers

A Complete Reference for Navigating, Researching & Publishing Online

Brian J. Thomas

SPIE
PRESS

SPIE—The International Society for Optical Engineering, Bellingham, Washington

IEEE
PRESS

The Institute of Electrical and Electronics Engineers, Inc., New York

The American Society of Mechanical Engineers, New York

Society of Automotive Engineers, Inc., Warrendale, Pennsylvania

The Institution of Electrical Engineers, London, UK

Library of Congress Cataloging-in-Publication Data

Thomas, Brian J.
    The World Wide Web for scientists and engineers : a complete
reference for navigating, researching, and publishing online / by
Brian J. Thomas.
        p. cm.
    Includes bibliographical references and index.
    ISBN 0-8194-2775-6 (softcover)
    1. Science—Computer network resources.   2. Engineering—Computer
network resources.   3. Online data processing.   4. Electronic
publishing.   5. World Wide Web (Information retrieval system)
I. Title.
Q179.97.T48   1998
004.67'8'0245—dc21   97-43434
                                                            CIP

Copublished by

SPIE—The International Society
    for Optical Engineering
P.O. Box 10
Bellingham, WA 98227-0010
Telephone: 360/676-3290
Fax: 360/647-1445
E-mail: spie@spie.org
WWW: http://www.spie.org

The Institute of Electrical
    and Electronics Engineers
445 Hoes Lane
P.O. Box 1331
Piscataway, NJ 08855-1331
Telephone: 1-800-678-IEEE
Fax: 732/981-9667
E-mail: customer.service@ieee.org
WWW: http://www.ieee.org

American Society of Mechanical Engineers
22 Law Drive, Box 290
Fairfield, NJ 07007-2900
Telephone: 1-800-843-2763
Fax: 201/882-1717
E-mail: infocentral@asme.org
WWW: http://www.asme.org

Society of Automotive Engineers
400 Commonwealth Dr.
Warrendale, PA 15096-0001
Telephone: 412/776-4841
Fax: 412/776-5760
WWW: http://www.sae.org

The Institution of Electrical Engineers
Michael Faraday House
Six Hills Way, Stevenage, Herts.
SG1 2AY United Kingdom
Telephone: +44 (0)1438 313311
Fax: +44 (0)1438 360079
E-mail: books@iee.org.uk
WWW: http://www.iee.org.uk

Printed in the United States of America.

10 9 8 7 6 5 4 3 2 1

For My Mother

CONTENTS

PART II: WEB AUTHORING & PUBLISHING

PREFACE

I wrote my first book, *The Internet for Scientists and Engineers*, in 1994. Back then, the Internet was a crazed amalgam of tools and technologies all held together with an epoxy of Unix and TCP/IP. Relatively user-hostile tools such as telnet, gopher, and FTP were the foundation, and the then-new World Wide Web was a bright yet minor star in the Internet constellation.

But today it is telnet and FTP that dwell in the distant corners of cyberspace, and the Web is a labyrinthine house of Gothic proportions. After two major revisions, my first book could no longer contain the ever-expanding Web as merely a chapter among many. And so, this book was born.

This book bridges a number of gaps in the Web's current state. While most of us have learned to point and click our way from site to site, the novelty of this limited exercise has worn off, as has its utility, and so now we're ready to step up to the next level. I define that next level as three distinct yet closely overlapping areas, and each is covered in this book's three major divisions as described below:

I.   Essential Tools & Applications

The emerging collection of software tools, applications, and services is enough to scare anyone away from cyberspace. The chapters in this section are designed to disentangle today's Web and focus on what's essential, beginning first with a comprehensive introduction to Web technologies and business directions as they relate to science and engineering. Following this are strategies for choosing an Internet service provider that's right for your needs (or shopping for a better one), and then a look at the essential tools for communicating with colleagues and co-workers on the Web, including e-mail and discussion lists, all using examples from today's Web browser environment. Finally we'll concentrate on the browser itself, which as one of the most sophisticated software applications available today is also often the most frustrating. Today's Web browsers try to be all things to all people, and so their strongest features can get lost among all the bells and whistles that marketing departments insist on adding. The chapter on Web browsers and applications cuts through all that and shows you how to leverage your browser to meet your needs, not someone else's.

II.   Web Authoring & Publishing

The opportunity to publish your own Web pages is one of the most exciting and potentially useful aspects of being online. The tools and technologies emerging today make it relatively easy to put essentially any type of information online. But beyond this utility are more profound socio-economic factors that will affect the scientific and engineering professions for decades to come. The chapters in this section therefore begin by providing some in-depth perspectives on electronic publishing in the sciences, and how the world of scholarly publishing is being changed by the advent of "personal publishing" on the Web. Also covered here are HTML standards and tips on problem areas and pitfalls. From this foundation we'll walk through the actual elements and processes involved in creating Web pages, including an introduction to HTML and other essential technologies. Then, for those who wish to tackle more complex Web authoring, the final chapter goes deep into the territories of advanced HTML, graphics, tables, and forms, concluding with a detailed summary of the most advanced applications available today, such as Java, JavaScript, CGIs, Cascading Style Sheets, image maps, and frames. This section concludes with an extensive reference list that tells you where to find some of the best online software resources and tutorials for all aspects of Web publishing.

III.   Searching & Researching

Nearly half of this book is devoted to using the Web as the ultimate information resource. I take two different but complementary approaches to this topic. First is a look at the big online search sites such as Yahoo, AltaVista, Excite, HotBot, Lycos, and InfoSeek. Learning to use these sites effectively is a key requirement for doing online research, and so this topic is covered in depth, starting with real-life comparisons of what I call the Big Six sites, with descriptions of how each collect and rank their contents. Then we'll look at search query construction practices for each of the sites, including advanced queries and advice on when to use which site, and how to get the best results. The chapter concludes with some sample searches on two different kinds of search engines, and features a comparison chart for all six sites in this book's Appendix. The second half of this section reflects a more traditional approach to Web-based research. It consists of a +200-page Resources section that offers hand-picked Web-site listings for 22 major technology areas. These listings attempt to take off where the online search tools end, giving the practicing scientist or engineer a comprehensive and prefiltered index to the best the Web has to offer. These resource listings are designed to be used either as a standalone reference or as a starting point for online exploration.

Beyond the practical nature of this book's many tutorials, examples, and resource listings, I have tried in all cases to place each topic within a larger context. The Web is much more than just a collection of links and cool sites. It is a sea-change in our professional lives and endeavors, particularly for those working in science, engineering, and education, for whom the Web was originally designed. The Web today represents a new way of communicating ideas, discoveries, research, and the interpersonal aspects that bind these all together. As such, the forest is still just as important as the trees.

Acknowledgments

This book would not have been possible without the contributions of many individuals. Many thanks first to the book's production team: Rick Hermann, editor; Carrie Binschus, compositor; Dixie Cheek, proofreading; Rodney Zeiler (Baron & Co.), cover design; and Eric Pepper, publisher. All had an important role in bringing this project to completion.

My respect and appreciation is also extended to the book's reviewers, James A. Harrington, Rutgers University, and Henri H. Arsenault, Université Laval, whose comments and insights contributed to the finished work. Finally, my sincere thanks to all my friends and colleagues who simply tolerated me these past few years, especially Andria Bader, Robert Dorsett, Melissa Eisenhauer, Marybeth Manning, Jayne Norton, and everyone at SPIE.

Part I

ESSENTIAL TOOLS
& APPLICATIONS

Chapter 1

INTRODUCTION

It could be argued that the World Wide Web was simply a vacuum waiting to be filled. This would certainly explain the Big Bang-like explosion that has swept most of this planet for the past few years. Any organization without a Web site today is the exception, not the rule. There are something on the order of 60 million references housed at some of the larger Web search sites like Excite and InfoSeek. Where did all this information come from? The only explanation is that it was there all along. It just needed a void to fill.

Enter the World Wide Web, the penultimate example of distributed computing, or "client-server" technology, as it is sometimes also called, because the Internet and World Wide Web are not really a repository, but rather a cooperative network consisting of millions of computers of all shapes, sizes, and operating systems. This is the first real accomplishment of the Internet: creating data ubiquity.

This ubiquity is at the heart of the Internet's success. While traditional publishing is still the foundation of scholarly discourse and technical communication, the model can no longer support the load. The world of science and engineering has simply gotten too large, complex, and fast. Journals, proceedings, transactions, dissertations, and other paper-based research continue to roll off the presses, but there is no room left on the library shelves. Compounding this is the fact that the process of scientific discovery has itself outpaced paper and ink's efficacy.

And so here I am, writing a book, the paper-and-ink entity you hold in your hands, about all this. The ultimate hypocrisy? I hope not. The book as an information tool is by no means dead. What is ailing, however, is the paradigm in which we think about information. After all, it's not that all those journals and proceedings are any less valuable today than they were 50 years ago. Of course they are not. The problem is access and timeliness. The promise of the Web is universal and instant access to all the information that may never see a bookshelf, despite its value to the professional scientist or engineer. The solution to the problem then is data ubiquity—that is, anytime, anywhere access to all information sources—coupled with smart tools to mine that data effectively. We've got the first part of this equation solved, at least in theory. It's the second part that's still troublesome.

A friend of mine authors an online webzine with the slogan, "All noise, all the time." This is an apt description of the World Wide Web. A simple search on AltaVista will show you just how noisy the Web can really be. This is not so much a criticism as it is simple fact, because while the strength of the Web is its ubiquity, this is also its Achilles' heel. What is needed most are tools and innovations that help you search, sort, and collect information spread across literally millions of archives with the same ease and transparency as if it were all there on your hard drive. Obviously this is a challenging task, and it is therefore where much of today's Web development is focused.

Publishing on the Web

The Web today is marked by turmoil more than ever. At the forefront are mega-players Netscape and Microsoft, who together dominate the browser market, and who continue their belligerent tug-of-war over standards, features, and even foundation technologies such as HTML. On the development side, Sun Microsystems' much-hyped Java programming language continues to swing wildly in the ever-fickle winds blown by Netscape, Microsoft, and a myriad of smaller developers. New technologies emerge literally every day, each trying to either usurp yesterday's announcement or pour it into a new bottle. All of this spells instability in an industry that has never known anything else. And for users and authors on the Web, it means continued bouts with buggy bloatware, mediocre performance, and rampant inconsistency.

But that's the bad news. The good news is much more interesting. Science and engineering are forging ahead stronger than ever on the Web, and in some ways (as we'll see) beyond it. For one thing, the fog that has been hanging over scholarly publishing for years appears to be lifting, albeit slowly, due in part to a confluence of technology and viable economic directions. Publishers are starting to "get it," as we say, by finally moving away from proprietary access solutions and arcane pricing models, and instead embracing more open standards as the HTML and PDF (arguably a de facto standard, despite its proprietary roots). They are also starting to recognize the value of being part of the bigger picture, and as such are beginning to offer their products in ever more bite-sized packages. After all, why buy the book when you only want one article? Enter online document delivery. The concept of on-demand delivery of journal and proceedings papers, technical abstracts, transactions, and other similar works has been limited to paper-based solutions until recently, but the major obstacle—technology—is finally stepping aside. Publishers can now convert existing and new content into digital formats for online delivery, and can collect a payment for that information before delivering it, all within minutes. Granted, this is still all relatively new technology to most of the world, but its adaptation offers some clear and viable directions here.

At the head of these liberating technologies is the Web itself. Most of us are now familiar with the process of clicking on a link and starting a download process. The next level of this is something many will also be familiar with: paying online. Thousands of companies today take payments online; whether they subsequently deliver their product online is dependent on the type of product. Obviously some things lend themselves to this model better than others. Software, for example, is ideal for online delivery, whereas hardware is not. But in either case, the customer's expectations are being met. When I buy hardware I know it's going to arrive FedEx the next day.

And so it should be with information, which lends itself eminently to real-time online delivery. Until now, the big technical obstacle in delivering information online has been lack of a universal container for it. Universal, in this case, encompasses two qualities: portability and readability. Before I purchase a technical paper online, I need to know that I can open it when it arrives on my hard drive. Once it's there, I need to have something to view the paper, something with acceptable fidelity, resolution, and utility.

After a few years of continuous product improvements (and dogged marketing), Adobe's Portable Document Format (PDF) is poised to be a universal container. While not a perfect technology by any means, PDF (aka Acrobat) has a tremendous user base, with free reader software being distributed by the millions, and more recently, seamless integration into browsers like Netscape. The Acrobat Reader is available for all major computer operating systems, which fills the ubiquity requirement. It has acceptable fidelity and utility, especially if the original document is available in some kind of ASCII-based format prior to conversion to PDF. (For more on this, see the section in Chapter 6 on PDF.)

The second big obstacle to online document delivery in the sciences has been economics. In the realm of scholarly and technical publishing, the subscription model has dominated. Institutional subscriptions have been especially critical, since libraries have traditionally been the primary access point for information. So naturally when the Web first emerged, many publishers dabbled with "online subscription" models. These of course all failed miserably, if only because the electronic commerce and security issues had not yet been resolved. But they also failed because they did not take into account a fundamental shift in the way information would be viewed in an online future.

Over the next few years, I believe we'll see an explosion of scientific and engineering documents available on the Web. Many if not most publishers are now gearing up for this or have already launched their "digital library" initiatives. Their motivation today is driven not only by the technology, which is opening up the doors, but also by the promise of a revenue model that might work: pay-per-view, or more accurately, pay-per-download. Online document delivery will become a reality.

After the Big Bang: HTML-Based Evolution

Beyond publishing, other developments are also showing great promise for science and engineering on the Web. The first is HTML itself, the foundation upon which the Web rests. As touched on throughout this book, HTML is a relatively limited page description language that at times seems to audibly creak under all the renovation it has undergone since the first days of the Web. Certainly, this reconstruction process has been hugely successful in making the Web something more than just a bunch of blue and red hypertext links on a flat gray background. But HTML was never designed to be much more than that, so the sooner we can hop onto the next wave, the better.

It seems clear right now that the next wave for HTML will involve other derivatives of SGML (Standard Generalized Markup Language), of which HTML is a subset. Dynamic HTML (DHTML) and Extensible Markup Language (XML) are the new derivatives of note. DHTML is the murkier of the two because it has different meanings depending on whom you ask. To Microsoft, DHTML is object technology being built into Internet Explorer that lets Web programmers develop programming elements that can be launched by plain vanilla HTML statements. Currently DHTML is being viewed with caution by developers because Netscape's definition is, of course, markedly different. However, this innovation does have long-term promise.

XML has even more potential. As a true subset of SGML and fully backed by the World Wide Web Consortium (W3C, the standards group that governs HTML), XML offers a way for developers to create their own custom HTML tags that will nevertheless be recognized by an XML-enabled browser. Both Netscape and Microsoft have made it clear that they intend to fully support XML. In fact, XML is already being implemented by some of the more innovative network managers in their intranets. A good example is a large metropolitan hospital system that has developed tags that are used to access the hospital's main patient database so that any authorized doctor or nurse can call up a patient's record from anywhere via a standard browser like Netscape, even from home or on the road via modem connection.

One specific use of XML bears elaboration: Mathematical Markup Language, or MathML, which is a proposed XML application for describing mathematical notation and capturing both its structure and content. The goal of MathML is to enable mathematics to be served, received, and processed on the Web, just as HTML has enabled this functionality for text.

Those of you who have tried to put anything more complicated than a super-script on your Web page know that equations on the Web simply don't exist in text form. This is because, as described in Chapter 6, HTML only supports the ASCII character set. The situation is not dissimilar to the world of mainstream computing, where complex markup languages like T$_e$X are used to define and display equations.

As I write this, since the XML standard itself is not yet finished, the launch of MathML is still pending. Once the initial MathML proposal is approved, we'll start to see first implementations in the form of browser applets or plug-ins that can parse and display the new markup codes, no doubt followed by HTML editing software that can generate MathML from probably a palette-based sys-tem. If done right and widely accepted, it will probably make T$_e$X and its de-rivatives obsolete. You won't see me crying over this one.

The most recent HTML-based promise for the future is something called Cas-cading Style Sheets (CSS), which are part of the current HTML 4.0 specification. While on the surface CSS appears to be something only a diehard HTML geek could love, it bears mentioning because it represents something much larger. The implementation of CSS fundamentally changes the way Web pages and sites are constructed. It is a workaround to the more exasperating problems that HTML's simple page description language induces. Style sheets take a Web page or site and turn it into something more like a complex word processing document. If you've ever worked with styles and macros in Microsoft Word or Corel WordPerfect, you'll understand style sheets on a conceptual level.

But this isn't the big news. The big news is that CSS-style page construction is in essence planned obsolescence for much of the HTML code on the Web today. A careful reading of the HTML 4.0 specification reveals this shift in direction. The truth is that HTML is getting further and further from the would-be Week-end Webber. Now, this statement may seem at cross-purposes with much of this book's content, which includes a whole section on Web authoring and pub-lishing. But it is not, or at least not yet. It would probably be more accurate to say that the world of Web page authoring is splintering. While individuals will still be able to create quite excellent Web pages using the tools of their choice—with or without style sheets—for quite some time, the world of professional site development is heading quickly toward the new models of CSS, CGIs and scripting, and dynamically generated content. But unless you're planning on becoming a professional Web site developer, this shift is simply something to be aware of and watch.

Much Ado about Java

And then of course we have Java, quite possibly the defining four-letter word of the Digital Age. Java has been both revered and ravaged by the industry that spawned it. Not a month goes by lately when some aspect of Java is not de-bated, touted, decried, and even sued for. Frankly, I'm quite weary of it all. From a user's perspective, it still appears to be much ado about nothing.

Yet, I know the promise and potential are there. Companies the size of Sun and Microsoft don't embrace any technology the way they have Java without fully intending to leverage it. It might be helpful to remember here that the best technology does not always win, so whether Java turns out to be digital ambrosia or just a mediocre technology with a marketing budget the size of a small country's GNP, it's clear it will be integral to the next wave of both the Web and corporate computing. However, since Java is in reality a hardcore programming language, in our use of the Web it won't affect most of us any more than the brand of server software a site uses. But it does promise to break through some of the limitations of HTML and the Web's rather primitive "click-and-view" technology, and as such will eventually affect many of our lives, whether we know it or not. In the end, the best technologies are the most transparent ones.

The Internet's Future: A Full Circle

Probably the most interesting development in science and engineering on the Web today is more political than technological: The Internet2. Announced late in 1996, this initiative is an effort to reestablish the goal of the original Internet, which was to foster communication among university and research facilities through a platform-independent information infrastructure. When the National Science Foundation (NSF) cut its ties with the Internet proper in 1995, a large hole was left. In stepped the U.S. government. As many will remember, the Clinton Administration soon announced the "Next-Generation Internet Initiative (NGII)," which declared three goals: interconnecting universities via high-speed links, promoting research of new networking technologies; and developing new Internet applications for use with high-speed links. And so, under the leadership of Vice President Al Gore and with the support of 34 major universities and some big corporate names like IBM and AT&T, the Internet2 was born.

Unlike previous efforts in the U.S. to implement a national network initiative (NII, 1992; GII, 1994), the Internet2 clearly has teeth. In fact, it already exists. The initiative has staked off as its starting territory the NSF's very high performance Backbone Network Service (vBNS). Begun in 1995 with an initial investment of $50 million, the vBNS links six NSF supercomputing centers and is designed to act as a gigabit testbed where advanced networking technologies can be developed and tested. These technologies include all the hottest geekspeak—ATM/SONET, HiPPI, GigaPoPs, and all-optical networking. Currently, a large and growing number of universities and national labs are making their plans to connect to and expand upon this base. Their goals are many-faceted, but all center on the development of educational and research tools that take advantage of high bandwidth connectivity. Some examples currently include high quality audio/video streaming for distance learning applications; virtual research using remotely located instruments such as electron microscopes and large telescopes; and transmission of high-resolution medical images for diagnosis and teaching.

In the Preface I describe my personal reasons for writing this book. But more important are my professional reasons. I have watched the Internet spin into something that has grown far beyond the scope of the original NSF initiative in 1985. And while as a consumer I marvel at and enjoy the changes the Internet has made to everyday living, I am also heartened to see that the original vision has not been lost, and is in fact reemerging from the ashes of the commercial sector's complete razing of the original NSFNet. The advancements now promised by such breakthroughs as online document delivery, HTML expansion, and alternative network systems will have a profoundly positive effect on the scientific and engineering communities. It has come full circle indeed.

Chapter 2

GETTING ONLINE

This chapter outlines the basic options for getting online, and offers some tips for choosing a service provider.

Who Provides Internet Access?

In the past few years Internet access has become big business, and just like any other big business, competition has brought us some good and some bad. On the good side, the cost of getting online has dropped to an affordable rate and has held steady. On the bad side, the businesses that provide access run the full spectrum of capabilities, service, and support.

Providing Internet access is still a very young industry. Beginning in 1994, thousands of companies were launched almost overnight, some of them being nothing more than two guys with a computer, a limited-bandwidth connection, a few incoming modems, and dreams of becoming rich. The reality is that the Internet access business has not turned out to be the cash cow that many thought it would. The more customers they signed, the more customer service and support they needed. Adding people costs money. The result is that there are many providers out there today for whom providing access to individuals is really a loss leader. They are essentially losing money on individual access accounts, but trying to make up for it by signing up whole companies that want access to the Internet.

Many pricing models have also been tried, with varying degrees of success. The most notorious of these was America Online's "unlimited access" option, for which customers would pay $19.95 per month. What backfired here was that America Online didn't anticipate both the immediate popularity of this smorgasbord approach, and so they didn't have enough food to sate their more than 8 million customers during the feeding frenzy that immediately followed. They also didn't count on all the customers simply never leaving the table. Customers came in droves and never logged off, leaving AOL's access lines clotted with busy signals.

Primary Options

Today there are two kinds of businesses offering complete Internet and Web access—Internet Service Providers, and Commercial Online Services.

Internet Service Providers (ISPs)

These are local, regional, or national organizations that sell various degrees of access to the Internet, both for businesses and individual users. This access will most likely be via a *PPP account*, which is software that runs on your computer to connect it to the Internet via modem. The best ISPs will give you a floppy or CD-ROM with an *installer* program specific to your computer operating system, and when you run this installer, the proper networking software, dialup phone numbers, and Internet addressing information is automatically installed on your computer. This type of setup is becoming increasingly common, so when searching for an ISP, look for one that can provide this level of service for your particular computer.

When you have an account with an ISP, you are essentially renting an address on the Internet, from which you can send and receive information directly from your computer. Your "address" usually includes both a temporarily assigned *IP number* so you can surf the Web using a browser like Netscape, and a more permanent e-mail address so you can send and receive e-mail. Most ISPs will now also provide you with space on their server computer to place your own Web pages for anyone to access. Some of the larger ones now offer toll-free access numbers for their customers who travel and wish to pick up their e-mail or even access the Web while on the road.

Commercial Online Services

These are self-contained online environments where users have access to services provided and maintained by the service, as well as access to the Web. These services usually require that you install and use software that they have developed to connect with and navigate their computer environment. This category is now dominated by the online behemoth America Online (AOL), although there are still a few surviving smaller players like CompuServe (now owned by AOL), Microsoft Network, and Prodigy.

Before the popularity of the World Wide Web, online services like AOL were really the only way to experience a complete online environment. They had e-mail, access to news and other resources, *chat rooms*, and a graphical user interface—all of which made them very popular in the few years preceding the Web. However, when the Web became popular and Web browsers got better, AOL and the others scrambled to hold onto their customers, especially in the beginning. Once these commercial services figured out how to "connect" to the Internet, they had a more viable service, since customers could still use both their service's unique online environment as well as "surf the Web."

What's the Difference?

So is there really a difference today between ISPs and commercial services? Absolutely yes. Commercial services like AOL and CompuServe have both disadvantages and advantages compared to an account with an ISP. The biggest disadvantage is that commercial services are generally slower, since you're really accessing the Web through their computer systems instead of having your own address, as with an ISP account. Another disadvantage is that they may force you to use their own e-mail software, news reader, and Web browser, which tend to be vastly inferior compared to the latest versions of established commercial software like Netscape or Eudora.

One advantage of a commercial provider is that they do provide a large online environment with thousands of magazines, companies, and services. While most of this same information can be found directly on the Web, the advantage of accessing it on the commercial service is that it's all organized for you. Another advantage of a commercial provider is that if you travel a lot, it's usually quite easy to access the service using a local or toll-free number. As mentioned previously, there are some larger ISPs providing this kind of access as well, however, most local providers can't offer such a service.

Which is Better?

At this point I'll take my stand. I've had an America Online account since 1989—long before the Web even existed as a twinkle in Netscape and Microsoft's eyes, and I cannot recommend such commercial online services if you're serious about using the Web for professional endeavors. If you need only e-mail access, then they are adequate, but for Web access services like AOL and CompuServe are slow, have a long history of access problems (busy phone lines), and are so large that their customer service is generally poor or difficult to contact. These services' real niche is the casual home user. They are good for that because they provide everything you need—software, local access number, and a self-contained online environment that offers a wide variety of easily accessible products and services. They are not, however, the World Wide Web per se, nor is their access to the Web as good as that offered by a quality ISP. (Certainly all of these problems can be experienced from an ISP, but a good ISP will have adequate bandwidth, incoming phone lines, and technical support.)

Choosing an Internet Service Provider

Shopping for an ISP is not much different than shopping for a computer. One good tactic is to make a list of what you want to do on the Internet, and also what you think you might want to do in the future. Here is a short checklist of questions to consider:

- Do you need or want a toll-free phone number?
- Do you need more than one e-mail account?
- Do you want telnet access to your e-mail?
- Do you want to author your own homepage or Web site?
- Do you want a place where other people can FTP files to you?
- Do you want to access to Usenet newsgroups?
- Do you need a flat-fee rate, or is hourly okay?

Something to keep in mind is that the business of providing Internet connectivity to individuals is generally considered a "loss leader" in the ISP industry. This means many ISPs offer individual dialup services only as a way of establishing credibility in the community, which will hopefully lead to contracts with commercial companies that need connectivity, or other business areas that have higher profit margins for the ISP. Therefore it pays to thoroughly investigate any ISP to see how well they service individual clients.

Travel Considerations

If you travel with a laptop and think you might want to access your e-mail on the road, you might want to investigate ISPs with toll-free access or "points of presence" in major cities (i.e., a local phone number). Usually this kind of service comes from large regional or national providers like UUNET, PSI, Netcom, or EarthLink. However, some local ISPs are now teaming up with these national providers to offer these kinds of access options.

You may also want to find a provider that can offer *telnet* access to your e-mail. Telnet is the lowest common denominator of e-mail access methods, and is often available at *cybercafes* in major international cities, and even at technical conferences where the sponsor provides Internet access. It is extremely valuable when traveling internationally, as computer and telephone connectivity become the major obstacles here. Cybercafes are thus a much easier option for checking your mail when far from home.

Make sure you get complete instructions from your ISP on how to read your e-mail via telnet. Usually this involves getting the telnet address of your ISP's mail server computer, and learning the software interface they provide for telnet e-mail access. You will also need to have telnet software on your laptop to make the connection. Among the many freeware and shareware telnet programs available, I recommend QTVNet for Windows computers, and NCSA Telnet for Macintosh computers. Current versions of these can be found at these (and many other) locations:

```
Windows:      http://wuarchive.wustl.edu/systems/ibmpc/
Macintosh:    ftp://ftp.ncsa.uiuc.edu/Mac/Telnet/
```

Finding Internet Access Providers (ISPs)

Once you have your shopping list ready, you'll next need to identify possible ISPs and then compare their services and fees. Note that the fees issue can be deceptive. Like most things in the world, as the saying goes, you get what you pay for. While you may be able to find an ISP who offers "unlimited access" for a very low fee, chances are good that you'll soon find out what the trade-offs are for such low fees. Usually this comes in the form of poor instructions for getting started, constant busy signals, slow network performance, and poor or nonexistent customer service.

The best way to find an ISP is to ask a friend or colleague who is already on the Internet, especially if you want a local provider. If you can't find someone to make a recommendation, then you can try looking in your local phone book, usually under "Internet" or "computers." Another option is to find a friend who already has Web access and ask them to go to this Web site:

`http://thelist.com`

The List is a well-established "killer site" on the Web that lists thousands of ISPs along with complete information about service levels, pricing, and contact information.

Finding Commercial Service Providers

America Online (AOL)	800/827-6364	
CompuServe (CIS)	800/524-3388	
Delphi	800/695-4005	617/491-3393
EarthLink	800/395-8425	818/296-2400
Microsoft Network	800/386-5550	
MindSpring (formerly PSI)	800/827-7482	703/709-0300
Netcom	800/353-6600	408/881-1815
UUNET	800/488-6384	703/206-5600
Whole Earth Networks		415/281-6550

Chapter 3

E-MAIL & MESSAGING

Why E-mail?

The Web is all about communication. Whether you're searching for information, publishing your own research online, or simply browsing the Web, the basic function is communication. Electronic mail, or *e-mail,* is the foundation of all that happens on the Internet and World Wide Web. The Web itself is generally a passive medium: you click on a link and the content of a Web page downloads into your Web browser. E-mail, on the other hand, is the active side of the Web. When you register for a conference using an online form, the results are usually e-mailed somewhere. When you purchase something online, you are often sent an e-mail confirmation of your order. When you join a discussion group via the Web, you're probably joining an e-mail forum. E-mail is fundamental to the Web, and the latest versions of popular Web browsers naturally incorporate increasingly sophisticated e-mail readers. It will not be long before we begin to view e-mail and the Web as one thing. Many do already.

What is E-mail?

The basic function of e-mail is the same as with regular postal service mail: to send and receive information. But e-mail is much more powerful than paper mail (or "snail-mail," as many online folks deride it). With e-mail you can send and receive just about anything you use or create on your computer—words, formatted documents, programs, photos, images, and sounds. It's all a matter of making sure that the contents of what you send are *encoded* correctly, and that the receiver of such information has the proper software to *decode* it.

E-mail Software

Whether you get online through your employer's direct Internet connection, a remote account on someone else's computer, or a personal PPP account, you'll be using some kind of e-mail software package.

On a Unix or VAX computer it might be called something like *Elm, Pine, Pegasus,* or just plain old *mail,* and often on large internal computer systems there will be a custom menu on your screen that lists something like *Mail,* which is probably the mail system your company or university has chosen for you.

On a PC or Macintosh computer, you might have something like Eudora, Microsoft Exchange, or BeyondMail. You may even have a choice. And if you have an account with a major commercial service like America Online or CompuServe, you have their proprietary e-mail software. The point is that there are many e-mail interfaces in use today, and they all look and act slightly different and have different bells and whistles.

Which brings us to the Web browser. While still not as popular as standalone e-mail software, the major Web browser developers like Netscape and Microsoft are banking on many of us switching to our Web browser for reading mail in the future. Historically, browser-based e-mail software has been clunky and lacking in features. However, this won't be the case forever, and the latest versions of Netscape Navigator and Microsoft Internet Explorer attempt to bridge that gap by offering more features and improved performance.

Addressing and Sending E-mail

Let's start with the basics of addressing and sending e-mail. As with paper mail, you need to know the address of the intended recipient of your letter. See the section on Finding Someone's E-mail Address at the end of this chapter for tips on this topic.

Electronic mail has its own addressing system, called *domain name addressing.* This is the electronic equivalent of postal addresses. Like postal addresses, e-mail addresses go from specific to general, in order to route the message to the right computer and person. Generally, e-mail addresses have a *username* (also called a *user ID,* often the person's account name on their computer system), one or more *location identifiers,* and a *domain.* There is also an @ ("at") symbol that separates the user ID from the locations and domain, and sometimes additional characters like % and ! symbols. My e-mail address is typical:

```
brian@mom.spie.org

brian                     is my user ID
```

`mom`	is a computer mailserver name
`spie`	is our location identifier
`org`	is a domain (nonprofit organization)

Note that in some cases the mailserver name ("mom" here) is not required if you wish to send me an e-mail message. It only appears as part of my e-mail address when I send you a message. This is because the software on my company's server automatically adds this mailserver name to all my outgoing messages.

Here are some other examples:

`jbreck@huey.jpl.nasa.gov`

`arseno@phy.ulaval.ca`

`sab@media-lab.media.mit.edu`

The portion of the address to the right of the @ symbol is referred to as the *domain name*. The domain name moves from most specific information at the left (often the computer's "name") to the most general (the type of site).

Let's break down that last address into its individual parts:

`sab`	is the user name (in this case, the owner's initials)
`media-lab`	is a mailserver computer name at MIT
`media`	is a subdomain at MIT
`mit`	is a location identifier
`edu`	is a domain (educational institution)

In the examples above, the address owners have used some portion of their name or a cognate for their user or account name. Some organizations require that names follow specific conventions. For example, some services combine the first three letters of your first and last name to create your account name. Others require the use of an account number rather than a name.

Your E-mail Address

When you subscribe to an online service, you are often given some degree of choice in choosing your user e-mail name—that is, what appears to the left of the @ symbol. Notice I said "some degree of choice." In other words, you can't always get what you want. The part you can never choose is everything to the right of the @ symbol, which is all the *domain* information, since that belongs to the service provider.

Some service providers give you more options than others. Whether this is good or bad is personal opinion. For example, everyone at CompuServe has a numerical user ID assigned by CompuServe. You don't have a say in the matter—you're just 77482.333, or whatever, and that's the end of it. On the Internet you become **77482.333@compuserve.com,** because that's their addressing scheme.

At the other end of the spectrum, there are service providers who let you pick your e-mail name, provided it's not already taken elsewhere on their service, and that it meets certain computer-designated criteria. So, for example, if you just got an account with a service provider called CTSNet, you could request the username *bob*, and if there were not already a user named *bob* at CTSNet, then they might approve the name and you would become

```
bob@ctsnet.com
```

There are, of course, some technical restrictions on e-mail names on the Internet, and these don't always match what is permitted or restricted on a commercial service provider. For example, on America Online, you can have a username that contains a space. This is because AOL's online environment allows spaces. So if I pick *bob atkins* as my AOL username, everyone else with an AOL account addresses messages to me at exactly that address.

However, if someone outside of the America Online environment tries to send a message to **bob atkins@aol.com,** their message will be returned as an error, because spaces are not permitted anywhere in an Internet e-mail address. (The historical reason for this discrepancy is that AOL started as a standalone online system before the Internet became popular.) The moral of the story is, wherever you get your online access, think globally when picking your e-mail address.

Choosing an E-mail Address

If you're given any degree of choice, I suggest picking an e-mail address that somehow relates to your real name so that others can better identify you by your address, and remember your address more easily. One common practice is to use a combination of your first name, middle initial, and last name.

Some examples, using my name:

- bjt
- bthomas
- b_thomas
- bjthomas
- thomasb
- thomasbj
- bthom

Things to avoid:

- spaces
- periods or any other punctuation marks
- long names or text strings
- special characters (!, %, *, #, etc.—most of these would be rejected by the service provider anyway)
- cute family names or nicknames

Also remember that e-mail addresses are not case sensitive. While you may see someone list their address as **PeNELopE@EARTHLINK.com**, the Internet's e-mail system does not differentiate between this and **penelope@earthlink.com**.

More about Domains

Every address has a domain that helps identify the type of organization it was sent from, or the geographical location of the organization. Typical domain types:

.com	commercial venture, such as **compuserve.com**
.edu	educational institution, such as **dartmouth.edu**
.org	a private or nonprofit organization, such as **spie.org**
.gov	government institution, such as **nasa.gov**
.mil	military site, such as **navy.mil**
.net	gateways or administrative hosts on the Internet, such as **nwnet.net**

In 1998 some new domains will be added, including:

.firm	Firms and businesses
.store	Online stores
.web	Entities emphasizing WWW related activities
.arts	Cultural and entertainment sites
.rec	Recreation and entertainment sites
.info	Information services
.nom	For those wishing individual or personal nomenclature

Remember that some of the usages noted above are just guidelines. No one on the Internet enforces them, so an organization with a **.org** domain might actually be a commercial venture.

Sites not in the U.S. sometimes end with a two-letter country code. Some examples:

.ca	Canada
.cn	China
.dk	Denmark
.de	Germany
.jp	Japan
.ch	Switzerland
.uk	United Kingdom
.se	Sweden

The United States actually has a country code (**.us**), but you won't see it very often. Similarly, many Web sites outside the U.S. are beginning to drop their country codes. This trend will likely continue.

Message Headers

The outgoing message header contains all of the address information for both the sender and recipient, as well as other information such as who else was "copied" on the message, and often a "Subject" line to help identify messages from only their headers.

Headers also pick up information as your message is sent to its recipient. Your e-mail software adds hidden text that itemizes the message size, origination location, and other miscellaneous information. By the time the message arrives at its destination, it may have a whole paragraph of cryptic text that recounts all the routers the message passed through, the message's unique ID number, and so on. See "Return Message Headers," below, if you're interested.

Here is an example of a typical outgoing message header as you might see it:

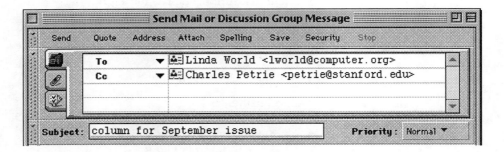

Note that with most e-mail software you don't see your own name in a From field. The software automatically inserts it for you.

In addition to the To and Subject fields, message headers may also contain any or all of these fields as well:

CC: Short for "Carbon Copy." This line shows who was also copied on the message.

BCC: Short for "Blind Carbon Copy." Same as CC, but names on this line are not seen by any of the message's recipients. It's somewhat stealthy. It's also a great way to send a message to a large list of people and protect everyone's identity, for example, on a subscription mailing list. This is a handy feature, but if you use it, make sure the people you blind copy understand what it's all about. If you just BCC someone out of the blue, they may be confused when they receive a message that does not show their e-mail address anywhere on it.

Reply to: If you want replies to be sent to a different e-mail address, that address goes in this field.

Attachments

Sometimes it is sufficient to write a message in plain ASCII text, no special fonts, formatting, or page layout required (see Chapter 6 for more background). When appearance is important, or if exchanging documents in their original file type is key, the attached document feature is handy. Most current e-mail software allows the user to specify the location of a file on their hard drive or network server and attach it to an e-mail message.

Broadly speaking, an attachment can be anything you can store on a computer. Because e-mail was originally designed to work on a wide variety of computers, it can only transmit basic types of data. Therefore, in order to send more complex types of information, such as graphics, spreadsheets, movies, etc., such files must be encoded prior to sending, and then decoded on the recipient's end. Thankfully, over the past few years a standard called MIME (Multipurpose Internet Mail Extensions) has been widely adopted and incorporated into most e-mail software today, so the process of attaching a file is relatively painless.

The attachment feature automatically encodes the file you wish to send, plus other information about the file that will help the receiver's mailer software decide how to handle it. MIME uses the file's extension to determine what to do with the file.

Here's what an outgoing attached file looks like in Netscape Communicator's outgoing e-mail window:

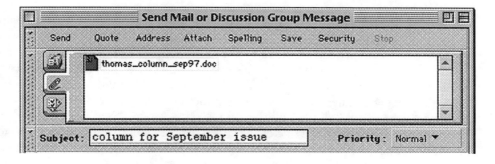

For more information on the MIME standard, see the chapter on Web File Formats.

Message Body

The message body is the area where you type your message. It appears below the header. To finish off the example above, here's what the whole message might look like:

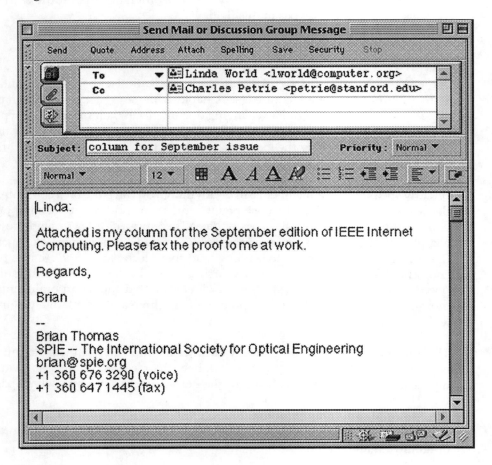

Signatures

The last few lines in the example above are called a *signature,* or "sig." As a courtesy to the recipients of your e-mail messages, you should "sign" your message with at least your full name and e-mail address at the end of the message. Most e-mail programs allow you to set up a signature that gets appended automatically to all your outgoing e-mail messages. The automated signature can be either a feature of the e-mail software or the computer operating system itself.

Some individuals choose to include extensive contact information in their signatures, such as phone, fax and street address. Others choose to add disclaimers emphasizing that the opinions they express in their e-mail are not necessarily the opinion of their Internet provider (often, the sender's employer). The general rule is to keep your signature useful and unobtrusive. Long quotations from your favorite author are not often appreciated in the spirit in which they are offered.

Return Message Headers

When you receive a message, you many notice that it not only contains the standard Date:, To:, From:, and Subject: lines, but also a whole bunch of other unsightly text strings. Like this:

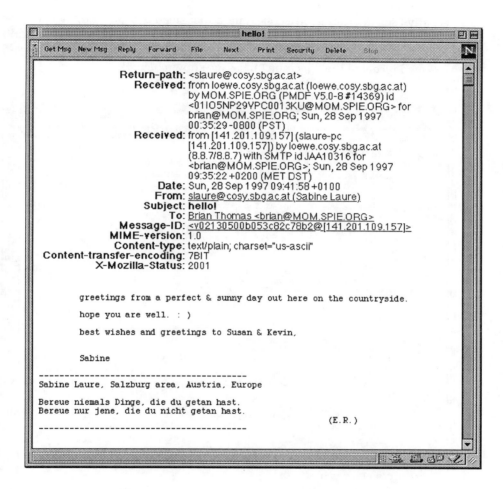

This is the return message header, and it contains routing and other information essential and unique to this e-mail message. Depending on what your e-mail software does with it, you may see it at the top or bottom of an incoming message, you may not see it at all, or you may even be able to display or hide it on the fly (Eudora, for example, does this).

For the most part, while it can be valuable in tracing e-mail transmission problems, you should be able to get by in life without ever having to use it. If you have the option to turn headers off, you'll probably want to as it makes reading e-mail much easier.

"Bounced" or Undeliverable Mail

If you send a paper letter to a friend but write down the address incorrectly, your letter comes back from the Post Office with big "ADDRESS UNKNOWN" stamped across it. E-mail has a similar mechanism, and it's quite common.

Recently I sent a message to a colleague, and instead of looking up her address in my address book, I simply typed it in from memory. Unfortunately, I didn't remember her address correctly. A few minutes after I sent my mis-addressed message I received the "daemon" message shown below:

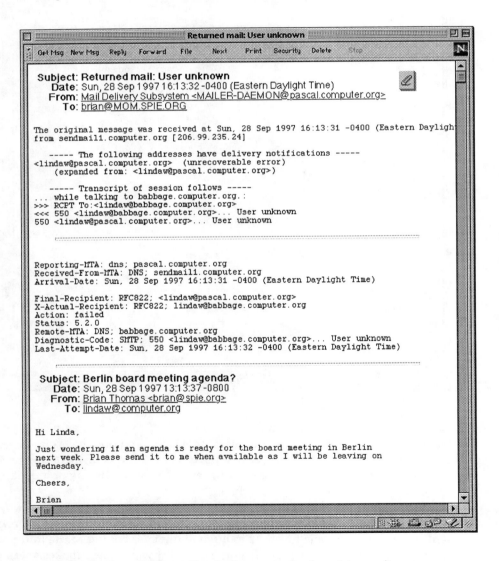

A mail *daemon* (see the From line in the example above) is a software program, in this case running on the mail server-computer at **computer.org**, that processed the incoming message and determined that there was no user named "lindaw@computer.org."

Daemons also reside at "higher levels" on the Internet to deal with message problems on those levels, such as invalid domain names. For example, an e-mail message sent to **brian@spie.com** will be intercepted by a daemon and returned as "site unknown," since **spie.com** does not exist (it's **spie.org**).

Composing E-mail Messages

While I'll be the last person to tell you *what* to write, I will offer some things to consider when composing your e-mail messages.

Structural Rules

Reading messages on a computer screen can be at best tolerable, and at worst, an utter nightmare. Consider these rules of the road when composing your e-mail to make it easier to read:

- Keep line lengths to 60 columns (or characters) or less.
- Use a monospace typeface such as Courier to display your e-mail.
- Use both upper and lower case just as you would in a letter, and only use ALL CAPS IF YOU REALLY MEAN TO SHOUT.
- Keep paragraphs short, and use two <returns> between them.
- Don't use tabs—they don't translate. Use spaces to indent instead.
- If responding to a previous message, clearly mark and quote the other message succinctly, if possible.
- Keep your signature short and useful. No cute sayings or "ASCII art."
- Send the message to yourself first (and save a copy) if you think formatting might be a problem.
- If your software has a "redirect" feature, be very careful with it as it can confuse your recipients very easily.

Netiquette

Writing e-mail can quickly become so commonplace that we forget its power to be misinterpreted or even to wound. E-mail is probably closer to spoken communication than written, despite its text-bound façade. Like verbal communications, e-mail runs the entire spectrum of tone and purpose, from sending a close friend a quick note on the latest *X-Files* episode to submitting a manuscript to a professional journal.

With that in mind, the best advice is to write for the occasion. For communications to close colleagues and friends, write as you would speak. For formal business correspondence, write as you would write a letter.

There is, I should note, a tendency toward the casual side with e-mail in business correspondence. This is partly because of the immediacy of e-mail, and partly because, as the *New Yorker* cartoon wryly pointed out, "On the Internet, no one knows you're a dog." In many ways the Internet is a classless society, where annual income and titles have no tangible value, and are generally frowned upon if stated overtly.

Propriety

- Always remember you are writing to another person. Treat people with respect.
- Always remember that the other person *might* forward your message to someone else (it happens).
- Use smileys judiciously and *special* characters (like asterisks) to clarify tone of voice.
- Don't use shorthand acronyms unless you know the reader will understand them.
- Sign with a short, informative signature block
- Review your message before sending it. It's easy to think you'll come back to check something and then forget.
- Read all the messages in your inbox before replying to any them. Sometimes messages received later preclude you from having to respond. This is especially true when you're on an e-mail *listserv*.
- Be concise.

And finally, my personal rule of thumb: Wait 24 hours before sending any message you write in distress or anger. Chances are you won't send it after reading it again the next day. E-mail's "instant gratification" is a dangerous and seductive blade.

Common Conventions

Since the nuances of a face-to-face conversation are lost in e-mail messages, most veterans of the Internet use *emoticons,* or *smileys,* as they are more commonly called. These can be used to convey some of the emotional nuance of a message.

While these may seem a little cute upon first encounter, after a while you may begin to see how important they are to avoid misunderstandings and convey tone of voice, which we often take for granted in face-to-face and phone conversations. And because e-mail can be so much less formal than a paper letter, it's important to make your message as clear as possible.

Generally, smileys are used as a kind of punctuation, most often at the end of a sentence. For example, if I sent this message to a friend,

```
The Mariners lost again last night. I'm quite upset.
```

I could be joking or serious. There are no clues given.

However, if I change it to

```
The Mariners lost again last night. I'm quite upset ;-)
```

then it's clear that I'm being sarcastic, and that I'm not really upset at all. In fact, I might be happy about it.

Some Common Emoticons ("smileys"):

:-)	smile
:-(	frown
;-)	smile and wink
:-o	oh oh!
:-D	big grin
:-|	neutral or disinterested
:-/	disconcerted

Another communication oddity unique to the Internet is a kind of Internet shorthand, using acronyms of phrases people say all time. These are very casual in tone, and are best used between friends or people you know will understand them.

Some Common Shorthand Acronyms

BTW	by the way
FYI	for your info
TIA	thanks in advance
TTFN	ta ta for now
ROTFL	rolling on the floor laughing
IMHO	in my humble/honest opinion
TFS	thanks for sharing (used sarcastically)
RTFM	read the @#$%! manual!
L8R	later (as in, goodbye)
TTYL	talk to you later (or TTYS for "soon")

Another common e-mail (and Usenet) practice is the use of some character, usually the > symbol, to show a direct and quoted reference to some previous message.

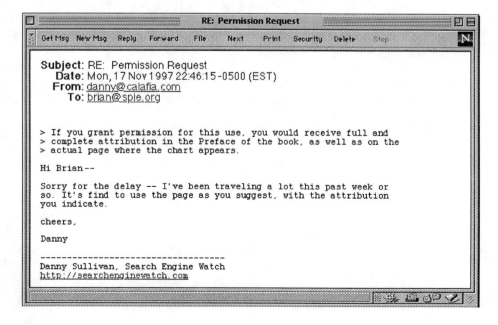

The e-mail message above shows a response to a message I sent to Danny Calafia requesting permission to republish a chart (found elsewhere in this book). In his message, Danny quoted three key lines from my original message, and then added his response below them. This is a good example of quoting because he quoted only enough of my original message that was necessary. Most e-mail software will automatically insert (or give you the option to insert) the > character in a message when you choose the Reply or Forward feature. Then you can delete those parts of the message that are not relevant for quoting (like the header!) and respond point by point if appropriate. This makes for highly effective communication. On the Usenet, such quoting is used extensively in message *threads* since there are often many messages posted every day, and you'll want to show what exactly you're referring to when you post your own messages to a newsgroup.

Finding Someone's E-mail Address

Listed below are a few Web sites that devote themselves to helping you find people on the net. However, there is no one central directory of everyone's e-mail address and no guarantee that the person you seek is listed. These services often search databases of people who have registered themselves (to help others find them), as well as relying on information retrieved from Web "crawlers" (see the chapter on searching the Web for more background on crawlers, spiders, robots, etc.).

```
http://www.switchboard.com
http://www.whowhere.com
http://www.four11.com
http://yahoo.four11.com
```

Note that the last listing is Yahoo's version of the Four11 service. This is a good example of where the Web is heading, with individual services formally collaborating with each other to expand their capabilities as well as make it easier for us to find information. I happen to prefer Yahoo's interface to the Four11 service, so I list it above. They do, however, search the same database of information.

If you try one of the sites above and don't find who you're looking for, save yourself the time and energy and just call the person directly (or at least someone who knows their address).

Chapter 4

Discussion Lists

Discussion lists, often called "listservs" (for software it's named after) or "mailing lists," are an essential communication tool on the Internet. Using only e-mail, discussion lists connect colleagues from around the world to discuss issues related to specific topics. The only requirement is that you have an Internet-accessible e-mail address. Discussion lists are especially useful in the sciences, since there are so many specialized interests that finding someone whose interests are similar is often difficult.

For the purpose of this chapter, I will use the term *discussion list* to refer to any e-mail type of list, including listservs and mailing lists. Later in this chapter I describe the different types of discussion lists.

When you join a discussion list, you are joining a group of people who also "subscribe" to the group. Basically, there's a "group e-mail address" that everyone sends messages to, and from there the message "explodes" to the entire group list. You and everyone else on the list receive messages sent to this e-mail address. You can choose to read, delete, or respond to any message you receive. You can also leave or "sign off" the list at any time.

Some people join a discussion list and never actually "talk," but rather just read the ongoing discussions. This is sometimes called "lurking," and is perfectly acceptable. In fact, it's a good idea to lurk on a new list for a while to see what the topics are, get the tone of the conversation, and watch for an FAQ posting. (Most discussion lists with an active Frequently Asked Questions document have it posted to the list on a regular basis.) On the other hand, you can jump into a conversation or "thread" on a list at any time. In many ways, dis-

cussion lists are like bulletin boards, except that you don't have to go somewhere to read them. They come to you instead.

Moderated v. Unmoderated Lists

The content and quality of the messages in a listserv are dependent on the
people participating. In some cases, a list will be *moderated* by one person knowledgeable in the subject area and will filter out unwanted or inappropriate messages. The moderator then forwards the messages to the subscribers.

Mailing Lists v. Listservs

As I've noted earlier, the terms "mailing list" and "listserv" are both used to
describe an e-mail discussion list. Note, however, that the term "listserv" itself
describes a specific and common set of software commands for using the **listserv** software on the BITNET computer network (see below). However, you
will also see "mailing list" or "listserver" used to describe listserv-like discussion groups that don't use the BITNET's listserv software. In some cases, the
mailing lists are handled manually by a list manager.

Despite the fact that they serve the same purpose, the difference between mailing lists and listservs in the way they operate is significant enough that we'll
discuss them separately here.

Mailing Lists

While most mailing lists today are managed automatically by software designed
for this purpose, some are still managed manually. In either case, mailing lists
usually have at least two addresses, a subscription address and an actual discussion list address. Many use the form

> **listname-request@an.internet.address**

for the subscription address. In this case the list is most likely managed manually (the subscription requests sent to the **-request** address are manually added
to the distribution list).

There are also other software programs that use addresses in the form of

> **majordomo@an.internet.address**

and

> **listproc@an.internet.address**

Though these are run by a software program, some elements may be run manually. In either case, a concise, syntactically correct subscription request is the
most efficient means to join a list.

The differences between mailing lists and listservs appear in the other features of the software. For example, to leave a list some mailing lists respond to the command **unsubscribe** or **unsub**. Others will only respond to the command **signoff**.

Most mailing lists will respond to the command **help** when sent to the subscription address, and will return to you a list of commands you can use for that list. Useful information about commands is also usually included in the "Welcome" message you receive after subscribing. Some welcome messages go so far as listing the name and e-mail address of the moderator or manager of the list.

Subscribing to Mailing Lists

Subscribing to a mailing list is not much different from subscribing to a listserv, except that there is no single standard. In most cases the addressing system is exactly the same; however, make sure you know what the proper address for subscribing is for every list you join. It may be completely different from anything you've seen before.

Usually, if your "subscribe" message is missing a phrase or is not listed in the correct order, the mailing list will simply send you an error message with more complete instructions. Remember to use the listserv-like address, not the discussion list address. Here is a sample subscription request to **gps@tws4.si.com**, a mailing list for anyone interested in global positioning systems. Note that we send it to **gps-request**, not the list name itself.

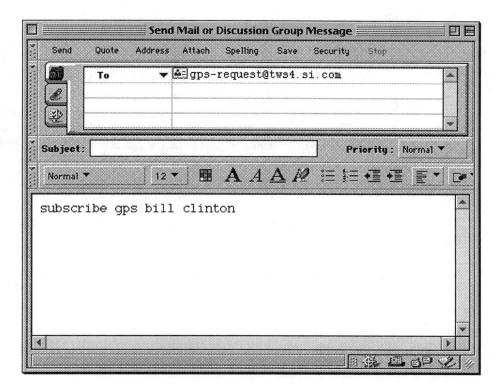

For a few more common commands, see the section on Discussion List Commands Review later in this chapter.

Listservs

When I first encountered listserv addresses on the Internet, I thought they were very confusing. Thus, I am motivated to explain them clearly here. Compounding my confusion was the fact that few books I've read tackle this issue with any breadth, yet for the science professional, listservs and discussion lists in general are one of the best tools for meeting colleagues with like interests in a useful forum. If you are interested in joining any of the thousands of listserv discussion lists active today in the scientific community, this section is here to save you a lot of time and confusion.

The term "listserv" refers to software developed for IBM/VM computers running on BITNET ("Because It's Time NETwork"), which for many years was a network unto itself, but which now is virtually indistinguishable from the Internet. The listserv software automates the process of managing a discussion list. This is why some Internet purists will squirm whenever the word *listserv* is used to describe a mailing list system that does not actually use the listserv software. However, for most of us the distinction is only a matter of knowing how to join (subscribe), participate in, and quit (unsubscribe) the list.

The other distinction is addressing. The key thing to remember about listserv discussion lists is that they're still somehow associated with BITNET, and therefore the Internet addresses you use to connect with the lists are not standard for everyone.

Understanding Listservs

Listservs usually have two addresses associated with each list. The *listserv address* begins with the word **listserv** and is used to subscribe and unsubscribe to the list. All other administrative type requests are also sent to the listserv address. The *list address* begins with the name of the list and is used when participating in discussions on the list. The thing to remember here is to send your subscription requests to the listserv address, *not* the list address. If you send your subscription request to the actual group address, your message may be sent erroneously to all the people in the group. Not a great way to introduce yourself.

Again—send your "subscribe" message to the **listserv@** address, not the list address itself. **This is very important.**

Here's an example. Let's say you've found a discussion list on astronomy you wish to join. The subscription information you've found might look like this:

> **astro**
> astro@gitvm1
> Astronomy Discussion List

The first line is the actual name of the discussion list—what they call themselves. The last line is obviously the list's discussion topic.

The second line is the important one—the *listserv address*. This is *not* the list address. If you send a message to this address, you are sending it to the entire list, therefore if you want to subscribe to the list, you would need to send your message to the *listserv address*, which would be **listserv@gitvm1**. I know I'm beating this topic into the ground, but it's important.

Now here's the other important part. Notice the Internet address for this list. There's something wrong. We learned in Chapter 4 that all Internet addresses have a domain suffix such as **.edu** or **.org**. The addresses above do not have domains, so unless you're actually on BITNET yourself, you'll probably need to add something to this address to make it a valid Internet address. I say *probably* because it's not true in all cases. This is where the topic gets a little murky.

Understanding Listserv Gateways

Here's what you need to know. In most books and resources that list listserv discussion lists, you'll find that they list addresses such as the one above. I suspect this is a legacy issue from when the BITNET was more of a closed system (there are still a lot of people who are on the BITNET system in some manner). Regardless, to subscribe to one of these lists (that is, one you find without a domain suffix), you'll need to add something to get your message over to the BITNET computer that controls the listserv.

There are two ways to do this. First, try adding **.bitnet** to the listserv address. For example:

listserv@gitvm1.bitnet

If this works—great. If it doesn't, it's because your particular location on the Internet doesn't quite mesh with BITNET. The alternative in this case is to try sending your message through one of the BITNET *gateways*, which are computers on the Internet that will (if you use the proper syntax) redirect your message to the BITNET computer that controls the listserv you're looking for. Here's the syntax using the example above and a gateway computer at City University of New York (CUNY):

listserv%gitvm1@cunyvm.cuny.edu

All you're doing now is changing **listserv@gitvm1** to **listserve%gitvm1**, and then sending the whole message to a standard Internet address (**cunyvm.cuny.edu**).

Here are some other listserv gateways that you can use:

cornellc.cit.cornell.edu

cunyvm.cuny.edu
mitvma.mit.edu
vm1.nodak.edu

Finally, I should note again that use of these gateways and the "trick" of adding **.bitnet** to the listserv address do not apply to anyone already on BITNET. In that case, you would simply send your message to the listserv address listed without the domain suffix (e.g., **listserv@gitvm1**).

Subscribing to Listservs

Subscribing to listservs is easy once you get the addressing issue out of the way. Continuing with our example above, you would send your subscription message to the listserv address, **listserv@gitvm1**, modified as necessary as noted above. Most listservs require only the word "subscribe," the *list name*, and a first and last name (or an e-mail address, if you prefer; however, some require *two* words). All of these go in the message body. The Subject line is ignored.

For example, if Al Gore wanted to join the **astro** listserv, his subscription message would look like this:

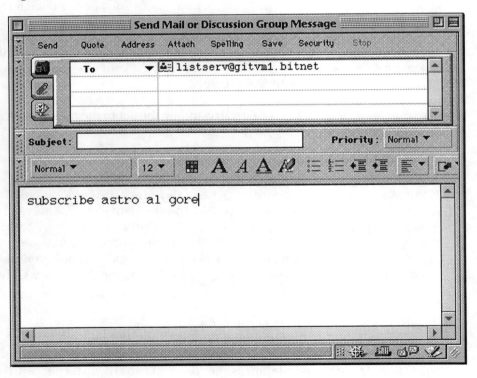

The listserv computer would then automatically send Gore a notification that it had received his subscription request.

There are a few different types of subscription processes. Some listservs will add you to their distribution immediately. Others will ask that you confirm your address by responding to their notification (within a specified amount of time). And others will refer your request to a person, moderator, or manager who will then add you to the list. I've even encountered some that send you a message that says something like, "Your subscription request has been received. To confirm, please enter a password in the space shown and forward this message back to xyz@some_address." This kind of procedure usually means the list is moderated and that the moderator wishes to control who subscribes, usually for the benefit of the legitimate listserv members.

Most likely, in addition to a subscription confirmation, you'll also receive an automated "Welcome" message. It will describe how to participate in discussions, list reference material if appropriate, and describe some of the listserv features. *Keep this message.* Save it in a e-mail folder or on your hard drive. Later on, if you decide you want to unsubscribe to the list, you'll need the information in this message.

Unsubscribing to a Listserv, and Other Commands

If you join a listserv and decide later to leave or *unsubscribe,* you need to send a **signoff** command to the listserv address (the same address you used to subscribe). Don't forget to tell the listserv computer the name of the list you wish to signoff from:

signoff astro

Listservs have many other services available through the e-mail system, such as file retrieval (e-mail servers). To learn more about these, send the word help to any **listserv@** address and you will receive more information.

For a few more common commands, see the section on Discussion List Commands Review later in this chapter.

Discussion List Netiquette

The same guidelines discussed for e-mail and Usenet *netiquette* ("net etiquette") apply here as well. Here are some additional guidelines to help you avoid the usual mistakes:

- Make sure you post your administrative requests (subscribe, help, etc.) to the correct e-mail address. There's nothing more annoying than seeing someone send a Help message to the actual discussion list address.

- Before ever posting to the discussion list, find out if there's an FAQ (Frequently Asked Questions) document for the group, and if there is, read it.

- Compose your postings carefully and be succinct. Don't "quote" a previous posted message in its entirety unless there's a very good reason to do so.

- If for some reason you start receiving lots of messages that are clearly erroneous—perhaps a temporary problem with the list software or another subscriber's e-mail system—don't start sending messages to the group saying, "Hey, what's going on?" All this does is exacerbate the situation. Just hang tight and wait for the list's administrators to fix the problem—and they will.

- Post only appropriate messages to the group. Keep personal messages between you and the other person. Sometimes you or someone else will start a valid discussion on the list that then becomes too specific or personal, at which point you should take the conversation "off line," which means "stop posting to the list and continue your discussion with the other person via e-mail directly." This is especially true if a more emotional discussion on the topic develops. Keep *flame wars* off line.

- Be careful about using the "Reply" feature of your e-mail software when reading a message posted to the group so that you don't accidentally send a personal message to the entire group. Make sure your message is going where you want it to.

- Keep blatant commercial messages out of the group unless you know the information is of interest to the group, or the information is in response to a request from someone else on the list. And even so, in the latter case, it's often best to send the information directly to the requester instead of to the whole group.

- Turn your e-mail "signature" off if you can, or at least trim it down to only the essentials—name, affiliation, address. Cute quotations and "ASCII art" are considered net noise.

- When you see someone else make one of the mistakes listed above, try to direct the person in the right direction. Don't ridicule them for their errors. It doesn't do anyone any good. If the list is moderated well, you'll never see inappropriate or misplaced messages. If the list is unmoderated, do your best to play "benevolent guide."

Digests

One variation on the standard discussion list is what's usually called a *digest*. Digests are one-to-many discussion lists, and there are at least two different kinds. The first is an electronic publication on a specific topic that is written and distributed by an individual or organization to a group of people who have subscribed to the digest. A high-quality "e-zine" digest is worth its weight in bytes. These are often compiled by individuals who are both passionate and knowledgeable about a specific technology area. This type of digest is also becoming increasingly popular in the commercial sector as a way of keeping users of a company's products or services informed of updates, tips, and other related information. Often you can sign up for a digest right from the company's homepage.

Another type of digest is a really a spin-off from the traditional discussion list. Popular discussion lists often generate significant traffic—sometimes upwards of hundreds of messages per day. Unless you live and die by the particular list's topic, you probably won't tolerate that kind of e-mail traffic very long. However, the topic may be important enough for you to subscribe to the list's digest version, if there is one. This usually means that instead of subscribing to the actual discussion list and seeing every single message posted in near-real-time, you instead get a daily or weekly message that is a compilation of all messages posted to the list during the period. Good digests in this category will also list the subject lines from each of the messages and append this at the top of the digest. That way you can quickly scan the various discussion topics and either read further, or just trash the digest. And of course, just because you subscribe to the digest version of a list doesn't mean you can't still post messages to it. It's just that you won't see any responses to your postings until you receive the next digest.

Discussion List Commands Review

Here are some of the basic commands for each of the three popular list types on the Internet today.

Majordomo Discussion Groups
To subscribe:
> `subscribe listname e-mail address`

To unsubscribe:
> `unsubscribe listname`

To receive the digest version:
> `subscribe listname-digest`

To list all subscribers:
> `who listname`

Listproc Discussion Groups
To subscribe:
> `subscribe listname yourfirstname yourlastname`

To unsubscribe:
> `unsubscribe listname yourfirstname yourlastname`

To receive the digest version:
> `set listname mail digest`

To list all subscribers:
> `recipients listname`

Listserv Discussion Groups

To subscribe:

```
subscribe listname yourfirstname yourlastname
```

To unsubscribe:

```
unsubscribe listname
```

To receive the digest version:

```
set listname digest
```

To list all subscribers:

```
review listname
```

Finding Discussion Lists

There are easily tens of thousands of discussion lists active today, and more are added all the time.

Despite all the noise on the net these days, there are some excellent resources out there for finding relevant discussion lists with a minimum of fuss. So while you can fiddle around with retrieving lists via e-mail servers or finding FAQs posted to Usenet newsgroups like **news.lists** and **news.answers,** I recommend instead going straight for the easiest interface: searchable Web databases. Following are a few of the most comprehensive online databases and resources for finding and joining active discussion lists.

Discussion List Resources

PAML: Publicly Accessible Mailing Lists

```
http://www.neosoft.com/internet/paml/
```

One of the original lists of lists.

Liszt: Searchable Directory of E-Mail Discussion Groups

```
http://www.liszt.com/
```

Contains over 65,000 listserv, listproc, majordomo, and independently managed lists from over 2000 sites.

Tile.Net

```
http://www.tile.net/
```

All the listserv discussion groups on the Internet.

InterNIC Mailing Lists

`http://www.internic.net/tools/list.html`

This is just a one-stop interface to some of the other searchable databases listed above.

In addition to searching the Web for discussion lists, listservs through the BITNET network are indexed and can be queried by e-mail. To find a listserv of interest send e-mail to:

`listserv@bitnic.bitnet`

with the message

`list global/keyword`

where the keyword is a topic you are interested in. For example:

`list global/sensors`

In response you will receive a roster of all the lists that use your keyword to describe their topical focus.

Finally, if you have access to the Web, try looking at some of the big search sites like Yahoo (**http://www.yahoo.com**) and Excite (**http://www.excite.com**), as they maintain numerous lists of links to Web-based mailing lists.

Chapter 5

WEB BROWSERS
& APPLICATIONS

The World Wide Web is an ingenious window to the millions of "pages" online today. It is also a way to access information available on other types of online information services, such as FTP and Usenet.

The Web was originally developed at CERN, the European Laboratory for Particle Physics. Its first stated purpose (from the original proposal) was to "provide a common (simple) protocol for requesting human readable information stored at a remote system, using networks." The overlying objective was simple: give scientists a way to exchange many kinds of data (text, graphics, figures, databases) using a concept known as hypertext for the purpose of advancing their research. From this testbed, the implementation and response from the online community has exploded into one of the biggest communications phenomena of the twentieth century.

Welcome to Hypertext

The Web is a radical departure from the hierarchical information systems that preceded it. For hundreds of years research has been conducted primarily at libraries, since that's where all the information was. There you might look up a subject or author in a card catalog, review relevant findings, from there compile a list of additional books and references to also review, and so on. This could be a very tedious and time-consuming process.

The Web is the new model that can vastly speed this process. The key to the Web is the use of hypertext, an idea that goes all the way back to Vannevar Bush in 1945. Twenty years later, Ted Nelson coined the term *hypertext*, but it's only been recently that the term and the implementation has made its way into the mainstream. The fundamental concept behind hypertext is that information can be stored and retrieved in a nonhierarchical structure (hence the term "Web"). So instead of moving through directories or card catalogs, you can instead jump from one place to the next through a series of hypertext links.

Web Foundation Elements

Much of what happens on the World Wide Web goes on behind the scenes using an Internet protocol called HTTP, or HyperText Transport Protocol. HTTP is extremely efficient at what it does because it does not have any "search" functions to slow it down. You simply click **here** and you go **there**. Not much to get in the way. This is not to say that Web servers or the Internet itself cannot be searched for information, because they can. However, such searches don't use the HTTP protocol to do the work; rather, the work is done by software either on your own computer or a server computer you're connected to. HTTP works together with many other Internet tools and services. In networking parlance it is the "transmission layer" of the Internet.

The language that HTTP "speaks" best is called HTML (HyperText Markup Language). HTML is a subset of SGML (Standard Generalized Markup Language), a powerful language for tagging documents with electronic formatting and structural definitions. Many scholarly and technical publishers today are tagging their publications in SGML, which makes them easily exportable for other uses, most notably the Web.

The Client-Server Model on the Web

The Web uses the client-server model of computer interaction. Any computer on the Internet that responds to HTTP requests is said to be a Web server, and any computer that can query using HTTP is a client, or more popularly, a browser. This conceptual model allows various types of computers to talk to each other. The client and server software, while designed to be used on a specific operating system such as Windows, Unix, or Macintosh, must still transmit and receive data using the HTTP protocol, and then display the information on your computer (which has the client software on it) according to the established standards.

Uniform Resource Locators (URLs)

An URL is basically a way of specifying the location of something on the Internet. That location can be as general as a computer name, or as specific as a single letter on a document on a server anywhere in the world. An URL is what's used in HTML to make hypertext links.

Let's look at an example. Right now I'm typing on a computer that is connected directly to the Internet. My computer's Internet domain name is **cozumel.spie.org**. In other words, if I were running Web server software from it, you could access my Web homepage by typing this address in your browser:

```
http://cozumel.spie.org
```

The same is true for other types of Internet services, such as FTP (File Transfer Protocol). If I were running FTP server software on my computer and was letting "anonymous" users access it, you could type

```
ftp://cozumel.spie.org
```

in your browser, and a directory of my server would display in your browser's window.

This is standard URL addressing. Note that the type of connection is shown by an addressing prefix such as **http://** or **ftp://**, which is used to define what kind of online server or service you're trying to access. Most of today's Web browsers have actually built in the assumption that you'll be visiting a Web site unless you say otherwise, so you don't need to type "http://" in front of an address, you simply type the server name (in the example above, **cozumel.spie.org**) and the browser will take care of the rest behind the scenes.

So, URLs can really be used to describe just about any kind of connection on the Internet, including FTP, telnet, gopher, Usenet, and e-mail, as show in these examples:

```
telnet://cozumel.spie.org
gopher://cozumel.spie.org
news://cozumel.spie.org
mail://cozumel.spie.org
```

Let's take this a step further. On my computer right now I'm typing in a document called web_chapter.html, which is stored in a directory called **book** directly on my hard drive. If I were running Web server software on my computer, you could directly access this specific document by typing the following address in your Web browser:

```
http://cozumel.spie.org/book/web_chapter.html
```

I could even go so far as to point you to a particular word on this page by marking the word with the HTML language, so you might type an URL something like this, where you would be taken directly to the word on the page:

```
http://cozumel.spie.org/book/web_chapter.html#word23
```

This is really the key to the Web's ability to use all of the Internet protocols in conjunction with HTML. By embedding addresses such as those above into hypertext links, the Web becomes an environment that draws on all kinds of connections from a single user interface—your Web browser. (See Part II of this book for specific tutorials on how to construct HTML links like the ones above for your own Web pages.)

Introduction to Web Browsers

As already mentioned, the Web browser is the client in the client-server model of the Web. In retrospect, it's rather unfortunate that the word *browser* stuck so well, since it more accurately describes the Web of 1994. Today's browsers do much more than simply browse the Web. The latest versions of the two leading browsers, Netscape Communicator (neé Navigator) and Microsoft Internet Explorer, comprise some of the most versatile software on the market today. They are being revised constantly, so much so that keeping up with their revisions is a full-time job.

There are also different kinds of browsers. If your computer is text-based (sometimes called a command-line interface), for example, through a Unix host, then a Web browser on that computer would be called a line or text browser. Alternately, if your computer has as a graphical operating system such as Windows, Macintosh, or XWindows, you'll likely be using a browser such as Netscape or Internet Explorer.

There is also a third category of browser, which can best be described as "service-specific." If you have an account with one of the major commercial online services such as America Online or CompuServe, or a major online service provider such as Netcom, you may be able to (or forced to) use their customized browser software for browsing the Web. However, most services like America Online today also let you use an alternate browser such as Netscape (which I highly recommend you do if you have an AOL account).

While the Web can certainly be accessed using a text browser, it's really designed to work best with the graphical browsers that take full advantage of the Web's ability to bring you all kinds of digital media such as pictures and sounds, as well as readable formats and interactive features such as online forms. The graphical browsers also rely heavily on the mouse for navigating and selecting information, whereas line browsers have you enter a selection number or skip from link to link using the arrow keys.

Two Browser Types

While many of us may take for granted having access to the latest versions of Netscape or Internet Explorer, I have seen evidence that there is still a significant number of people who, for various reasons, access the Web via a text browser such as Lynx, either on their own network or via telnet. I've also found that when traveling, there are times when I really need to look something up on a Web site (especially my own company's site), and the only access I can find is through a university or laboratory computer with a text browser or telnet capabilities. For both these reasons, I'm going to demonstrate accessing the Web via a text browser before moving on to the more glitzy graphical browsers.

Text Browsers

As already noted, there are two kinds of text browsers common on the Web today. The only real difference between the two is that one uses numbers in brackets like this [1] to denote a link, and the other uses boldface type like **this**. This last type is known as the Lynx browser and seems to be the most common text browser in use today, so we'll use it for our example.

To use a Lynx browser, you either need to have it installed on your Internet host computer, or telnet to another computer that lets you use their public Lynx browser. The best way to find out what your options are is to ask a knowledgeable colleague, your network administrator, or your Internet Service Provider.

For our example, we'll telnet to a public Lynx browser at the University of Kansas (The U of K just happens to also be the place where Lynx was developed.) The login name we use for this site is **lynx**, as they tell us on this opening screen:

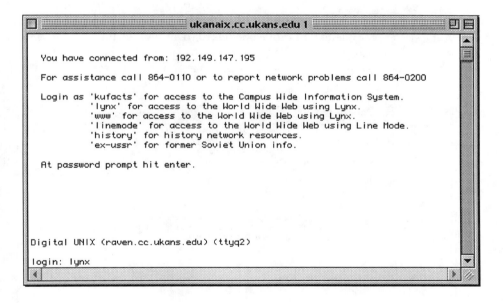

```
                        ukanaix.cc.ukans.edu 1

    You have connected from: 192.149.147.195

    For assistance call 864-0110 or to report network problems call 864-0200

    Login as 'kufacts' for access to the Campus Wide Information System.
             'lynx' for access to the World Wide Web using Lynx.
             'www' for access to the World Wide Web using Lynx.
             'linemode' for access to the World Wide Web using Line Mode.
             'history' for history network resources.
             'ex-ussr' for former Soviet Union info.

    At password prompt hit enter.




Digital UNIX (raven.cc.ukans.edu) (ttyq2)

login: lynx
```

Pressing Return now tells the remote computer that we'll accept the default VT100 terminal type, resulting in the following text display:

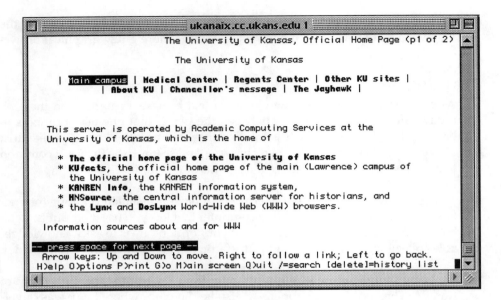

Note the use of boldface type here. Every word or phrase that is bold is actually a hypertext link. The commands at the bottom of the screen tell us that we can use the up and down arrow keys to skip to the next hypertext link, and we can use the right and left arrow keys to either select a link (and therefore take you to wherever it leads) or move backward to a previous link, or the spacebar to view the next screen. Pressing Enter or Return accesses the link indicated by the blocked text. I first used the spacebar to get to the next screen:

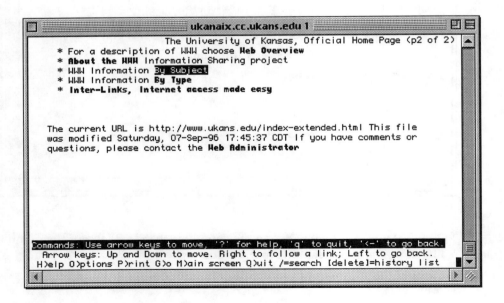

From here I chose the "WWW Information by Subject" link, which brings us here:

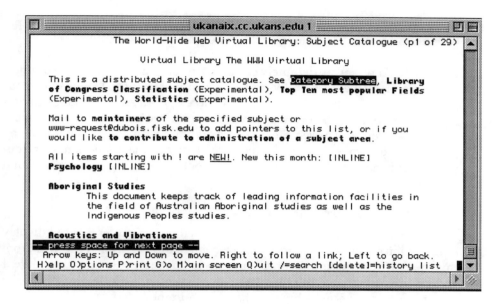

Now, as it turns out, this took us to the WWW Virtual Library at Stanford University, a very familiar starting point for new Web users, with hundreds of topical area sites managed by individual experts in their fields all over the world. I then used the spacebar to find a link to the Artificial Intelligence Virtual Library, which took me here:

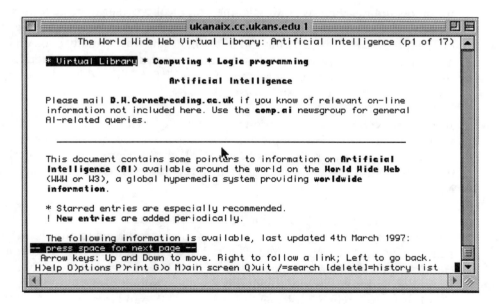

Although it may look like we're still at the University of Kansas where we started, we're actually at the University of Reading, home of the WWW Virtual Library for Artificial Intelligence. From here we could continue down the page to find additional links to many AI facilities, or use the arrow keys to retrace our path and look at other virtual libraries. Of course, we could also simply type the G key for "Go", enter an URL, and go directly there.

Lynx-style browsers are definitely crude when compared to Netscape or Internet Explorer, as we'll see in the remainder of this chapter. However, if your access to the Web is limited to this kind of access, from an information gathering standpoint these text browsers are still useful. The biggest problem usually arises when you're at a Web site that uses graphics for navigation without any alternative text links. But most major sites today in the sciences have recognized this common design flaw and offer both text and graphic navigation systems.

Graphical Browsers

The Web was originally designed to be accessed via a browser that can display both graphics and text, the first of these being a browser called Mosaic. From this starting point more effort has gone toward increasing the graphic content and capabilities of the Web than any other aspect of it. Certainly part of the reason for this is because humans have such immediate responses to visual cues. So it goes without saying that an attractive Web site that mixes text and graphics well will be more popular than one that is merely a massive wall of text. Of course, as most of us have seen, some Web designers simply don't know when to stop with graphics. Some of the most heinous examples of bad design ever conceived were born on a Web page.

Browser Wars

In the beginning, there was Mosaic, the graphical browser developed at the National Center for Supercomputing Applications (NCSA) and distributed freely on the Internet. However, by the end of 1995, Mosaic was virtually overrun by an influx of new browsers, led first by the enormously successful Netscape from the new company of the same name, and later followed by Microsoft's Internet Explorer. Thus began Browser Wars.

At present, Netscape and Microsoft absolutely dominate the browser market. While there are still a few people out in cyberspace who continue to use obsolete versions of browsers like Mosaic and WinWeb, the overwhelming majority of the graphical browsers on the Web today are from either Netscape or Microsoft.

There is good news and bad in this situation. The good news is that this is one area of the computer industry that Microsoft hasn't managed to muscle out or simply buy all of its competitors. The bad news is that these two companies couldn't agree on a feature specification if their lives depended on it. There is simply no end to the lack of standardization across their respective browsers. This is even true when implementing actual HTML standards, which are governed by the Internet Engineering Task Force (IETF), of which both Microsoft and Netscape are primary members.

This all may sound like a tangential discussion in a book like this, but it's not. The browser you choose to access the Web will absolutely dictate what you can do and see online. For example, if you choose to use a browser (or version) that does not support tables, a feature that allows information to be displayed in a grid-like manner, you may visit a site that has information you wish to read, but all the text there will appear as a jumbled mess in your browser window. Taken to the extreme, your choice of browser can dictate whether you'll have features such as online shopping or perhaps the ability to view certain images or figures.

This feature war is also a major headache for Web site designers. It is getting increasingly difficult to design Web pages that will display correctly on both Navigator and Internet Explorer while using the more advanced features available to designers. Recent surveys among Web designers continue to show that they are designing for both Netscape and Microsoft browsers, which means they are leaving out some features they could include that would be useful to readers. It also means they are spending more money and resources to create and maintain their Web site, money that might be better spent improving their site's contents.

There is no easy resolution to the Browser Wars situation. I still hold hope that it's just a growing pain that the Internet community just has to endure. As with any industry, commercialization of the Internet has brought with it increased capabilities as well as much confusion.

Exploring the Web with Netscape

As I write this, despite Microsoft's indefatigable marketing efforts, Netscape still accounts for almost 60% of the browsers in use on the Internet, and maintains versions for over 17 operating systems. As such, it is an obvious choice for demonstrations throughout this book. If you have chosen Internet Explorer for your window to the Web, most of the examples and tutorials herein will be equally applicable, albeit with some changes due to obvious differences such as menu items and preferences windows.

The Windows, Macintosh, and XWindows versions of Netscape all undergo continual facelifts, but they all look and act basically the same, and support the same features. The differences are mostly in menu titles and other interface aspects that are more a function of what is "normal" for each of these computer types, and in fact even those standards have changed along the way, so that no two versions of Netscape are the same, regardless of computer type. For the examples in this book, I use Netscape 4.0, which at the time of writing is the most current version (and just released, actually).

The first thing you can do after installing Netscape is go somewhere with it. You don't really need to configure anything before starting, providing your computer is already set up to access the Internet. There are certainly things you may want to customize later, as we'll see, but you don't have to do anything to get started surfing. The installation process will ask for all of the basics required.

Netscape comes with a "Search Internet" menu option that connects you directly to a page on the Netscape Web site which has instant connections to most of the major Internet search engines such as InfoSeek and Yahoo (and those companies pay lots of money to be featured on that page.) This can be a good place to start if it's your first time on the Web.

However, since you're holding a book full of interesting places to go, we'll use one of them instead. Like everything on the Internet, we can type an URL into the browser's URL window to go where we want on the Web, although one of the major advantages of the Web is that you often do not need an address, since everywhere you go can be a jumping off point, using hypertext links, to other locations.

From the Computer Science section of this book, I found the URL for Silicon Graphics (**http://www.sgi.com**), a developer of high-end computer hardware and software.

As I suspected, their homepage reflects some of the more advanced features of the Web. First off is that they offer alternate "paths" for users who want a text-only version of their site, and even more interesting, for those who want a Java-enabled version. The Web designers at SGI are ahead of their time in offering this Java option. Most sites simply foist Java applets onto your computer without warning, so making this an option path is a considerate design feature. (More about Java applets later in this chapter and in Part II of this book.)

All in all, the SGI homepage is good example of some of the better-designed sites you'll find on the Web today. It provides lots of navigation options, and doesn't clutter up the page with a lot of extraneous bells and whistles.

Customizing Your Web Browser

As mentioned earlier, most Web browsers have default settings designed to get you started on the Web immediately. However, if you do a lot of Web surfing, customizing your browser environment can make your time on the Web even more productive and enjoyable. Most of the current browsers support some truly innovative ways to allow you to personalize your online environment, and so we'll look at some of the most popular ones here.

Link Colors, Background Colors, and Image Maps

A relatively common feature found on the SGI homepage above is an *image map*. In fact, there are two image maps on this page. The upper left-hand corner has an image map graphic for major navigation choices such as Find and Archives, whereas the graphic on the right margin of the main page has more specific navigation links such as Products & Services. Each of these is an image map, which means that you can simply click on various locations of the graphic to take you to other locations, just like a hypertext link. The Web server (in this case, SGI's) interprets the *x-y* coordinates of your mouse-click on the image and translates it into an URL location. So actually it's the same process as clicking on a hypertext link. Image maps used for navigation also mean that you must load the image in order to navigate to the site, which is why SGI smartly offers a text-only version of their site. Note that image maps are not the same as a simple linked graphic. The main graphic on this page ("Partners in Integration") is a simple linked graphic, meaning that if you click anywhere on the graphic you will be linked to a single location. The distinction here is subtle but important, since you'll find both kinds of links on Web pages.

In addition to the image maps and linked graphics there are also some regular hypertext links on this page in the lower left-hand corner. As is standard to most browsers, text links to other places are usually underlined and in a color different from the static text on the page. In the not-so-distant past, you could count on a blue link to signify someplace you had not yet visited, and a red link to show a place you visited recently. All that has changed, however. With most Web browsers today you can customize the colors of the links, or let the Web sites you visit control those colors. This is also true for the background of your browser window. Again, you can often dictate a color of your choice; however, most people allow the Web sites they visit to control the background colors, since many sites are designed to take advantage of this feature. Many of the more sophisticated sites will try to change the background color and link colors of your browser when you visit them, and some even change the background to a custom texture or graphic. The difference on a visual level can be quite dramatic, much like the difference between a black-and-white newspaper and a full-color glossy magazine. However, if you wish to control the link colors or backgrounds yourself, look in your browser's Preferences menu for Link Colors and Background options.

Saving Text and Printing

One of the best things about browsing the Web with Netscape or most other graphical browsers is the ability to perform so many functions from just one interface. For example, if you arrive at a Web site that has lots of interesting documents you want to read later, you have a number of options. First, you could save the document as a text file on your hard drive. Some of the more advanced browsers let you save as formatted text as well, and you'll want to use this option if available, because even when stripped of their HTML tags, documents on the Web are often long strings of text that run together without breaks. The formatted text option can be a real eye saver.

As an alternative, if you prefer the look of a document as viewed in your Netscape browser, you can usually save the document on your computer as an HTML-encoded file (usually called "Save as source"), which means you can come back later and view it with your Netscape browser software with all the nice formatting and readable text still intact. The process of viewing HTML-formatted files directly from your own computer is usually done using a menu option called Open Local or Open File, meaning "open a file that's already on a local hard drive, not on the Internet."

Still another option is to print a Web document you're viewing directly to your printer. Some browsers even let you save a Web page as a PostScript file so that you can then send it to a PostScript-compatible printer, where even the graphics will be faithfully reproduced.

Viewing Text and Graphics

Netscape and most other browsers allow you to select your favorite typeface (font) and size for your browser's display. Be careful about what you choose, however. There are usually two choices to be made: proportional font and fixed font. Remember that it's your browser that usually determines the actual typeface displayed; however, it's the Web server that tells the browser the relative size and style of the typeface. What happens is, you tell your browser to use Times Roman to display proportional text at 12 points. This is your default text size, which is scaled up and down in your browser, depending on what the server you are visiting tells your browser to do.

For example, there are six relative sizes of headlines in the HTML standard (H1, H2, H3, etc.). When you access a page on a Web server, the HTML tags your browser "reads" may tell the browser to display a particular headline as an "H1". This means whatever font you've chosen as your proportional font will be scaled up to display as a large headline, probably two or three times the size of the 12-point default you've designated. This is how Web browsers work with the HTML tags to create a semi-customized viewing environment. You choose the typeface and basic text size, and the browser scales it up and down, or adds bold or italics for emphasis. My personal preference is to set up my browser with a 14-pt. Helvetica or Arial default font. I've found that, for me, the slightly larger sans serif base font induces less eye strain, and if you spend a lot of time on the computer, this is important.

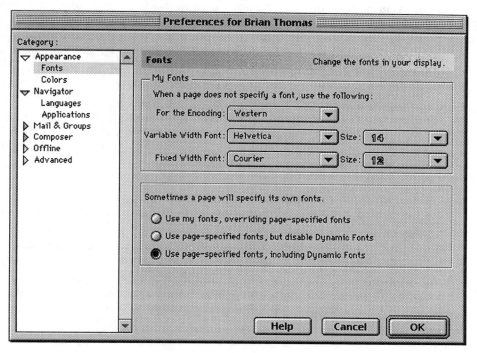

Choice of a fixed font is just as important. Fixed fonts are used by Web browsers to display text that needs to maintain the formatting of the original document. For example, if you wanted to serve up a document that had four separate columns of numbers, and you wanted those numbers to stay in well-defined columns to make the document easy to read, you would choose this approach. Choosing a monospace typeface such as Courier will display information correctly when it is designated by the server as fixed (the HTML tag is actually called preformatted). Of course, the increased use of the tables feature (see Tables, below) is replacing the need for preformatted text in many situations.

Image Loading

Finally, you'll need to make some choices about how images are handled when encountered on the Web. The main point here is, if you're connected to the

Internet via a modem, you'll probably want your browser to not automatically load graphics; instead, you would choose which individual graphics should load by clicking on them with your mouse. Many new Web surfers opt to load every graphic as it's encountered, and then wonder why the Web is so slow.

The truth is, many of today's Web sites are filled with graphics. From a modem connection, or when connecting to a Web site far away, this can make for very slow browsing. Turning off your browser's auto-load feature may not be the prettiest way to view the Web, but it's certainly the most efficient. In the worst-case scenario, choosing to load all the graphics can even mean that you can't access a certain site, because the download time will exceed the server's time-out limit and will abort the transfer in midstream. This can be very frustrating.

Older versions of Netscape gave you the ability to turn automatic image loading on or off from a main menu item. However, in 4.0 they've decided to move it to the Advanced Preferences window, which I think is a bad decision. Sometimes when I'm on the Web I like to turn off image loading just for a little while, such as when I know I'll be going through a number of graphics-intensive sites before finding what I'm looking for, and then turn them back on when I'm done with that task. This is still a good surfing tip, despite Netscape's making it a little more difficult to do on the fly.

Bookmarks and Hotlists

One of the first things you can do when you start using a Web browser is create a personal list of favorite places to go. Such lists are called by a variety of names—bookmarks, hotlists, favorite places, etc. They are nothing more than a way of saving an URL address for future retrieval—the equivalent of a personalized online phone book. Web browsers continue to get more sophisticated in the ways they let you create, edit, and display bookmarks. Most let you create any number of separate lists and load them on the fly, or create lists that have sublists attached.

The first time you go somewhere on the Web you think you'll want to come back to at some other time, just find the menu option that lets you "Add Bookmark" (under the Bookmarks menu in Netscape), and it will be appended to the default list in your Web browser. When you want to see what's in your bookmarks, find something similar to Netscape's "Bookmarks" command to display a window listing all the addresses you have saved.

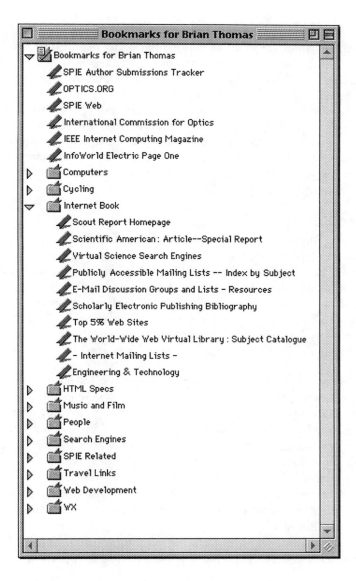

From here you can add, edit, or delete links as you wish. You can even give it a name that's easier for you to remember than the often lengthy and convoluted URL address. For long URLs, bookmarks are an especially handy feature. One tip that I'll add here from hard-learned experience: as with any other important digital information that would be difficult to recreate, back up your bookmark files regularly to some other location.

When your Web exploring gets more extensive and your bookmarks list starts getting unwieldy, you can start using the customized menu features of your browser to organize the information into smaller groups of bookmarks, as shown in the figure above, in what's called a hierarchical or cascading menu.

Another browser feature that I find especially helpful is one that allows you to click on a hypertext link in a document and, if you continue to hold down the mouse button for a second or two (or use the right mouse button), a pop-up menu displays. This menu gives you options not only to connect to the link in the normal way, but also to retrieve the entire document it links to and save it on your computer's hard drive. For anyone interested in the HTML tagging language or starting their own Web server, this is useful information. It may also let you add the link as a bookmark without actually loading the link location, as well as save an image or graphic directly to your computer. Finally, it lets you copy an URL address to your computer's clipboard and then paste it into a document directly.

Helper Applications & Plug-ins

Helper Applications are applications on your computer that you tell your Web browser to launch when you run across something in your Web explorations that your browser cannot handle. Plug-ins have the same purpose, except that they allow the helper application to be "opened up" inside your browser window, which makes for a more integrated Web environment. Netscape today ships with a wide variety of plug-ins, and new ones are available periodically. To add a new plug-in on most computers it is simply a matter of downloading the plug-in module and moving it to the Netscape Plug-ins directory.

Let's follow an example. If you were visiting an online music archive and clicked on an AIF or WAV file (both are audio formats used with computers), the audio-clip file would automatically be transferred to your computer's hard drive. However, your browser's work might then be done if it can't play audio clips directly, but as a shortcut, you can tell your browser to launch a certain application (in this case, one that can play audio files) whenever it sees a certain type of file or filename extension (in this example, .aif or .wav). This same concept is used to launch external graphics viewers, video players, and other applications that work with your browser to create a seamless working environment while you're on the Web.

On the next page is an example of what Netscape's Applications window looks like.

In the left-hand column is a description of many types of files you can encounter on the Web, and in the right is a designated "handler" for each. The ones that say "Netscape (internal)" are files that Netscape can read without any other application. The rest require either a helper application defined, or a plug-in such as the LiveAudio ones shown in the figure.

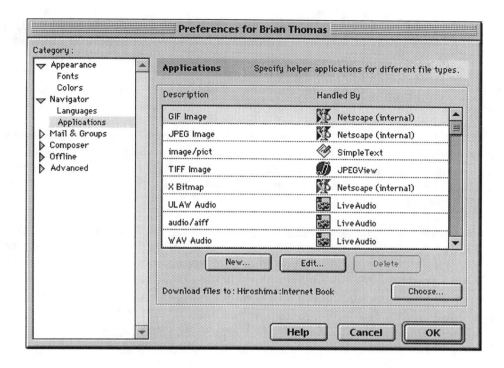

MIME: Multipurpose Internet Mail Extensions

Don't let the name fool you. While originally developed for e-mail attachments, MIME is now integral to your Web browser's ability to identify and deal with the myriad and ever-growing list of file types on the Web today. MIME uses a filename's extension to determine what to do with it. When you view a Web page, the first thing your browser reads is the page's file extension—*.html*. Then it looks up *.html* in its list of MIME types, which tells the browser that *.html* is a MIME type of "text/html," and therefore it should display the file's contents in the browser window. A start tag of <html> on the actual page then tells the browser to convert everything that follows into text with corresponding HTML features and display characteristics. (For more background on HTML, see the chapters in Part II of this book.)

After loading the text and formatting attributes from the HTML tags on the page, the browser then starts parsing the rest of the elements on the page, looking at all the pointers, links, actions, scripts, etc. References to filenames with the extensions *.gif* or *.jpg* will be recognized as the MIME types image/gif or image/jpg and, since these are formats that the browser can display on its own, will be loaded and displayed. If, however, these graphics had a file extension of *.tif* or *.eps*, the browser would recognize these as the MIME extensions for image types that it cannot display in the browser, and therefore would either download the images to the hard drive, or prompt the user for a decision. Files of completely unknown type will also elicit the "What do you want to do?" dialog box (see figure on following page). This is the basic function of MIME in action, whether it be applied to e-mail attachments or Web pages.

What this all means for you is control. Let's look at a real-life example: I've personally lost all patience with sites that foist unwanted audio or video clips at me, not only because bandwidth and time are precious commodities but, moreover, because these offending files often crash my browser, my connection, or my computer. And even when these "multimedia" elements do work correctly, I've yet to see one I couldn't have lived without.

Now MIME certainly can't stop people from creating useless sound bites, but it does give us the power to shunt such "enhancements" off into the ether before they do any damage. MIME's adaptability here gives us the tools to stop such files from automatically loading, and instead just download or cancel them altogether.

So let's say you want to stop WAV audio files (a very popular format) from playing automatically. Using Netscape 4.0 (for example) select the Navigator:Applications option from the Preferences menu. Locate the listing for WAV files, choose Edit, and then click the Unknown: Prompt User option (see figure below). If there isn't already an entry for WAV files in the list, just create a new one using the New button, then type **application/wav** in the Description and MIME Type fields, and *.wav* in the Suffixes field.

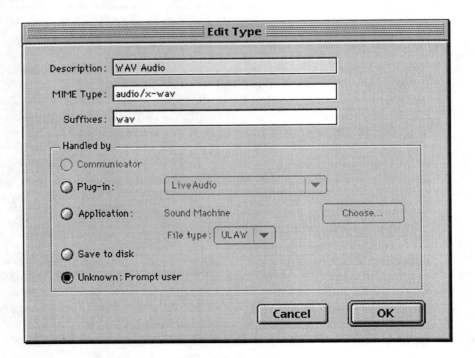

The next time you encounter a link to a WAV file on the Web, instead of automatically loading and playing it via the LiveAudio plug-in, you will see a message like the one shown below. Here you're not only given the option of downloading or launching the sound file, but also to simply cancel the download altogether.

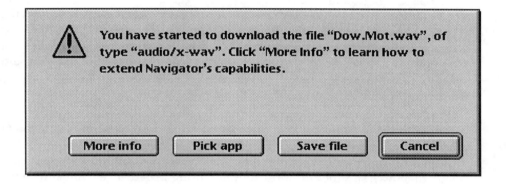

Looking back at the main Preferences: Applications window on the previous page, we can see some of the other controls we're given for handling files encountered on the Web. As mentioned already, based on the file's MIME extension, the browser can be set up to load a file internally (if it can), automatically launch a file with another application, or save it to the hard drive. The plug-in option is a relatively new and important one. It goes back to my earlier comments on how browsers are expanding their feature-set to handle functions that would normally require separate applications. Plug-ins are application-specific modules that allow certain file types to be opened from within the browser instead of requiring another application. For example, Netscape 4.0 now comes with plug-ins for playing many types of audio files via a LiveAudio plug-in. In the Preferences window above where we change the WAV MIME type, the "Handle by Plug-in" pulldown menu will automatically become active if a chosen MIME type can be handled by an available plug-in.

Web Page Enhancements

Some of the most important innovations in Web browsers recently have been those that attempt to organize and display information more efficiently, as well as make it easier to navigate. Following is a look at some of the most important ones. More detailed background on these elements can be found in Part II of this book.

Tables

The *tables* feature is one that most browsers now support. Originally it was a simple solution to organizing information that is best suited for tabular display—such as numerical tables or spreadsheet information. However, Web designers quickly picked up on tables as a way of constructing whole pages, often using numerous tables nested inside of other tables, and all tagged as "invisible" so the reader doesn't see any of the table borders. From a user's perspective, tables are usually not a problem unless they are designed poorly. For example, a newer tables feature is the ability to specify a colored background for each table cell or area. This can become a problem if the designer specifies a cell or area as "background=black," and then necessarily also specifies that the text in that area be "color=white" so the text can be seen against the black background. This kind of HTML tagging can be problematic when, for example, a user's browser fails to execute both design elements when the page is loaded, leaving either black text on a black background, or white text on a white or default gray background. This is also an example of why it's not a good idea to designate a specific background color for your browser and have it set to override whatever a Web site is trying to set the background to.

Frames

One of the most hotly debated features introduced by Netscape in 1996 was and continues to be frames. While frames give Web designers more control over site design by allowing the creation of "windows within windows," each with their own specific attributes, they also bring with them a number of negatives. The frames feature is a significant change in the way Web browsers work, not only for the reasons noted above, but also because it changes some of the standard browser features, such as navigation and formatting tools. For example, if you're viewing a page formatted with frames, the "Back" button on your browser may no longer work the way you expect. Instead, you'll have to click and hold your mouse inside the frame you want to go back from, wait for a little pop-up menu to appear, then select the Back option from there. This is all because the browser's Back button doesn't know which frame to switch backward. While this is a seemingly minor issue, it continues to confuse Web users when encountered.

But the biggest argument against frames centers on performance, or lack thereof. Depending on their implementation and extent, frames often have a significant effect on the speed of your browsing because they simply take a long time to lay out and load. The other oft-cited argument against frames is that they're often complex and poorly designed, and so in fact make it more difficult for users to navigate a site. Slower and more confusing are not features most designers would choose for their sites, but often the novelty of frames seduces them into using (or overusing) them. Thankfully, some of the best sites that have chosen to use frames also offer a nonframes version of the site, usually as a link from the homepage.

Online Forms

The use of online forms is commonplace on the Web today. The forms feature allows users to type in information in database-style fields, and then when all the information is entered, a button is usually activated to send the information to the Web server, where it is processed. Typical uses for online forms include querying a database, registering for a service, or purchasing goods.

Above is an example of a simple database search form. The user enters the requested information into each field by clicking the mouse in the first field, and then using the tab key to jump to successive fields. In this example the user would click the Search button, after which the information from the form is sent to the Web server, and in a few seconds the results of the search are displayed back to you.

When forms are used to submit information permanently, such as when registering for an event or purchasing something online, it's becoming increasingly common to also receive an e-mail confirmation of your registration or purchase. However, in many cases you won't know if you'll be getting an e-mail confirmation, so it's always a good practice to save a copy of any message you receive in your browser window after initiating a transaction. For example, if you register for a conference using an online form, after submitting the registration form you will receive some kind of message from the server saying your registration was received. With this message in your browser window, select the "Save" menu option and save the message as text somewhere on your hard drive. That way you have a record of what the server told you in case there are disputes later.

Multimedia on the Web

The promise of true multimedia functionality on the Web is well-advertised in the popular literature. In reality, the word *multimedia* is often stretched to include just about anything new or not "straight HTML." Below are a few of the most promising technologies being implemented on the Web today. Note that nearly all of these nascent technologies depend on the ability to make the browser (client) take on as much work as possible, in an effort to resolve performance issues caused by limited bandwidth.

Java and JavaScript

Java is Sun Microsystems' hybrid of C and C++ languages optimized for handling client/server actions on the Web. All this really means is that with a Java-enabled browser, you can download small *applets* of computer code that will automatically launch on your computer, which is then continually fed or updated by the Web server if necessary. Some common examples of what this technology can do include continuously updated stocks and mutual funds data that can automatically update a client's portfolio, or real-time animations played directly inside your browser's window. Obviously, this is sophisticated technology and has as many obstacles as it does potential uses. But there is tremendous movement and financial support behind this technology, and it seems clear it will find the applications necessary to make it successful.

JavaScript is not Java, but rather a scripting language that works largely as an extension to the HTML tagging language. It is gaining increasing acceptance among site designers as a way of adding features that you can't do with plain HTML.

While Java and JavaScript are not something that you have any direct control over when you're surfing the Web, you can in fact disable them in your browser if you wish. Many people choose to do this because of security or stability reasons. By turning Java and/or JavaScript off, your browser will refuse to load any Java applets or JavaScripts that you encounter while on the Web. If your browser is Java-enabled, you can turn it off via the Preferences: Advanced menu option, which in Netscape 4.0 looks like this:

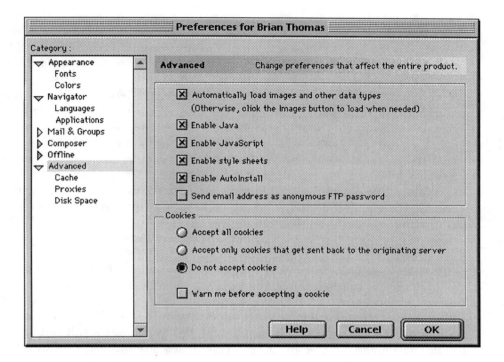

Note also that this Preferences window is also where you can choose to turn on or off the automatic loading of all graphics (if you turn it off, then you'll need to click on any graphic's generic icon to view it—a useful option if you're in a hurry and on a slow connection.)

Java and JavaScript are discussed further in Part II of this book.

Cookies

In the previous figure there are options for controlling cookies as well. Cookies are small data packets collected by most Web servers in the background. They can be good or evil, depending on your perspective and level of Web privacy paranoia you have. Basically, cookies can make it so that when you revisit a Web site, the site "remembers" certain things about you from your last visit. For example, a server might use cookie information to determine how many connections to a site have come from different computers (so multiple connections from the same computer are only counted once). Cookies cannot, contrary to folklore, gain access to information on your computer. Note also that just because a Web server "requests" a cookie from your browser, this doesn't necessarily mean that the people managing that server are going to do anything with the cookie. Most servers just collect them automatically as part of the connection process.

You can choose to turn off cookie granting, or to have an alert pop up every time one is requested. My recommendation is to either leave them on or off. The alert feature will become an annoyance very quickly.

VRML and QuickTime VR

Virtual Reality Modeling Language (VRML—pronounced "vermil") from Silicon Graphics and InterVista Software, is now touted as a standard for transmitting navigable 3D models over the Web. With VRML, Web authors can construct entire sites, or "worlds," with infinite space and depth. Objects in these worlds can be links to text, audio, or video files, HTML files or sites, or links to other VRML worlds. The challenge here, as with most other Web innovations, is to keep the playback speed acceptable. Right now most implementations are such that the VRML movie is downloaded first, then viewed via the browser or helper application. For real-time applications, the VRML environment works by transmitting dimensions and texture commands to the Web browser, which handles the actual rendering and manipulation. So all the server is really doing is sending mathematical descriptions of objects and their locations, and the browser fills everything in, thereby reducing the amount of bandwidth needed.

Currently there are a number of companies developing VRML players, plug-ins, and demonstrations. Netscape itself has purchased a VRML software engine that they call Live3D. They are currently developing plug-ins that will work within Netscape to view VRML applications. The key thing to remember at this point is that, despite any media hype, this technology is still very much in its infancy, and is therefore not yet an essential tool. However, if you're interested in knowing more about it, visit the VRML repository at this address.

```
http://www.sdsc.edu/vrml/
```

Audio and Video Online

Microsoft's RealAudio technology (purchased from Progressive Networks in 1997) has been widely embraced by the browser development community, and promises to deliver near-real-time audio over the Web using a technique called streaming. Like Java, this technique again involves establishing a somewhat direct connection with a browser and then feeding the highly compressed audio data to the browser, where it is decompressed and played on the fly. RealAudio has in recent months progressed into a usable technology, and many CD music sites offer small sound samples to preview music selections.

In the video world, technologies such as Xing Technologies' StreamWorks are aiming to deliver FM-quality audio and lower-quality video to Web browsers, but admittedly the bandwidth requirements here still look relatively upscale. Much like VRML, this technology is also still in a nascent stage of development. An ISDN connection will probably be the entry level for anything in video for quite some time.

Finally, Netscape again is trying to lead the pack by their recent integration of what they call Netscape Conference, which is part of Netscape Communicator 4.0. Conference is the first browser-integrated attempt at creating "live" audio and video interactions between two or more browsers. Conference consists of a whiteboard feature that lets you and other "conference attendees" exchange image files and information pasted from your computer's clipboard, and a two-way audio system to converse with someone else (who must also have Netscape 4.0) over the Internet. Once again, my litany here is that these are very young technologies and still have many issues to be worked out before they become mainstream applications, not the least of which is performance. The Internet's packet-switched networking principle was never designed with video transmission in mind. In fact, it's the opposite type of technology you would want to have available if you were designing a network for video or audio transmission. Therefore, speaking as someone who gets paid to test 1.0 versions of software on the Internet, my advice here is unless you really have a viable need to talk or see someone via the Internet, it's best to avoid these technologies for now. A good example is the "chat" feature in Conference. Before you can even use it, your computer must be configured and capable of managing the audio requirements involved, including a compatible sound card and installed audio drivers, a good noise-condensing microphone, and plenty of RAM to handle the requirements. Add to this the vagaries of a packet-switched network like the Internet, and you have a recipe for frustration.

More information and software about these technologies, as well as software, can be found at these Web sites:

```
http://www.realaudio.com
http://www.streamworks.com
http://www.netscape.com
```

Reading Usenet Discussion Groups

Although in recent years the Usenet has been plagued by overload and rampant commercial spam (unsolicited e-mail, usually promotional), if used judiciously it can still be an important tool for scientists and engineers today. Current Web browsers offer the ability to read and post Usenet news in an efficient manner, so we'll discuss here how to set up Netscape to read Usenet news.

What is Usenet?

But first, some background on the Usenet system, which is one of the oldest messaging systems on the Internet. Usenet, conceptually, is a global bulletin board system. People send e-mail style messages, which are processed and interpreted by computers running appropriate software. These messages are collected into newsgroups, which are topical associations of like interests, and which anyone with a news account can then read.

Usenet has one major advantage over mailing lists: when you send out a message to a newsgroup, you're mainly sending one copy to each of the machines that subscribe to Usenet. This one copy is archived, and users can reference that one copy. In a certain amount of time (ranging from one day to one month), the machine automatically deletes the file, to make room for new files.

This is much more efficient than mailing lists, which could conceivably send a hundred copies of a post to each of a computer's one hundred users. This is horribly wasteful, in terms of disk storage.

There are two types of newsgroups: moderated and nonmoderated. Moderated groups are effectively edited by one or more people, who scan and process submissions before posting: this way, the quality of a newsgroup can be ensured.

Nonmoderated groups, which include most groups, are just like bulletin board systems, gab-fests in which anyone can speak their mind on absolutely anything. Want to talk about aerospace engineering in **sci.bio**? Go for it! But just be prepared for the flame mail when you do.

Conduct on Usenet is complex, mainly because you don't know who you're dealing with. To address these issues, the notion of "netiquette" has arisen, with individuals listing recommended rules of contact, most intended to reduce the phenomenon of *flaming*. The netiquette rules for Usenet are similar to those for e-mail. Therefore see the previous chapter on e-mail for further background.

Lastly, it's important to remember that what few rules that exist on Usenet are purely artificial and arbitrary. There's an anarchistic "consensus" on certain things, but the bottom line is, the written rules are written by people who just felt like sitting down and writing rules. Some important rules, such as those pertaining to newsgroup creation, are similarly arbitrary, but are tolerated solely because nobody else has offered better solutions. Nobody owns anything, and nobody has enforcement power (although whoever provides your access to the Internet can control what you see). It's not even clear whether the usual laws of libel apply, since anyone can forge a Usenet message, usually pretty easily.

Setting Up Netscape to Read Usenet News

Before you can access the Usenet, you'll need to make sure your Internet Service Provider (ISP) offers a "news feed" as part of your subscription. If they do, then they should be able to tell you their news server's address, either as a numerical IP address, such as 192.143.324.12, or its domain name, such as **news.barditch.com**. You may also need a username and password to access the news server.

Once you have this information in hand, you can then set up your browser software to access Usenet newsgroups. Using Netscape as our example, in the Preferences window find the Groups Server option. The window will look something like this:

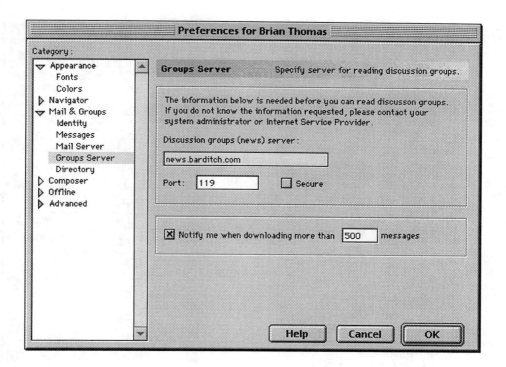

In the server name field, type the domain name or numerical IP address of the news server at your ISP. Unless your ISP told you a specific port number or other information, this is all you need to do for now. Later you may want to raise or lower the number in the "Notify me when..." field if you regularly read newsgroups with high traffic volume.

Next, go to the Netscape menu and choose the Message Center option. This displays a window that you may already be familiar with if you read your e-mail using Netscape as well. From here choose the Join Groups menu option. You'll see the window you'll use to select which newsgroups you wish to "subscribe" to. You may also be asked for your username and password at this point. Subscribing to a group means nothing more than designating it as a group you want to bookmark for future access. It in no way commits you to anything as would subscribing to an e-mail discussion group.

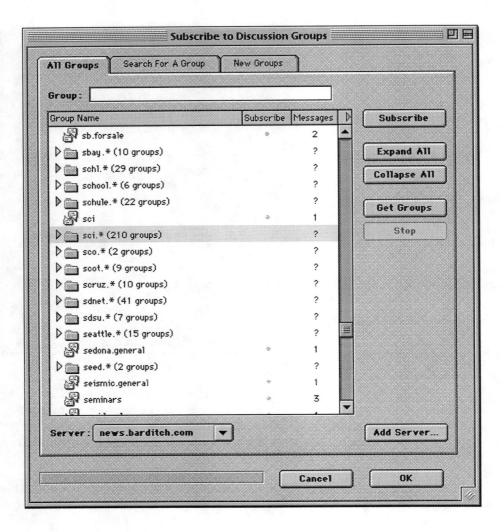

The first thing Netscape will do here is query your news server to build a master list of all groups available. This may take a few minutes, and is the reason you want to create a custom list of groups that you subscribe to so you won't have to go through this procedure each time. Once you subscribe to a few groups, as we'll see, they will be the only ones the server has to look for whenever you want to read news.

From the master list above, I scrolled down to the "sci" hierarchy of groups to find some science groups to subscribe to, then clicked on its icon to list the groups it contains.

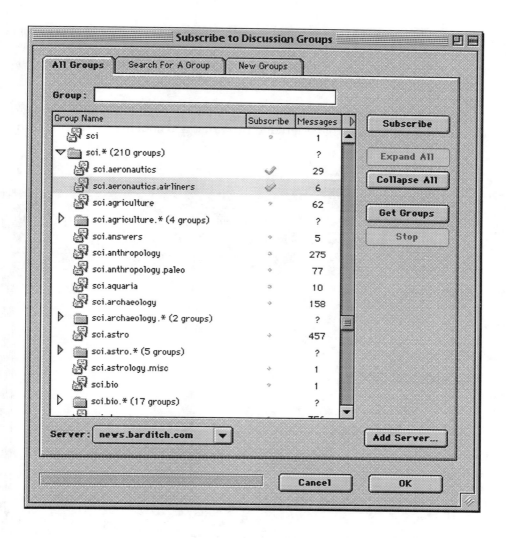

The Usenet system consists of thousands of individual newsgroups each categorized under some major groupings, such as **sci** and **comp** (for computers). Here's a list of some the major top-level groups and their purposes:

alt	Alternative groups
comp	Computer-related topics
misc	Anything that doesn't fit elsewhere
news	Usenet administration
rec	Recreational topics
sci	Science and technology (non-computer)
soc	Social chatter, sociology, cultural issues
talk	Miscellaneous politics and rhetoric, mostly.

In the figure above note that I've already subscribed to two groups, as denoted with a check mark. I simply double-clicked on the two **sci.aeronautics** groups to subscribe to them. After adding a few more groups further down in the list, I clicked the Okay button to finalize my subscriptions.

Back in our Message Center window, I now find that my news server (**news.barditch.com**) has been added to the list, and underneath it are the groups I subscribed to:

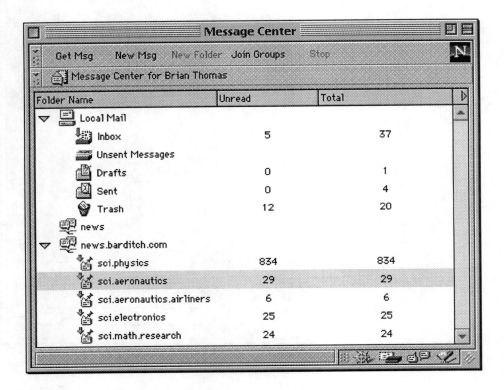

From here I can see that there are 29 messages posted to the **sci.aeronautics** newsgroup that I haven't read yet. Double-clicking on the group then brings up a list of these messages. The arrows next to some of the messages show first the original posting, followed by any responses made to it. This lets you follow a message thread more easily. Here's what the newsgroup window looks like:

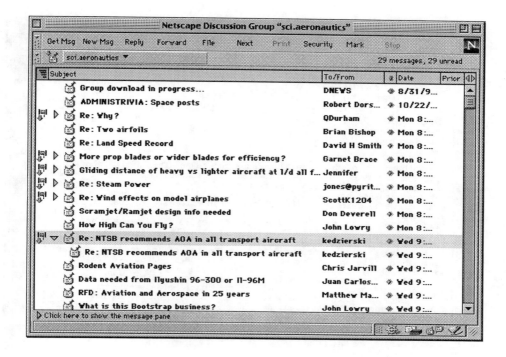

Now I can scan for messages I'm interested in. I've selected a message about an NTSB recommendation, shown below. Note that in the actual message you can also see the header information and links to previous or related postings. This is a handy feature if you read a message in the middle of a thread and wish to see previous or subsequent messages; however, keep in mind that news messages reside on a news server for only a finite period of time, usually anywhere from a day to many weeks, so while you might see a reference to a previously posted message, the message itself may have been deleted from the server (your Internet Service Provider controls this setting).

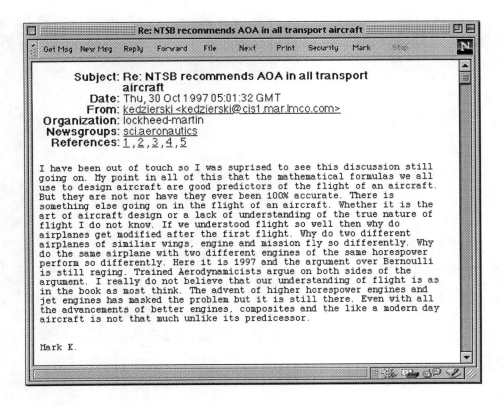

If I wished to respond to this post, the procedure is very much like responding to e-mail. In fact, Netscape has very tightly integrated the e-mail and news-reader functions. This has both positive and negative results. On the positive side, it creates an integrated environment for the user. On the negative, it can be confusing at times, since Usenet and e-mail are very different things. Also, to date these browser-based newsreaders are simply inferior to standalone soft-ware for reading news. I'm not sure why this is, but Netscape and Internet Explorer's newsreading software is very slow and cumbersome to use when compared to software such as Free Agent for Windows or Newswatcher for Macintosh.

Where to Find Browser Software

Netscape Navigator and Communicator

You can get the latest version of Netscape from the following online archives:

```
ftp://ftp.netscape.com
ftp://ftp.pu-toyama.ac.jp/pub/net/WWW/netscape (Japan mirror)
http://www.netscape.com/
```

Or contact Netscape Communications via telephone:

From Europe: +33 1/46.92.27.25
From everywhere else: +1 415/528-2555

Microsoft Internet Explorer

```
ftp://ftp.microsoft.com
http://www.microsoft.com
```

Where to Find Standalone Newsreaders

Windows95 and Windows NT

```
http://cws.internet.com/
```

Search for "newsreader"

Macintosh

```
http://www.shareware.com/
```

Search for "newsreader"

Part II

WEB AUTHORING & PUBLISHING

Chapter 6

WEB FILE FORMATS

This chapter is an essential primer for the Web publishing chapters that follow. It discusses the basic building blocks of the Web—specifically, the many different types of information you will encounter and may want to use for your own Web pages. While the topics covered here might seem somewhat esoteric at first glance, they are extremely important for anyone who wishes to use much of the scientific and engineering reference material available on the Internet.

Beyond this, even if you never plan to create your own Web pages, the information in this chapter may also be helpful in clarifying much of what is often hidden from casual view, but is nevertheless useful when exploring the Web and its myriad file types and formats. As is often true, knowledge of the parts makes it easier to understand the whole.

Documents, Images, and File Types

For the purposes of this book and especially this chapter, I use the term *document* to mean the computerized version of the word *page*—something that can store text, images, and other formatting information, and can be "read" somehow on the computer. This is in contrast to the word *image,* which specifically means a storage format for a visual image type that can be included within a document or stand alone. Finally, the term *file type* refers to the actual format of a document, image, multimedia element, or other format, including (but not limited to):

- simple ASCII text documents, including HTML
- complex documents stored in a proprietary format such as MS Word, WordPerfect, Excel, or PageMaker

- digital images stored in either proprietary formats such as Photoshop or Illustrator, or in one of many standard compression formats such as GIF, TIFF, EPS, and JPEG
- digital sound files stored in a variety of formats, such as MIDI, AIFF, AU, and WAV
- digital movies or animations stored as QuickTime, AVI, MPEG, Shockwave, or a similar formats
- *executable* files that are part of, or complete, software programs, including Java applets

On the Web you will encounter a barrage of file types. Some of them, such as TXT, HTML, and JPEG, will be relatively generic. However, many other file types on the Web are in some kind of proprietary format. There are literally hundreds of these, each usually requiring some special software that you may or may not have on your computer. Increasingly, plug-ins are available for these files, so that you can access them from within your browser (see previous chapter on Web Browsers & Applications for more information on plug-ins).

Document Formats

ASCII v. Binary

ASCII (American Standard Code for Information Interchange) is the accepted standard for information exchange. The elemental unit in computer communications is the *byte*, which can represent 256 values, so correspondingly there are 256 ASCII characters (also known as "8-bit ASCII"). ASCII is used to map a value to a character. So, for example, letter A is 65, and therefore the letter Z is 90 (25 letters after A).

While different computers never seem to agree on anything, one thing they do generally agree on is what is represented in the first 128 values of ASCII, sometimes called "low ASCII" or "7-bit ASCII." The first 33 values are control codes, which are used by terminals and interfaces in consistent manners. For example, ASCII character 7 is a "bell," and therefore to make a computer terminal beep, all a program has to do is output an ASCII value of 7. The remaining 95 values of the 128 are used to represent printable characters such as letters of the alphabet, numerals, and basic punctuation marks.

On the other side of the spectrum, there are still the 128 *additional* ASCII characters that signify different things to different computers, so that an umlaut over the letter *u* on one computer might translate to a little rabbit symbol on another. Typographers have a field day with this last 128.

This is where the binary part comes in. Messaging systems intended for use on multiple computer types (e.g., e-mail) use the first 128 characters of ASCII. These are the *lingua franca* of computers. Programs and non-text images are represented with ASCII as well, but these use all 256 possible characters, and therefore if viewed as "raw" text they would look like garbage. These files are normally called *binary* files to distinguish themselves from human-readable, or ASCII, files. (Minor point: this refers to the *elemental* relationship: a binary file, when parsed through a suitable word processor, may be entirely readable.) In addition to being called binary, files that use the full 256 values of ASCII are sometimes referred to as "high ASCII" or "8-bit ASCII."

The important thing to remember in all this is that binary files often require special handling. In the realm of e-mail, binary files need to be encoded before attaching and then decoded at their destination, since the e-mail transmission protocol (SMTP—Simple Mail Transport Protocol) does not recognize any characters beyond the first 128 of ASCII. In the realm of the Web, which uses a more sophisticated transport protocol (HTTP—Hypertext Transport Protocol), binary characters are permitted (but only if they are coded correctly in HTML; more about this in the chapters that follow). However, this opens the doors to a whole new set of issues, which all culminate in the recognition of file types so that they can be handled appropriately on the user's computer, as we'll see later.

Formatted Text

We've already talked about ASCII text and binary files. A formatted text file is any file saved in a format that uses anything more than just the ASCII letters, numbers, and punctuation. This means any file that isn't specifically saved as "text only" in your word processing software, and it definitely means any spreadsheet, desktop publishing, drawing, painting, or presentation software. Basically, you have to go out of your way nowadays to save something that doesn't use some kind of formatting.

As you will learn in the chapters that follow, files formatted in anything other than strict ASCII will have problems on the Web. Therefore it is very important to understand the difference between a simple ASCII file and a document formatted in Word, WordPerfect, or any number of software programs. The reality is that you cannot put such files on the Web for viewing. They must be converted first to a simple ASCII file, and then tagged appropriately in HTML (as described in the chapter that follows).

PostScript

PostScript is a remarkable *page description language* developed by Adobe Systems to describe pages of text and images with ASCII-based coding. It is perhaps the most versatile and universal language for communicating with printers. It is capable of drawing to computer screens and any kind of drawing device.

Many documents available on the Internet are available in both ASCII text and PostScript versions. PostScript is also the format of choice for saving figures and images for journal submissions, as well as other publications. PostScript files usually have a *.ps* filename extension.

If you download a PostScript file, you'll need to send it to a PostScript-compatible printer, which will have the necessary software to "decode" and print it. While there are some PostScript *previewing* programs available (GhostScript is one example), most are still under development.

Although some PostScript files are supposed to be 7-bit ASCII, don't count on it. Always transfer using methods appropriate for binary files.

Like any good universal standard, there's more than one version. In fact, with PostScript, there are not only multiple versions (PostScript1, PostScript2, etc.), but different *flavors* of those versions. So, if your document doesn't print correctly, it's probably because the file is formatted in a version of PostScript that your printer doesn't speak, or because there are fonts encoded in the PostScript document that your printer does not have. Sometimes missing fonts will be converted to a similar available font, and other times they'll be converted to something really hideous, like Apple's Monaco typeface.

T_eX and Derivatives

T_eX (pronounced "tek") is a software system used to typeset text, especially text containing mathematics. It is quickly becoming the de facto standard format for submitting manuscripts for most scientific journals and reference publications.

Over the years the original T_eX standard has been converted to numerous sets of *macros* with names like LaT$_e$X, RevT$_e$X, VorT$_e$X, and BibT$_e$X, all designed to make it easier for the writer to format a paper or other typeset documents in T_eX.

There are also style sheets distributed by publishers that can be used to format a paper for a particular publication. For example, the American Mathematical Society publishes and distributes style sheets for submitting to the AMS's journals. For the truly determined, there is even a program called METAFONT that allows users to design their own fonts.

Adobe Acrobat PDF

In the last few years a number of new document formats have hit the street, all designed to be the next "killer app" on our way to the elusive paperless office. The most notable of these is a category loosely called *portable documents*.

One of the biggest hassles with computers is that there are so many of them, and so any document you create with your software requires that someone else have either the same software or some other software that will translate it correctly and completely. Portable documents are supposed to change all that by letting you first convert your WordPerfect or Photoshop or Mathematica documents as a generic "cross-platform" document, which can then be read on any computer. And then not only can you create multipage archives, but you can add hypertext links, electronic sticky notes, and all sorts of other features. Needless to say, the technical obstacles here are not negligible.

In the early years of the World Wide Web, a number of companies raced to develop the standard for portable documents. By 1997 it was clear that Adobe's product, called *Acrobat,* was the winner. Acrobat draws on that company's already pervasive PostScript language, and requires that you have a *reader* or *browser plug-in* on your computer in order to use a file formatted in Acrobat's *PDF* (Portable Document Format). The PDF documents can be read on any computer with a reader module installed, or a reader plug-in that works with your Web browser. Adobe distributes free reader software and plug-in modules for many types of computer operating systems.

Acrobat files are next-generation in concept. When Acrobat version 1.0 was launched, I admit that I was first in line to buy it. I was immediately impressed by the program's promise to break through so many of the existing limitations for online publishing. Yet still, Adobe was smart to recognize and attempt to maintain the paper paradigm that so many of us grew up on. The result is that PDF files are poised to fill a long-standing need for a file format versatile enough to enable true electronic publishing.

You can create Acrobat PDF files by purchasing one of the software packages sold by Adobe. However, increasingly common are export filters for word processing and desktop publishing software that allow you to essentially "save" a file as PDF. Usually this is done through the Print function of your computer. In other words, you can download what acts like a printer driver from Adobe (**http://www.adobe.com**), install it on your computer, and then when choosing Print from the menu options, instead of choosing an attached or networked printer, you choose the PDF driver, which converts and saves your file to your hard drive. You could then send this file to someone who has a completely different computer system than you, and as long as they have the free Acrobat Reader or a browser with a PDF plug-in, they will be able to read your document.

If you wish to add some of the more advanced features to your PDF documents, such as a table of contents, bookmarks, and automatic threading, you will need to purchase Adobe's Acrobat Exchange software. Further, if you have large documents to convert, such as Pagemaker or Quark files, you'll probably need to export your documents as PostScript, convert them using the Acrobat Distiller, then modify them in Acrobat Exchange.

Image and Graphic Formats

There are hundreds of software programs that will create some kind of picture—black-and-white drawings or illustrations, color pictures, digital photographs, and so on. Therefore there are also hundreds of *formats* in which to save image files (I use the terms *image* and *graphics* interchangeably).

Image files are almost always binary, (i.e., high ASCII) and they take up huge amounts of space. A full-screen (640×480 pixel resolution), photographic quality (24 bits per pixel), uncompressed photograph will occupy more than one megabyte (1MB) of your hard drive. Compressed, its size drops to 100 K (your mileage may vary).

The other reason to compress is, of course, speed. A 1MB file will take ten times longer than a 100 K file to get from point A to B. And since a lot of us pay by the hour for our online endeavors, compression can translate directly into money saved.

So, on the Internet, compression is king, and the vast majority of images you'll find will be in one of three common image types: GIF, JPEG, and TIFF. All of these have become file format and compression *standards,* and as such are also used extensively outside of the Internet, especially in the desktop publishing and digital imaging industries. Some, such as GIF, are always compressed, whereas others, such as TIFF, have uncompressed formats as well.

GIF Images

GIF stands for Graphic Interchange Format and is a standard format for images that was developed by CompuServe to be a device-independent method of storing pictures. It includes Lempel-Ziv-Welch (LZW) compression, which makes the files fairly small (generally a 3:1–5:1 compression ratio). GIF is a *lossless* compression, meaning that the act of compressing/decompressing does not degrade the image quality in any way. The GIF format is by far the most prevalent for displaying graphics on the World Wide Web. GIF files are usually recognizable by a *.GIF* or *.gif* filename extension.

There are two standards for GIF file formats: the original 87a format, and a newer 89a format. The latter allows for one-bit transparency (a pixel is either transparent or opaque). It allows a palette of a maximum of 256 colors, so representation of 24 bit color images in GIF involves loss. The general rule therefore is that GIF is only used for images of 8 bits (256 colors) or less. This makes it the format of choice for most graphics that are not color photographs, which JPEG (see below) does better.

GIF also supports interlaced images: if saved in an interlaced format, every eighth row in an image is displayed first, then every fourth, then every second, and so on. Interlacing was invented to allow users to visualize images as they are being downloaded over slow modems, instead of having to wait for the entire graphic to load before you can see what it is. The downside of interlaced graphics is that they actually take slightly longer to load.

Animated GIFs

The GIF89a format also supports animation. Most of the animations you see on the Web today are animated GIFs. The reason they are so popular is that they are now supported by both Netscape and Internet Explorer, and that once they load, they use the browser's own cache to repeat the animation, so that once the initial loading is completed, there is no more delay or connection to the server required. (Of course this also means that if you have your browser's disk cache set to zero, animated GIFs will not load.)

Animated GIFs are simple animations involving successively displayed images, just like the original cartoon animations. They are a self-contained format for which the artist can specify a number of parameters, such as a single-play or looped (continuous) play, or even a finite number of cycles. There are special software programs available for creating animated GIFs. The two most popular right now are GIF Construction Set for Windows, and GIF Builder for Macintosh. You can find both of these and other free and shareware software for creating animated GIFs at **http://www.shareware.com**.

JPEG Images

JPEG stands for Joint Photographic Experts Group (the original name of the committee that wrote the standard). Its increasing popularity is based on its high (variable, up to 10:1) compression ratio. Unlike GIF, however, JPEG files are usually *lossy*, meaning that they sacrifice some of their resolution during the compression process, due to dithering or averaging of individual pixel groupings in an image. This makes JPEG most effective for images with a pixel depth of at least four bits (16 grays or colors). JPEG files usually have *.JPG* or *.jpg* as filename extensions.

Because it supports images with more than 256 colors and offers a variable compression method, JPEG is the standard format for photographic images on the Web. Some of the better tools for creating or converting JPEG images actually let the artist try varying degrees of compression with the resulting image displayed in real-time, which is an excellent means for creating the smallest possible image without losing too much fidelity.

PNG Images

Unless you're already involved with Web development, the PNG format will probably be news to you. However, as a currently proposed standard to the W3 Consortium, it is poised to possibly replace the GIF format on the Web, and as such is worth mentioning even at this early juncture.

PNG stands for Portable Network Graphic (or, as the joke goes, "PNG Not GIF"). The original impetus for PNG was a legal fracas back in 1996 involving GIF's proprietary roots as the original graphics format developed by and for CompuServe. However, CompuServe quickly realized that the negative publicity stemming from trying to enforce some kind of usage parameters around the already widely accepted GIF standard would far outweigh anything they stood to gain, so they backed off with their legal proceedings.

Today, however, PNG is still a proposed standard because it offers a number of advantages to the GIF format, including higher resolutions (up to 48 bits for true color support), and a number of other technical nuances that only a serious digital artist would appreciate (esoteric features such as true alpha channel support, gamma correction, chromaticity data, and integrated corruption recognition).

PNG will not likely become a serious movement for another year or so, and even then, there will be a lengthy transition period because of the universal prevalence of GIF. However, the latest high-end graphics tools are starting to support PNG, so this is a sign that it's being accepted in the development communities.

TIFF Images

TIFF stands for Tagged Image File Format. It is widely used in the desktop publishing field because of its flexibility and compatibility with a variety of software programs. However, for a number of reasons it has not become a common format for image files on the Internet. Currently no Web browsers can read TIFF files directly, so if you encounter a TIFF file on the Web, you will need another application to view the image, or a browser plug-in if available. TIFF files usually have .*TIF* or .*tif* file extensions.

Encapsulated PostScript (EPS)

Finally, there's *EPS*, or Encapsulated PostScript. This is a separate standard for importing and exporting PostScript language files in all environments. It is usually a single-page PostScript language program that describes an illustration. The purpose of the EPS file is to be included as an illustration in other PostScript language page descriptions. You probably won't run into too many of these on the Internet, but if you ever want to convert a manuscript or other publication to the PostScript format, you might use the EPS format to save your figures and images. EPS files usually have an .*eps* or .*EPS* filename extension.

Multimedia Formats

The popularity of the Web has brought with it an explosion of all types of software trying to deliver sound and video, separate or synchronous, to the Web. The result is that there is no single standard for audio or video transmission, and even worse, there is nothing even close. Everyone is vying for dominance in a marketplace that is so young it literally reinvents itself every six months. So what we're left with is a confusing array of software types and applications to read them. This confused picture is further compounded by hardware-related solutions, as in the 3D graphics fields, where the newest 3D modeling programs require specific hardware on your computer to either read or at least optimize viewing.

The key thing to remember about audio and video on the Web is that these are nascent technologies. The technique of streaming audio and video has come a long way in the past year or so, but the Internet's underlying technology was never designed to support audio or video, and so the workarounds are just that—workarounds. If you have a low-bandwidth connection to the Web, the limitations will be obvious the first time you download an audio or video file.

Perhaps the best news in this arena is that browser developers have recognized that one of the biggest obstacles to audio and video on the Web is simply recognizing and utilizing the vast array of formats available, so they are building "universal" players directly into the browser. Netscape 4.0, for example, has developed plug-ins called LiveAudio, LiveVideo, and Live3D, which can recognize and play many of the major multimedia formats found on the Web today. For less common formats, developers can create their own Netscape plug-ins, which you can download from Netscape or other sources and install on your computer.

Audio Formats

Here is an overview of the most common audio formats you will find on the Web. Also included are the MIME types/subtypes, and common extensions, so that you can both recognize and add each of these types to your browser, if required. (See the following section on MIME for more background.)

Format	Description
AIFF	Older but still common format for distributing music files and sound bites.

	MIME Type/Subtype:	audio/x-aiff
	Extensions:	*.aiff, .aif, .aifc*

AU	An older audio format also known as ULAW. Quality is relatively poor.

	MIME Type/Subtype:	audio/basic
	Extensions:	*.au*

MIDI	Musical Instrument Digital Interface. The de facto standard for musicians that enables synthesizers, sequencer hardware, personal computers, drum machines, lights, and hard disk recorders, etc., to interconnect through a standard data protocol via an inexpensive serial hardware interface.

	MIME Type/Subtype:	audio/midi
	Extensions:	*.mid, .xmid*

MPEG	MPEG (Moving Picture Experts Group) is an ISO standard for audio (and video) compression. MPEG audio layer 3 is part of that standard, and is now a popular format for both self-contained and streaming audio. It is also used as a component technology for other multimedia files, such as Shockwave. MP2 is the older version of the MPEG audio standard.

	MIME Type/Subtype:	audio/x-mpeg
	Extensions:	*.mp2, .mp3*

RA   RealAudio, from RealNetworks, is now highly integrated with Microsoft's Internet Explorer. It is the de facto standard for audio streaming, which works best with a higher bandwidth connection.

MIME Type/Subtype: audio/x-pn-realaudio
Extensions: *.ra, .ram*

SND   An older sound format, soon to be obsolete.

MIME Type/Subtype: audio/snd
Extensions: *.snd*

WAV   A very popular sound format, mostly for Windows.

MIME Type/Subtype: audio/x-wav
Extensions: *.wav*

Video and Animation Formats

Here is an overview of the most common video formats you will find on the Web. Also included are the MIME types/subtypes, and common extensions, so that you can both recognize and add each of these types to your browser, if required. (See the following section on MIME for more background.)

Format   **Description**

AVI   AVI stands for Audio Video Interleave. AVI is defined by Microsoft, and file format is a central part of Video for Windows. As such it is one of the most common formats for audio/video data.

MIME Type/Subtype: video/msvideo
Extensions: *.avi*

MPEG   MPEG (Moving Picture Experts Group) is an ISO standard for video (and audio) compression. MPEG video is known as one of the best and most promising technologies for digital video, and is even the codec (code/decode) chosen for upcoming standards for HDTV.

MIME Type/Subtype: video/mpeg
Extensions: *.mpeg, .mpe, .mpg*

MOOV   QuickTime, developed by Apple, is a multiplatform industry-standard multimedia architecture. It is a long-reigning standard for digital movies and compression, as well as virtual reality renderings via QuickTime VR. Almost all built-in video support for Netscape 4.0 is handled by the QuickTime plug-in (included with Netscape). According to *New Media* magazine (September 1997), over 50% of all video on the Web is in QuickTime format. QuickTime software also supports most other sound and video formats, including AIFF, WAV, and MPEG.

MIME Type/Subtype: video/quicktime
Extensions: *.mov, .qt, .qtv*

Shockwave   Shockwave, from Macromedia, is a well-supported standard for authoring and delivering multimedia on the Web. As such it is not really a video format per se, but rather a true multimedia development environment. To create Shockwave animations, developers usually use a tool such as Director (also from Macromedia) and then convert it to the Shockwave format for viewing on the Web.

MIME Type/Subtype: handled by Shockwave installer
Extensions: handled by Shockwave installer

VRML   The Virtual Reality Modeling Language is the standard for rendering virtual reality animations on the Web. It is quickly receiving integrated support from both Netscape and Internet Explorer.

MIME Type/Subtype: model/vrml
Extensions: *.wrl*

Identifying File Types and Formats

The Role of MIME

Over the past few years a standard called MIME (Multipurpose Internet Mail Extensions) has been implemented across most of the Internet. MIME provides a way for software such as Web browsers to recognize different file types by their extension, such as *.html* or *.pdf*. Once recognized, the software can then decide what to do with it.

For example, typically a web browser can only display ASCII text and certain image types, specifically JPEG and GIF. Everything else a browser encounters on the Web must be handled in some other manner. So when a browser encounters a reference to an entity named "picture.gif," it recognizes the *.gif* extension as something it can display in the browser window and goes ahead and parses the image code (which is binary, by the way) and the image displays. However, if it encounters a reference to "picture.tif," it will need to do something else with this file since it cannot display the TIFF image format (browsers are still remarkably limited in what they can actually deal with themselves). In this situation, the browser will rely on a table of MIME types that it keeps in its own settings file to decide what to do with the TIFF file. This settings file can tell the browser to either download TIFF image files automatically to the user's computer, or pick another application or plug-in to display the image. This settings file is user-configurable, so you can set up your browser to handle specific file types exactly how you want.

More information on the MIME standard can be found in the chapter on Web Browsers & Applications.

Common File Types and Extensions

Here is a sample of file format types and their extensions. Note that not all files you encounter on the Web will have proper extensions. It's still up to the person putting the file online to name it properly. Not all files will have a three-letter extension, since this a vestige of the DOS operating system and is therefore not necessarily a standard for all computers.

.arc	ARCed file (archive file that contains many other files)
.arq	DOS compression format (competes with ARC and ZIP)
.bin	Binary file, used in many situations
.doc	Document file (ambiguous, often ASCII text or MS Word)
.exe	Executable program file (either system specific or self-extracting)
.eps	Encapsulated Postscript, normally used in desktop publishing applications
.gif	GIF (Graphics Interchange Format) image format, common for Web graphics
.gz	GNU compress (popular Unix format)
.gzip	GZIP is a popular compression format for Unix
.hlp	Help file (sometimes ASCII)
.hqx	BinHex file (binary data coded to ASCII—typically Macintosh)
.jpg	JPEG image format (for photographs on the Web)
.me	Not really a format, but usually stands for text, as in "read.me"
.pdf	Acrobat Portable Document Format
.ps	PostScript file
.pkg	Applelink Package file
.png	Portable Network Graphic, an emerging graphics format on the Web
.sea	Self-expanding archive file (unstuffs itself)
.sit	Stuffit file(s) from Aladdin
.tar	Compressed with Unix tar (tape archive) utility
.tex	T_eX source file
.tif	Tagged Image File Format (TIFF)
.txt	Text file (generic ASCII)
.uue	Uuencoded (binary data coded to ASCII) file
.wrd	WordPerfect document
.Z	Compressed using Unix *compress* software
.zip	Popular Windows compression format using PKZip, WinZip, or similar
.zoo	Zoo file(s) compressed (a Unix format)

Chapter 7

INTRODUCTION TO WEB PUBLISHING

This chapter addresses the growing capabilities for "personal publishing" that the Web has brought to all of us through an Internet connection at work, home, school, or even a hotel room. These opportunities may be especially interesting to scientists and engineers because of the traditionally strong ties between publishing and research. Opportunities for communicating and publishing individual work, ideas, and projects via the Web are quickly becoming an everyday part of our professional lives.

Let me begin this chapter by saying that creating your own Web pages and even a basic Web site is easy. HTML, as we'll see later in this chapter, is not a programming language, but rather is a very simple tagging language. And once you learn a few of the basic tags you will be well on your way to creating your own Web pages. Of course, there are also real programming languages such as C, C++, Perl, and Java used in the creation of complex Web sites. However, they are beyond the scope of this book. In the chapter that follows—Advanced Web Publishing—we will address many of the more complex HTML tools for those of you who wish to expand your Web publishing skills.

Before we launch into the hands-on part of this chapter, I feel compelled to provide some background that I think useful, as it provides an important context, particularly for science and engineering professionals for whom writing and publishing is sine qua non.

Scholarly Publishing: Past, Present, & Future

The growing popularity of the World Wide Web has turned the publishing industry upside down. Why? Because the scholarly publishing industry—especially in science and engineering—has not only formed the backbone of professional communication for more than a century, but has in many ways controlled and directed scientific research as a whole. The familiar "publish or perish" litany has real teeth behind it. Journals and other peer-review communication systems have long been the established standard upon which people have built their research, reputations, and careers.

All of that is changing now, yet no one knows exactly how. For publishers, the situation today is not unlike it was in the late 1980s. At that time, the business of typesetting and composition was controlled by a few big companies like Interleaf, Varitype, and Compugraphics. The equipment was expensive, the operating systems were closed and proprietary, and the user interfaces required specially trained compositors. Everyone was locked into these systems. And then of course traditional graphic artists were needed to design, cut, wax, and paste all the little strips of typeset words onto flats that created the books, magazines, journals, and everything else destined for publication. An extremely time-consuming process all around.

Then came the first "desktop publishing" (DTP) systems from Apple. At first, the publishing industry refused to take notice. They blindly considered these systems to be mere "toys." They continued to push their expensive, proprietary systems into the marketplace with all the arrogance of a classic industry monopoly. A lot of companies died or are near death today because of this arrogance. In less than ten years, those proprietary systems have been almost completely replaced by desktop publishing systems that have revolutionized the publishing industry.

Let's think about that for a moment: less than ten years. Now think about the Web, and how far it has come in less than *five* years. This is an incredible timeframe for a phenomenon that has virtually revolutionized communication in the industrialized world.

So why are publishers not only taking notice but retooling their publishing strategies this time around? Because the revolution that desktop publishing brought about in the past decade is about to be repeated, except this time it's not only a technological revolution, it's also a *contextual* revolution. The Web makes it possible for anyone to not only compose their own publications, but also to publish them on a global scale rivaling that of any traditional publisher.

Well, almost.

The Mythology of Personal Publishing

That at least is the vision. The reality is as usual something much more complicated. Remember that desktop publishing's vision was to make the concept of "personal publishing" come true. We were all going to be graphic designers and book publishers. The reality is, for a few years in the beginning, the world saw some of the worst designed and edited works that ever put ink to paper. This simply proved that computers can't replace the talent and experience of professional designers, writers, and editors. The technology is still just a tool.

Now it's déjà vu all over again. Companies like Corel and Microsoft are doing their marketing-best to convince the world that everyone can be a "webmaster" (a term I loathe, actually), and that the playing field is irrevocably leveled. And it's not just the big software corporations that believe this. A good example from the inside is Paul Ginsparg's e-print archive at Los Alamos National Lab. Launched in the early days of the Web, the LANL "xxx" project is funded by the U.S. National Science Foundation (at least through February 1998) for the purpose of improving communications within specific scientific communities such as high-energy physics, mathematics, and nonlinear sciences. The concept is relatively simple: create an automated archiving system that allows users to submit, search, and download research papers and other materials both for the purpose of inviting online peer review, as well as accelerating communications outside the traditionally slow scholarly journals publishing cycle. The LANL archive can be found at **http://xxx.lanl.gov.**

The success of Ginsparg's project was the first wake-up call for the publishing industry. Of course, not all scientific circles have a LANL-style e-print archive created for them, nor would they want one. It just happens to work well for some communities. However, the paradigm could be easily modified to one that works for, say, the electrical engineering community. In its most basic incarnation, that paradigm is the concept of personal publishing on the Web. After all, the Web makes location irrelevant. To some degree, it makes format and software irrelevant, since if created correctly, everyone on the Web can read what's published there. Further, references in a paper I've posted on my personal Web site can be linked to other papers posted on colleagues' personal Web pages. For readers, the location of these papers is transparent. Taking this concept to the extreme, we can start to see the incredible power behind the Web. Who needs an archive when the Web itself is an archive?

An Introduction to Publishing on the Web

Beyond the ease and utility of creating simple Web pages, the larger topic of Web authoring and publishing is itself both broad and complex. At the root of this complexity is the computer industry itself, which exhibits about as much consistency as U.S. foreign policy. I challenge anyone to show me two computers on this planet that have exactly the same hardware, software, operating system, configuration, and Internet connection. Even when companies try to "standardize" their systems, the inevitable exceptions start to creep in immediately. It is simply a fact of life in today's burgeoning computer industry, and it is likely to get worse before it gets better, if ever.

The Web is a particularly fertile breeding ground for this lack of standardization. On the one side, the sprawl of computer systems makes it virtually impossible to approach the topic of Web authoring from the standpoint of the specific software or hardware you may have on your desk at any particular moment in time. There are simply too many variables. On the other, as a Web publisher this same variability will greatly affect how your published works appear to others on the Web.

So with these issues in mind, my approach in this chapter will focus on the basics of creating Web pages and sites "by hand," which means learning the fundamentals of HTML (HyperText Markup Language), the tagging language used to create Web pages, and also some tricks of the trade that will help make your Web pages readable for everyone on the Web, not just those who happen to have software similar to yours.

Building Blocks of Web Publishing

What do you need to create a Web presence? First we'll define the basics, and then we'll construct a simple homepage. In the next chapter we'll look at some more advanced pages and general site design issues, as well as how to get found.

Internet Connectivity

This means not only the ability to surf the Web, which you may already have, but also access to a Web server where you can put your Web pages for others to see them. If your Internet connection is through your school or work, most likely you will need to get permission and instructions from the network administrator there. If your connection is through a private Internet Service Provider, contact their customer service staff to see if they offer such services.

In all cases, keep in mind that every Web server setup is different, so it's essential that you get all the information you need from the place you get your Internet connection. Remember also that it's not a foregone conclusion that just because you have Web access it also means that your provider offers Web *server* access.

HTML Editing Software

As we'll soon see, HTML files are nothing but simple ASCII text. In fact, they must be only simple ASCII text. You cannot, for example, take a page saved in standard Wordperfect or Microsoft Word file formats and put them on the Web for others to read. They will be appear as text garbage in a Web browser. This is because standard word processors like WordPerfect and Word add hidden "high ASCII" characters to the page that cannot be parsed by a Web browser (for more background on ASCII text, see the earlier chapter on Web File Formats).

Of course, this doesn't mean you can't use a word processor like Word or WordPerfect to create your Web pages; it just means you have to save them in a Web-compatible format before putting them on the Web, specifically, the "Text

Only with Line Breaks" option. Most of the newer versions of popular word processors actually have an "Export as HTML" or "Save as HTML" option for this very purpose, which will in fact attempt to convert any formatting such as paragraph breaks, boldface, etc., in your document to HTML tags.

This brings me to a thorny topic: HTML editing software. In this chapter, the examples I use will show "raw" HTML coding. This is because it's quite possible to create even the most sophisticated Web pages using a very simple text editor such as Windows' Notepad, Macintosh's SimpleText, or a Unix editor like vi or Emacs. Again, this is because HTML tags use only the basic ASCII characters, as we'll soon see.

However, as HTML has become both popular and more complex, a barrage of "HTML editors" have hit the software shelves in the past year, all claiming to make HTML composition and editing as easy as plain old word processing. And in many respects most of them do. However, what isn't nearly as well known is that these editors bring about their own specific sets of problems, the first and foremost being that the HTML code they create is almost universally nonstandard, as well as being very difficult to modify unless you always use the software that created it.

So what does this mean? As a Web site developer from its early days, my personal bias is to create HTML coding by hand. What that means is that I don't use any of the newer "WYSIWYG" editors like HotMetal, Microsoft FrontPage, Adobe PageMill, or hundreds of others on the market (WYSIWYG, pronounced "wizzywig," stands for "what you see is what you get," in this case meaning the actual HTML code is hidden from you by a graphical interface). For most professional developers, these types of programs still create more problems than they cure, especially in an environment where you are trying to support many different browsers, and where you have more than one person who may need to edit a Web document.

But it won't be this way forever, and even today's young WYSIWYG editors are perfectly fine for anyone wanting to create a small Web site for themselves. So my advice is this: if you want to use one of the WYSIWYG editors like Microsoft FrontPage, keep these few things in mind when doing so:

1. Test your pages on other browsers and computer platforms. Granted, this advice is prudent for any Web author regardless of editing software being used, but it's especially important if you're using an editor that creates most of the actual HTML tags for you. These programs have a well-documented tendency toward platform and browser specificity, meaning that pages they create may look great on your Windows computer using Internet Explorer, but for someone on a Sun or Macintosh workstation using Netscape, they may be virtually unreadable. This is particularly important in the science, engineering, and education realms, where Windows doesn't command the huge market share that Microsoft enjoys in the business sector.

2. Once created, don't try to edit your pages using something other than what you created them in. Nearly all of the fancy software editors create HTML code that is a nightmare to modify by hand, let alone with another software editor that probably won't recognize half the coding on the page. Again, lack of standards plague this industry.

3. Watch out for "features" that are vendor specific. A good example of this is Microsoft FrontPage, which offers a whole bunch of really nifty features that only work if your Web server is running the server software for FrontPage, and the person reading your Web pages just happens to have the latest version of Microsoft Internet Explorer.

Graphics Software

Finally, unless you're planning on a text-only Web site (which is perfectly acceptable!), you'll need some type of software to either create new graphics, convert existing graphics or photos, or both. There is a wide variety of high-quality freeware, shareware, and commercial software for these purposes today (some references to online recommendations can be found at the end of the chapter on Advanced Web Publishing).

At a minimum, you'll need software that can create or modify other image formats into both the GIF and JPEG formats. If you plan to include a lot of images on your site, or if some of them are large or are photographs, then you'll really want to look for something more powerful that will let you edit an image's palette or compression ratio in order to optimize them for the fastest download times. More information on creating and modifying graphics is covered in the next chapter.

Introduction to HTML

HyperText Markup Language was originally supposed to be a "device independent" system designed to sidestep all the problems mentioned above concerning the endless variety of computer platforms, operating systems, and software configurations. In the parlance of the industry, it was supposed to be a "write once, read anywhere" system. In its purest and most basic form, this goal has been realized. Unfortunately, while this idea was appropriate for the original target audience—scientific researchers—the Web as we know it today is driven far more by commercial interests, and commercial interests are far more interested in the look and image of the Web than the original audience ever was. After all, if the company's documents were going to be viewable by millions of people all over the world, they had better look good. This is the original locus of the biggest problem on the Web today—conflicting standards.

So, since the original HTML specification offered very little control over layout and presentation, browser vendors like Netscape and Microsoft took it upon themselves to "extend" HTML to include more controls, and while many of these controls have made it into some of the more recent official HTML standards, the browser vendors continue to develop new extensions outside any real agreed-upon standards. Just as bad, caught in this crossfire are services like America Online, whose browsers are consistently well behind (and inferior to) anything from Netscape or Microsoft, yet with a user base of over eight million people, this is a significant obstacle for anyone who wishes to author Web documents viewable by the majority of people on the Web today.

For the purposes of this introduction, therefore, I am going to concentrate on HTML coding that is virtually bulletproof for the vast majority of browsers on the Web today. In the next chapter we'll take a look at some of the advanced features like Cascading Style Sheets that, if all goes well, should offer a better workaround to the current problems with presentation control.

As a side note, I need to say a bit about HTML's roots. HTML is actually a subset of SGML (Standard Generalized Markup Language), a well-established ISO standard that provides a means for defining markup languages. As HTML has evolved it has also been moving into closer step with SGML, which means that in some ways HTML is becoming more strict. This is why, for example, tags like <italic> and <bold> are being "deprecated" in HTML 4.0 and replaced with more SGML-conformant tags like <em> and <strong>. (A deprecated element or attribute is one that has been outdated by newer constructs. While they will still "work" in current browsers, the intent is to make them obsolete in the future, so you shouldn't use them when creating new HTML code. Many elements on the "deprecation list" are those that are being replaced by the Cascading Style Sheets specification being introduced with HTML 4.0. More on style sheets in the next chapter).

Basic HTML Tags

At the heart of every Web page are HTML tags, which define the structural elements of a page, such as the size of text and headlines, and any associated attributes, such as bold and italic typefaces. Let's take a look at a headline:

<h1 align=center>This is a big, centered headline</h1>

The tag above would render the text in between them as a large (level 1) headline centered on the page. HTML tags always begin with a left bracket < and end with a right bracket >. The Web browser uses these to interpret and display a page properly. Every time a browser encounters a left bracket, it knows that everything after will be HTML coding, that is, until it sees the closing (right) bracket. Browsers therefore know to follow the instructions between all the brackets, and to actually display the text for everything else.

In addition, some tags come in sets of two, a beginning tag and a closing tag (as shown above), whereas others must stand alone. Tags that require a closing tag add a slash mark to that closing tag, as in the </h1> above.

By the way, HTML tags are case-insensitive. Generally, however, you'll want to be consistent with your coding using either all upper- or all lower-case. This will make your coding easier to edit.

A Basic Web Page

Next, let's look at a basic Web page, including all the required tags for any HTML page:

```
<html>
<head>
<title>My Homepage</title>
</head>
<body>
<h1>Brian's Homepage</h1>
<p>
Welcome to my homepage.
<p>
If I really had something to say, I would say it here in
this second paragraph.
</body>
</html>
```

That's it. The HTML tags and text for a complete, albeit simple, Web page. The <html> tag at the top of the document is there to tell the browser that the information that follows will be in HTML-tagged format. The <head> tag comes next. It contains information such as the page <title>, which is also required, plus some optional elements that could be included, such as meta-tags (more on meta-tags later). By the way, the contents of the <title> tag are what appear as the title of the browser window, much like a document name. Search engines like AltaVista often use this information to help index your page, so it's important to title your pages well. Next we have the <body> tag, which takes over where the <head> leaves off, and finally there are all the closing tags for each of these required elements.

The other elements on this basic page are optional. In the example above, these include the <h1> headline tags that we saw in the previous example, and also the paragraph marker tag, <p>. Note that the <p> tag does not require a closing </p> tag, although for some reason many Web page construction programs include them.

The <p> tags are very important in HTML, because HTML pages ignore any physical spacing you see in your text editor. That is, carriage returns in HTML are ignored, and multiple spaces are collapsed into a single space by your browser. The <p> tag is the perfect way to create the look of a carriage return and line feed on a page, but only one at a time. Using multiple <p> tags in succession, like this

```
<p><p><p><p><p>
```

is not a good way to create vertical "white space" or leading on your page, if only because it's messy HTML. A better way to do this is to use a set of <pre></pre> tags, which signify "preformatted" text, and which will convert anything in between them to exactly how you see it on your source HTML page. For example, if you wanted to created a couple inches of vertical white space on your page, you could just insert an opening <pre> tag, then add a few carriage returns, and then the closing tag, like this:

```
<pre>



</pre>
```

The browser will interpret this as that much white space because everything between <pre> tags is translated literally.

At this point you could be making your own page. Type the Basic Web Page example shown above into a simple text editor on a computer where you also have a Web browser available. By "simple text editor" I mean something like Notepad, SimpleText, or Emacs, depending on your specific computer type. After you've typed in the text from the Basic Web Page, save the file with a filename containing the extension *.html*, such as *myfile.html*. Next, use your browser's Open File (or similar) command to open the file "locally," meaning from your hard drive (as opposed to opening a file elsewhere on the Web). This is how you can view any HTML file you've created before ever putting it on the Web for others to view.

Now is a good time to mention a great tool available to everyone for learning HTML. Next time you visit someone's Web site and you like their page, use your browser's "View Source" (or similar) command to view the HTML coding that composes the page you're looking at. This is a fantastic way to learn HTML since you can save someone's page on your own computer and even re-use someone else's code on your own pages. (And by the way, this isn't considered pirating or inappropriate at all. It's just the way of the Web. If someone really wanted to hide their code from others on the Web, there are ways they can protect it.)

URLs and Links

As noted in the chapter on Web browsers, "URL" stands for Uniform Resource Locator, which is just a geeky way of talking about an Internet address. Every resource available on the Web—HTML document, image, video clip, software program, etc.—has an address that may be encoded by an URL. So in the largest sense, an URL can be used to link us to just about anything on the Web. Here are some examples:

Web Site Homepage	http://www.computer.org
Specific File on Web	http://www.stanford.edu/pub/schedule.html
FTP Site	ftp://rtfm.mit.edu
Image	http://www.sun.com/logo.gif
Database Query	http://www.excite.com/search.gw?trace=a&search=laser+diode

That last example shows the real utility of an URL. The next time you visit a search site like AltaVista or Excite, take a look at the URL displayed in your browser's address window. What you'll see is a long string of what seems like garbage, but upon closer examination, you'll be able to see how your query was constructed into an URL, which is how their Web server needs to see it before it can respond to the search query.

So an URL is just an address. What, then, is a link? A link is the HTML coding surrounding an URL that makes it work for everyone on the Web. If you simply type an URL like the ones above onto your Web page, it won't be "live" for anyone to use. In order to make it a live hypertext link, you need to format it in HTML coding. The tag used is called the <a> tag ("a" stands for "anchor").

Here, for example, is how you would make the first link I showed above into a live hypertext link:

```
Visit the <a href="http://www.computer.org/">IEEE Com-
puter Society</a> homepage.
```

This is rendered as:

Visit the <u>IEEE Computer Society</u> homepage.

Note that there's a start tag (<a href="http://www.computer.org">) and an end tag (</a>), and that everything in between these two tags ("IEEE Computer Society") is rendered as the link the user can click on—often colored and underlined in your Web browser.

Links to Images

Images or graphics that are in either the GIF or JPG format will be directly displayed in a Web browser, provided you put the right HTML coding around them. The basic tag is the <img> tag:

```
<img src="http://www.sun.com/logo.gif">
```

Note here and in the previous example that the name of the file or image is in quotation marks. This is very important as not all browsers will tolerate file or image references without quotes. An even bigger trap is an URL with only one quote, which will often make the rest of the Web page "disappear" in the browser window. Make sure you always have both opening and closing quotes.

There are some important attributes that can be added to image tags. First, if you know the size of your graphic's width and height in pixels (e.g., 50×100), you might want to include it in the link tag because it will speed the loading of that graphic for anyone visiting your page. Here's an example:
ZZZZZZ
```
<img src="http://www.sun.com/logo.gif" width="50"
height="100">
```

The ALIGN attribute is also useful. You can insert align=top, align=middle, or align=bottom to control where the image will appear on the page. For example, if you choose:

```
<img src="http://www.sun.com/logo.gif" width="50"
height="100" align=right>
```

then the graphic will automatically flush itself to the right-hand margin of the page, even after resizing the browser window.

The ALT attribute is a good thing to include in many situations. It specifies the text that will be shown if a browser is unable to show the graphic, for example if someone has set up their browser to not load images (to save time), or for someone on a Lynx-style text browser. Here's the example:

```
<img src="http://www.sun.com/logo.gif" width="50"
height="100" align="right" alt="Sun Logo">
```

You may be wondering: Does the order of the attributes as they appear in a tag really matter? It doesn't.

Finally, you can of course put an <img> between <a> and </a>, so the user can click on the picture to follow the link. In other words, a "clickable graphic."

Here's what the final URL would look like:

```
<a href="http://www.sun.com"><img src="http://
www.sun.com/logo.gif" width="50" height="100"
align="right" alt="Sun Logo"></a>
```

In this final example, the graphic logo would appear, and if someone clicked on it, it would take them to the Sun Web site just like a text link.

E-Mail Links

We've all seen examples of a link that when you click it, instead of taking you to a Web page, it brings up an e-mail window with an address in it, ready to go. This is a simple variation of the <a> tag sometimes called a "mailto" link (for obvious reasons):

```
Send an e-mail message to <a
href="mailto:henry_kim@mit.edu">Henry Kim.</a>
```

This would appear as

Send an e-mail message to <u>Henry Kim</u>.

Relative v. Absolute Links

All of the examples above used what are commonly called absolute, or full, URLs. This means that the places referenced by the URLs could be accessed from anywhere on the Web. You would have to use this kind of an URL if you wanted to create a link to a place outside your own Web site. However, from within your own Web site you can instead use relative URLs, which are shorter and easier to manage. If, for example, you have three pages named *one.html*, *two.html*, and *three.html*, and if they are in the same directory on your website, to create a link to *three.html* from the *one.html* page, you could type the relative URL:

```
<a href="three.html">Click Here for Page Three</a>
```

Similarly, if you had another file named *four.html*, but it resided in a subdirectory named "otherfiles," you could reference it with this URL:

```
<a href="otherfiles/four.html">Click Here for Page
Four</a>
```

To reference a directory above the one your file is in, you will often see the "../" convention used, which is somewhat of a DOS and Unix convention, used to refer to the next directory up. For example, if your file were already in the "otherfiles" directory referenced above, and you wanted to refer to the directory that contained the *three.html* file located in a directory named "mainfiles," you could reference it like this :

```
<a href="../mainfiles/three.html">Click Here for Page
Three</a>
```

There are of course other ways of referencing files or images outside your current directory. So if you wish to use relative URLs like these on your Web site, make sure you check with your Web administrator first to find out the correct ways to construct relative URLs for your server.

Link Anchors

Up until now we've looked at links to specific pages or graphics. However, you can also create a link that is more specific than that. You can create a link that takes the reader to a specific location on any page. This is usually called an anchor (technically, it's called a fragment identifier). You've probably seen this done with really long pages, where the author offers you an "Up to Top" button that takes you back to the top of the page.

Here's how to do that. First, create a named anchor at the top of the page. You can name it anything you want, but make it something short. It's just a reference. Do this with the <a> tag and the name attribute:

```
<a name="up"></a>
```

Since the anchor just marks a point on the page, you don't need to put anything between <a> and </a>.

Once the anchor exists at the target location, if it's on the same page (as in this example), you just create a simple <a href> link wherever you want one, using the # symbol to denote a "name" location:

```
<a href="#up">Up to Top</a>
```

You can also make this same link from a different page, but to do so you'll need to use a full URL or at least a valid relative URL, such as

```
<a href="otherfiles/four.html#up">Top of Page Four</a>
```

Text Formatting and Attributes

Formatting text is easy in HTML. Just make sure you use closing tags in all cases. If you write the following:

```
<em>This would be seen in italics</em>
<strong>This would be seen in bold</strong>
```

here's what you would probably see:

```
This would be seen in italics
This would be seen in bold
```

There are many other attributes not covered here. Be aware also that many older attributes, such as bold, italic, underline, etc., are no longer part of the official HTML specification (as I write this, HTML 4.0 is under review).

Headlines of six relative sizes can be chosen. Headings are usually shown in bold with H1 having the largest font size and H6 the smallest. Remember that the key word in any text formatting scheme is "relative." Ultimately it is up to the individual browser to determine the exact typeface and size used.

```
<h2>Here's an example of a Level 2 headline's HTML
coding.</h2>
```

Numbered or Bulleted Lists

Since lists are so important to scientists and engineers, HTML provides a simple way to create them. There are "ordered lists," (i.e., numbered), and "unordered lists" (i.e., bulleted). Use <ol> and <ul> to make ordered lists and unordered lists, and then for both use the <li> tag to denote the start of a list item.

```
This is an ordered list:
<ol>
<li>First item
<li>Second item
<li>Third item
</ol>
```

Which looks like this in the browser:

This is an ordered list:

> 1. First item
> 2. Second item
> 3. Third item

Next, an unordered list:

```
This is an unordered list:
<ul>
<li>First item
<li>Second item
<li>Third item
</ul>
```

Which looks like this in the browser:

This is an unordered list:

> • First item
> • Second item
> • Third item

Inside the list items, you can put whatever you want—links, images, tables (more on those in the next chapter), or even other lists. Nested lists are actually quite common, useful for outlines or cascading menus.

Less common, but still useful, are "definition lists," which contain an alternating set of terms and definitions. Enclose the entire list in the <dl> container tag, and use <dt> and <dd> to denote the start of terms and definitions, respectively. For example,

```
Here's a definition list:
<dl>
<dt>Term 1
<dd>Definition of Term 1
<dt>Term 2
<dd>Definition of Term 2
</dl>
```

Which looks like this in the browser:

Here's a definition list:

Term 1
> Definition of Term 1
Term 2
> Definition of Term 2

Be sure to end your lists with </ol>, </ul>, and </dl>, or the rest of your page will show up as part of the final list item (if at all).

Comments

You can "comment" your HTML pages with text that won't display in the browser window. This is great for remembering why you did some HTML coding a certain way, or for text that you want to temporarily remove from being public, or if you want to leave some notes for anyone else who may modify your pages. One of my favorite uses for comments is on pages I've composed that are very complex—for example, ones with multiple tables nested inside each other. I use the comments to help me find specific parts of the page quickly.

Start a comment with <!-- and end it with -->, For example:

```
<!-- This is my comment, and won't display to the user -->
<!-- Start second column of third table in Contents -->
```

Comments can be as long as you want. Just remember to use the closing tag exactly where you want the comment to stop, and to not put any HTML tags inside your comments, since most browsers will think the comment ends with the first ">" character.

Putting It All Together

We've just covered a lot of the basic HTML construction set. In the next chapter we'll tackle some more advanced features, but for now, let's put them all together to create a real homepage.

I've created a page in my personal directory to list some astronomy links that might be interesting to some of my colleagues. Compare the HTML code below to the image shown to see how all of the tags work together and appear in the Web browser. By the way, I downloaded the image of Saturn from one of NASA's imaging libraries. Since they are funded by the U.S. government, all images posted there are public domain. Also look carefully at the HTML code for the image. Since the original image was too large for my page, I resized it using the WIDTH and HEIGHT tags. When you do this, make sure you keep the original image's proportions or your image will look skewed. Also note that I made the image into a link back to a description of the image at the NASA Web site, so if you click on the image you can read the caption.

```
<html>
<head>
<title>Brian's Astronomy Page</title>
</head>
<body>

<a name="top"></a>

<!--insert image from NASA's web site here-->
```

```
<a href="http://oposite.stsci.edu/pubinfo/gif/
SatStorm.txt"><img src="SatStorm.jpg" alt="Storm on
Saturn" align=top width="400" height="250" border="0">
</a>

<h1>Brian's Astronomy Gateway Page</h1>

<p>
Welcome to my <strong>Astronomy Gateway</strong>. I've
created this page of interesting links for all my
friends interested in astronomy.
<p>
<h2>Astronomy Links</h2>
<ul>
<a href="http://www.cfht.hawaii.edu/">
<li>Canada-France-Hawaii Telescope</a>

<a href="http://cea-ftp.cea.berkeley.edu/HomePage.html">
<li>Center for Extreme Ultraviolet Astrophysics</a>

<a href="http://www.coseti.org">
<li>Columbus Optical SETI (COSETI) Observatory</a>

<a href="http://http.hq.eso.org/eso-homepage.html">
<li>European Southern Observatory</a>

<a href="http://cass.jsc.nasa.gov/lpi.html">
<li>Lunar and Planetary Institute</a>

<a href="http://www.mtwilson.edu/">
<li>Mount Wilson Observatory</a>

<a href="http://umbra.gsfc.nasa.gov/sdac.html">
<li>NASA Solar Data Analysis Center</a>

<a href="http://sao-www.harvard.edu/home.html">
<li>Smithsonian Astrophysical Observatory</a>

<a href="http://stsci.edu/top.html">
<li>Space Telescope Science Institute</a>
</ul>

<p>
If you have links you think should be here, please send
me an e-mail message at <a
href="mailto:brian@spie.org">brian@spie.org</a>.
<p>

<a href="#top">Top of Page</a> | <a href="/home.html">My
Homepage</a>
</body>
</html>
```

In the next chapter we'll take this page and further enhance it with some of the more advanced HTML features.

Chapter 8

ADVANCED WEB PUBLISHING

In the previous chapter, I described and applied some of the more basic HTML constructs to create a simple homepage. In this chapter, we'll expand on some of the more complex elements of HTML, and then apply them to our original page to make it more dynamic and interesting. Along the way we'll look at some of the "tricks" experienced Web designers employ to work around some of HTML's more perplexing problems. Remember that HTML was never designed to be a page layout and design language. In fact, it's just the opposite. It was designed to share information first and foremost, leaving the task of deciding basic design issues to the user's browser. HTML is "platform irrelevant," meaning that anyone with a browser can view the pages.

But before we get started, some background is pertinent. Specifically, the issue of HTML's various versions is important. As a specification, HTML has a short but colorful history. As I write this, HTML v.3.2 is the current standard approved by the World Wide Web Consortium (W3C), which now governs the HTML standards development process. However, a working draft of HTML 4.0 has been published for two months now, and it's 4.0 that is important since many of the features in 3.2 were supported by the major browsers long before it became official in early 1997.

Much the same is true for HTML 4.0. For example, Cascading Style Sheets, which are easily the most significant new HTML specification since the introduction of tables, have already been adopted by many current-version browsers, despite the fact that they are part of a specification that isn't even approved yet, and that it's incompletely implemented in the recent release of Netscape 4.0. This is, in fact, the heart of the issue. The HTML specification is extremely fluid. It is in practice more derivative than innovative, since most if not all next-generation specifications stem directly from the two major browser developers, Netscape and Microsoft.

This works somewhat against the system because, as statistics show, users themselves take much longer to actually upgrade to the next browser version following its release. So what is essentially happening is that browser development is getting further and further from the end user, with only a handful of people actually using the current version of their favorite browser. This gap continues to widen as users get tired of new versions of software that is buggy and released before it's stable. The rationale behind early release is simple: market positioning. As I write this, both version 4.0 releases of Microsoft Internet Explorer and Netscape Navigator/Communicator suffer greatly from this ailment. No one I know who is serious about using the Web on a daily basis is upgrading to the newest version of either browser. As the old saying goes, "Fool me once, shame on you. Fool me twice, shame on me." We've all played the software upgrade game too many times.

This leaves Web authoring in a particularly difficult place. If we wish to be read and accessible widely, we must design our Web pages to meet the capabilities of a broad range of browsers, and that means making choices about what version or versions of HTML we are going to support. Yet this is not something easily discerned. There is gray everywhere in the level and depth to which any browser version actually conforms to any HTML standard.

Here's a very common example: you recently surveyed a number of colleagues on a particular topic, and now have the results in a spreadsheet format on your computer. The results lend themselves to spreadsheet-style formatting because it makes them easy to compare. Now you wish to put these results online for others to review. The obvious solution for Web publishing is to convert your spreadsheet into Web tables. But guess what? Not everyone has a browser that is capable of reading tables. Tables weren't officially introduced until HTML 3.2 in early 1997. So all those older browsers out there that people haven't felt compelled to upgrade or who are still working on character-based terminals will interpret and hence display your nice neat tabular data as an incomprehensible string of textual garbage. And perhaps just as bad, some older but still popular browsers support tables per se, but not the entire feature-set, and not with the same results. So someone looking at my table in Netscape 1.1 will see some of my table's features whereas someone with v.3.2 will see all of them. If, for example, my table relies on background colors in some of the cells to be read clearly, then the person with Netscape 1.1 will have problems because cell colors weren't supported until v.3.0.

There are of course workarounds to almost everything, and Web authors have been ingenious at implementing them. So as we work through some of the more advanced applications of HTML in this chapter, I will be pointing out some techniques and all-out tricks that will in future versions of HTML be different or hopefully even unnecessary. The direction HTML standards are currently going is toward increased control over design and layout. Style sheets are particularly aimed at this goal. The downside is that in the transition, it is necessary to "code" for multiple possibilities if you really wish to have your Web pages be readable by the widest possible audience, which in the sciences is almost a given.

For the purpose of writing this book, I am adhering to the current published HTML 3.2 specification as a foundation. I considered using the draft HTML 4.0 specification, which based on history would be a good bet, since once something is added to a specification, it is rarely removed. But the problem with this is that 4.0 "deprecates" a number of tags and attributes from 3.2, which means that these elements are planned for obsolescence in some future version of HTML. The conflict however is that while these elements are being deprecated on the promise that new 4.0 elements like Cascading Style Sheets will be able to adequately replace them, at the present time style sheets are immature in the current versions (4.0) of both Netscape and Internet Explorer. It goes without saying that Web authors won't give up their hitherto important tags such as WIDTH and ALIGN until browsers fully support their replacements (more on these later in the Tables section).

Painting the Canvas

In the last chapter, we created a homepage for some of my astronomy links. In this chapter we'll do a makeover of that page using some more advanced HTML features.

One of the easiest and most striking ways to customize your pages is to add a custom background, either in the form of a solid color, which is specified by some simple HTML, or by specifying an image to display as your page background.

Let's take the colored background option first. Creating a colored background for your page is very easy. All you need to do is add an attribute to a tag that is found on every valid HTML page, the <body> tag. The attribute can describe the colors in the form of a word, such as *blue*, *fuchsia*, or *green*, or as a six-character definition that represents the color's RGB value (see next page). The first example is easy. There are currently 16 colors you can "name" as your page's background: aqua, black, blue, gray, fuchsia, green, lime, maroon, navy, olive, purple, red, silver, teal, white, and yellow. These colors were originally picked as being the standard 16 colors supported with the Windows VGA palette. Not exactly a rainbow of colors, but certainly better than standard "Netscape Gray." Here's how you would specify a blue background for your page:

```
<body bgcolor="#blue">
```

That's it. Just make sure the # symbol precedes the color name, and that the quotation marks are included as always.

But suppose you don't like the 16 "named" colors. No problem. Most browsers now support 216 colors. That is to say they agree on 216 colors, which means they don't agree on 40 other colors in the 256-color (8-bit) palette, and so you shouldn't use them as they'll look markedly different on different browsers. These 216 color values are sometimes called "browser safe" because they'll look right on all browsers.

The standard color model used on the Internet is RGB, which consists of a set of three values from 0 (zero) to 255 in decimal notation, or 0 – FF in hexadecimal notation. One of these values is for red, one is for green, and one is for blue, in this format:

```
#RRGGBB
```

Here RR, GG, BB are the hexadecimal digits specifying the red, green, and blue values of the color. Hexadecimal is what's used universally on the Web. The colors you create depend on the mixture of these three colors, which are indicated by their respective numerical values. For example, a notation of "00" indicates the total absence of that color, and the FF indicates a full-strength value. Thus, we can see that pure red is #FF0000 in hexadecimal, pure green is #00FF00, and pure blue is #0000FF.

The reality is, if you're working within a graphic design program such as Adobe Photoshop, the standard practice is to work from a customized (browser safe) palette of these 216 colors when creating any kind of image (not a photo, however, as we'll discuss later). That way any graphics you create will look the same on most of the current browsers on the Web in use today. For now, however, suffice it to say that specifying a nice red-orange color would look like this:

```
<body bgcolor="#FFCC00">
```

How did I know this? I looked it up on a Web site I use as a reference occasionally. See the end of this chapter for some URL pointers.

Graphics on the Web

This seems like a good time to talk more about Web graphics. This is a topic worthy of a book all its own, and in fact there are many good books on the topic (see the Bibliography for some suggestions). I'll try to cover some of the most important basics here to get you going.

As introduced in Chapter 5, Web browsers currently can display only two types of graphic formats, GIF and JPEG. While both formats offer internal compression (which makes them ideal for the Web), the primary difference between these two formats is that GIF uses lossless compression, and JPEG uses a lossy compression, which means image quality can be somewhat degraded in an effort to compress it further.

The general rule of thumb is to use JPEG for photos and GIF for almost everything else. I say "almost" because there are exceptions. GIF images are limited to 256 colors (8 bits), which is why GIF is not suitable for photos. JPEG, on the other hand, is great for photos because its compression algorithm is specifically designed for them.

The actual process of creating graphics or photos is of course software-specific. There are hundreds of software programs—freeware, shareware, and commercial—that you can use to manipulate and convert graphics and photos to GIF or JPEG formats. Some of the more popular freeware or shareware programs include LView and Quick View Plus for Windows, and GIF Converter and Graphic Converter for the Macintosh (see the end of this chapter for pointers).

If you're interested in converting some of your photos to JPEG format, you'll of course need to scan them into digital format to get them on your computer.

Regardless of the software you use to create or prepare your Web graphics or photos, there are some simple guidelines to follow to help make your graphics both look good and load fast. The first is probably obvious: Keep your images small. I'm not referring to an image's physical size (although that's important too), but rather to its binary size, or "byte size." Most graphics programs will tell you how "big" an image is in bytes or megabytes. Remember that on a 28.8 modem connection, an image will normally transfer and display at a rate anywhere from 1 to 2 kilobytes per second. This means a 30K image can take up to 30 seconds to view.

There are of course some tricks to help get the smallest possible byte size without sacrificing image quality too much. With GIF images, the best trick is to save the graphic with an optimized palette, meaning that out of the 256 possible colors in GIF's 8-bit palette, any colors your image doesn't use are not saved with the graphic. Most good Web graphic programs will offer this option. For JPEG images, it's even easier. JPEG is a variable compression format, so you can save your image in varying degrees of compression and see which one offers the best compromise between image quality and byte size. Some of the more sophisticated Web graphics programs today even let you see the results of a certain compression value "on the fly" so you can quickly pick the best value.

Another standard practice of experienced Web designers is to use WIDTH and HEIGHT tags in an image's HTML tagging. I referred to this in the previous chapter with this example:

```
<img src="http://www.sun.com/logo.gif" width="50"
height="100">
```

The way this speeds up the image's loading is by providing the sizes in advance so the browser doesn't need to interpret the image's size on its own. Tagging this way also means that if visitors have their browser set to not load images, the page layout will still look correct since the browser will draw a box-outline the size of the unloaded graphic and display it.

Background Images

Earlier we learned how to create a solid color background. You can also create a background for your page using a graphic. HTML uses a process called tiling to create backgrounds, which means any graphic you specify will repeat itself indefinitely. So if you use a really small graphic, it will display all over the page background in a grid. Some people have used this effect to create some great backgrounds that look totally seamless. But other backgrounds show tiling's limitations. One trick that many sites use is a single background image that consists of two or more "stripes" that then tile downward to create colored columns. This is a neat trick to create "zones" on a Web page to help the reader. The graphic in this case is very simple: usually only about 5 pixels high, but make sure it's at least 1024 pixels wide so that it won't "repeat" on larger monitors. Here's a page I created using a graphic just like that, where the first 150 pixels are dark red, and the rest of the image is black. Both colors were chosen from a browser-safe palette.

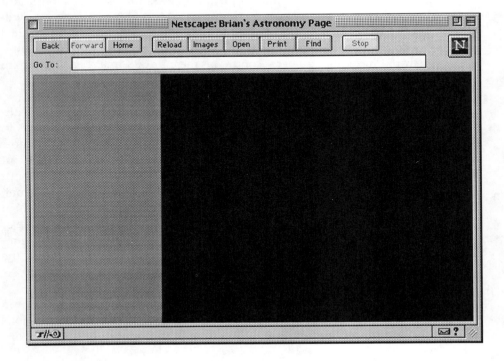

The HTML tag for the page above would be coded as follows:

<body background="astrobackground.gif">

There are numerous archives on the Web with background images for you to download and try out, and of course you can make your own. When choosing a background image, don't choose something with a lot (or any) detail. A background design that looks like a Jackson Pollock painting will render your text and links unreadable. Now, admittedly, I've chosen a rather dramatic background for my page, but I did this because the topic is astronomy and a dark background just seems apropos.

Text and Link Colors

Like backgrounds, the color of text and hypertext links on your page can also be controlled (remember, however, that users can override your specifications if they wish via their own browser's settings). The text and link attributes include the following, and they use the same color-naming scheme as that used for background colors:

TEXT
: Controls the color of all the "normal" text on the page. This basically consists of all text that is not specially colored to indicate a link.

LINK
: Controls the color of an unvisited link (usually defaulted to blue).

ALINK
: Controls the color of the link when clicked on with a mouse (stands for "Active Link"). I personally don't ever modify this color as no one really notices it.

VLINK
: Controls the color of a link that has been "visited." Remember that the "visited" attribute is usually a function of the number of days the user has set up in their browser to trigger expiration of their links.

Here's an example I created for our new astronomy homepage, using white for text, bright yellow for links, and gray for visited links.

```
<body bgcolor="#000000" background="astrobackground.gif"
text="#FFFFFF" link="#FFFF00" vlink="#CCCCFF">
```

An important point here: be careful when specifying text and link colors, since they depend heavily on whatever background is behind them for their legibility. They should contrast well. For example, the specification above virtually requires the user to load images because if they don't, then my white text will be displayed against a standard Netscape gray background, which won't work at all. But since this is an astronomy page and I want to make it dramatic, I'm willing to risk this nuance.

Introduction to Tables

Tables were first introduced by Netscape and then later accepted as part of HTML 3.2. They are the fundamental building blocks for most of today's Web pages, and you would be hard-pressed to find a professional site that doesn't utilize them. At their most basic, tables are a simple way of creating a grid—either visible or invisible—within which you can better control the alignment of text and graphics. They're not perfect, but they work, and there are myriad tricks to help you get whatever desired effect you're after on your pages.

There are only three tags required for building a table. These define the table itself, the number of rows, and the number of cells in each row. Everything else is optional. It helps to keep this in mind once you start delving into the many available modifying attribute options. Once you understand the basic concepts of table construction, building even complex tables becomes relatively easy.

Every table consists of the first tag <TABLE>, followed by the row tag <TR> (Table Row), and then any number of cell tags, either <TD> (Table Data) or <TH> (Table Header). The only difference between <TD> and <TH> is that the latter will make any text in the cell boldface. The paradigm here is of course a spreadsheet, where <TR> is the table row and <TH> or <TD> are cells. The number of columns is defined by either the total number of cells in the row, or by using some additional tags (more on these later).

So, here's the most basic table you can build:

```
<table>
<tr>
<td>This is the only cell.
</td>
</tr>
</table>
```

The table above really has no special purpose, since it doesn't do anything different format-wise from plain text HTML. However, if we were to add a second cell, the concept of tables should become clear. I'll also add a tag here to show the border so you can see what's happening:

```
<table border=2>
<tr>
<td>This is Cell One.
</td>
<td>This is Cell Two.
</td>
</tr>
</table>
```

Here's what this would look like in a browser:

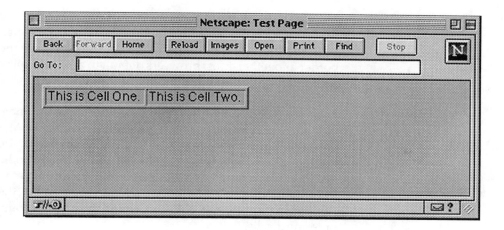

This is a basic table. One row, two cells—and therefore two columns. The cells' sizes would expand to accommodate whatever is inside them (text or graphics). As we'll see, many times you'll wish to control the column sizes with some additional tag attributes.

The options and variety of possible table configurations is beyond the scope of this book. However, for the purpose of this tutorial, we will modify my original Astronomy Links page to a table, which exemplifies a common application. By converting a whole page to a table format, we can control the page layout significantly better than without the table. It's especially useful when using the "sidebar" background that we created earlier, as we'll see.

But first let's outline most of the basic table, row, and cell attributes and what they do.

The <TABLE> element always requires both start and end tags. It supports the following attributes:

ALIGN   This takes one of the case insensitive values: LEFT, CENTER or RIGHT. It specifies the horizontal placement of the table relative to the current left and right margins. The default is left alignment, but this can be overridden by an enclosing DIV or CENTER element.

WIDTH   In the absence of this attribute the table WIDTH is automatically determined from the table contents. You can use the WIDTH attribute to set the table WIDTH to a fixed value in pixels (e.g. WIDTH="212") or as a percentage of the space between the current left and right margins (e.g., WIDTH="80%").

BORDER

This attribute can be used to specify the WIDTH of the outer border around the table to a given number of pixels (e.g., BORDER="4"). The value can be set to zero to suppress the border altogether. Most browsers default to zero to display no border.

CELLSPACING

In traditional desktop publishing software, adjacent table cells share a common border. This is not the case in HTML. Each cell is given its own border that is separated from the borders around neighboring cells. This separation can be set in pixels using the CELLSPACING attribute, (e.g., CELLSPACING="10"). The same value also determines the separation between the table border and the borders of the outermost cells.

CELLPADDING

This sets the padding in pixels between the border around each cell and the cell's contents.

The <TR> or table row element requires a start tag, but the end tag can always be left out. <TR> acts as a container for table cells. It has two possible attributes:

ALIGN

Sets the default horizontal alignment of cell contents. It takes one of the case insensitive values—LEFT, CENTER, or RIGHT—and plays the same role as the ALIGN attribute on paragraph elements.

VALIGN

This can be used to set the default vertical alignment of cell contents within each cell. It takes one of the case insensitive values—TOP, MIDDLE, or BOTTOM—to position the cell contents at the top, middle, or bottom of the cell, respectively.

There are two elements for defining table cells. <TH> is used for header cells and <TD> for data cells. As previously mentioned, the difference between the two is cosmetic; it allows browsers to render header and data cells in different fonts, and enables speech-based browsers to do a better job. The start tags for <TH> and <TD> are always required, but the end tags can be left out (personally, I like to use end tags as they make it easier for me to decipher my own coding). Table cells can have the following attributes:

NOWRAP

The presence of this attribute disables automatic word wrap within the contents of this cell (e.g., <TD NOWRAP>). This is equivalent to using the   text code for nonbreaking spaces within the content of the cell.

ROWSPAN

This takes a positive integer value specifying the number of rows spanned by this cell. It defaults to one.

COLSPAN	Used to specify the number of columns spanned by this cell. Default is one.
ALIGN	Specifies the default horizontal alignment of cell contents, and overrides the ALIGN attribute on the table row. It takes the same values: LEFT, CENTER, and RIGHT. If you don't specify an ALIGN attribute value on the cell, the default is left alignment for <TD> and center alignment for <TH>, although you can override this with an ALIGN attribute on the <TR> element.
VALIGN	Specifies the default vertical alignment of cell contents, overriding the VALIGN attribute on the table row. It takes the same values: TOP, MIDDLE, and BOTTOM. If you don't specify a VALIGN attribute value on the cell, the default is MIDDLE, although you can override this with a VALIGN attribute on the <TR> element.
WIDTH	Specifies the suggested WIDTH for a cell content in pixels excluding the cell padding. This value will normally be used except when it conflicts with the WIDTH requirements for other cells in the same column.
HEIGHT	Specifies the suggested height for a cell content in pixels excluding the cell padding. This value will normally be used except when it conflicts with the HEIGHT requirements for other cells in the same row.

Building a Page with Tables

Now it's time to apply a table or two to our astronomy page. Since we created a page background with two distinct columns (red and black), we'll also want to control the text that appears in each of these areas. A table is perfect for this. Since our background graphic has a red stripe that is 150 pixels wide, we'll create a table with two columns, the left-hand column being fixed at 120 pixels wide, and the right-hand column being unfixed, which means it will expand to fill whatever the browser's WIDTH is. The reason for using 120 pixels (instead of 150) as the column WIDTH is to make sure that any text in this column doesn't overlap into the black background. In other words, we're creating a 30-pixel buffer between the two colored areas.

Here's the basic table coding:

```
<table border=2>
<tr>
<td width=120>
</td>
</tr>
</table>
```

Here's what it looks like:

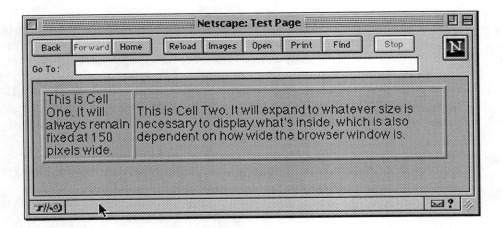

Now let's apply the table to our astronomy page, putting all the text from the page inside the right-hand column. Later we'll also add some new elements to our red left-hand column, starting first with a horizontal rule tag with a size attribute of 120 to make sure that our fixed-sized left-hand column stays fixed. Some browsers are rather sloppy at implementing this tag, often resizing it somewhat depending on what's in the other columns in the table. Adding a fixed size rule or graphic is a workaround to this inconsistency.

The HTML code for our rule looks like this:

```
<hr width=120>
```

Below this we'll add three small graphic "thumbnails," meaning that they ex-pand to much larger images when clicked on. This is an especially good way to help keep your site fast if you're putting up some technical drawings or images that not everyone will want to see, but you want to make available. The trick is to make separate smaller graphics (usually around 1"×1") from your larger originals, then display these on the page with an <a href> link tag around them so that users can simply click on them and connect to the larger image.

Here's the coding for one of our thumbnails:

```
<A HREF="http://oposite.stsci.edu/pubinfo/jpeg/
SN1987A_Rings.jpg"><IMG SRC="94-22T.gif"></A>
```

Notice what we've done here is to have the thumbnail image reside on our Web server, but the link to the larger image takes you to the original image on the NASA server. Since both thumbnail and the large image are available on the NASA server, I could have linked to them both there, but having the thumbnail image actually reside on my own server is a good practice, because if the NASA server just happened to be offline or very slow when someone tries to view your page, not only will your thumbnails not display, but it might take a long time for your entire page to display. This is because your page will sit there trying to contact the NASA server until it times out, which may take a long time.

Now we'll put our <HR> and three thumbnail tags in the first <TD> of our table, and put the rest of our page into the second <TD> (the right-hand column).

Here's what our final page looks like. I've left the BORDER="2" tag in the TABLE tag so that you can see the actual table borders. In the final version of my page I would probably turn the borders off (BORDER="0") to give it a cleaner look.

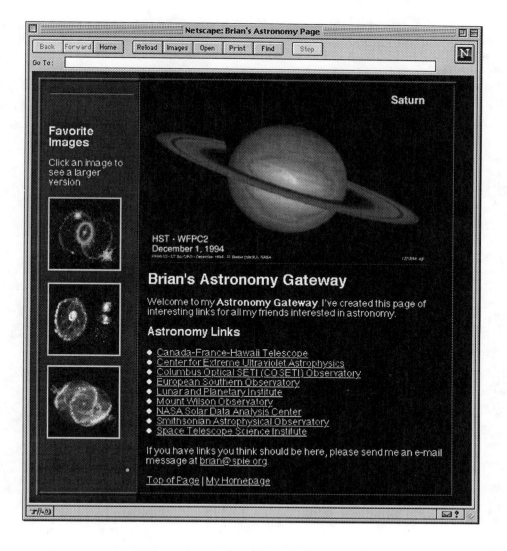

Here is the complete HTML page for my page above:

```
<HTML>
<HEAD>
<TITLE>Brian's Astronomy Page</TITLE>
</HEAD>
<BODY BGCOLOR="#000000" BACKGROUND="astrobackground.gif"
TEXT="#FFFFFF" LINK="#FFFF00" VLINK="#CCCCFF">

<TABLE BORDER="2" CELLPADDING="10">
<TR VALIGN="top">
<TD WIDTH="120">
<HR WIDTH="120">

<PRE>
</PRE>

<H3>Favorite<BR>Images</H3>

Click an image to see a larger version.<P>

<A HREF="http://oposite.stsci.edu/pubinfo/jpeg/
SN1987A_Rings.jpg"><IMG SRC="94-22T.gif"></A>
<P>
<A HREF="http://oposite.stsci.edu/pubinfo/jpeg/
Cartwheel.jpg"><IMG SRC="95-02Tx.gif" ALIGN=TOP
WIDTH="100" HEIGHT="100"></A>
<P>
<A HREF="http://oposite.stsci.edu/pubinfo/jpeg/
NGC6543a.jpg"><IMG SRC="95-01ATx.gif" ALIGN=TOP
WIDTH="100" HEIGHT="100"></A>
</TD>
<TD>
<A NAME="top"></A>

<!--insert image from NASA's web site here-->

<A HREF="http://oposite.stsci.edu/pubinfo/gif/
SatStorm.txt"><IMG SRC="SatStorm.jpg" ALT="Storm on
Saturn" ALIGN=TOP WIDTH="400" HEIGHT="250" BORDER="0">
</A>

<H2>Brian's Astronomy Gateway</H2>
<P>
Welcome to my <STRONG>Astronomy Gateway</STRONG>. I've
created this page of interesting links for all my
friends interested in astronomy.
<P>
<H3>Astronomy Links</H3>
<A HREF="http://www.cfht.hawaii.edu/">
<LI>Canada-France-Hawaii Telescope</A>
<A HREF="http://cea-ftp.cea.berkeley.edu/HomePage.html">
<LI>Center for Extreme Ultraviolet Astrophysics</A>
<A HREF="http://www.coseti.org">
<LI>Columbus Optical SETI (COSETI) Observatory</A>
<A HREF="http://http.hq.eso.org/eso-homepage.html">
```

```
<LI>European Southern Observatory</A>
<A HREF="http://cass.jsc.nasa.gov/lpi.html">
<LI>Lunar and Planetary Institute</A>
<A HREF="http://www.mtwilson.edu/">
<LI>Mount Wilson Observatory</A>
<A HREF="http://umbra.gsfc.nasa.gov/sdac.html">
<LI>NASA Solar Data Analysis Center</A>
<A HREF="http://sao-www.harvard.edu/home.html">
<LI>Smithsonian Astrophysical Observatory</A>
<A HREF="http://stsci.edu/top.html">
<LI>Space Telescope Science Institute</A>
</UL>
<P>
If you have links you think should be here, please send
me an e-mail message at <A
HREF="mailto:brian@spie.org">brian@spie.org</A>.
<P>
<A HREF="#top">Top of Page</A> | <A HREF="/home.html">My
Homepage</A>

</TD>
</TR>
</TABLE>

</BODY>
</HTML>
```

Special Text Characters

As with e-mail, high ASCII characters (explained in detail in Chapter 6) on the Web require special tagging in order to be displayed correctly. Some of the most common examples are the symbols above the numbers on your keyboard, accented characters such as Å and é, and smart or "curly" quotes. All of the high ASCII characters have HTML equivalents that you can use. Below are a few examples. See the end of this chapter for a complete table of all special HTML characters.

Character	Text Code	ASCII Code
©	&copy;	&#169;
&	&amp;	&#38;
®	&reg;	&#174;
nonbreaking space		
à	&agrave;	&#224;
ñ	&tilde;	&#241;

Note that there are two ways to display these characters in HTML, either by their text code, such as " " or by their actual ASCII value, such as "t". Note that in all cases, a special character must be preceded by an ampersand (&) symbol and followed by a semicolon (;). (And therefore the ampersand and semicolon have their own special symbols.) See pages 135–137 for a complete chart of all special characters.

More HTML Features

As noted earlier, HTML has a lot of features available—far more than can be covered here in examples. Some of the more common ones are explained below so you can at least get a picture of what features like forms and frames are. For tutorials on these more advanced constructions, see the references at the end of this chapter.

HTML Forms

We've all seen them. Those Web pages that have forms with fields, check-boxes, and pull-down menus where we input information to answer a survey, sign up for a service, or purchase a product. The deceiving thing about forms is that there are really two elements to them. First, the obvious formatting, which is straightforward HTML coding. For example, every form starts with a "form action" declaration, which the browser passes on to the Web server as a software instruction, and then continues with standard HTML tags for inputting data, selecting options, etc. Here are some typical form elements in code, following by what they look like in the browser:

```
<form action=/cgi-bin/register.acgi method=POST>
Your Name:
<input type=text name=name><br>
Your Personal Homepage (if available):
<input type=text name=home value=http://><br>
Your E-Mail Address:
<input type=password name=email><br>
I am interested in the following:<p>
<input type=checkbox name=binary>Binary Stars<p>
<input type=checkbox name=quasar>Quasars<p>
<input type=checkbox name=pulsar>Pulsars<p>
<input type=submit value="Sign Me Up!">
<input type=reset value="Clear Form">
```

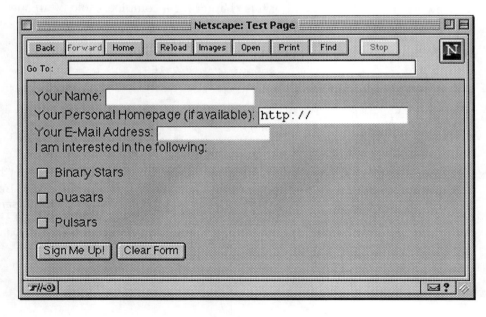

The first tag above is what's commonly called the "action statement," for obvious reasons. It defines what will happen when the user clicks the "Sign Me Up" button. In this case, the contents of the form will be processed by a small software application on the server called "register.acgi." (More about CGIs below.) The rest of the tags all define both what the users sees, and what "value" is passed by the CGI to the Web server for processing. For example, the <input type=text name=name> tag tells the browser to display a text entry box (type=text), and whatever is in that box will be passed via CGI to the Web server as a data field called "name."

CGI: Common Gateway Interface

The second part of a form is invisible to the user. Behind every form is some kind of software that is programmed to pass the information from the form to the Web server via your browser, and then pass the results back to your browser all nicely formatted for you to read. This software element is usually a CGI, short for Common Gateway Interface, and is typically written in a traditional programming language such as Perl, C, or Java. What this all means is that, despite the fact that you can create a truly beautiful online form for someone to interact with on your site, you still need to create the CGI programming element to connect your form to the Web server, and from there probably some other action, such as creating an e-mail message or adding data to a database. In other words, forms require specific privileges and knowledge of the Web server your pages are hosted on, and usually the assistance of a programmer familiar with that system.

If you wish to create forms for your site, refer to the links suggested at the end of this chapter for formatting tutorials, and contact your Internet Service Provider for information on technical requirements and programming assistance.

Frames

Frames were first developed and implemented by Netscape, and it didn't take long for them to catch on. If you've done a little surfing on the Web, chances are good you've already encountered them. Frames are those pages that have different sections, often with scroll bars between them. A typical use is to provide a list of links at the left or bottom of a page that act as an index. This section remains static while other areas of the page change as you click on them. Here's a page that uses a lot of frames:

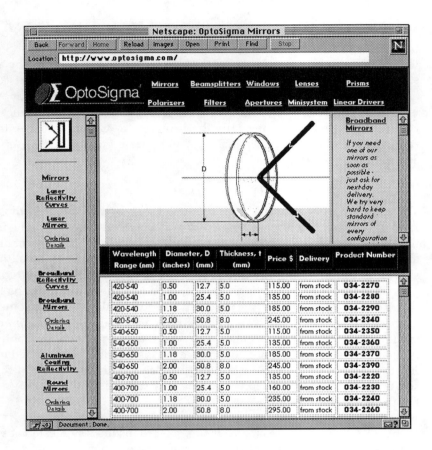

In the page above, not only is there an index frame at the left, but the right-hand area of the page is further divided into two scrolling frames on the top and bottom of a static frame. This is a solution to the problem of displaying complex tabular data while also providing an image for reference.

Despite their obvious utility, I'm not a big fan of frames. They require a lot of extra (and sometimes convoluted) coding to implement, and older browsers don't support them, so you end up having to create essentially two Web sites. They're also relatively slow to load, especially on modem-speed connections, and can be confusing for the user. But I will admit that if they're well thought out and not overdone, they can be a good solution to complex navigation and display problems.

Image Maps

Image maps allow you to specify areas of an image that when clicked on will act as a hypertext link to some other page or site, or initiate some other kind of action such as a file download or sound file playing.

There are two types of image maps:

Server-side Image Map

When a user activates a region of a server-side image map with a mouse, the pixel coordinates of the click are sent to the server where the document is housed. The server interprets the coordinates and performs some action.

Client-side Image Map

When a user activates a region of a client-side image map with a mouse, the pixel coordinates are interpreted by the browser. The browser selects a link that was specified for the activated region and follows it.

Client-side image maps are preferred over server-side image maps because they require no additional software on the Web server, and because they're simple to code. Almost all current versions of popular browsers support client-side image maps, so server-side maps are slowly disappearing, although you still see a lot of sites that offer both, letting the browser itself decide what to do. Browsers that can read client side image maps will recognize the specific tagging used for them, while browsers that cannot will simply ignore the client-side tags and recognize the server-side image map if one is available.

Here's an example of a typical client-side image map's HTML tags:

```
<IMG src="index.gif" usemap="#index1"></IMG>

<MAP name="index1">
 <AREA href="contents.HTML"
        alt="Table of Contents"
        shape="rect"
        coords="0,0,118,28">
 <AREA href="search.HTML"
        alt="Search"
        shape="rect"
        coords="184,0,276,28">
 <AREA href="textonly.HTML"
        alt="Text-Only Version"
        shape="circ"
        coords="184,200,60">
 <AREA href="Other Links"
        alt="Other Links"
        shape="poly"
        coords="276,0,373,28,50,50,276,0">
</MAP>
```

The <MAP> tag is the one that tells the browser that a client-side image map will follow. The image "index.gif" is divided into four individual "areas," which are referenced to corresponding pages by describing these areas with the shapes and x-y coordinates specified. It's really quite a simple system; however, I recommend using software designed to create image maps if you want to add one to your site. It will make creating the areas infinitely easier.

In either case, since not everyone loads or uses graphics when accessing the Web, it's important to make sure you offer textual alternatives to graphical image maps. This means providing either text alternatives to the links included in your image maps, or at least a link to a "text only" version of your site. It's also standard practice to use the image's ALT attribute to at least explain what the image is (e.g., "This is an image map used to navigate our site. Please load this graphic or use the text links below.").

For more information, tutorials, and pointers to software for image maps, see the links provided at the end of this chapter.

Cascading Style Sheets (CSS)

It seems clear right now that Cascading Style Sheets (CSS), or style sheets, as they're sure to be called eventually, are going to be the first major renovation to Web publishing since HTML was originally designed. One look at the HTML 4.0 specification will affirm this. However, as I mentioned in this book's Introduction, as I write this the CSS specification is only partially implemented in the just-released 4.0 versions of Netscape Communicator and Microsoft Internet Explorer, as well as treated differently in each of these. As a result, they are still regarded with some skepticism among professional Web developers, who have been burned in the past by "standards" that are only partially embraced by Netscape and Microsoft.

Style sheets are a large but still only partial answer to many of the more problematic elements of managing a Web site and its HTML coding. Their greatest potential is for large or complex sites. At their most basic level, style sheets will offer a way to create page-format templates that can be easily called from throughout a Web site. In this way, style sheets are a lot like the "styles" feature found in many word processors and desktop publishing software. You specify master page elements, text styles, and other elements, and then pick them up throughout your Web site. So, for example, if you at some later time decide that all the photo captions need to be a point size smaller, you simply change the style specification and all captions with that style are instantly modified.

For more information and tutorials on using Cascading Style Sheets, see the links provided at the end of this chapter.

Java and JavaScript

While the topics of Java and JavaScript would seem to be obvious ones for a chapter on advanced Web authoring, they are in fact not. Unlike HTML, which is a page description language, Java is a programming language. It is heavily derivative of C++, and while it shows great promise as a way of extending the Web's functionality, such work will necessarily be done by Java programmers. The reason Java has been so overhyped is because its development coincided nicely with the popularity of the Web, not—as some may think—because it was designed solely for the Web. It was not.

Part of the problem with the public confusion over Java is that it is actually many different things to different people, depending on which Java we're talking about. Today's Java can be used to build and run standalone applications, embedded "applets" on HTML pages, and even animations and 3D objects and scenes (VRML). Of course, most of the interest in Java does not involve application development. It focuses instead around Java applets: little pieces of Java that are downloaded automatically to run on a Web page. But regardless of the application, the key point is that unlike HTML, Java is not something most people are going to run out and learn. It will continue to be used by professional programmers and site designers to bring new features to Web sites.

Further confusing the issue is JavaScript, which is not really Java at all, but rather a scripting language developed by Netscape (and then later muddled by Microsoft's own bastardization, JScript). Unlike Java, which is used to create standalone applications or applets, JavaScript interacts specifically with HTML and a JavaScript-aware Web browser. JavaScript can be used to add "client-side" features to Web sites without a great deal of programming. Contrary to popular belief, JavaScript was not meant to be a poor-man's version of Java, nor was it intended to replace functions normally handled by CGIs. Instead, JavaScript can be used to augment these functions and more. And unlike Java, because JavaScript is a scripting language, while certainly more difficult than HTML, it is nevertheless much easier to learn than Java or any other programming language.

JavaScript can do some very nifty things, and its potential is just now being explored. However, on the flip side, JavaScript is currently plagued by lack of universal browser support. Worse, those browsers that do support it don't always do so completely. As I mentioned, Microsoft is (as usual) off doing their own thing with their version called JScript, which while close to JavaScript is not the same thing. So Web designers who wish to use JavaScript have to deal with two issues: first, they must provide alternate features for browsers or versions that don't support JavaScript, and second, they must be aware of Microsoft's Internet Explorer, which recognizes JScript and therefore some functionality may be lost.

If you're interested in learning more about Java and JavaScript, follow the pointers at the end of this chapter.

Some Final Advice

Whether you're just creating a single homepage for yourself or an entire Web site, there are a few practices that can help keep you moving toward your goal. The first is: use the Web. There is no better resource for learning how to create Web pages and sites than the Web itself. True to the original spirit of the Internet, on the Web you can find some truly excellent tutorials and resources that some kind and knowledgeable people have constructed to help. While books on HTML programming and such have their place, they can never be as current as a well-maintained Web site. And with the speed of change on the Web today, timeliness is paramount.

When I say "use the Web," it also means learn by example. Almost all good HTML authors learned their skills by reverse-engineering existing Web pages and sites. It's so easy—just find a page you like, select "View Source" in your browser, and start walking through their code to see how they did it. Some of the more fastidious sites even comment their code (often so others working on the site can add new copy more easily). You may even want to save the page as HTML (often called "source") and then open it in your favorite HTML editor to fiddle with the code and even use pieces of it for yourself. There's no law against this, and in fact most authors would be flattered. Just make sure you don't use their graphics unless you get permission.

HTML is getting increasingly unforgiving. In the "old days" you could get away with some sloppy work, but not anymore. Hence, use an HTML checker or validator. Functionally these fall somewhere between a spell checker and a software debugger. They comb through the code you've written and point out where you've done something wrong or "illegal." Most professional HTML authoring programs have an HTML checker built in (much like a spell checker), or you can also use a separate software package specifically designed for this purpose. There are even some useful online checkers. Just remember that HTML standards are fluid and somewhat subjective, so you'll need to keep your HTML validator up to date with the latest releases. It's a never-ending but essential task.

Some parting words about HTML editing software. While still somewhat kludgy and problematic, these products will get better with time. Recent surveys by *Web Week* magazine show use of programs like Allaire's HomeSite, Microsoft Frontpage, NetObjects Fusion, and Adobe PageMill is on the rise. However, so is use of high-end text editors like BBEdit. What this means is that many professional site developers are using one of the former to "rough out" a site and its pages, and then going back in with a text editor like BBEdit to fine tune the code to get exactly what they want. This in fact underlines one of the biggest problems with WYSIWYG editors like HomeSite: they're still difficult to tweak. By "tweak" I mean that when you are using one of these, your ability to make subtle changes to your code is limited to the software you're using. A text-based editor like BBEdit gives you complete control over your code, since you're actually editing it instead of working with a bunch of menus and palettes that are built into a graphical editor. The key here is to use what makes sense for your situation, and be prepared to perhaps not get exactly what you want in your page design. There are trade-offs, definitely, with all Web design.

Finally, if you're going to want a lot of graphics on your site, find a good Web graphic software package and learn it well. While Adobe Photoshop is certainly the choice of the pros, it also has a steep learning curve, so you may want to check out one of the less full-featured products. Again, you might not be able to get exactly what you want, but as with most things in the world, it's often that last 10% that takes 90% of the effort.

Getting Found on the Web

There's not much point in spending your time and energy creating a Web site if no one knows about it. Sure, you can tell you friends about it and reference it on your business card, but part of the value of having your own Web page is the possibility of letting others find you because they have similar interests. In other words, you want your page to be found when someone searches the Web. The Astronomy Links page we created is a good example of this well-established Web tradition.

There are of course many ways to announce a new Web page or site. You can post a short notice to any appropriate discussion lists you subscribe to, as well as Usenet newsgroups (be careful, however, not to overdo your announcement, lest someone take offense and publicly denounce—aka flame—you).

But these methods won't get your site found when someone searches the Web using one of the many public search sites. As discussed in detail earlier in this book, these search sites compile and update their databases in one of two ways, or a combination of both. The first method is registration, meaning that they learn of new sites or updated pages from people visiting their site and registering the new URL, or requesting that an existing URL be updated. The second method is through the use of a robot crawler or spider, which goes to your homepage and pages linked to it at your site, and through various software techniques, creates an index of your site to be added to the search engine's database (see the chapter on Searching & Researching for more complete background on the major search sites).

With this all in mind, there are a few things you can do to get your site indexed at the major search engines. The first is to register it with those sites that accept registrations, which nowadays is just about all of them. Some sites, such as Yahoo, rely solely on registration to collect or update links, whereas most others use registration as a way of scheduling their robot crawler's activity. Your registration actually functions as a request to be indexed by their crawler very soon, as opposed to the randomly scheduled updates that these crawlers do on their own. Registration is usually simply a matter of finding the "Register Your Site" link, usually found on a search site's homepage. You can register with as many sites as you wish. In some cases they will ask you for keywords and other information about your site, whereas in others they'll just ask you for your name, e-mail address, and the URL of your homepage. Each search site varies.

For those search sites that use robot crawlers, there is another trick you can do to help get your site indexed. Some (but not all) of the crawler-based sites will recognize and use a special set of HTML tags called META tags if present on your homepage. These tags are very simple to create, and you have nothing to lose by adding them. There are two basic tags, plus a number of optional ones that are mostly for record-keeping. The two essential tags are <META NAME="DESCRIPTION"> and <META NAME="KEYWORDS">. The first tag is where you add a short paragraph describing your site. This is what some search engines will display in search results when your site comes up in a search. The second tag is for a list of keywords that you think best describe the contents of your site. In both cases, don't abuse the META tags feature with long descriptions or endless lists of keywords. Most search engines will view this as the HTML version of spamming and will penalize your site for doing this, and possibly your site won't get indexed at all. A 25–50 word description and that many keywords as well is usually sufficient. Remember to pick keywords that are "root" words. That is, don't use plurals or multiple constructions. For example, include "optic" instead of "optics," and if you write "laser diode" you don't need to also say "excimer laser," since you've already said laser.

Here is an example of META tags, showing how it would appear on our Astronomy homepage. Note that the tags should appear as part of the <HEAD> element on the page, not in the <BODY>, and that of course these tags are invisible to anyone visiting your homepage.

```
<HTML>
<HEAD>
<TITLE>Brian's Astronomy Page</TITLE>

<META NAME="KEYWORDS" CONTENT="astronomy, star, optic,
planet, solar, radiation, telescope, x-ray, gamma">

<META NAME="DESCRIPTION" CONTENT="The Astronomy Links
site is designed as a starting point to help guide those
who are relatively new to astronomy on the Web.">

<BODY BGCOLOR="#000000" BACKGROUND="astrobackground.gif"
TEXT="#FFFFFF" LINK="#FFFF00" VLINK="#CCCCFF">
```

Remember also that HTML tags are not case sensitive, but in the case of the Description tag, you'll want to punctuate your description as you would like it to be read, since many search sites will use what you put here verbatim.

As mentioned, there are a few more optional things you can do with META tags; however, the two explained here are the most critical. There is one other tag worth mentioning here—the NOINDEX tag. This can be used if you have a Web page that you do not want to be crawled and indexed. Remember that many search engine crawlers will traverse and index your entire site without ever asking you for permission. By including this tag

```
<META NAME="ROBOTS" CONTENT="NOINDEX">
```

some search engine's robots will not index this page. Some, not all. Another way to help stop search engines from indexing your pages is to use what's called a *robots.txt* file on your Web site, more technically known as the Robots Exclusion Protocol. A *robots.txt* is a plain ASCII text file containing a coded list of all directories and files that are not public and therefore should not be indexed. It must reside in the root directory of your Web server, which means it governs the entire Web site, and therefore must be implemented by the site's administrator. If your pages are being served by an Internet Service Provider or your employer, chances are good you won't have any control over the *robots.txt* file, so your best bet is to use the NOINDEX tag above on all pages you don't want public.

For more information on META tags and the Robot Exclusion Protocol, see the Resources section that follows.

References and Resources

Here are some tools and resources related to HTML composition that can be found on the Web.

Major Reference Sites

WebReference
http://www.webreference.com/

Netscape Guide to Building Net Sites
http://cgi.netscape.com/assist/net_sites/

Web Mastery
http://union.ncsa.uiuc.edu/HyperNews/get/www/html/lang.html

Web Developer's Virtual Library
http://www.stars.com/

HTML Authoring

A Beginner's Guide to HTML
http://www.ncsa.uiuc.edu/General/Internet/WWW/HTMLPrimer.html

HotWired's HTML Tutorial
http://www.hotwired.com/webmonkey/teachingtool/

HTML Primer—A Complete Tutorial
http://www.htmlgoodies.com/primers.html

Bare Bones Guide to HTML
http://werbach.com/barebones/barebone.html

Advanced HTML
http://www.geocities.com/SiliconValley/Park/7476/advancedhtml.htm

HTML Made Really Easy
http://www.jmarshall.com/easy/html/

HTML Editors

Adobe PageMill
http://www.adobe.com

BBEdit
http://barebones.com

HomeSite and Cold Fusion
http://www.allaire.com

HoTMetaL PRO
http://www.sq.com/products/hotmetal/hmp-org.htm

Macromedia Dreamweaver
http://www.macromedia.com/software/dreamweaver/

Microsoft FrontPage
http://www.microsoft.com

Yahoo HTML Editors Index
http://www.yahoo.com/Computers_and_Internet/Software/Internet/World_Wide_Web/HTML_Editors/

HTML Validators

CSE 3310 HTML Validator
http://www.htmlvalidator.com/

Doctor HTML
http://www2.imagiware.com/RxHTML/

A Kinder, Gentler HTML Validator (online)
http://ugweb.cs.ualberta.ca/~gerald/validate/

WebTechs Validation Service
http://www.webtechs.com/html-val-svc/

Tables

The Table Element
http://www.webreference.com/html3andns/table.html

Basic Tables
http://ncdesign.kyushu-id.ac.jp/html/Table/table.html

The Table Sampler
http://cgi.netscape.com/assist/net_sites/
table_sample.html

Frames

Frames: An Introduction
http://cgi.netscape.com/assist/net_sites/
frames.html

Frames Tutorial
http://www.htmlgoodies.com/fram.html

HotWired Frames Tutorial
http://www.hotwired.com/webmonkey/
html/96/31/index4a.html

Image Maps

Client-Side Image Maps
http://WWW.Stars.com/Authoring/HTML/
Body/csmap.html

Image Map Tutorials
http://www.htmlgoodies.com/im.html

Servers-Side Image Maps
http://WWW.Stars.com/Authoring/HTML/
Body/ismap.html

Cascading Style Sheets

Getting Started with Cascading Style
Sheets
http://www.cnet.com/Content/Builder/
Authoring/CSS/index.html

Web Review Style Sheets Reference
Guide
http://www.webreview.com/guides/style/
index.html

WebReference Cascading Style Sheets
http://www.webreference.com/dev/style/

The W3 Guide to Style Sheets, Level 1
http://www.w3.org/TR/REC-CSS1

Cascading Style Sheets Tutorial
http://webreview.com/97/05/30/feature/
tutorial.html

Graphics Creation and Editing

GIF Animation on the WWW
http://members.aol.com/royalef/
gifanim.htm

Graphics Tools, Techniques,
Examples and Resources
http://WWW.Stars.com/Authoring/
Graphics/

Lynda's Homegurrl Page
http://www.lynda.com/

Graphics Software

Adobe Photoshop (Windows &
Macintosh)
http://www.adobe.com/prodindex/
photoshop/

GIFConverter for Macintosh
http://hyperarchive.lcs.mit.edu/
HyperArchive/Archive/gst/grf/

GraphicConverter for Macintosh
http://www.lemkesoft.de/

GIF Construction Set for Windows
http://www.mindworkshop.com/alchemy/
gifcon.html

Graphic Workshop for Windows
http://www.mindworkshop.com/alchemy/
gww.html

JPEGView for Macintosh
http://hyperarchive.lcs.mit.edu/
HyperArchive/Archive/gst/grf/

LView Pro for Windows
http://www.lview.com/

Paint Shop Pro
http://www.jasc.com

Quick View Plus for Windows
http://www.inso.com

XLoadImage for XWindows
ftp://ftp.x.org/R5contrib/
xloadimage.4.1.tar.gz

Beyond HTML

Authoring JavaScript
http://WWW.Stars.com/Authoring/
JavaScript/

Java Home Page
http://java.sun.com/

Java FAQ Archives
http://www.www-net.com:80/java/faq/

Javascript 411 Resource Center
http://www.freqgrafx.com/411/

JavaScript Resource Center
http://jrc.livesoftware.com/

JScript Homepage
http://www.microsoft.com/jscript/

Virtual Reality Modeling Language (VRML) Repository

http://www.sdsc.edu/vrml/

Dynamic HTML (DHTML)

http://www.insideDHTML.com/home3.htm

META Tag Tutorials

META Tagging for Search Engines

http://WWW.Stars.com/Location/Meta/Tag.html

Robots Exclusion Protocol (ROBOTS.TXT)

http://info.webcrawler.com/mak/projects/robots/exclusion-admin.html

Search Engine Watch Guide to META Tags

http://searchenginewatch.com/meta.htm

HTML Special Characters Reference Chart

Description	Character	ASCII Code	Text Code*
quotation mark	"	&#34;	&quot;
ampersand	&	&#38;	&amp;
less-than sign	<	&#60;	&lt;
greater-than sign	>	&#62;	&gt;
non-breaking space			
inverted exclamation	¡	&#161;	&iexcl;
cent sign	¢	&#162;	&cent;
pound sterling	£	&#163;	&pound;
general currency sign	¤	&#164;	&curren;
yen sign	¥	&#165;	&yen;
broken vertical bar	¦	&#166;	&brvbar;
section sign	§	&#167;	&sect;
umlaut (dieresis)	¨	&#168;	&uml;
copyright	©	&#169;	&copy;
feminine ordinal	ª	&#170;	&ordf;
left angle quote, guillemotleft	«	&#171;	
not sign	¬	&#172;	&not;
soft hyphen	−	&#173;	&shy;
registered trademark	®	&#174;	&reg;
macron accent	¯	&#175;	&macr;
degree sign	°	&#176;	&deg;
plus or minus	±	&#177;	&plusmn;
superscript two	2	&#178;	&sup2;
superscript three	3	&#179;	&sup3;
acute accent	´	&#180;	&acute;
micron sign	µ	&#181;	&micro;
paragraph sign	¶	&#182;	&para;
middle dot	·	&#183;	&middot;
cedilla	¸	&#184;	&cedil;
superscript one	1	&#185;	&sup1;
masculine ordinal	º	&#186;	&ordm;

*missing elements denote no text code equivalent is available

right angle quote, guillemotright	»	&#187;	
fraction one-fourth	*	&#188;	&frac14;
fraction one-half	*	&#189;	&frac12;
fraction three-fourths	*	&#190;	&frac34;
inverted question mark	¿	&#191;	&iquest;
capital A, grave accent	À	&#192;	&Agrave;
capital A, acute accent	Á	&#193;	&Aacute;
capital A, circumflex accent	Â	&#194;	&Acirc;
capital A, tilde	Ã	&#195;	&Atilde;
capital A, dieresis or umlaut mark	Ä	&#196;	&Auml;
capital A, ring	Å	&#197;	&Aring;
capital AE diphthong (ligature)	Æ	&#198;	&AElig;
capital C, cedilla	Ç	&#199;	&Ccedil;
capital E, grave accent	È	&#200;	&Egrave;
capital E, acute accent	É	&#201;	&Eacute;
capital E, circumflex accent	Ê	&#202;	&Ecirc;
capital E, dieresis or umlaut mark	Ë	&#203;	&Euml;
capital I, grave accent	Ì	&#204;	&Igrave;
capital I, acute accent	Í	&#205;	&Iacute;
capital I, circumflex accent	Î	&#206;	&Icirc;
capital I, dieresis or umlaut mark	Ï	&#207;	&Iuml;
capital Eth, Icelandic	‹	&#208;	&ETH;
capital N, tilde	Ñ	&#209;	&Ntilde;
capital O, grave accent	Ò	&#210;	&Ograve;
capital O, acute accent	Ó	&#211;	&Oacute;
capital O, circumflex accent	Ô	&#212;	&Ocirc;
capital O, tilde	Õ	&#213;	&Otilde;
capital O, dieresis or umlaut mark	Ö	&#214;	&Ouml;
multiply sign	x	&#215;	&times;
capital O, slash	Ø	&#216;	&Oslash;
capital U, grave accent	Ù	&#217;	&Ugrave;
capital U, acute accent	Ú	&#218;	&Uacute;
capital U, circumflex accent	Û	&#219;	&Ucirc;
capital U, dieresis or umlaut mark	Ü	&#220;	&Uuml;
capital Y, acute accent	†	&#221;	&Yacute;
capital THORN, Icelandic	fi	&#222;	&THORN;
small sharp s, German (sz ligature)	ß	&#223;	&szlig;
small a, grave accent	à	&#224;	&agrave;
small a, acute accent	á	&#225;	&aacute;
small a, circumflex accent	â	&#226;	&acirc;
small a, tilde	ã	&#227;	&atilde;
small a, dieresis or umlaut mark	ä	&#228;	&auml;
small a, ring	å	&#229;	&aring;
small ae diphthong (ligature)	æ	&#230;	&aelig;
small c, cedilla	ç	&#231;	&ccedil;
small e, grave accent	è	&#232;	&egrave;
small e, acute accent	é	&#233;	&eacute;
small e, circumflex accent	ê	&#234;	&ecirc;
small e, dieresis or umlaut mark	ë	&#235;	&euml;
small i, grave accent	ì	&#236;	&igrave;
small i, acute accent	í	&#237;	&iacute;
small i, circumflex accent	î	&#238;	&icirc;
small i, dieresis or umlaut mark	ï	&#239;	&iuml;
small eth, Icelandic	›	&#240;	&eth;

small n, tilde	ñ	&#241;	&ntilde;
small o, grave accent	ò	&#242;	&ograve;
small o, acute accent	ó	&#243;	&oacute;
small o, circumflex accent	ô	&#244;	&ocirc;
small o, tilde	õ	&#245;	&otilde;
small o, dieresis or umlaut mark	ö	&#246;	&ouml;
division sign	÷	&#247;	&divide;
small o, slash	ø	&#248;	&oslash;
small u, grave accent	ù	&#249;	&ugrave;
small u, acute accent	ú	&#250;	&uacute;
small u, circumflex accent	û	&#251;	&ucirc;
small u, dieresis or umlaut mark	ü	&#252;	&uuml;

Part III

SEARCHING & RESEARCHING ON THE WEB

Chapter 9

SEARCHING & RESEARCHING

Introduction

It was not so long ago that searching the World Wide Web was impossible, and custom indexes maintained by individuals were really the only way to find information in an organized manner. However, there are now a number of fast, innovative, and—best of all, free—search sites to help point to Internet resources using anything from simple keywords to full-fledged Boolean search queries. Most of these search engines work by preindexing and regularly updating pointers to a huge number of URLs on the Web, so when you enter your search criteria, you're only searching a powerful database, not the Web itself, which would be impossibly slow.

Search sites now come in all sizes and shapes, and are under constant renovation, as well as mergers and collaborative agreements. It is a full-time job just keeping up with their changes, so above and beyond anything else I say, the most practical advice I can give to anyone is to experiment with some of the sites mentioned here, find one or two you like, and delve into their online Help documentation so that you fully understand how the site works, and how to construct effective search queries.

Surveying the Landscape

For the purposes of this book, I've chosen to recognize six search sites as the current leaders—AltaVista, Excite, InfoSeek, Lycos, HotBot, and Yahoo. While there are others that could be included here, these represent the full range of what is on the Web today, both in terms of functionality and quality.

While all search engines are designed to do the same basic function, each of them has a slightly (or radically) different approach, which means their results can and do vary widely. A few factors that influence search results include database size, the type of content the site indexes, how often it's updated, and the search software's capabilities. Search engines also differ in performance, user interface, results display, and the quality of their online help. Clearly there's something for everybody today, and learning what works best for your needs is of paramount importance.

Searching the Web has become big business. In fact, it's arguably the biggest profit-making venture on the Internet today. Search sites have become the crossroads where users and companies can connect, and therefore companies are viewing search sites as a way to reach potential customers on the Web via "banner advertising." While banner ads may be annoying to some people, the reality is that someone has to provide the financial backing for these search sites to survive and remain free to everyone on the Web.

Searching the Web has also become frustrating, exhilarating, and everything in between. Each of the major search sites have unique and often cryptic ways of cataloging, indexing, and querying their vast databases. As I write this, AltaVista claims that their database currently indexes 30 million pages found on 275,600 servers, and four million articles from 14,000 Usenet newsgroups. This deserves repeating: 30 million pages. And that's Web pages, not paper pages. Web pages are not bounded in size like their paper counterparts. Web pages are digital documents that can contain thousands of words, in addition to the hidden HTML coding on them. I've seen entire doctoral dissertations put up on the Web as a single document, which is an affront to the user since many browsers will crash while trying to download documents or images that exceed 200 K. However, a well-managed Web site will not let page sizes get out of control, and most Web documents contain less than 5,000 words. The average is probably closer to 1,000 words. So let's do the math: even if we say the average web page contains 1,000 words, that means AltaVista's searchable index covers over 30 billion words.

My point here is based on experiences I've had with colleagues trying to search the Web. It is a common practice for those new to the Web or search engines to visit a search site like AltaVista, type in a word like *medicine*, and then wonder why the American Medical Association doesn't appear at the top of the search results. The reality is, a search on *medicine* returns over a half-million hits on AltaVista, and worse, the search results appear to be organized in a random manner.

The truth is, the major Web search sites are incredibly sophisticated databases that run on multimillion-dollar hardware and software that's under continuous development. In my search above on the word *medicine*, the search results were returned in less than 2 seconds, and probably 1.5 of those were the time it took to transmit the information across the Internet. This is the kind of performance that information managers everywhere can only dream about.

Most if not all of these sites provide detailed instructions on how they collect and categorize the contents of the Web, and how to get the best results when searching a database. It's important to read these instructions for each different search site you use, as they can vary slightly. Of course few of us have the time or patience to learn every site's idiosyncrasies, so my suggestion would be to experiment a little with some of the major search sites first to find one or two that you like, for whatever reason, and then dig deeper into their online help and instructions. As you use the web more and more, this research will pay off over time as you become an expert Web searcher.

Getting Started

To help get you started, I'll first outline the various types of search engines on the Web today, examine some of their similarities and differences, and then offer some insight into when to use which type of site.

Powerful tools require powerful controls, and most search sites have them. Unfortunately, they're all pretty much worlds unto themselves, and there is very little one can say about these sites as a group before the exceptions start flying. It's perhaps somewhat ironic that one of the most visible aspects of the Web is also one of the least standardized. So as with any complex system, it's up to the user to learn the controls to get the best results. So now that we have a sense of the landscape, we can zoom in on some simple guidelines to help make searching the Web relatively easy and fast.

Perhaps the most important difference among search sites is how they are structured. Some sites have a highly structured system of categories to help users find sites via the traditional "drill down" method (as well as by searching), whereas others offer no categorical structure or browsing at all—you can only search. And then there are those that offer a combination with some variations to set them apart; each has a searchable database, but also ranks or rates some of the sites in their database in an effort to offer visitors a way to search among only "prequalified" sites. And finally there are the so-called "meta-search" sites, which have no indexes of their own, but rather they search only other search sites.

Registration Sites

Perhaps the most important thing to understand is how search sites build and maintain their database indexes. There are two primary methods in use today: registration and robot crawlers. Both have their own strengths and weaknesses, and consequently a place in every researcher's toolbox.

Let's look at registration sites first. At its most conceptual level, a registration site is one where you must register your site using an online form. By registering, you are requesting that your site be indexed by the search service. Sometimes this indexing is done manually—that is, you supply keywords and a description that will define how your site is to be "found," and then someone at the search site places your site's information in their online database. Yahoo is an example of an almost pure registration site. Yahoo has made its niche by collecting and hand-indexing a huge index of sites that they have reviewed to some degree. By "reviewed" I mean that while anyone can submit their site to be indexed, the Yahoo staff first evaluate all submissions both for propriety and for proper categorization. Not every site is accepted, and the criteria used to judge a site's "worthiness" is often relatively subjective. However, my experience with the folks at Yahoo is that they try very hard to be the "best of the best," and this means that many sites simply aren't popular enough to merit a listing.

There are some advantages as well as disadvantages to a registration site such as Yahoo. Some obvious strengths are that they do not generate a raft of irrelevant links when searching, and that they are easy to browse and "drill down" into, much as you might search a traditional library card catalog. On the disadvantage side, they cover a much narrower slice of what's actually on the web, and are probably less up-to-date than a pure robot crawler site. They also inevitably reflect an indexing structure that may not sync up with everyone's view of the world, and therefore if precautions are not taken, you might miss an important link. We'll cover such techniques in more depth later in this chapter.

Robots, Spiders, and Crawlers

The other primary type of search engine is the robot crawler (or spider) site. Because of the Web's size, being a Web crawler is no small job. The Web has become the largest construct of information in all of human history, and creating a complete searchable index of it requires significant resources.

AltaVista is the purest example of a robot crawler site. It employs a highly sophisticated software agent developed to do one specific job: crawl the Web far and wide to collect and index its contents. More recently, sites like AltaVista have programmed their robots also to respond to human input—that is, you can specifically "ask" (via a Web form) their robot to revisit your site soon, presumably because you've made major changes to it. It will then schedule itself to check out your site earlier than its next regularly scheduled visit, which normally may not happen for weeks. In this sense, AltaVista is a bit like a registration site; however, the similarities end quickly. AltaVista is and will probably continue to be the definitive crawler site.

Robot crawlers revolutionized the Web. Before AltaVista and WebCrawler emerged on the scene, the Web was just a giant labyrinth of disjointed information. Sure, there were a lot of great "subject guides" like the W3 Virtual Library that mapped out hundreds of well-categorized sites. But these sites only represented a skeleton of the Web. Crawler sites were the first to map the whole body, with simple searches bringing back thousands and even millions of hits found deeper in the Web than anyone could have previously imagined.

The most often heard complaint about robot crawler sites is a familiar litany in modern life: too much information. They yield thousands of hits, but in no apparent order or ranking. At least on the surface this is what it seems like. As we'll see though, these sites can be mined effectively, just like registration sites.

Hybrid Search Engines

Yahoo and AltaVista represent well the two extremes of registration and crawler sites. Most of the other major search sites operate as hybrids. While sites like Excite, InfoSeek, Lycos, and many others actively solicit site registrations, they then also send out their robot crawlers to dig through those sites, as well as others. Many hybrid sites also offer reviews of many of their most popular sites, and then offer searches of these reviewed sites only, in addition to Web-wide searching. In short, all of the major search sites are constantly looking for ways to differentiate themselves from the pack, either by offering unique services, or by trying to muscle into the mold as the biggest or best overall. The truth is that they all have their laurels and their thorns.

Focused Subject Guides: A Viable Alternative

Subject guides are basically smaller, more focused versions of Yahoo and other registration sites. They are often managed by volunteers or groups of volunteers who are considered experts in their fields both on and off the Web. Some are housed on one Web site, while others link to guides located at various remote sites (often the "expert's" own site). Many subject guide sites have been around long before Yahoo and the other big services existed, and they're especially prevalent in the sciences. An excellent example is the W3 Virtual Library (see URL at the end of this chapter), which originated and still exists as a grassroots volunteer effort in the true tradition of the Internet.

Meta-Search Sites: Best of All Worlds?

Finally, there is another kind of search site that developed not long after search sites were first launched on the Web. These are often called "meta-search" sites. Conceptually, the approach is both smart and simple: you submit a query to one site that in turn goes out and searches sites like Yahoo and AltaVista, merges the results, and brings them back to you .

Such a search of searches can only work because the main search sites themselves are so speedy. Nevertheless, meta-search sites typically have a user-controllable timeout value (such as one minute), and a also a limit on the number of hits to be returned. The logic underlying these limits stem from the site's dependence on multiple sites for results, and because those results are weighted amongst themselves to yield a "best of the best" list of hits. Another oft-cited problem with meta-searches is that they offer very little control over queries, since they are not sophisticated enough to take a single complex query and recast it correctly before submitting to each queried site. Despite these limitations, meta-search sites are great for getting a quick overview of what's on the Web in a give topic. It won't be long either also before intelligent agents become sophisticated enough to overcome the search query limitations.

The original meta-searcher is MetaCrawler, which was created at the University of Washington and which now simultaneously searches Lycos, Infoseek, WebCrawler, Excite, AltaVista, and Yahoo. Other popular meta-search sites are listed at the end of the chapter.

How Search Engines Rank Web Sites

This is by far the most convoluted and hence perplexing subject on the Web today. The variety and weighting of criteria used by each search engine is a topic worthy of a separate book. I will simply outline some of the most significant factors that can be involved in ranking Web sites. Later in this chapter we'll look in more detail at how the Big Six search engines work internally, and how engine functionality in combination with search interface options determine what your final search results will be.

Words on the Page

The location and frequency of words on a page are generally the most important factors involved in how a site ranks search results. Words that appear in the page title ("title" is an HTML tag that tells the browser what to "name" the browser window) or among the first headlines or paragraphs on the actual page are given the most weight.

The frequency of a word on a page is also often used to rank its importance, but webmasters have to be careful about using a word too many times (such as filling up a page with hundreds of the same words), since search engines will almost always catch on to this version of spamming and will penalize the offending sites. Note also that the frequency of a word is relative to the rest of the content on the page. If you only have 50 words on your homepage and 10 of them are *astronomy*, your page will probably rise to the top of searches on the word *astronomy* more readily than others.

And then there's the issue of what exactly has been indexed. Some sites index only the words that can be seen when someone visits the site, while others index "hidden" text such as ALT tags, comments, and meta-tags. The latter are a set of structured tags on a Web page that are hidden to the user, but that some search engines use specifically to help categorize a site's contents. Notice I say "some search engines." Many people erroneously believe that meta-tags are more important than they really are. The reality is that they are just one tool among many, and that some sites such as Excite don't even use them. (According to Excite, the reason they don't use meta-tags is that they are easy to abuse, to the disservice of readers.)

See the chapters on Web authoring for more information about these hidden HTML tags.

By the way, there's one common trap that a few sites fall prey to: a homepage consisting of one giant graphic (usually a clickable image map). Such a homepage gives search engines nothing or very little to index, and in many cases no way for a crawler to index any farther into the site, since most crawlers cannot follow image map links.

Popularity

Search engines are clever in that they can work in reverse. By this I mean that they can use their robot crawlers' indexes to determine roughly how many links have been created to a specific Web site from everywhere on the Web. Some use this information to help determine a site's ranking during searches, with the more popular sites rising to the top of the results. The logic here is that the more links extant on a given site, the more valuable it must be, and therefore it deserves a higher rating.

Search engines that actually review and rate sites as part of their service may also use this information when ranking search results. A site with a favorable review may therefore show up first in all results.

Depth

Simply put, some search engines' crawlers don't dig as deep as others when indexing a site. For example, AltaVista and InfoSeek will only sample pages, whereas Excite and HotBot will attempt to follow all the links on a site and index everything (which explains why their databases are larger).

The Secret Formula

Some or all of these elements are used by each search engine to rank Web sites. The key to the complexity is in the mix. Each search engine has its own special formula for ranking criteria, which is why no two sites will ever yield the same results for a given set of search parameters.

Search Engine Basics

Just as you wouldn't use an electron microscope to read the daily newspaper, you don't need a monster index like Excite or AltaVista to find something as simple as IBM's homepage. A lot of people often miss the forest for the trees when it comes to searching the Web. As with any research, a little forethought as to what you're trying to accomplish can save you a lot of time in the long run.

As a general starting point, a registration site like Yahoo will be most effective when searching within a broad topical area. Even if you don't find what you're looking for, the predetermined categories can sometimes help you better formulate a search query by giving you ideas about what other topics or keywords might relate to your search. Better yet, Yahoo incorporates an AltaVista designed search engine, wherein a search that yields no results at Yahoo is automatically submitted to AltaVista, with the results coming back to you automatically.

Contrastingly, giant index sites collected by robot crawlers such as Excite and AltaVista are usually the best tool for conducting a very narrow search. This is especially true if you can construct a reasonably specific query statement. All of the major search engines offer certain basic Boolean operators that can be used to help focus your search results. Some of these are standard expressions that most users are already familiar with, such as *and*, *or*, and *not*. Most sites also have two levels of searching, usually called Simple and Advanced. Obviously the procedures and results for using a Simple Query will be different than those for the Advanced Query. Just how different varies from site to site.

For example, at AltaVista you can just type words into the Simple Search field, they'll be searched as if connected with an *or* operator, and the results will be ranked according to AltaVista's algorithm, which you can't control. With the Advanced Search, however, you must type a Boolean operator between words and phrases, and you can control how the results are returned to you. For example, if you search for *(laser near diode) and semiconductor* and put the word *semiconductor* in the Results Ranking field, your search results will first display any documents with high occurrences of the word *semiconductor* in them.

Searching More Than Text

As search sites have become more sophisticated, some now offer the ability to focus on other kinds of data besides text. Some common examples are searches for images, URLs, domains, even Java applets.

For example, it's becoming increasingly common to find images on the Web that are useful to a researcher. These might include technical specifications, CAD drawings, and other types of images. So now on AltaVista you can search for *image:spectrum* to find all images with the word *spectrum* as part of their title. Similarly, on Lycos you select *image* from a pull-down menu to limit your search to images only. Of course, searching for an image by its name is probably not going to yield fantastic results, since not everyone names their images that way, but it's a place to start, which is sometimes all you need.

Common Search Elements

This section provides an overview covering some of the most common search functions.

Boolean Operators

These form the foundation for creating good search queries.

Boolean Operator	Function	Example
and	*match all words*	*"laser and diode"*
or	*match any words*	*"laser or diode"*
and not	*exclude these words*	*"laser and diode and not sapphire"*
near	*proximity required*	*"laser near diode"*
( )	*search inside first*	*"(laser and diode) and . . ."*

It's very important to know what each search engine's default settings are since they will greatly affect your results. AltaVista and Excite use *or* as the default operator, whereas HotBot, InfoSeek, and Lycos each use *and* as their default. Personally, I'll take an *and* search almost any time, since it narrows the search instead of expanding it. The *or* operator is good, however, for more complex queries like the *and not* example above.

Increasingly common is the use of pull-down menus to create all or part of a Boolean construction, instead of having you enter all your query parameters into a single search field.

While at first this type of search form might seem more noisy, I've begun to prefer such an interface because it takes some of the guesswork out of creating a good search query. For example, search engines that require you to type in Boolean operators often use slightly different variations from each other, such as requiring *not* instead of *and not* (the former is a Lycos convention). Some also require or allow as optional some symbols to be used as shorthand for some operators. The most common symbols are shown below:

Symbol	Meaning	Example
+	and	+laser +diode
-	or	laser -diode
&	and	laser & diode
|	or	laser | diode
!	and not	laser & diode !sapphire

These symbols are even more dangerous for beginning users because not only are they touchy (e.g, you must make sure that the + symbol is in front of the first word, and that there are no spaces between it and the word), but also because they are not standardized. A great example of this is InfoSeek, for which the pipe symbol (|) means something closer to *and* than to *or*.

Unfortunately, every search site seems to have made its own rules, so check the specific search site's Help documentation to see which operators and symbols are recognized. I cannot overemphasize this.

Field Search

As mentioned above, some search engines let you narrow your search for specific data types, such as sounds or images, or to specific parts of a Web page, such as the page title. Including a field search as one search parameter can greatly increase the relevance of the results, as well as give you the ability to find out how many other pages link to a certain page (a great tool for webmasters).

Search for a Phrase

You can usually indicate a specific phrase (like a proper noun) to be searched by either enclosing it in quotation marks ("IEEE Internet Computing") or via a menu option on the search page.

Relevance Ranking

Assignation of a numerical "score" showing how relevant each hit compares to your actual query within the context of the documents found. Usually the numerical scale is either 0–100 or 0–1000, with the highest numbers being most relevant. Note that the key word here is "relevance," which refers to how relevant your search terms are not only within the context of all the hits returned, but also within the individual documents found. For example, if you search on "laser and dental and surgery," any hit that contains all three terms would receive a relatively high score. However, the relative number of times each of those words appears within each hit's source also affects the ranking, so that a one-page document where those three words occur numerous times will receive a higher ranking than a ten-page document where they only appear once.

Truncated or Wildcard Searches

Surprisingly few search engines support true wildcard searching. I highly suspect this is because it would be easy for someone to create a wildcard search that brings a search engine's performance to its knees. The only site I know of that supports true wildcarding (with the * symbol) is AltaVista, which again supports my theory since they are known to have probably the best and fastest hardware on the planet.

Some sites do offer ways to at least create truncated search stems, which are useful where in situations you aren't sure of a spelling, or there is more than one possible spelling (e.g., *color* and *colour*), or you want to account for plurals and other suffixes in your search. For example, to search on *optics*, *optical*, *opto-electronics*, and *opto-electronics*, you might simply search for the root *opt*, which when combined with some other limiting terms should yield good results.

The Big Six Search Engines

Compiled below are my views of the six major search engines. They are based on my personal experience with each of the services and include some historical and business perspectives. This is not a features comparison. Such comparisons are quickly dated because these search services change on a weekly basis, sometimes quite significantly. As I've said elsewhere, the best way to compare search engines is to read their current online documentation and try some sample searches. A typical sample search is shown later in this chapter. A features comparison is also included in the Appendix.

AltaVista (http://www.altavista.digital.com)

When it first launched, AltaVista, sponsored by Digital Equipment Corporation (DEC), made its mark on two fronts. First, it was the ultimate junkyard of web indexes. DEC made no apologies for this position, and it served them well as it was a niche hitherto unfilled.

AltaVista's second mark was as the fastest search engine, a claim which for a long time was substantiated by raw performance. Again, this was a smart marketing move on DEC's part, since their real business is selling high-performance computer hardware, and especially since they used AltaVista to promote their then-new Alpha workstations. Unfortunately, the same techno-prowess that created those speedy searches has also leached into its interface design and help facilities, which are busy and overloaded with technical explanations. The search results also need a retuning to something a bit less dense.

Today, AltaVista's landscape hasn't changed much. While InfoSeek and Excite have surpassed AltaVista in overall content indexed (55 million v. 30 million pages), the latter still seems to have the highest garbage ratio on the Web, and for some reason this seems to be why people still like AltaVista. I have to confess to this irrational behavior myself. When I want to search on something really off the wall, like "the music of Hildegard of Bingen" (a 12th-century nun), I'll try AltaVista first just to see what it finds. I suppose it's this surprise factor that makes AltaVista still attractive at times. Clicking the Search button at AltaVista is the Internet equivalent of pulling a slot machine handle in Vegas: you take your chances.

A little trivia about AltaVista. Notice that their URL is not simply **www.altavista.com**, because it requires the primary domain "digital". This is because when DEC registered AltaVista with the InterNIC, the domain **altavista.com** was already taken by a Web design firm.

Excite (http://www.excite.com)

Excite turned out to be a bit of a sleeper. Founded in 1995 by six Stanford graduates, Excite has become something of an enfant terrible, as it were, not the least because of its voracious appetite for mergers, acquisitions, and strategic deals. First they bought both Magellan and WebCrawler, then they started cutting deals with everyone from Netscape to AOL (when you use AOL's NetFind, you're really using Excite). And like AltaVista and Yahoo, they are quickly expanding on the international market with regionally specific points of presence outside the United States.

On the technology side, Excite's patented ICE search technology is their claim to fame. ICE stands for Intelligent Concept Extraction, which means that when you enter a search query, Excite searches the entire Web for documents containing related concepts, not just the keywords you entered. For instance, when you search for *integrated circuits*, Excite will bring you pages containing *semiconductor manufacturing*, even if the words *integrated* and *circuit* are not actually on the page. While this is more a trick of statistics than any kind of new artificial intelligence agent, it nevertheless seems to work to the searcher's advantage. Excite has consistently fared very well in the industry press, getting the highest marks for smart, easy, and relevant searching.

Like Yahoo, Excite also offers what they call Channels, which consist of over 140,000 pre-selected Web site listings, 25,000 of which include short reviews and are ranked by an actual person. You can also search Usenet postings on Excite, a feature that is quickly becoming de rigeur for any big search site.

HotBot (http://www.hotbot.com)

Clearly the up-and-coming contender in the search engine ring, HotBot is gaining market share and recognition very quickly. While I couldn't find an explicit reference to its origins on the HotBot site, a little sleuthing at the InterNIC site (where domains are registered) revealed that the HotBot domain is registered to HotWired, which is in turn owned by Wired Ventures, Ltd., the company that also owns *Wired* magazine.

It appears to be money well spent. Unlike AltaVista and Yahoo, which seem to be concentrating their resources on acquisitions, deals, and international expansion, HotBot is working hard to enhance its user services. Their search interface is currently my favorite, primarily because it has tons of options while making it very easy to use (unlike the simple "fill in the blank" search fields of AltaVista and Yahoo, which are ambiguous and easily misused).

It appears I'm not alone in this opinion. During my research for this chapter I ran across a review of search engines in the September 1997 edition of *Internet World* magazine, which said "In our tests, HotBot's search results were unmatched. It also provides what is arguably the simplest-to-use and most customizable user interface in the group." They concluded by saying, "If we could use only one search engine, it would be HotBot."

Interestingly, HotBot's search engine is actually not their own, but one licensed from Inktomi Corporation, an ARPA spin-off that pioneered the concept of "network of workstations," or NOW, which implements clusterings of inexpensive PC computers to achieve supercomputer processing levels.

InfoSeek (http://www.infoseek.com)

I've never been quite sure how to interpret this, but when I look at the Web server logs for the two scientific/engineering Web sites I manage, InfoSeek represents an inordinate amount of traffic when compared to all other search sites. That is, more people are finding our Web site through searches on InfoSeek than anywhere else.

This could of course be related to InfoSeek's quantum leap in 1996 from a few million indexed URLs to now over 50 million, which puts InfoSeek at the top of the heap right next to Excite.

Infoseek maintains its directory services separate from its search engine. Sites are listed by topic, which are automatically generated using categorization software. They also have an agreement with DejaNews so you can search Usenet postings directly from the InfoSeek homepage. And of course they have the usual links to Yellow Page, White Page, and Stock Ticker services. These are becoming ubiquitous among the major search engines.

InfoSeek started out with a subscription-based revenue model, which means they tried to get individual users to pay a fee to search the site. Like most subscription models on the Web to date, it failed. The good news though was that as part of their subscription service they had set up an infrastructure to collect additional information about Web sites, and to review them. They now claim to have over 500,000 sites with expanded listings, and they use a single red check mark to denote "InfoSeek Select" sites that they've both reviewed and recommend.

Lycos (http://www.lycos.com)

I have to admit up front that I've never been a big Lycos fan. Not that there's anything wrong with Lycos. It just seems to suffer from mediocrity in a business that makes Madison Avenue marketing look like a lemonade stand. To survive in the Web search business, it would seem that you need at least one of three things: a loyal following (like Yahoo), a substantial niche (like AltaVista), or sheer utility (like HotBot and InfoSeek). Lycos appears to have none of these handholds.

Yet it certainly merits a place in this book. I've heard Lycos described as your basic four-door sedan of search sites—comfortable and solid feeling. And perhaps this is why it still represents 16% of all search site traffic and is consequently the fourth largest service at this time, and is the ninth most visited site on the Web overall. (Lycos actually gets more traffic than AltaVista, the latter being in the fifth most visited search engine and tenth in overall Web traffic.)

However, Lycos is clearly not taking their middling position lying down. In September 1997 they launched Lycos Pro, which features a search algorithm designed to give users the most relevant results on the Web and a spidering algorithm capable of visiting up to 10 million Web pages per day. In addition to these technology changes, Lycos' business managers have been aggressively signing strategic alliances with everyone from Microsoft and Lotus to Barnes & Noble and the Discovery Channel.

Yahoo (http://www.yahoo.com)

Yahoo is still the Big Kahuna of search engines. It attracts over 35% of the total search traffic, and is the single most visited site on the Web today. This is an incredible position for any company in any industry.

Thankfully, it hasn't gone to their heads. Yahoo continues to be both useful and fun. Their "My Yahoo" service was a pioneer in user-customizable services, and the company continues to grow its user services despite a healthy dose of expansion going on in the background. Yahoo has partnered with some big names, including Microsoft and Amazon.com. One of Yahoo's biggest coups is being the default search engine link built into Microsoft Internet Explorer.

Remember that Yahoo is not a search engine per se, since it relies solely on user registrations to build its content. Of course you can still search Yahoo, and in fact when you do so you are searching with AltaVista's search engine. But the key to Yahoo's success is still founded on two major elements. The first is longevity. Yahoo is the grandfather of all Web directory services, and has built an extremely large and loyal user base. Second, it's smart. I'll be the first to admit that its indexing catagories can be confusing or misleading at times, but overall the site continues to give the impression that every single link has some human thought behind its existence. This is unique among the major search sites, since all the others use some level of randomized URL scooping a la robot crawler.

This human touch concept carries through on all their other services. A good example is the regional Yahoos, currently called World Yahoos and Yahoo! Metros. These are simply cool. From the homepage I quickly drilled down to the town where I live (Bellingham, Washington), and what I received was a customized page built from all the various places on Yahoo that somehow related to my town, including local weather, business yellow pages, local news (via UPI), local sports scores and stories, and a list of related links such as the *Seattle Times*, The Rough Guide, and Movie Link. This is the same technology they employ for the aforementioned "My Yahoo" service, which lets users create customized resource pages that can be accessed any time for an instant snapshot of things you're interested in. It's the closest thing to having an intelligent agent on the Web today.

As a technical resource, Yahoo has a few quirks, but in general is a good starting place for any broad search. High on my list of squawks would be search results, which are cluttered with references to Yahoo's highly structured indexing. However, once you get used to the results pages they're not nearly so bad, and if you're going to use Yahoo a lot, they can actually be useful because they show you the root path for all the links you find. This can give you ideas about what other areas you might want to look under for your searching.

A Sample Search: HotBot

Now that we have some insight into how search engines work and what their capabilities are, it's time to practice. I'm going to use HotBot for my test search, because they just recently announced the ability to search document date ranges (before, between, and after), as well as some new field search options, and I wanted to try these out. I designed a specific search scenario not uncommon to science and engineering professionals. The scenario goes like this: I am preparing references for a paper I've just written on pattern recognition software. I know that a colleague of mine, Henri Arsenault, who is at the University of Laval, edited a book on the topic a couple years back. I'm relatively certain it was published before 1996. I also remember that one of the topics covered in the book was *rotation invariant pattern recognition*, which is fairly specific and should therefore serve well as a starting point for constructing a search query.

So here is the query I constructed:

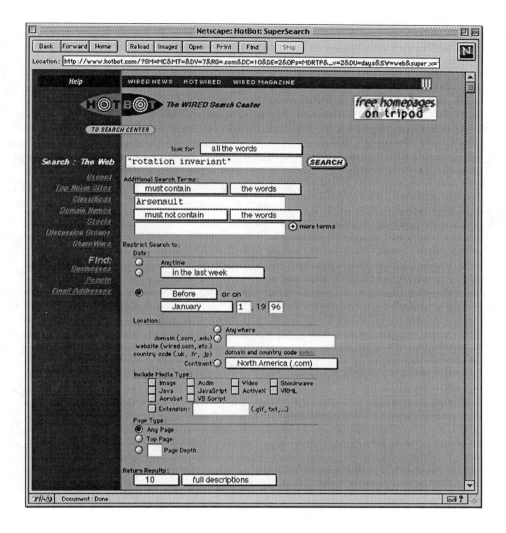

The first thing that strikes me about HotBot's user interface is the wealth of options available. As I mentioned, this might seem like a lot of noise at first, but really, it's a very elegant solution to constructing highly complex searches in their database without introducing all the ambiguities that traditional Boolean search queries bring.

My primary search terms, *"rotation invariant"*, are entered with quotes because I know from reading the HotBot Help file that this will force the search to look for these words in that specific order. I do not enter the words *"pattern recognition"* as I'm not sure that they would appear in the string, and if I removed the quotes because of this uncertainty I would get a lot more hits because these words are fairly common. Note that I also use the pull-down menu to designate "all the words" as the first Boolean operation (same as an *and* search).

Next, I see that the Additional Search Terms fields offer "the person" as an option. This is a new feature and I wanted to check it out. It's a first for a Web search engine, and a smart option especially for scientific research, since citations always have names to search. So I enter the last name of my colleague using mixed case because most search engines ignore case unless you specifically enter something besides all lower case.

Finally, I use the Restrict Search to Date option to direct my search to only those documents dated before 1 January 1996.

As I mentioned, this is a fairly well defined search. In general, the better you can refine the search up front, the better your results will be. Sometimes this can be counterproductive, of course, and yield results that stray from your intent because of misinterpretation by the software, especially when it comes to ranking lots of results. Then again, if you have too many results you'll have to narrow your search anyway.

Other Search Options

Before looking at the results of my search, let's review some of the other options offered in the search form shown. First, notice the little circled + symbol with the words *more terms* next to it. If you click this, it refreshes the search form and adds another search field with the accompanying pull-down options above it. This allows you to enter as many additional search terms and Boolean parameters (via the pull-down menus) as you like.

Next are all of the items under "Restrict Search to". They are all for the most part self-explanatory, although I needed to consult the Help guide to find out how the search engine is determining the date of a document (date created or last modified, whichever is later). The Domain and Continent restriction options could be useful in many situations, especially if you wished to find sites authored in a particular language (e.g., a domain **.de** and continent "Europe" would certainly bring up more sites authored in German).

Next is the Media Type restrictions, which could drastically narrow a search to one or more specific data types. Page Type is a new option, and I have to admit I cannot think of a situation where this would be useful. Narrowing my search to a specific number of directory levels in a Web site would seem to presume that I have some knowledge of a site before I've found it, which is not usually the case.

Finally, the Return Results is a standard limiting factor, and can greatly speed or slow a search's progress. Either go with the minimums and be prepared to modify your search, or raise the number to bring back a lot of results and then use your browser's built in Find feature to scan the big page of results you receive.

Now on to my search results:

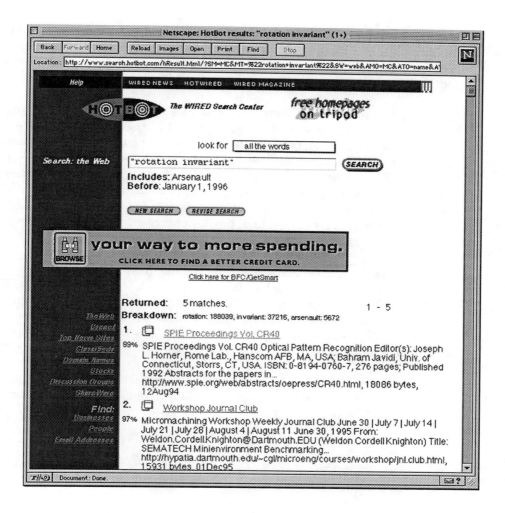

My search yielded a total of five hits, and the first one is actually the one I was looking for. I wish all my searches went so well!

While this is only one example from one search site, the concepts behind effective Web searching are the same no matter where you are. There are no magic formulas. Knowing a site's capabilities, learning its search query syntax, and constructing logical queries are the keys to finding resources and information as quickly and painlessly as possible.

A Sample Search: Yahoo

Now that we've seen how a hybrid search engine works, it's time to look at the other kind of search engine. Yahoo is the purest example of a registration site because it's the only major search site that does not use robot crawlers (actually, they do use a limited type of crawler, directed only to specific places where new Web sites are announced). To collect their database, they rely primarily on user registrations, and to some degree on a staff of people at Yahoo who watch for appropriate sites, as well as evaluate incoming registration requests. Because they don't clutter their site with the random cullings of a robot crawler, the Yahoo site is without question the "cleanest" search site on the Web today. (The intended irony here is that the word "Yahoo" comes from Jonathan Swift's *Gulliver's Travels*, where the Yahoos were a race of "filthy brutes.")

Because Yahoo has no robot crawlers, it provides a different view of the Web. In our HotBot search, we wanted to find something very specific—a book title— that we knew had a listing on the Web for quite some time, and therefore were confident it could be found because the robot crawlers would have indexed it automatically by now. Contrastingly, Yahoo's database, while certainly massive, would not be a place I would expect to find such a discrete reference. As I mentioned early in this chapter, Yahoo is a place to start when you want to get either an overview of an interest area, or a list of the best possible resources in that area.

At Yahoo, most people generally search by drilling down through the various levels of categorizations, all of which have been devised—for better or worse— by Yahoo staff. Of course, you can also search Yahoo just like you can HotBot or the other crawler-based sites. But the real value of Yahoo is that it's structured so rigidly, and cross-referenced extensively. This latter feature can also be confusing if you're new to Yahoo, as we'll see.

To frame our sample search, we'll propose that we're looking for more resources in the area of electrical engineering, specifically integrated circuit design. Here's the Yahoo homepage:

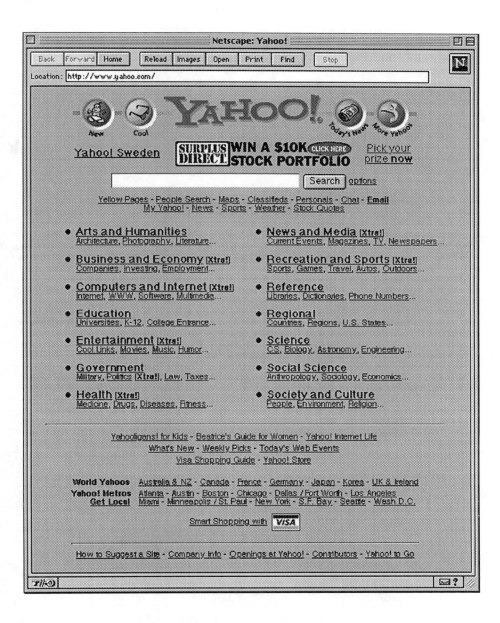

The categories listed here are the major areas of the site. From here, once you start drilling down, you will always know where you are because Yahoo always lists at the top of each page a path index to the that page, such as **Top:Science:Engineering:Electrical Engineering:Circuits**. This feature becomes very important if you use Yahoo on a regular basis, again because of the extensive cross-referencing of links.

Notice also at the top of the page there is a button to "Add URL". This is where you go to register an URL.

From the homepage I clicked the link to Science:

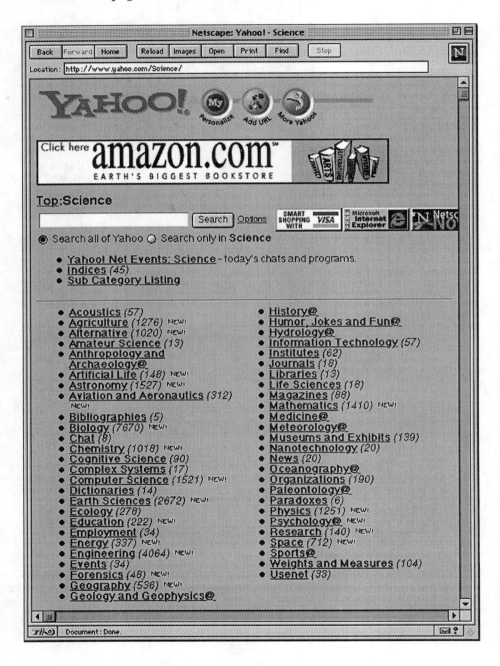

This is the master list of science subcategories. Above the listings are some standard Yahoo features. First, the path index I mentioned, here **Top:Science**. As we drill down deeper into Yahoo's archives, you'll see this path grow with each new level. Another standard feature here is the small search field, plus radio buttons below to denote a search of all Yahoo, or just the subcategory you're currently in. This is handy for quickly narrowing a search. For example, you could drill down to an engineering subcategory such as optical engineering, and then search only within that area, thereby lessening the chances of irrelevant hits. Of course, when you search Yahoo you get a lot less garbage than you do with any of the search sites, since every link on the site has been reviewed by a Yahoo staff member. This doesn't mean you won't find irrelevant hits; it just means you won't find all the dreck you would with an AltaVista search.

One final feature at the top of the page is something you'll find only at this level: the link to Sub Category Listing. This is an example of a Yahoo feature that has grown out of control and is basically useless. Here's where that link takes you:

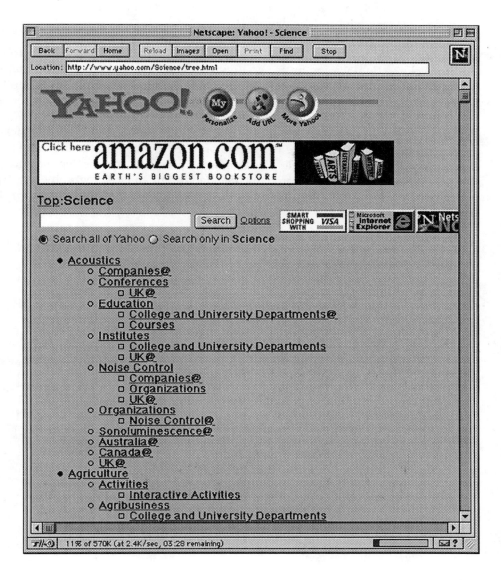

This is obviously a way of viewing the entire Science directory and all its subdirectories at a glance. Anyone familiar with the File Manager in Windows will relate to this view. However, while this feature was probably nice when Yahoo was first launched, it's now become ridiculous. Look at the lower left-hand corner of the Netscape window frame. I stopped this listing from loading after about 11% of it had already loaded because I noticed that the actual page size was 570K! Not only would this take (according to the Netscape estimate) another 3:38 minutes to load, but it would almost certainly hang my browser after about 300K (based on experience). And I have 20MB of memory allocated to my Netscape application.

My reason for pointing this out is not only to save you from crashing your browser, but also to point out how search engines, just like every other major service have suffered from the explosive expansion of the Web. This is also why it's good to pick a couple of search engines you like and become familiar with their strengths and weaknesses.

Now onto the actual Science subcategories. Two things to notice here before we click the Engineering link to go down a level. First are the italicized numbers next to most of the subcategories. These denote how many links you'll find in that subcategory. Second is the asterisk (@) symbol appended to some of the subcategory names, such as Oceanography@. This means that this sub-category heading is listed in multiple places within the Yahoo hierarchy. Clicking on the heading will take you to the primary location in the hierarchy for that heading. In this example, Oceanography is actually a subcategory under Earth Sciences. Yahoo staff probably decided to put an Oceanography link on the main Science page because many people wouldn't think of looking for it under Earth Sciences.

Now let's drill down into the Engineering subcategory, and then from there to Electrical Engineering:

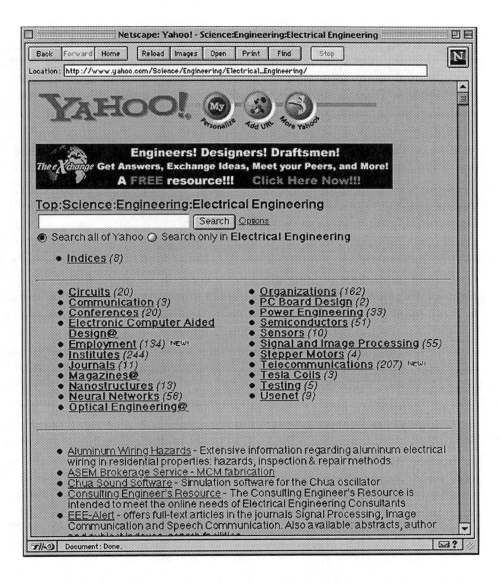

At this point we're finally hitting some actual links to places outside of Yahoo. Below the list of further subcategories are links that are officially indexed as **Science:Engineering:Electrical Engineering**. This is the basic construction throughout Yahoo. You can keep drilling down, and on every new level there are first links to further subcategories (or cross-references, as noted by the @), plus the actual site listings for that category. Many times there are only one or two actual links to sites on a level, which at first can seem a bit limited, at least when compared to the millions of hits you would get at AltaVista. For example, here is a page two levels further from the Electrical Engineering page, from which I clicked first on links to Circuits, then Integrated Circuits—Digital.

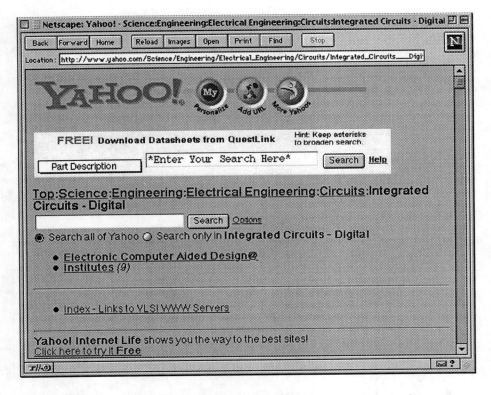

Here we have only three links, the first of them being a cross-reference to a subcategory actually under Computer Science, the second a link to nine "Institutes"—both still pages on Yahoo, and then finally one link to a VLSI links page at the University of Idaho.

The key thing to remember about Yahoo is that it is not, at least when compared to sites like AltaVista or HotBot, a mega-search engine. It is instead a relatively tight index to major places on the Web in a wide variety of disciplines. So while it may at times seem a little weak on actual links—as it can be—the links it does have are usually excellent starting points for further exploration. It really all comes down to the type of information you're looking for. Yahoo is a place for exploring and discovery, especially when you only have a vague or incomplete idea of what you're looking for. Yahoo could be called the "Lazy Person's Guide to the Web." Unlike the robot-crawler-based sites, which for the most part rely on you to structure the search process, Yahoo attempts to do all of this for you, which is no doubt why it's still the most popular site on the Web. Sometimes you just want someone else to drive.

Primary Internet Search Sites

Below is a list of the major search sites on the Web today. Note that some even allow you to search archives of Usenet newsgroup messages, which can be good for finding current discussions on a topic, as well as someone's e-mail address.

Robot Crawler Sites

AltaVista
http://www.altavista.digital.com/

WebCrawler
http://webcrawler.com/

Registration Sites

Yahoo
http://www.yahoo.com

Hybrid Sites

DejaNews
http://www.dejanews.com/

Excite
http://www.excite.com/

InfoSeek
http://www.infoseek.com

Lycos
http://www.lycos.com

Magellan
http://www.mckinley.com/

Meta-Search Sites

CUSI
http://web.nexor.com/public/cusi/

Cyber 411
http://cyber411.com

Inference Find
http://www.inference.com/ifind/

MetaCrawler
http://www.metacrawler.com

My Virtual Reference Desk
http://www.refdesk.com

SavvySearch
http://savvy.cs.colostate.edu:2000

search.com
http://www.search.com

Science-related Specialized Subject Guides

Industry Net
http://www.industry.net/

W3 Virtual Library
http://vlib.stanford.edu/Overview.html

SCIENCE & ENGINEERING RESOURCES

Resource Listings Index

Aeronautics & Aerospace

See also Astronomy & Astrophysics, Engineering, Medicine, Optics, Physics

Advanced Air Transportation Technologies
http://www.nas.nasa.gov/AATT/

Aerodynamic Facilities and Simulation
(Wind Tunnel)
http://ccf.arc.nasa.gov/ao/index.html

Aeronautical Radio, Inc. (ARINC)
http://www.arinc.com/

Aeronautical Simulation Facilities
http://scott.arc.nasa.gov/code_a/code_ao/

Aeronet UK
http://www.aeronet.co.uk/

Aerospace Business Development Center
http://arganet.tenagra.com/Tenagra/
aero_bd.html

Aerospace Colleges and Universities
http://macwww.db.erau.edu/www_virtual_lib/
aerospace/universities.html

Aerospace Mechanisms Symposium
http://www.lmsc.lockheed.com/ams/

AeroWEB Italy
http://aeroweb.lucia.it/

Air & Space Magazine (Smithsonian)
http://airspacemag.com

Airborne Science & Flight Research
Division
http://airsci-www.arc.nasa.gov/

Airbus Industries Consortium
http://www.oden.se/~ulle/airbus.html

Aircraft Homepage
http://macwww.db.erau.edu/www_virtual_lib/
aviation/aircraft.html

Air Chronicles Magazine (USAF)
http://www.cdsar.af.mil/air-chronicles.html

Airmen Knowledge Test Information
http://acro.harvard.edu/GA/
airmen_test_links.html

Ames Research Center
http://www.arc.nasa.gov/

American Helicopter Society
http://vortex.ae.gatech.edu/rcoe/ahshome/
ahshome.html

American Institute of Aeronautics and
Astronautics
http://www.aiaa.org/

AMR
http://www.amrcorp.com

Andrews Univ.
http://www.andrews.edu/AVIA/

ARPA - Advanced Research Projects
Agency
http://ftp.arpa.mil/

Aviation and Aerospace Outlook, including research resources
http://macwww.db.erau.edu/aero_forecast/
assess.html

Aviation Airworthiness Alerts
http://acro.harvard.edu/GA/aaa_links.html

Aviation Colleges and Universities
http://macwww.db.erau.edu/www_virtual_lib/
aviation/universities.html

Aviation Image Archives
http://acro.harvard.edu/GA/
image_archives.html

Aviation Museum Locator
http://www.brooklyn.cuny.edu/rec/air/
museums/museums.html

Aviation Publications
http://acro.harvard.edu/GA/av_publ.html

Aviation Week Group
http://www.datapro.mgh.com/

Boeing Company
http://www.boeing.com

Breault Research Organization
http://www.widdl.com:80/bro/

BTG Inc.
http://www.btg.com/

CIRA, the Italian Aerospace Research Centre
http://www.cira.it

College of Aeronautics, Laguardia Airport, NY.
http://www.mordor.com/coa/links.html

Computational Human Engineering Research Office
http://ccf.arc.nasa.gov/af/aff/midas

Cranfield Univ., College of Aeronautics (United Kingdom)
http://www.cranfield.ac.uk/aero/aero_menu.html

Daimler-Benz Aerospace
http://www.daimler-benz.com/dasa/dasa_e.html

DLR German Aerospace Research Establishment
http://www.dlr.de/

Douglas Aircraft Company
http://www.dac.mdc.com/

Dryden Flight Research Ctr.
http://mosaic.dfrf.nasa.gov/dryden.html

Dryden Research Aircraft Photo Archive
http://www.dfrf.nasa.gov/PhotoServer/photoServer.html

Embry-Riddle Aeronautical Univ.
http://macwww.db.erau.edu/

EnviroNET
http://envnet.gsfc.nasa.gov/

European Space Agency
http://www.esrin.esa.it/

European WWW Aviation Server
http://ourworld.compuserve.com/homepages/osprey_sw/

FAA Center for Aviation Systems Reliability
http://www.cnde.iastate.edu/faa.html

FAA Education
http://web.fie.com:80/web/fed/faa/

FAA Human Factors Home Page
http://www.faa.gov/aar/human-factors/welcome.htm

FAA Library at FEDWORLD
http://www.caasd.org/

FAA Mike Monroney Aeronautical Center
http://www.mmac.jccbi.gov/

FAA Office of Commercial Space Transportation
http://www.dot.gov/dotinfo/faa/cst/ocst.html

FAA Program Analysis and Operations Research Lab
http://www.orlab.faa.gov

FAA Technical Center
http://www.tc.faa.gov/

Federal Aviation Administration
http://www.faa.gov/

Federal Aviation Regulations
http://acro.harvard.edu/GA/fars.html

Flight Safety Foundation
http://www.flightsafety.org/

Flight Simulator News
http://bigben.larc.nasa.gov/fltsim/simnews.html

Florida Institute of Technology
http://www.fit.edu/soa/soa.html

French Research Ctr. on Air Traffic Control
http://www.cenatls.cena.dgac.fr/English/index.html

German Aeronautics and Aerospace Association
http://www.dlr.de/DGLR/Welcome_e.html

General Electric
http://www.ge.com

Glenn L. Martin Wind Tunnel, at University of Maryland
http://windvane.umd.edu

Goddard Space Flight Ctr.
http://hypatia.gsfc.nasa.gov/GSFC_homepage.html/

GPS Overview
http://wwwhost.cc.utexas.edu/ftp/pub/grg/gcraft/notes/gps/gps.html

GPS/MET Program
http://pocc.gpsmet.ucar.edu/

Graduate Aeronautical Labs.
http://www.galcit.caltech.edu/

Gravitational Fluid Mechanics Laboratory at UC Boulder
http://iml.colorado.edu/

Ground and Flight Instrumentation
http://pslwww.nmsu.edu/GIF.html

Hang Gliding/Para Gliding and other foot launch aircraft.
http://cougar.stanford.edu:7878/
HGMPSHomePage.html

High Powered Rocketry
http://seds.lpl.arizona.edu/ROCKET/
rocket.html

IEEE Aerospace and Electronic Systems Society
http://rsd1000.gatech.edu/public_html/bobt/
AESS_Home_Page.html

IEEE Control Systems Society
http://eewww.eng.ohio-state.edu/~yurkovic/
css.html

Institute for Computer Applications in Science and Engineering (ICASE)
http://www.icase.edu/

International Association for Computational Mechanics
http://www.ncsa.uiuc.edu/Apps/SE/mechanics/usacm/usacm.html

International Association for Unmanned Vehicle Systems
http://asrt.cad.gatech.edu/AUVS/

International Aviation Events Calendar
http://acro.harvard.edu/IAC/int_airshows.html

Jane's Information Group
http://www.janes.com/janes.html

Jet Propulsion Laboratory
http://www.jpl.nasa.gov/

Johnson Space Ctr.
http://www.jsc.nasa.gov/jsc/
JSC_homepage.html

Joint University Program for Air Transportation Research
http://www.princeton.edu/~stengel/JUP.html

Jonathan's Space Report
http://hea-www.harvard.edu/QEDT/jcm/
space/jsr/jsr.html

Kennedy Space Ctr.
http://www.ksc.nasa.gov/ksc.html

Langley Research Ctr.
http://mosaic.larc.nasa.gov/larc.html

Lewis Research Center
http://www.lerc.nasa.gov/
LeRC_homepage.html

Lockheed Martin Corporation
http://www.lockheed.com/TRW

Marshall Space Flight Ctr.
http://hypatia.gsfc.nasa.gov/
MSFC_homepage.html

McDonnell Douglas Aerospace - Houston
http://pat.mdc.com/

Meteorology Index
http://www.met.fu-berlin.de/DataSources/
MetIndex.html

Mig-29 tours (commercial)
http://www.interedu.com/mig29/mig29/

MIT Rocket Society
http://www.mit.edu:8001/activities/mitrs/
home.html

MIT Soaring Association, a WWW server dedicated to soaring.
http://adswww.harvard.edu/MITSA/
mitsa_homepg.html

MIT Weather Radar Lab.
http://graupel.mit.edu/Radar_Lab.html

Mooney Aircraft
http://www.vero.com/mooney.htm

NASA Ames Aviation Operations Branch
http://olias.arc.nasa.gov/

NASA Dryden
http://www.dfrf.nasa.gov/

NASA Engineering
http://epims1.gsfc.nasa.gov/engineering/
engineering.html

NASA Langley Technical Report Server
http://techreports.larc.nasa.gov/ltrs/ltrs.html

NASA — National Aeronautics and Space Administration
http://www.nasa.gov/

NASA Scientific and Technical Information Program
http://nova.sti.nasa.gov/STI-homepage.html/

NASA Technical Report Server
http://techreports.larc.nasa.gov/cgi-bin/NTRS/

National Oceanics and Atmospheric Administration (NOAA)
http://www.noaa.gov/

New Space Network
http://www.newspace.com/

NLR National Aerospace Laboratory of the Netherlands
http://www.nlr.nl/

Numerical Aerodynamic Simulation
http://www.nas.nasa.gov

Parks College, St. Louis Univ..
http://www.slu.edu/PARKS/parks_home.html

Part-Task Simulation Laboratory
http://olias.arc.nasa.gov/facilities/part-task/part-task.html

Penn State Univ., Aerospace Engineering
http://www.psu.edu/aero/aero.html

Piper Aircraft Co.
http://www.newpiper.com

Purdue Univ.
http://roger.ecn.purdue.edu

Raytheon and E-Systems
http:www.raytheon.com

rec.aviation newsgroup.
http://adswww.harvard.edu/MITSA/news_groups.html

Rockwell International
http://www.rockwell.com/

SAIC Science Applications Intl. Corporation
http://www.itl.saic.com/

Scaled Composites
http://www.portal.com/~scaled/

sci.aeronautics.airliners archive
http://www.chicago.com/airliners/archives.html

Society of Automotive Engineers
http://www.sae.org

Southern Illinois Univ. at Carbondale
http://www.siu.edu/departments/ctc/aviation

Space Activism Home Page
http://muon.qrc.com/space/start.html

Space Colonies
http://www.nas.nasa.gov/RNR/Visualization/AlGlobus/SpaceColonies/spaceColonies.html

Space Studies Institute
http://www.astro.nwu.edu/lentz/space/ssi/home-ssi.html

SPACEHAB, McDonnell Douglas in Huntsville.
http://hvsun4.mdc.com:1025/SPACEHAB/SPACEHAB.html

Space Shuttle Clickable Map
http://seds.lpl.arizona.edu/ssa/space.shuttle/docs/homepage.html

St Cloud State Univ. Aviation
http://condor.stcloud.msus.edu/aviation/

Stanford Univ.
http://aero.stanford.edu/aeroastro.html

Students for the Exploration and Development of Space (SEDS)
http://seds.lpl.arizona.edu/

TecQuipment
http://www.tecquip.co.uk/

United States Air Force
http://www.af.mil/

United Technologies
http://www.utc.com/

University Aerospace Departments
http://macwww.db.erau.edu/www_virtual_lib/aerospace/universities.html

Universities Space Research Association (USRA)
http://www.usra.edu/

Unofficial L-1011 Home Page
http://users.aol.com/tristar500/l1011/

Value Engineering Database
http://libra.wcupa.edu/ValuLink

Weather, Weather maps, and other weather related must see items
http://rs560.cl.msu.edu/weather/

Western Michigan Univ.
http://www.wmich.edu/aviation

WWW.Flight.Com
http://www.flight.com/enter.html

Airlines

Aer Lingus
http://www.hursley.ibm.com:80/aer/

Aeroflot
http://www.seanet.com/Bazar/Aeroflot/Aeroflot.html

Air Canada
http://www.aircanada.ca/

Air Cruise America
http://www.webcom.com/~aca/

American Trans Air
http://www.xmission.com/~aoi/fata.html

Austrian Airlines
http://www.aua.co.at/aua/

Big Island Air
http://www.ilhawaii.net:80/pt/bigair.html

Canada 3000 Airlines
http://vanbc.wimsey.com/~gordona/cmm.html

Canadian Airlines International
http://www.CdnAir.CA/

Cathay Pacific
http://www.cathay-usa.com/

China Northwest Airlines
http://www.demon.co.uk/virtual/China-Northwest.html

Comair, Delta Connection
http://www.iac.net/~flypba/oh.home.html

Delta Airlines
http://www.delta-air.com

Eagle Canyon Airlines
http://cybermart.com/eagle/

Federal Express
http://www.fedex.com/about_fedex.html

Frontier Airlines
http://www.cuug.ab.ca:8001/~busew/frontier.html

KLM
http://www.ib.com:8080/business/klm/klm.html

Lauda Air
http://www.laudaair.com/engl/indexe.htm

Lufthansa
http://www.tkz.fh-rpl.de/tii/lh/lhflug-e.html

Mexicana Airlines
http://www.mexicana.com/index.html

Northwest Airlines
http://www.winternet.com/~tela/nwa-info.html

Õslandsflug
http://www.mmedia.is/eng/loccomp/icebird.html

Qantas Airways
http://www.anzac.com/qantas/qantas.htm

Singapore Airlines
http://www.technet.sg/InfoWEB/communications/industry.html

Southwest Airlines
http://www.iflyswa.com/

TWA
http://www.inlink.com/~jack/twa.html

United Airlines Flight Center
http://www.ualfltctr.com/

Virgin Atlantic
http://www.fly.virgin.com/atlantic/

Agricultural Sciences

See also Biology & Biotechnology

Ag-Links
http://www.gennis.com/aglinks.html

Ag Sites Around the World
http://ipmwww.ncsu.edu/cicp/countries/international.html

Agricultural Biotechnology Ctr., Hungary
http://www.abc.hu/

Agriculture Economics
http://www.ttu.edu/~aecovl

Agricultural Genome WWW Server
http://probe.nalusda.gov:8000/index.html

Agriculture Online
http://www.agriculture.com/

Agriculture Virtual Librarian
http://galaxy.einet.net/galaxy/Engineering-and-Technology/Agriculture.html

Agriculture Weather
http://ipm_www.ncsu.edu/weather/weather.html

Agriculture WWW Virtual Library
http://ipm_www.ncsu.edu/cernag/cern.html

American Small Farm Journal
http://www.smallfarm.com/

American Society of Agricultural Engineers
http://asae.org/

Asia Regional Agribusiness Project
http://www.milcom.com/rap/

Beef Today
http://www.smartnet.net/BeefToday

Biological Control Virtual Information Center
http://ipmwww.ncsu.edu/biocontrol/biocontrol.html

Biofuels Information Network (U.S. Dept. of Energy)
http://www.esd.ornl.gov/BFDP/BFDPMOSAIC/binmenu.html

Biotechnology WWW Virtual Library
http://www.cato.com/interweb/cato/biotech/

CENET, the Cornell Extension NETwork
http://galaxy.einet.net/hytelnet/OTH085.html

Center for Integrated Pest Management
http://ipmwww.ncsu.edu/cipm/Virtual_Center.html

Cereal Rust Lab
http://www.umn.edu/rustlab/

Chickadee Creek Cattle Services
http://www.teleport.com/~chick/

Crop Production Science
http://ekolserv.vo.slu.se/

Department of Plant Breeding WAU
http://www.spg.wau.nl/pv/

European Bank of Glomales - (BEG)
http://www.ukc.ac.uk/biolab/beg/index.html

Farm Journal Today
http://www.FarmJournal.com/

Florentine CNR Institutes - Agriculture and Forest
http://www.area.fi.cnr.it/agris.htm

Florida Agricultural Information Retrieval System
http://hammock.ifas.ufl.edu/

Florida Entomologist
http://www.fcla.ufl.edu/FlaEnt/fehmpg.htm

Florida State Univ. Agriculture Index
http://www.cs.fsu.edu/projects/group3/agri.html

Frescargot Farms Snail Farming Ventures
http://www.paccon.com/snails/

Genome & Genetics - Agricultural Genome
http://probe.nalusda.gov:8000/index.html

High Plains Journal
http://www.hpj.com

IFA Nurseries, Inc.
http://www.ifainc.com/~ifainc/

Iowa Farmer Today
http://www.infi.net/fyiowa/ift/index.htm

Irrigation and Hydrology WWW Virtual Library
http://www.wiz.uni-kassel.de/kww/projekte/irrig/irrig_i.html

Livestock Homepage
http://www.ansi.okstate.edu/library/

Maize Genome Database
http://teosinte.agron.missouri.edu/top.html

Meat Animal Research Ctr.
http://sol.marc.usda.gov/

Milling Journal
http://www.grainnet.com/mj.htm

Missouri Univ.
http://ssu.agri.missouri.edu

Munich Univ. of Technology
http://www.edv.agrar.tu-muenchen.de/hello.html

National Agricultural Library
http://www.nalusda.gov/

National Dairy Database
http://www.inform.umd.edu:8080/EdRes/Topic/AgrEnv/ndd/

National Farmers Organization
http://www.agriculture.com/agworld/nfo/nfoindex.html

National Institute of Animal Health, Japan
http://ss.niah.affrc.go.jp/index.html

National Taiwan Univ.
http://flood.hy.ntu.edu.tw/ntuae/home.html

NCSU Soil Sciences
http://www.soil.ncsu.edu/

NetVet Veterinary Resource Line
http://netvet.wustl.edu/

NewCROP
http://newcrop.hort.purdue.edu

North Carolina Agricultural & Technical State Univ.
http://rhema.ncat.edu/

North Carolina State Univ. Cooperative Extension Service
http://gopher.ces.ncsu.edu/

Norwegian Implement Company Store
http://athos.phoenixat.com/power/store.html

NSF SUCCEED Agricultural Engineering Visual Database
http://succeed.edtech.vt.edu/Indexes/Agricultural%20and%20Env.html

NYSAES WWW Server
http://aruba.nysaes.cornell.edu:8000/geneva.htm

Oklahoma State Univ. Agronomy
http://clay.agr.okstate.edu/agrover.htm

Ostriches On Line
http://www.achiever.com/ostintro.html

OSU Agricultural Sciences
http://www.orst.edu/mc/coldep/agrsci.htm

Oxford Univ. Plant Sciences
http://ifs.plants.ox.ac.uk/

Pasteur Institute
http://web.pasteur.fr/welcome-uk.html

Pesticide Action Network North America (PANNA)
http://www.panna.org/panna/

Poultry Science Virtual Library
http://gallus.tamu.edu/1h/posc/dother.html

SAC (The Scottish Agricultural College)
http://www.sac.ac.uk/

Salmon Select Distributors Home Page
http://rampages.onramp.net/~salmon/index.html

Science of Food and Agriculture Index
http://www.netins.net/showcase/cast/sfae_ndx.htm

Science of Soils
http://www.hintze-online.com/sos/

Sea Urchin Harvesters Association - California
http://seaurchin.org/

Southwest Agricultural Weather Service Center
http://swami.tamu.edu/

Strategic Management in Agribusiness
http://128.146.140.187/ae601/

Technical Univ. of Nova Scotia Agricultural Engineering
http://www.tuns.ca:80/ae/

Texas A&M Univ.
http://ageninfo.tamu.edu/

Texas A&M's AGropolis
http://agcomwww.tamu.edu/agcom/agrotext/agcommap.html

UCR - Biological, Agricultural and Medical Resources
http://lib-www.ucr.edu/bioag/

Univ. of Arizona College of Agriculture
http://ag.arizona.edu/aginfo.html

Univ. of Calif. Coop. Ext. Livestock/Natural Resources
http://www.ucop.edu/anrhome/coop-ext/Uccelr/uccelr.html

Univ. of Florida Institute of Food
http://gnv.ifas.ufl.edu/

Univ. of Tennessee Institute of Agriculture
http://solar.rtd.utk.edu/campuses/utia.html

USDA Homepage
http://www.usda.gov/

USDA-ARS National Soil Erosion Lab
http://purgatory.ecn.purdue.edu:20002/NSERL/nserl.html

USDA GrainGenes Database
http://wheat.pw.usda.gov/graingenes.html

USDA Research Database
http://medoc.gdb.org/best/stc/usda-best.html

USDA Soil Conservation Service - Missouri
http://www.mo.scs.ag.gov/

Artificial Intelligence

See also Computer Science, Linguistics & Natural Language, Virtual Reality

ACIA—Cataloan Association for Artificial Intelligence
http://www.iiia.csic.es/ACIA/ACIA.html

ACM SIG on Artificial Intelligence
http://sigart.acm.org/

Adaptive Behavior
http://www-mitpress.mit.edu/jrnls-catalog/adaptive.html

Agent Info
http://www.cs.bham.ac.uk/~amw/agents/index.html

Agents and Mediators
http://www-ksl.stanford.edu/knowledge-sharing/agents.html

AI and Statistics Electronic Mailing List
http://www.vuse.vanderbilt.edu/~dfisher/ai-stats/mailing-list.html

AI Discussion Lists
http://ai.iit.nrc.ca/ai_archives.html

AI Resources on the Internet
http://ai.iit.nrc.ca/ai_point.html

AI, Cognitive Science, and Robotics WWW Resources
http://www.cs.ucl.ac.uk/misc/ai/

AI FAQs
http://ai.iit.nrc.ca/ai_faqs.html

AI-related Job Posting Archives
http://www.cs.cmu.edu/Web/Groups/AI/html/other/jobs.html

American Association for Artificial Intelligence
http://www.aaai.org/

Annotated Blackboard-Systems Bibliography
http://www.bbtech.com/bibli.html

Applied Logic Lab - Univ. of Idaho
http://www.cs.uidaho.edu/lal/homepage.html

ARPA Knowledge Sharing Effort public library
http://www-ksl.stanford.edu/knowledge-sharing/README.html

Artificial Intelligence at TNT
http://www.tnt.uni-hannover.de/data/info/www/tnt/subj/sci/ai/overview.html

Artificial Intelligence Resources
http://ai.iit.nrc.ca/ai_point.html

Artificial Intelligence Subject Index
http://ai.iit.nrc.ca/misc.html

Association for Computing Machinery
http://www.acm.org/

ASTAP
http://www.demon.co.uk/ar/ASTAP/

Austrian Research Institute for Artificial Intelligence (OFAI) and Dept. of Medical Cybernetics and Artificial Intelligence at the Univ. of Vienna
http://www.ai.univie.ac.at/

Bibliography of Research in Natural Language Generation
http://liinwww.ira.uka.de/bibliography/Ai/nlg.html

Boston Univ.
http://web.bu.edu/CNS/CNS.html

Center for the Neural Basis of Cognition
http://www.cs.cmu.edu/afs/cs/project/cnbc/CNBC.html

Clarkson AI Lab Pages
http://jupiter.ece.clarkson.edu:5050/

CMU Artificial Intelligence Repository
http://www.cs.cmu.edu/Web/Groups/AI/html/repository.html

CMU SCS OZ Project
http://www.cs.cmu.edu/afs/cs.cmu.edu/project/oz/web/oz.html

Cogent Prolog and Amzi! Things
http://world.std.com/~amzi/

Cognition and Affect Project
http://www.cs.bham.ac.uk/~axs/cogaff.html

Computational Intelligence Research Lab.
http://cirl.uoregon.edu/cirl.html

Computational Intelligence Research Laboratory
http://cirl.uoregon.edu

Computer Based Learning Unit: Univ. of Leeds
http://cbl.leeds.ac.uk/~www/home.html

Computer Generated Writing
http://www.uio.no/~mwatz/c-g.writing/

Computer Science Technical Reports Archive Sites
http://www.rdt.monash.edu.au/tr/siteslist.html

Computer Vision
http://www.cs.cmu.edu/afs/cs/project/cil/ftp/html/txtvision.html

Computing as Compression
http://www.sees.bangor.ac.uk/~gerry/sp_summary.html

Computing Research Association
http://cra.org/

Connectionist Natural Language Processing
http://www.cs.bham.ac.uk/~jah/CNLP/cnlp.html

CSCW Research Group
http://orgwis.gmd.de

Ctr. for Artificial Intelligence Research, Korea
http://cair-archive.kaist.ac.kr/

Ctr. for Biological and Computational Learning at MIT
http://www.ai.mit.edu/projects/cbcl/web-homepage/web-homepage.html

Dave Brown's AI Page
http://cs.wpi.edu/~dcb/

Decision/Risk Analysis Page
http://www.lumina.com/lumina/DA.html

DFKI
http://www.dfki.uni-sb.de/

Distributed Artificial Intelligence and Multi-Agent Systems
http://www-lgis.univ-savoie.fr/~stinckwi/sma.html

Distributed Artificial Intelligence Lab
http://dis.cs.umass.edu/

Distributed Object Computing
http://info.gte.com/ftp/doc/doc.html

DSI Neural Networks group home page
http://www-dsi.ing.unifi.it/neural/home.html

Ecole Polytechnique, la bibliotheque
http://www.polytechnique.fr/htbin/bcx.pl

EEB
http://www.eeb.ele.tue.nl/index.htm

ELIS Speech Lab
http://www.elis.rug.ac.be/ELISgroups/speech/

Eliza
http://www.cl.cam.ac.uk/users/mh10006/eliza.html

EPFL-MANTRA
http://didecs1-e.epfl.ch:80/w3mantra/

ESSIR
http://www.dcs.gla.ac.uk/essir/

European Neural Network Society
http://www.neuronet.ph.kcl.ac.uk/neuronet/organisations/enns.html

First Australian Workshop on Commonsense Reasoning
http://frey.newcastle.edu.au/~is/ai95wshop.html

First International Conference on Multiagent Systems
http://centaurus.cs.umass.edu:80/ICMAS/

FLAIRS
http://www.cis.ufl.edu/~ddd/FLAIRS/

Forschungsgruppe Neuronale Netzwerke
http://www.hrz.uni-kassel.de/fb17/neuro/

GA Visualisation Questionnaire
http://kmi.open.ac.uk/~trevor/Quest1.html

Genetic Programming
http://www.salford.ac.uk/docs/depts/eee/genetic.html

Genetically Programmed Music
http://nmt.edu/~jefu/notes/notes.html

Georgia Tech Artificial Intelligence
http://www.gatech.edu/ai/ai.html

Gerry Wolff's WWW Pages
http://www.sees.bangor.ac.uk/~gerry/

Goddard AI/IT Conference
http://defiant.gsfc.nasa.gov/aiconf/AI-conf-General.html

Graduate Students Who's Who in Robotics
http://www.sm.luth.se/csee/ra/sm-roa/Robotics/WhoSWho.html

Graphic Presentation of Subjects
http://ACS.TAMU.EDU/~jpf6745/subjects.html

Gunnar Blix's AI Page
http://www-ilg.cs.uiuc.edu/~blix/

Handwriting Recognition
http://hcslx1.essex.ac.uk/

Human Cognition Research Lab. at The Open Univ., UK
http://hcrl.open.ac.uk/

Human-Languages Page
http://www.willamette.edu/~tjones/Language-Page.html

IEEE Neural Networks Council
http://www.ieee.org/nnc/index.html

IJCAI
http://ijcai.org/

IlliGAL
http://gal4.ge.uiuc.edu/illigal.home.html

IMKAI/OFAI Homepage
http://www.ai.univie.ac.at/

Indiana Univ. - Knowledge Base of Computing Information
http://scwww.ucs.indiana.edu/kb/search.html

Inductive Inference at Monash
http://www.cs.monash.edu.au/research/inference.html

Information and Computation
http://theory.lcs.mit.edu/~iandc/

Information Extraction
http://ciir.cs.umass.edu/info/ie.html

Institut Dalle Molle d'Intelligence Artificelle Perceptive (IDIAP)
http://www.idiap.ch/

Intelligent Software Agents
http://www.cl.cam.ac.uk/users/rwab1/agents.html

International Journal of Applied Expert Systems
http://www.abdn.ac.uk/~acc025/ijaes.html

IRCS
http://www.cis.upenn.edu/~ircs/homepage.html

ISSCO, Univ. of Geneva
http://issco_www.unige.ch/

JNNS
http://jnns-www.okabe.rcast.u-tokyo.ac.jp/jnns/home.html

Joel's Hierarchical Subject Index
http://www.cen.uiuc.edu/~jj9544/index.html

Jon Iles' AI Page
http://www.cs.bham.ac.uk/~jpi/

Jrnl. of Artificial Intelligence Research
http://www.cs.washington.edu/research/jair/home.html

Juan Carlos Santamaria Information Page
http://www.cc.gatech.edu/ai/students/Ai-students/carlos/home.html

Julia's AI Page
http://fuzine.mt.cs.cmu.edu/mlm/julia.html

Knowledge Sharing
http://logic.stanford.edu/knowledge.html

Knowledge Sharing Effort
http://www.cs.umbc.edu/kse/

Knowledge Systems Lab. (Canada)
http://ai.iit.nrc.ca/home_page.html

KQML - Knowledge Query and Manipulation Language
http://www.cs.umbc.edu/kqml/

KQML Mailing Lists
http://www.cs.umbc.edu/kqml/mail/

KRUST
http://www.scms.rgu.ac.uk/research/kbs/krust/

Linguistic Geometry
http://ucdacm.cudenver.edu/cse/boris.html

Lockheed Artificial Intelligence
http://hitchhiker.space.lockheed.com/aic/README.html

Logic Group
http://Logic.Stanford.edu

London Parallel Applications Centre Web Server
http://www.lpac.ac.uk

Mathematics For Computer Generated Spoken Documents
http://www.cs.cornell.edu/Info/People/raman/aster/aster-toplevel.html

Medical Cybernetics and Artificial Intelligence at the Univ. of Vienna and the Austrian Research Institute for Artificial Intelligence
http://www.ai.univie.ac.at/

MIT Artificial Intelligence Lab
http://www.ai.mit.edu/

Morgan Kaufmann, Publishers
http://market.net/literary/mkp/index.html

NASA
http://www.gsfc.nasa.gov/NASA_homepage.html

Neural and Multimedia Center
http://synap.neuro.sfc.keio.ac.jp/

Neural Networks at UT Austin
http://www.cs.utexas.edu/~sirosh/nn.html

Neural Web
http://www.erg.abdn.ac.uk/projects/neuralweb/

NEuroNet
http://www.neuronet.ph.kcl.ac.uk/

Nicole English's AI Page
http://cctr.umkc.edu/user/nenglish/index.html

NIPS: Neural Information Processing Systems
http://www.cs.cmu.edu/afs/cs/project/cnbc/nips/NIPS.html

Northwestern Univ. - Learning Through Collaborative Visualization Project
http://www.covis.nwu.edu/

NSF Strategic Planning Workshop for Design Engineering
http://cs.wpi.edu/~dcb/NSF/NSF-wkshp.html

OFAI Library Information System Biblio
http://www.ai.univie.ac.at/biblio.html

Optics and Machine Vision Application Engineering Services
http://www.iti.org/eoe/index.htm

Outsider's Guide to Artificial Intelligence
http://www.mcs.net/~jorn/html/ai.html

Parallel Computing and Imaging Laboratory
http://teal.ece.jhu.edu

Parsing Techniques - A Practical Guide
http://www.cs.vu.nl/~dick/PTAPG.html

Prehistory of AI
http://www.mcs.net/~jorn/html/ai/prehistory.html

QRNET
http://www.dcs.aber.ac.uk:80/QRNET/

Qualitative Reasoning at U Texas
http://www.cs.utexas.edu/~qr/

Qualitative Reasoning Group at Northwestern Univ.
ftp://multivac.ils.nwu.edu/pub/MOSAIC/qrg.html

Ralph Becket's AI Page
http://www.cl.cam.ac.uk:80/users/rwab1/

Research Group Autonomous Mobile Robots
http://ag-vp-www.informatik.uni-kl.de/

Robin Burke - Univ. of Chicago
http://cs-www.uchicago.edu/~burke/

Robot Web - Robotics resources on the WWW
http://www.sm.luth.se/csee/ra/sm-roa/RoboticsJump.html

Robot Wisdom
http://www.mcs.net/~jorn/home.html

Sandip Sen's AI Page
http://euler.mcs.utulsa.edu/~sandip/sandip.html

SEL-HPC Article Archive
http://www.lpac.qmw.ac.uk/SEL-HPC/Articles/index.html

SGAICO — Swiss Group for Artificial Intelligence and Cognitive Science
http://expasy.hcuge.ch/sgaico/

SIGART Electronic Information Service
http://sigart.acm.org/

SPIE — The International Society for Optical Engineering
http://www.spie.org

SRI Artificial Intelligence Ctr.
http://www.ai.sri.com/aic/

Stanford Concurrency Group
http://boole.stanford.edu

Stanford Knowledge Systems Laboratory
http://www-ksl.stanford.edu/

Steven Woods' AI Page
http://logos.uwaterloo.ca/sgwoods/

Supercomputing & Parallel Computing:
Conferences & Journals
http://www.cs.cmu.edu/Web/Groups/scandal/
www/conferences.html

UCI Machine Learning Group
http://www.ics.uci.edu/AI/ML/Machine-
Learning.html

UCL-DICE Neural Net Group
http://www.dice.ucl.ac.be/neural-nets/
NNgroup.html

UCSD Neuroscience
http://salk.edu/NeuroWeb/

Univ. of Edinburgh Artificial Intelligence
http://www.dai.ed.ac.uk

Univ. of Essex
http://www.essex.ac.uk

Univ. of Leeds
http://lethe.leeds.ac.uk/

Univ. of New Hampshire Cooperative
Distributed Problem Solving Research
http://cdps.cs.unh.edu/

Univ. of Sussex at Brighton - School of
Cognitive and Computing Sciences
http://www.cogs.susx.ac.uk/

Univ. of Washington
http://www.cs.washington.edu/research/
projects/ai/www/

Univ. Video Communications
http://www.uvc.com/

VLSI Vision Chips
http://www.eleceng.adelaide.edu.au/Groups/
GAAS/Bugeye/visionchips/

William Ward Armstrong's AI Page
http://web.cs.ualberta.ca/~arms/

WPI AIDG — AI in Design Webliography
http://cs.wpi.edu/Research/aidg/AlinD-
hotlist.html

WWW Virtual Library: Artificial Intelligence
http://www.comlab.ox.ac.uk/archive/comp/
ai.html

Yahoo AI Resources
http://www.yahoo.com/Science/
Computer_Science/Artificial_Intelligence/

YODA at Temple Univ.
http://yoda.cis.temple.edu

Astronomy & Astrophysics

See also Aeronautics & Aerospace, Optics, Physics

AAO Telescope Information
http://aaoepp.aao.gov.au/telescope.html

Abstracts of Astronomical Publications
http://fits.cv.nrao.edu/www/
yp_library.html#abstracts

ADS Einstein Archive Service
http://adswww.harvard.edu/
einstein_service.html

Advanced Computing Research Institute
http://www.tc.cornell.edu/InBriefs/ACRI.html

Albert-Ludwigs-Univ.Freiburg - Fakultät
für Physik
http://hpfrs6.physik.uni-freiburg.de/

American Astronomical Society
http://www.aas.org

American Physical Society
http://www.aps.org

Anglo-Australian Observatory
http://aaoepp.aao.gov.au/aaohomepage.html

Anne's CyberJunk Drawer
http://as.arizona.edu/~aturner/home.html

Anti-matter Research Through the Earth
Moon Ion Spectrometer
http://polhp5.in2p3.fr:8000/u1/data/www/
artemis.html

Apache Point Observatory
http://www.apo.nmsu.edu/

Archive of Starlink Newsgroups
http://cast0.ast.cam.ac.uk/starnews/

Arizona State Univ.
http://info.asu.edu/asu-cwis/las/phys-astro/

Armagh Observatory
http://star.arm.ac.uk/

ASA Goddard Space Flight Center's Solar
Data Analysis Ctr. (SDAC)
http://umbra.gsfc.nasa.gov/sdac.html

Aspen Ctr. for Physics
http://www-aspen.het.brown.edu/aspen/

Astronet - Navigation in Astronet
http://www.pd.astro.it/Astronet/Home-
Page.html

Astronomer's Bazaar
http://cdsweb.u-strasbg.fr/Cats.html

Astronomer's Guide to On-line Biblio-
graphic Databases and Information
Services
http://fits.cv.nrao.edu/www/temp-cd.ps

Astronomical Anonymous FTP Sites
http://seds.lpl.arizona.edu/pub/faq/
astroftp.html

Astronomical Data Analysis Software and
Systems
http://ra.stsci.edu/ADASS.html

Astronomical Image Processing Center
http://www.cv.nrao.edu/aips/

Astronomical information on the Internet
http://ecf.hq.eso.org/astro-resources.html

Astronomical Internet Resources
http://nearnet.gnn.com/wic/astro.08.html

Astronomical Internet Resources (CFHT)
http://www.cfht.hawaii.edu/html/
astro_info.html

Astronomical Journal
http://www.astro.washington.edu/astroj/
index.html

Astronomical League
http://bradley.bradley.edu/~dware/al.html

Astronomical Societies List
http://www.w3.org/vl/astro/astroweb/
yp_society.html

Astronomical Society of the Pacific
http://maxwell.sfsu.edu/asp/asp.html

Astronomical World Wide Web Resources
http://anarky.stsci.edu/astroweb/net-www.html

Astronomie im Internet
http://aquila.uni-muenster.de/astro-im-net/astronomy.html

Astronomy & the Web
http://cast0.ast.cam.ac.uk/overview.html

Astronomy and Astrophysics Journals
http://cnidr.org/other_links/astronomy.html

Astronomy and Astrophysics Sites
http://kudzu.cnidr.org/astronomy.html

Astronomy at ADFA
http://www.adfa.oz.au/physics/astro/astron.htm

Astronomy Cafe
http://www2.ari.net/home/odenwald/cafe.html

Astronomy Index at the USGS
http://info.er.usgs.gov/network/science/astronomy/index.html

Astronomy Information Systems
http://fits.cv.nrao.edu/www/yp_infosys.html

Astronomy Magazine
http://www.kalmbach.com/astro/astronomy.html

Astrophysics Data System
http://adswww.harvard.edu/

AstroWeb Consortium
http://www.w3.org/vl/astro/astro.html

Australia Telescope Compact Array
http://www.atnf.csiro.au/ATNF/Narrabri-Site-information.html

Australian National Univ. - Mt. Stromlo & Siding Spring Observatories
http://meteor.anu.edu.au/home.html

Australian Working Group for Antarctic Astronomy
http://newt.phys.unsw.edu.au/~mgb/awgaa.html

AVHRR Land Pathfinder Data Set
http://xtreme.gsfc.nasa.gov/

AXAF [Advanced X-ray Astrophysics Facility] Science Ctr.
http://hea-www.harvard.edu/asc/axaf-welcome.html

Backgrounds Data Ctr.
http://bradbury.nrl.navy.mil/

Be Star Newsletter
http://chara.gsu.edu/BeNews/intro.html

Berkeley Illinois Maryland Association
http://bima.astro.umd.edu/bima/home.html

Bernhard Beck-Winchatz, Astronomy
http://www.astro.washington.edu/bbeck/

Board on Physics and Astronomy
http://www.nas.edu/0/bpa/bpa.html

Bologna 152cm Telescope - Schedules
http://boas3.bo.astro.it/loiano/schedula.html

BONNAREL François
http://cdsweb.u-strasbg.fr/people/fb.html

Boston Univ. Center for Space Physics
http://bu-ast.bu.edu/csp.html

Bradford Robotic Telescope
http://www.eia.brad.ac.uk/

Bradley Observatory
http://www.algorithm.com/~asadun/bradley.html

Brittany Ctr. of Informatical Resources
http://www.univ-rennes1.fr/ASTRO/astro.english.html

Brookhaven National Lab.
http://suntid.bnl.gov:8080/bnl.html

Brown Univ. Astronomy
http://www-astro.physics.brown.edu/astro/

Cagliari Astronomical Observatory
http://caosun.unica.it/welcome.html

Caltech Astronomy
http://astro.caltech.edu/astro.html

CalTech - High Energy Astrophysics Group
http://www.ccsf.caltech.edu/astro/heastro.html

CalTech - Infrared Astrophysics Group
http://www.cco.caltech.edu/~rknop/ira.html

CalTech - Physics, Mathematics and Astronomy
http://www.caltech.edu/caltech/PMandA.html

CalTech - Pulsar Group
http://kaa.caltech.edu/

CalTech - Space Radiation Lab.
http://www.srl.caltech.edu/srl/

CalTech Submillimeter Observatory
http://www.cco.caltech.edu/~hunter/csotext.html

CalTech - Submillimeter Wave Astrophysics Group
http://www.cco.caltech.edu/~hunter/submm.html

CalTech -Theoretical Particle Physics
http://www.theory.caltech.edu/

Cambridge LFST
http://cast0.ast.cam.ac.uk/MRAO/mrao.clfst.html

Cambridge Ryle Telescope
http://cast0.ast.cam.ac.uk/MRAO/mrao.ryle.html

Cambridge Univ. Astronomy
http://cast0.ast.cam.ac.uk/

Campus Universitaire de St Martin d'Hères.
http://www.grenet.fr/campus.html

Canada France Hawaii Telescope
http://www.cfht.hawaii.edu/

Canadian Astronomy Data Centre
http://cadcwww.dao.nrc.ca/

Cardiff Star Formation
http://www.astro.cf.ac.uk/local/groups/starform/

Catalog of Galactic SNR's
http://cast0.ast.cam.ac.uk/MRAO/snrs.intro.html

CCD Images of Messier Objects
http://zebu.uoregon.edu/messier.html

CDS
http://cdsweb.u-strasbg.fr/astroweb.html

Centre de Données Astronomiques de Strasbourg [English]
http://cdsweb.u-strasbg.fr/CDS.html

CERN Preprint Server
http://darssrv1.cern.ch/

Cerro Tololo Interamerican Observatory
http://ctios2.ctio.noao.edu/ctio.html

CfA Optical and Infrared Astronomy Division
http://oir-www.harvard.edu/oir.html

CfA Radio and Geoastronomy Division
http://cfa-www.harvard.edu/cfa/rg.html

CfA Whipple Observatory
http://cfa-www.harvard.edu/cfa/whipple.html

CFHT at CADC
http://cadcwww.dao.nrc.ca/cfht/cfht.html

CNAM (French National Conservatory of Arts & Works)
http://www.cnam.fr/astro.english.html

Compton Observatory Science Support Ctr.
http://enemy.gsfc.nasa.gov/cossc/cossc.html

Conservatoire National des Arts et Métiers (English text)
http://web.cnam.fr/astro.english.html

Cornell Univ. Theory Ctr.
http://www.tc.cornell.edu/ctc.html

Corporate Research Institute
http://www.tc.cornell.edu/InBriefs/CRI.html

Cracow Observatory - Solar Radio Emission
http://www.oa.uj.edu.pl/sol/

Ctr. for Advanced Space Studies NASA Johnson SC
http://cass.jsc.nasa.gov/CASS_home.html

Ctr. for Applied Parallel Processing
http://www.cs.colorado.edu/mcbryan/home/capp/Home.html

Ctr. for Earth and Planetary Studies
http://ceps.nasm.edu:2020/homepage.html

Ctr. for Extreme Ultraviolet Astrophysics
http://cea-ftp.cea.berkeley.edu/HomePage.html

Ctr. for Subatomic Research
http://inuit.phys.ualberta.ca/

Daedalus
http://mimas.ethz.ch/Daedalus/daedalusdoc.html

Daily Planet
http://www.atmos.uiuc.edu/

DAO Virtual Library
http://www.dao.nrc.ca/librarymap.html

Dark Matter
http://www-hpcc.astro.washington.edu/simulations/DARK_MATTER/

Data Reduction Expert Assistant
http://lor.stsci.edu/draco/draco.html

Defense Meteorological Satellite Program Data Archive
http://www.ngdc.noaa.gov/dmsp/dmsp.html

Design Research Institute
http://dri.cornell.edu/Info/DRI.html

Deutsches Elektronen-Synchrotron
http://info.desy.de/

Distributed Astronomical Data Archives
http://cnidr.org/cnidr_papers/archives.html

Dominion Astrophysical Observatory
http://www.dao.nrc.ca/DAO-homepage.htm

Dutch Astronomy Services
http://eems.strw.leidenuniv.nl/astroned.html

Earth & Sky
http://www.quadralay.com/EarthSky/
es_home.htm

Earth Satellite Ephemeris Service
http://chara.gsu.edu/sat.html

Edinburgh Royal Observatory
http://www.roe.ac.uk/

Effelsberg Radio Telescope
http://www.mpifr-bonn.mpg.de/effberg.html

EINET Astronomy Listings
http://galaxy.einet.net/galaxy/Science/
Astronomy.html

Einstein Data Archive
http://hea-www.harvard.edu/einstein/
Ein_home/ein_welcome.html

Electronic TextBook
http://bovine.uoregon.edu/text.html

ESIS on-line image (GIF) files
http://ecf.hq.eso.org/ESIS-GIF.html

ESO / ST-ECF Data Archive
http://arch-http.hq.eso.org/ESO-ECF-
Archive.html

ESO Preprints Database
http://arch-http.hq.eso.org/cgi-bin/wdb/eso/
preprints/form

ESRIN - European Space Agency
http://www.esrin.esa.it/htdocs/esrin/esrin.html

ETH
http://www.ethz.ch/

ETH Solar Radio Spectrometer
http://mimas.ethz.ch/catalogs.html

European Incoherent Scatter
http://seldon.eiscat.no/homepage.html

European Southern Observatory
http://www.hq.eso.org/eso-homepage.html

European VLBI Network
http://rzmws10.nfra.nl:8081/jive/header.html

EUVE Guest Observer Ctr.
http://cea-ftp.cea.berkeley.edu/EGO/
EGOProgram.html

Extreme UltraViolet Explorer
http://cea-ftp.cea.berkeley.edu/

Fermilab
http://fnnews.fnal.gov/

FITS
http://fits.cv.nrao.edu:/FITS.html

Five College Radio Astronomy Observatory
http://donald.phast.umass.edu/Docs/
GradProg/fcrao.html

Flexible Image Transport System
http://fits.cv.nrao.edu/

FNAL
http://fndauh.fnal.gov:8000/

Freie Univ.Berlin - Institut für
Meteorologie [English]
http://www.met.fu-berlin.de/english/

Front Range Consortium
http://www.cs.colorado.edu/mcbryan/home/
frc/Home.html

Galactic PNe data base Innsbruck
http://ast2.uibk.ac.at/index.html

Gemini 8m Telescopes Project
http://www.gemini.edu/

George Smoot Astrophysics Research
http://spectrum.lbl.gov

Glasgow Univ.
http://info.astro.gla.ac.uk/

Global Land Information System
http://sun1.cr.usgs.gov/glis/glis.html

Global Oscillation Network Group
http://helios.tuc.noao.edu/gonghome.html

GOES Image Sequences of Solar Eclipse on
May 10, 1994
http://ageninfo.tamu.edu/eclipse/

Gravitational Lensing Conference
http://www.ph.unimelb.edu.au/astro/
glconf.html

Grenoble Image and Line Data Analysis
Software
http://iraux2.iram.fr/www/doc/gildas.html

Hafak Astronomical Society
http://www.csn.net/~emorse/haf/haf.html

Hard Labor Creek Observatory
http://chara.gsu.edu/hlco.html

Harvard Astrophysics Data System
http://adsabs.harvard.edu/

Harvard College Observatory
http://cfa-www.harvard.edu/hco-home.html

Harvard-Radcliffe Student Astronomers
http://hcs.harvard.edu/~stahr/

Harvard-Smithsonian Center for
Astrohysics
http://cfa-www.harvard.edu/cfa-home.html

Hat Creek Radio Observatory
http://bima.astro.umd.edu/bima/hatcreek/

Haystack Observatory
http://hyperion.haystack.edu/haystack/
haystack.html

HEAT (High-Energy, Antimatter Telescope)
http://tigger.physics.lsa.umich.edu/www/heat/
heat.html

High Energy Astrophysics Science Archive
Research Ctr.
http://heasarc.gsfc.nasa.gov/

Hiraiso Solar Terrestrial Research Ctr./
CRL
http://hiraiso.crl.go.jp/

Hubble Space Telescope
http://ucluelet.dao.nrc.ca/hst.html

Hubble Space Telescope Astrometry
Science Team
http://dorrit.as.utexas.edu/

IAU: Minor Planet Center
http://cfa-www.harvard.edu/cfa/ps/mpc.html

Icarus
http://astrosun.tn.cornell.edu/Icarus/
Icarus.html

IDL Astronomy User's Library
http://idlastro.gsfc.nasa.gov/homepage.html

Image Reduction and Analysis Facility
http://iraf.noao.edu/iraf-homepage.html

Imperial College, Univ. of London -
Theory Group: Preprints
http://euclid.tp.ph.ic.ac.uk/Papers/

Indiana Univ.
http://astrowww.astro.indiana.edu/

Infra-Red Telescope Facility
http://irtf.ifa.hawaii.edu/

Infrared Processing & Analysis Ctr.
http://www.ipac.caltech.edu/

Infrared Sky Survey Atlas
http://brando.ipac.caltech.edu:8888/ISSA-PS

Infrared Space Observatory
http://isowww.estec.esa.nl/

Infrared Subnode
http://esther.la.asu.edu/asu_tes/

Innsbruck - Galactic Planetary Nebulae
Database
http://ast2.uibk.ac.at/

Institut d'Astrophysique Spatiale (1)
http://www.ias.fr/

Institut de Radio Astronomie
Millimétrique
http://iraux2.iram.fr/www/iram.html

Institut National de Physique Nucléaire et
de Physique des Particules
http://info.in2p3.fr/

Institut National de Recherche en
Informatique et en Automatique
http://zenon.inria.fr:8003/

Institute for Astronomy Innsbruck
http://ast7.uibk.ac.at/

Institute for Space and Terrestrial Science
http://www.ists.ca/Welcome.html

Instituto de Astrofísica de Canarias
http://www.iac.es/home.html

Inter Univ. Ctr. for Astronomy and
Astrophysics
http://iucaa.iucaa.ernet.in/

Intl. Astronomy Conferences and Meetings
http://cadcwww.dao.nrc.ca/meetings/
meetings.html

Ionia 1 km AVHRR Global Land Data Set
Net-Browser
http://shark1.esrin.esa.it/

IRAF (preliminary)
http://iraf.noao.edu/iraf-homepage.html

Istituto di Astrofisica Spaziale - C.N.R.
http://titan.ias.fra.cnr.it/ias-home/ias-
home.html

Istituto di Fisica Cosmica e Tecnologie
Relative
http://www.ifctr.mi.cnr.it/

Istituto di Radioastronomia, Bologna -
C.N.R.
http://trantor.ira.bo.cnr.it/HomePage.html

Istituto Nazionale di Fisica Nucleare -
Astrofisica
http://hpl33.na.infn.it/Astr/Astr.html

IUE Data Analysis Ctr.
http://iuesn1.gsfc.nasa.gov/iue/
iuedac_homepage.html

James Clark Maxwell Telescope
http://malama.jach.hawaii.edu/
JCMT_intro.html

Joint Astronomy Centre
http://jach.hawaii.edu/

Joint Australian Centre for Astrophysical
Research in Antarctica
http://newt.phys.unsw.edu.au/~mgb/
jacara.html

Joint Institute for VLBI in Europe /
European VLBI Network
http://www.nfra.nl/home_jive.html

JPL Space Very Long Baseline Interferometry Project
http://sgra.jpl.nasa.gov/

Keck Observatory
http://astro.caltech.edu/keck.html

Kernfysisch Versneller Instituut
http://kviexp.kvi.nl/

Kestrel Institute
http://kestrel.edu/pub/mosaic/kestrel.html

Kitt Peak National Observatory
http://www.noao.edu/kpno/kpno.html

Konkoly Observatory
http://ogyalla.konkoly.hu/

La Palma - Isaac Newton Group
http://cast0.ast.cam.ac.uk/~lpinfo/

La Palma - Nordic Optical Telescope
http://nastol.astro.lu.se/Html/not.html

La Palma - Telescopio Nazionale Galileo
http://www.pd.astro.it/TNG/TNG.html

La Silla - All Telescopes
http://lw10.ls.eso.org/lasilla/Telescopes/
Telescopes.html

Lab. for Atmospheric and Space Physics
http://laspwww.colorado.edu:7777/
lasp_homepage.html

Lab. for Computational Astrophysics
http://zeus.ncsa.uiuc.edu:8080/
lca_home_page.html

Laboratoire d'Astrophysique de Grenoble
http://gag.observ-gr.fr/

LAI Olivier
http://www.obspm.fr/~lai/

LaRC
http://mosaic.larc.nasa.gov/nasaonline/
nasaonline.html

Large Binocular Telescope (LBT) Project
http://as.arizona.edu/lbtwww/lbt.html

Lawrence Berkeley Lab.
http://www.lbl.gov/LBL.html

Leeds Univ. Astrophysics
http://ast.leeds.ac.uk/

Loiano Telescopes - Bologna
http://boas3.bo.astro.it/loiano/
LoianoHome.html

Los Alamos National Lab Preprint Server
http://xxx.lanl.gov/

Low Surface Brightness galaxies
http://zebu.uoregon.edu/paper/lsb.txt

Ludwig Maximilians Univ.München -
Institut für Astronomie und Astrophysik
http://www.bl.physik.tu-muenchen.de/sektion/

Lund Observatory
http://nastol.astro.lu.se/Html/home.html

Magellan Image Browser
http://delcano.mit.edu/cgi-bin/midr-query

Malin Space Science Systems, Inc.
http://barsoom.msss.com/

Mars Atlas
http://fi-www.arc.nasa.gov/fia/projects/bayes-
group/Atlas/Mars/

Max-Planck-Institut für Astrophysik
http://www.mpa-garching.mpg.de/

Max-Planck-Institut für Extraterrestrische
Physik
http://hproe1.mpe-garching.mpg.de/

Max-Planck-Institut für Radioastronomie
http://www.mpifr-bonn.mpg.de/index.html

McGill Univ. - Earth and Planetary Science
http://stoner.eps.mcgill.ca/AboutEPS/
abouteps.html

McMaster Univ.'s Dept. of Physics and
Astronomy
http://www.physics.mcmaster.ca/

Mees Observatory
http://www.solar.ifa.hawaii.edu/mees.html

Microcomputer Image Processing System
http://fits.cv.nrao.edu/www/news_mips.txt

Millstone Hill Observatory
http://hyperion.haystack.edu/homepage.html

MIT - Massachusetts Institute of Technology
http://hyperion.haystack.edu/mit/mit.html

MIT Lab. for Nuclear Science
http://marie.mit.edu/

MIT Microwave Subnode
http://delcano.mit.edu/

Mopra Antenna
http://www.atnf.csiro.au/ATNF/
Coonabarabran-Site-information.html

Mount Laguna Observatory/San Diego
State Univ.
http://mintaka.sdsu.edu/

Mount Stromlo and Siding Spring Observatories - Schedules
http://meteor.anu.edu.au/dave/schedule/
schedule.html

Mount Wilson Observatory
http://www.mtwilson.edu/

MPA Galaxy Formation Group: Preprints
http://www.mpa-garching.mpg.de/Galaxien/
Prep.html

MPA Gravitational Lensing Group:
Preprints
http://www.mpa-garching.mpg.de/Lenses/
Prep.html

MPA Hydro Gang: Preprints
http://www.mpa-garching.mpg.de/Hydro/
Prep.html

MPIfR - Bonn 100-m Telescope Surveys
http://www.mpifr-bonn.mpg.de/survey.html

MSSS Viking Image Archive
http://barsoom.msss.com/http/vikingdb.html

MSSSO
http://meteor.anu.edu.au/anton/
astronomy.html

Mullard Radio Astronomy Observatory
http://cast0.ast.cam.ac.uk/MRAO/
mrao.home.html

Multi Telescope Telescope
http://chara.gsu.edu/mtt.html

Multiple Mirror Telescope Observatory
http://oir-www.harvard.edu/MMT/mmto.html

Munich Image Data Analysis System
(WWW)
http://http.hq.eso.org/midas-info/midas.html

NASA ADC Online Information System
http://hypatia.gsfc.nasa.gov/about/
adc_online.html

NASA Homepage (with Links to Everywhere Else at NASA)
http://www.nasa.gov/

Nation River Observatory
http://hydra.carleton.ca/nro/nrohome.html

National Climatic Data Ctr.
http://www.ncdc.noaa.gov/ncdc.html

National Consortium for High Performance Computing
http://info.lcs.mit.edu/

National Ctr. for Atmospheric Research
http://http.ucar.edu/metapage.html

National Ctr. for Supercomputing
Applications - Publications
http://www.ncsa.uiuc.edu/Pubs/
NCSAPubs.html

National Geophysical Data Ctr.
http://www.ngdc.noaa.gov/ngdc.html

National Information Infrastructure
Testbed
http://www.esi.com/niit/

National Institute of Space Research
http://www.inpe.br/astro/home

National MetaCenter for Computational
Science and Engineering
http://www.ncsa.uiuc.edu/General/
MetaCenter/MetaCenterHome.html

National Optical Astronomy Observatories
http://www.noao.edu/

National Radio Astronomy Observatory
http://info.aoc.nrao.edu/

National Solar Observatory
http://argo.tuc.noao.edu/

Naval Research Lab.
http://www.cmf.nrl.navy.mil/home.html

NEMO Stellar Dynamics Toolbox
http://bima.astro.umd.edu/nemo/

Nerd World Astronomy Links (massive)
http://www.tiac.net/users/dstein/nw37.html

Netherlands Foundation for Research in
Astronomy
http://www.nfra.nl/home_nfra.html

New Mexico State Univ.
http://charon.nmsu.edu/

Nicolaus Copernicus Astronomical Ctr.
http://www.ncac.torun.pl/

Nine Planets
http://seds.lpl.arizona.edu/nineplanets/
nineplanets/nineplanets.html

NOAA - National Oceanographic and
Atmospheric Administration
http://www.ncdc.noaa.gov/noaa.html

North Carolina State Univ. - Mars Mission
Research Ctr.
http://www.mmrc.ncsu.edu/

Northwestern Univ. - Astronomy
http://www.astro.nwu.edu/home.html

Numerical Algorithms Group
http://www.nag.co.uk:70/

Oak Ridge National Lab.
http://jupiter.esd.ornl.gov/home.html

OAT Astronomical Services
http://www.oat.ts.astro.it/astro-services/
overview.html

Observatoire du Mont Mégantic
http://ftp.astro.umontreal.ca/omm/
omm_eng.html

Observatories and Astronomical Institutions on WWW
http://sousun1.phys.soton.ac.uk/
Institutions.html

Optical Astronomy Group at Leeds Univ.
http://ast.leeds.ac.uk/opti-home.html

Optical Gravitational Lensing Experiment
http://www.astrouw.edu.pl/~udalski/ogle.html

OPTICS.ORG - The Photonics Resource
Center
http://optics.org/

Orbiting Very Long Baseline Interferometry
http://info.gb.nrao.edu/ovlbi/OVLBI.html

OSSE
http://enemy.gsfc.nasa.gov/cossc/OSSE-
desc.html

Osservatorio Astrofisico di Arcetri
http://helios.arcetri.astro.it/

Osservatorio Astrofisico di Catania
http://convex.ct.astro.it/

Osservatorio Astronomico Collurania di
Teramo
http://terri1.te.astro.it/oact-home/home.html

Osservatorio Astronomico di Bologna
http://boas3.bo.astro.it/

Osservatorio Astronomico di Padova
http://www.pd.astro.it/

Osservatorio Astronomico di Palermo
http://www.astropa.unipa.it/

Osservatorio Astronomico di Roma
http://oar.rm.astro.it/home.html

Osservatorio Astronomico di Trieste
http://www.oat.ts.astro.it/oat-home.html

Oxford Workshop on Evidence for Tori in
AGN
http://www-astro.physics.ox.ac.uk/torus/

Pacific Northwest Lab.
http://romana.crystal.pnl.gov/

Padova: Ekar 182cm Telescope - Schedules
http://www.pd.astro.it/CurrentSchedule.html

Parallel Tools Consortium
http://www.llnl.gov/ptools/ptools.html

Parkes Radio Telescope
http://www.atnf.csiro.au/ATNF/Parkes-Site-
information.html

PASP Abstract Service at CDS
http://cdsweb.u-strasbg.fr/PASP.html

PDS Planetary Rings Node
http://ringside.arc.nasa.gov/

Pennsylvania State Univ. - Dept. of
Astronomy and Astrophysics
http://www.astro.psu.edu/

Peora Astronomical Society
http://bradley.bradley.edu/~dware/

Physikalisch-Astronomisch-
Technikwissenschaftliche Fakultät
http://www.physik.uni-jena.de/

Pico Veleta
http://iraux2.iram.fr/www/veleta.gif

Pine Mountain Observatory
http://zebu.uoregon.edu/pine.html

Pittsburgh Supercomputing Ctr.
http://pscinfo.psc.edu/

Planetary Astronomy
http://fits.cv.nrao.edu/www/yp_planetary.html

Planetary Society
http://wea.mankato.mn.us/tps/

Pomona College
http://shanti.pomona.claremont.edu/

Princeton Univ. Astrophysics Library
http://astro.princeton.edu/library/

Princeton Univ. Observatory
http://minos.princeton.edu/

Princeton Univ. - Pulsar Group
http://pulsar.princeton.edu/

Radio Astronomy Group (RAG)
http://mimas.ethz.ch/home.html

Rennes' Univ.
http://www.univ-rennes1.fr/

Rensselaer Polytechnic Institute
http://www.rpi.edu/dept/phys/astro.html

Repository Based Software Engineering
http://rbse.jsc.nasa.gov/eichmann/rbse.html

Research Institute for Computing and
Information Systems
http://rbse.jsc.nasa.gov/

RGSC
http://tdc-www.harvard.edu/software/
rgsc.html

Rice Univ.
http://spacsun.rice.edu/

Robert Lentz's Astro Resources
http://www.astro.nwu.edu/lentz/astro/home-astro.html

Royal Greenwich Observatory
http://cast0.ast.cam.ac.uk/RGO/RGO.html

Royal Observatory, Edinburgh
http://www.roe.ac.uk/

Rutherford Appleton Lab.
http://www.rl.ac.uk/home.html

RVSAO
http://tdc-www.harvard.edu/iraf/rvsao/
rvsao.html

Sac Peak Preprint Library
http://www.sunspot.noao.edu/Library/
preprints/

Sacramento Peak Observatory
http://sunspot.noao.edu/SP-home.html

Saint Mary's Astronomy and Physics
http://mnbsun.stmarys.ca/www/
smu_home.html

Saint-Louis Nicole
http://ftp.astro.umontreal.ca/membres/
stlouis.html

San Diego Supercomputer Ctr.
http://gopher.sdsc.edu/Home.html

Sandia National Labs.
http://www.cs.sandia.gov/pub/WWW/
Sandia_home_page.html

SAO Telescope Data Ctr.
http://tdc-www.harvard.edu/TDC.html

sci.astro.research Archive
http://xanth.msfc.nasa.gov/xray/sar.html

Science on the Edge of Chaos Cosmology
http://arti.vub.ac.be/www/chaos/cosmology/
description.html

Seoul National Univ.
http://astrox.snu.ac.kr/

Set of Identifications, Measurements, and
Bibliography for Astronomical Data
http://cdsweb.u-strasbg.fr/Simbad.html

SETI Institute
http://www.metrolink.com/seti/SETI.html

Sidewalk Astronomers
http://lausd.k12.ca.us/~npatteng/sa.html

SIS junctions lab
http://iraux2.iram.fr/www/sis.html

Sky & Telescope magazine
http://www.skypub.com/

SKYMAP
http://tdc-www.harvard.edu/software/
skymap.html

SkyView
http://skyview.gsfc.nasa.gov/skyview.html

Sloan Digital Sky Survey
http://astro.princeton.edu/

Small Astronomical Image Library
http://donald.phast.umass.edu/gs/
wizimlib.html

Smithsonian Astrophysical Observatory
http://cfa-www.harvard.edu/sao-home.html

Solar and Heliospheric Observatory
http://umbra.gsfc.nasa.gov/soho/anglais/
soho.html

Solar Astronomy
http://fits.cv.nrao.edu/www/
yp_areas.html#solar

Solar Workshops
http://www.oat.ts.astro.it/isps/
sworkshops.html

Southampton Univ. Astronomy Group
http://sousun1.phys.soton.ac.uk/

Southern Columbia Millimeter Telescope
http://ctiot6.ctio.noao.edu/

Space Astrophysics Lab.
http://nereid.sal.ists.ca/Welcome.html

Space Environment Lab.
http://www.sel.bldrdoc.gov/

Space Infrared Telescope Facility
http://kromos.jpl.nasa.gov/sirtf.html

Space Physics Resources on the Internet
http://www.esrin.esa.it/htdocs/esis/
sp_resources.html

Space Telescope - European Coordinating
Facility
http://ecf.hq.eso.org/ST-ECF-homepage.html

Space Telescope Electronic Information
Service
http://stsci.edu/top.html

Space Telescope Science Institute
http://www.stsci.edu/top.html

SPIE-The Intl. Society for Optical Engineering
http://www.spie.org/

Stanford Public Information Retrieval
System
http://www-spires.slac.stanford.edu/FIND/
spires.html

STAR
http://tdc-www.harvard.edu/software/star.html

Star*s Family
http://cdsweb.u-strasbg.fr/~heck/sf.htm

StarBits
http://cdsweb.u-strasbg.fr/~heck/sfbits.htm

Starcat
http://arch-http.hq.eso.org/starcat.html

StarHeads
http://cdsweb.u-strasbg.fr/~heck/sfheads.htm

STARLINK (at UCL)
http://zuaxp6.star.ucl.ac.uk/mainindex.html

StarTrax: an Astrophysics Information
System
http://heasarc.gsfc.nasa.gov/StarTrax.html

StarWorlds
http://cdsweb.u-strasbg.fr/~heck/sfworlds.htm

Statistical Consulting Ctr. for Astronomy
http://www.stat.psu.edu/scca/homepage.html

STECF
http://ecf.hq.eso.org/astro-resources.html

STELAR project
http://hypatia.gsfc.nasa.gov/Welcome.html

Sterrewacht Leiden
http://eems.strw.leidenuniv.nl/

Steward Observatory
http://as.arizona.edu/www/so.html

STScI
http://stsci.edu/net-resources.html

STScI-EPA HST Images
http://ra.stsci.edu/EPAimages.html

Students for the Exploration and Development of Space
http://seds.lpl.arizona.edu/

Study of Electronic Literature for Astronomical Research
http://hypatia.gsfc.nasa.gov/
STELAR_homepage.html

SUNY Stony Brook Astronomy Group
http://sbast3.ess.sunysb.edu/home.html

Superconducting Super Collider Lab.
http://www.ssc.gov/

Sussex Starlink
http://star-www.maps.susx.ac.uk/index.html

Texas Astronomical Society - Dallas
http://fohnix.metronet.com/~cajun/tas.html

THE Star
http://www.oat.ts.astro.it/isps/isps.htm

TIPSY
http://hermes.astro.washington.edu/tools/
TIPSY/

TL Systems - Astronomy & Satellite
Products
http://PoliticsUSA.com/PoliticsUSA/news/

Today's Solar Weather
http://www.sel.bldrdoc.gov/today.html

Two Micron All-Sky Survey
http://scruffy.phast.umass.edu/GradProg/
2mass.html

UK Infra-Red Telescope
http://malama.jach.hawaii.edu/
UKIRT_intro.html

UMASS Astronomy Image Library
http://donald.phast.umass.edu/gs/
wizimlib.html

UniPOPS
http://info.cv.nrao.edu/html/unipops/unipops-
home.html

Univ. di Bologna - Dipartimento di
Astronomia
http://boas3.bo.astro.it/dip/DepHome.html

Univ. di Roma " Tor Vergata" Astrophysics
http://itovf2.roma2.infn.it/

Univ. of Adelaide - Astrophysics Group
http://bragg.physics.adelaide.edu.au/
astrophysics/home.html

Univ. of Alabama
http://crux.astr.ua.edu/AlabamaHome.html

Univ. of Amsterdam - Astronomical
Institute
http://helios.astro.uva.nl:8888/home.html

Univ. of Birmingham - Space Research
http://www.sr.bham.ac.uk:8080/

Univ. of Bradford - Engineering in
Astronomy Group
http://www.eia.brad.ac.uk/eia.html

Univ. of Calgary
http://bear.ras.ucalgary.ca/department.html

Univ. of California, Berkeley
http://astro.berkeley.edu/home.html

Univ. of California, Los Angeles
http://www.igpp.ucla.edu/

Univ. of California, San Diego
http://www.ucsd.edu/

Univ. of California, Santa Cruz - UCO/
Lick
http://ucowww.ucsc.edu/

Univ. of Cantabria - Departamento de
Física Moderna
http://esanu1.unican.es/

Univ. of Chicago
http://bio-3.bsd.uchicago.edu/htbin/lookup-
building?AAC

Univ. of Colorado Astrophysics Data
System
http://adswww.colorado.edu/adswww/
adshomepg.html

Univ. of Edinburgh
http://www.ph.ed.ac.uk/index.html

Univ. of Groningen - Kapteyn Astronomical Institute
http://kapteyn.astro.rug.nl/

Univ. of Hawaii - Institute for Astronomy
http://www.ifa.hawaii.edu/

Univ. of Hawaii IfA: 2.2m Telescope
http://www.ifa.hawaii.edu/88inch/88inch.html

Univ. of Leicester
http://www.star.le.ac.uk/

Univ. of Manchester
http://axp2.ast.man.ac.uk:8000/

Univ. of Maryland
http://pdssbn.astro.umd.edu/

Univ. of Maryland, College Park
http://www.astro.umd.edu/

Univ. of Massachusetts
http://www-astro.phast.umass.edu/

Univ. of Massachusetts, Amherst
http://donald.phast.umass.edu/
umasshome.html

Univ. of Melbourne
http://www.ph.unimelb.edu.au/

Univ. of Minnesota
http://ast1.spa.umn.edu/

Univ. of Montréal
http://ftp.astro.umontreal.ca/index_eng.html

Univ. of Nevada, Las Vegas
http://pauli.lv-physics.nevada.edu/

Univ. of New Mexico
http://wwwifa.unm.edu/

Univ. of New South Wales
http://newt.phys.unsw.edu.au/

Univ. of Oxford - Astrophysics
http://www-astro.physics.ox.ac.uk/

Univ. of Oxford - Atmospheric, Oceanic & Planetary Physics.
http://www-atm.atm.ox.ac.uk/index.html

Univ. of Pennsylvania
http://dept.physics.upenn.edu/

Univ. of Pittsburgh
http://artemis.phyast.pitt.edu/

Univ. of Rochester - Near Infrared Group
http://sherman.pas.rochester.edu/URNIRHome.html

Univ. of Southampton - Astronomy Group
http://sousun1.phys.soton.ac.uk/

Univ. of Texas, Austin - McDonald Observatory
http://www.as.utexas.edu/

Univ. of Tokyo - Gravitational Wave Group
http://www.phys.s.u-tokyo.ac.jp/local/research/tsubono/res94-e.html

Univ. of Tokyo - Theoretical Astrophysics Group
http://www.phys.s.u-tokyo.ac.jp/local/research/astrophys/res94-e.html

Univ. of Tokyo - X-Ray Astronomy Group
http://www.phys.s.u-tokyo.ac.jp/local/research/maxima/res94-e.html

Univ. of Toronto - Canadian Institute for Theoretical Astrophysics
http://www.physics.utoronto.ca/department/groups_partners/cita.html

Univ. of Toronto Astronomy Library Book and Software Reviews
http://www.astro.utoronto.ca/reviews1.html

Univ. of Tübingen - Theoretische Astrophysik ünd Computational Physics
http://aorta.tat.physik.uni-tuebingen.de/

Univ. of Utrecht - Sterrenkundig Instituut
http://stkwww.fys.ruu.nl:8000

Univ. of Victoria
http://info.phys.uvic.ca/uvphys_welcome.html

Univ. of Vienna - Institut für Astronomie
http://charon.ast.univie.ac.at/index.html

Univ. of Virginia
http://www.astro.virginia.edu/

Univ. of Wales at Cardiff
http://www.astro.cf.ac.uk/

Univ. of Washington
http://www.astro.washington.edu/

Univ. of Western Ontario
http://phobos.astro.uwo.ca/

Univ. of Wisconsin-Madison
http://www.astro.wisc.edu/

Uppsala Astronomical Observatory, Sweden
http://www.astro.uu.se/

UUNA Astronomy Listings
http://sturgeon.mit.edu:8001/uu-nna/meta-library/index.html?astronomy

Vassar College
http://noether.vassar.edu/

Viking Orbiter
http://www.gsfc.nasa.gov/planetary/Viking.HTML

Warsaw Univ. - Astronomical Observatory
http://www.astrouw.edu.pl/

Warsaw Univ. - Optical Gravitational Lensing Experiment
http://www.astrouw.edu.pl/~udalski/ogle.html

Weather World
http://www.atmos.uiuc.edu/wxworld/html/top.html

Weaving the Astronomy Web
http://cdsweb.u-strasbg.fr/waw.html

WebStars: Astrophysics in Cyberspace
http://guinan.gsfc.nasa.gov/WebStars.html

Westerbork Synthesis Radio Telescope
http://kapteyn.astro.rug.nl/UserDoc.html

Whipple Gamma-Ray Observatory
http://egret.sao.arizona.edu/index.html

Whipple Observatory
http://oir-www.harvard.edu/FLWO/FLWO/whipple.html

Williams College
http://albert.astro.williams.edu/

Wilson Synchrotron Lab.
http://w4.lns.cornell.edu/

Woodman Astronomical Library
http://uwast.astro.wisc.edu/~astrolib/
WoodmanLibrary.html

World Data Ctr. A for Rockets and Satellites
http://hypatia.gsfc.nasa.gov/about/
about_wdc-a.html

X-Ray WWW Server
http://xray.uu.se/

Xerox Palo Alto Research Ctr.
http://pubweb.parc.xerox.com/

Biology & Biotechnology

See also Agriculture, Chemistry, Medicine, Optics, Physics

Aachen Institute of Physiology
http://www.physiology.rwth-aachen.de/

AAnDB
http://keck.tamu.edu/cgi/aandb/anid.html

ABtDB
http://keck.tamu.edu/cgi/bov/bov.html

Addison-Wesley
http://www.germany.eu.net/shop/AW/

Aging Server
http://www.hookup.net/mall/aging/
agesit59.html

AGsDB
http://keck.tamu.edu/cgi/agsdb/
agsdbserver.html

Alces
http://alces.med.umn.edu/start.html

ALSCRIPT and AMPS manuals
http://geoff.biop.ox.ac.uk/manuals.html

American Institute of Biological Sciences
http://www.aibs.org

American Society of Plant Physiologists
(ASPP)
http://www.aspp.org/

American Type Culture Collection (ATCC)
http://merlot.welch.jhu.edu/11/Database-local/
cultures/atcc

Arabidopsis cDNA Sequence Analysis
Project
http://lenti.med.umn.edu/arabidopsis/
arab_top_page.html

Arabidopsis thaliana Data Base
http://weeds.mgh.harvard.edu/

Argonne National Lab.
http://www.anl.gov/

Artificial Life & Complex Systems
http://www.seas.upenn.edu/~ale/cplxsys.html

Artificial Life Online
http://alife.santafe.edu/

Auburn College of Veterinary Medicine
http://www.vetmed.auburn.edu/

Australian Herpetological Directory
http://www.jcu.edu.au/dept/Zoology/herp/
herp2.html

Australian National Botanic Gardens
http://155.187.10.12/index.html

Australian National Univ.
http://life.anu.edu.au/

Avery Lab Caenorhabditis elegans Server
http://eatworms.swmed.edu/

Bacterial Species Nomenclature
http://www.ftpt.br/cgi-bin/bdtnet/bacterianame

Barton Group
http://geoff.biop.ox.ac.uk/

Base de Dados Tropical
http://www.ftpt.br/

Baylor College of Medicine
http://www.bcm.tmc.edu/

Baylor Molecular Biology Information
Resource
http://mbcr.bcm.tmc.edu:8080/home.html

Beekeeping
http://alfred1.u.washington.edu:8080/~jlks/
bee.html

Berkeley Molecular and Cell Biology
http://mendel.berkeley.edu/homepage.html

Berkeley Plant Biology
http://mendel.berkeley.edu/pb/
pbhomepage.html

Bermuda Biological Station for Research
http://www.bbsr.edu/

BEST North America
http://best.gdb.org/best.html

Bio-wURLd
http://www.ebi.ac.uk/htbin/bwurld.pl

BioBanco
http://fiss.org.ec/

Biobox
http://shamrock.csc.fi/brochure.html

BioCatalog
http://www.ebi.ac.uk/biocat/biocat.html

BioCatalogue
http://www.genethon.fr/exterieur/
bio_catal_resume.html

Biochemical Metabolism Pathway
Database
http://www.mcs.anl.gov/home/towell/
metabhome.html

Biocomputing and Modeling
http://www-bio.unizh.ch/xmosaic.home

Biocomputing Survival Guide
http://www.ch.embnet.org/jam/jam.html

BioData
http://www.biodata.com/

Biodiversity and Biological Collections
Web Server
http://muse.bio.cornell.edu/

Biodiversity and Ecosystems Network
(BENE)
http://straylight.tamu.edu/bene/bene.html

Biodiversity around the World
http://www.igc.apc.org/igc/ian.html

Biodiversity at Australia National Univ.
http://life.anu.edu.au/biodiversity.html

Biodiversity Consortium
http://www.bio.bris.ac.uk/sbsbd.htm

Bioinformatics at Australia National Univ.
http://life.anu.edu.au/

Bioline
http://www.ftpt.br/cgi-bin/bioline/bioline

Bioline Publications
http://golgi.harvard.edu/biopages/
all.html#Brazil

Biological Databases Online
http://www.abc.hu/bio/part2.html

Biological Evolution
http://perpmc1.vub.ac.be/BIOEVOL.html

Biological Journals
http://golgi.harvard.edu/journals.html

Biological Molecules
http://golgi.harvard.edu/sequences.html

Biological Resources
http://biomaster.uio.no/biological.html

Biological Software and Data FTP Archives
http://www.gdb.org/Dan/softsearch/
softsearch.html

Biologist's Control Panel
http://gc.bcm.tmc.edu:8088/bio/
bio_home.html

Biology Indexes
http://gulib.lausun.georgetown.edu/blommer/
biology/

Biology WWW Sites
http://calvin.stemnet.nf.ca/subjects/
biology.html

BioMedNet
http://www.cursci.co.uk/BioMedNet/
biomed.html

BioMolecular Engineering Research Ctr.
http://bmerc-www.bu.edu/

Biomolecules Virtual Library
http://golgi.harvard.edu/sequences.html

BIONET Software Archives
http://www.ch.embnet.org/bio-www/info.html

BiOS - The Biomedical Optics Society
http://www.spie.org/web/working_groups/
biomedical_optics/bios_desc.html

BIOSCAN Sequence Similarity Search
http://www.cs.unc.edu/bioscan/bioscan.html

BIOSCI/bionet Electronic Newsgroup
Network for Biology
http://www.bio.net/

Biosciences WWW Virtual Library
http://golgi.harvard.edu/biopages.html

BioSciences (en Espaniol)
http://fiss.org.ec/BioBanco/BioCuentas/
BioSciences.html

Biosequence comparison
http://twod.med.harvard.edu/seqanal/

BioSpace Biotechnology Center
http://www.biospace.com/

Biotechnology Ctr. of Oslo, Norway
http://biomaster.uio.no/

Biotechnology Information Ctr.
http://www.inform.umd.edu/EdRes/Topic/
AgrEnv/Biotech

Biotechnology Lab, Univ. of British
Columbia
http://bc-education.botany.ubc.ca/
biotech_lab/biotech.htm

Biotechnology Resources
http://biotech.chem.indiana.edu/

BioViz
http://bioviz.biol.trinity.edu/

Birding on the Web
http://
compstat.wharton.upenn.edu:8001?~siler/
birding.html

BITMed
http://bitmed.ucsd.edu/

BLITZ protein database searches
http://www.embl-heidelberg.de/searches/
blitz.html

BLOCKS Server
http://www.blocks.fhcrc.org/

Boston College
http://darkstar.bc.edu/

Boston College Bio-Inorganic Chemistry
Server
http://chemserv.bc.edu/Bioinorganic/
BioInorganic.html

Boston Univ. Biophysics
http://med-biophd.bu.edu/

Boston Univ. School of Public Health
http://www-busph.bu.edu/

Boston University
http://bio.bu.edu/

Brain Mapping Database Conference
http://biad38.uthscsa.edu/brainmap/
brainmap94.html

BRASS
http://mbisg2.sbc.man.ac.uk/brassp.html

Breast Cancer Information Clearinghouse
http://nysernet.org/bcic/

Brigham and Women's Hospital
http://golgi.harvard.edu/biopages/
all.html#HMS

Brock U. Biology Department
http://aqueous.labs.brocku.ca/

Brookhaven National Lab.
http://suntid.bnl.gov:8080/bnl.html

Brown University
http://biomedcs.biomed.brown.edu/

Caenorhabditis elegans Data Base
http://moulon.inra.fr/acedb/acedb.html

Caenorhabditis elegans WWW Server at
UTSW
http://eatworms.swmed.edu/

California Academy of Sciences Museum
http://www.calacademy.org/

Caltech Molecular Neuroscience
http://www.cns.caltech.edu/molecula/

Cambridge Dept.of Biochemistry
http://www.bio.cam.ac.uk/

Cambridge Scientific
http://www.camsci.com/

Canadian Genome & Analysis Technology
Bioinformatics
http://cgat.bch.umontreal.ca

Canadian Medical Research Council
http://hpb1.hwc.ca:8100/

CancerNet
http://biomed.nus.sg/Cancer/welcome.html

Candida Biology
http://alces.med.umn.edu/Candida.html

CAOS
http://www.caos.kun.nl/

Carleton Biology/Ecology Jrnl.
http://journal.biology.carleton.ca/

Carthew Drosophila Lab
http://flies3.bio.pitt.edu/

Catalogue of Molecular Biology Programs
http://www.genethon.fr/exterieur/
bio_catal_resume.html

CELLS Alive
http://www.comet.chv.va.us/quill/

CEPH-Genethon Human Genome Physical
Map
http://gc.bcm.tmc.edu:8088/bio/
ceph_genethon_interface.html

CGSC: E.coli Genetic Stock Ctr.
http://cgsc.biology.yale.edu/top.html

Cold Spring Harbor Lab
http://www.cshl.org

Collaborative BioMolecular Tools
http://www.dl.ac.uk/CBMT/HOME.html

Collaborative Clickable Biology
http://s-crim1.dl.ac.uk:8000/HOME.html

Colorado State Univ. Entomology
http://www.colostate.edu/Depts/Entomology/ent.html

Colorado Univ. Institute for Behavioral Genetics
http://ibgwww.colorado.edu/

Columbia Univ. Biochemistry and Molecular Biophysics
http://cuhhca.hhmi.columbia.edu/

Columbia-Presbyterian Medical Ctr.
http://www.cpmc.columbia.edu/

Computational Biochemistry Research Group
http://cbrg.inf.ethz.ch/

Cooperative Human Linkage Ctr.
http://www.chlc.org/

Cornell Cooperative Extension
http://empire.cce.cornell.edu/

CSUBIOWEB
http://arnica.csustan.edu/

CSUBIOWEB - Biotechnology
http://arnica.csustan.edu/biotech.html

CSUBIOWEB - Cell Biology
http://arnica.csustan.edu/ce.html

CSUBIOWEB - Microbiology
http://arnica.csustan.edu/mi.html

CTI Centre for Biology
http://www.liv.ac.uk/ctibiol.html

Dana-Farber Cancer Institute
http://golgi.harvard.edu/biopages/all.html#HMS

Daniel Hartl Lab
http://golgi.harvard.edu/hartl/

DELTA Project - Biological Sciences
http://www.calpoly.edu/delta.html

Dendrome, A Genome Database for Forest Trees
http://s27w007.pswfs.gov/

DENTalTRAUMA
http://www.unige.ch/smd/orthotr.html

Developmental Biology (Biosciences) Virtual Library
http://golgi.harvard.edu/biopages/develop.html

Developmental Studies Hybridoma Bank
http://www.gdb.org/Dan/DSHB/dshb.intro.html

Dialog Information Services, Inc
http://www.dialog.com/

Dinosaur Exhibit
http://www.hcc.hawaii.edu/dinos/dinos.1.html

Division of Refuges
http://bluegoose.arw.r9.fws.gov/

Dog Genome Project
http://mendel.berkeley.edu/dog.html

Domestic Animal Endocrinology
http://www.ag.auburn.edu/dae/dae.html

Drosophila Server
http://flies3.bio.pitt.edu/

Duke Univ. Center for In Vivo Microscopy
http://wwwcivm.mc.duke.edu

Duke Univ. Medical Ctr.
http://www.mc.duke.edu/

Duke Univ. Medical Informatics
http://dmi-www.mc.duke.edu/

E. coli Genetic Stock Ctr.
http://cgsc.biology.yale.edu/top.html

Eccles Institute of Human Genetics
http://www-genetics.med.utah.edu/

EcoNet
http://www.igc.apc.org/

EcoWeb
http://ecosys.drdr.virginia.edu/EcoWeb.html

Edinburgh Univ. Chemical Engineering Dept.
http://www.chemeng.ed.ac.uk/

Educational Technology Branch
http://wwwetb.nlm.nih.gov/

EGCG manuals
http://biomaster.uio.no/gcgman/egcgmain.html

Eli Lilly and Company
http://www.lilly.com/

EMBL Data Library & European Biocomputing Institute
http://www.embl-heidelberg.de/

EMBL Nucleotide Sequence Database
http://www.ebi.ac.uk/ebi_docs/embl_db/
embl_db.html

EMF-Link
http://archive.xrt.upenn.edu:1000/emf/top/
emf-link.html

Encyclopedia Radiologica
http://www.xray.hmc.psu.edu/
EncyclopediaRadiologica.html

EnviroLink Network
http://envirolink.org/about.html

Environmental Information Services
http://www.esdim.noaa.gov/

Environmental Protection Agency
http://www.epa.gov/

Environmental Resources Information
Network
http://kaos.erin.gov.au/erin.html

EnviroWeb
http://envirolink.org/

Enzyme Nomenclature Database
http://www.gdb.org/Dan/proteins/ec-
enzyme.html

European Biocomputing Institute
http://www.ebi.ac.uk/

European Bioinformatics Institute
http://www.embl-heidelberg.de/
ebi_home.html

European Molecular Biology Network
http://beta.embnet.unibas.ch/embnet/
info.html

European Synchrotron Radiation Facility
http://fox.esrf.fr:3600/

ExPASy Molecular Biology Server
http://expasy.hcuge.ch/

Experimental Searchable Index for the
WWW VL Biosciences
http://golgi.harvard.edu/htbin/biopages

EXtension TOXicology NETwork
http://sulaco.oes.orst.edu:70/1/ext/extoxnet

Finnish Forest Research Institute
http://www.metla.fi/

FINS
http://www.actwin.com/fish/index.html

FireNet - Landscape Fire Information
http://life.anu.edu.au/firenet/firenet.html

Fish, and other Aquatic Animals
http://www.actwin.com/WWWVL-Fish.html

Flea News!
http://www.public.iastate.edu/~entomology/
FleaNews/AboutFleaNews.html

Florida Agricultural Information
http://hammock.ifas.ufl.edu/

Forestry College
http://www.environment.sfasu.edu:1080/

Fred Hutchinson Cancer Research Ctr.
http://www.fhcrc.org/

French Genomics Server, Moulon
http://moulon.inra.fr/

Frog Dissection Server
http://george.lbl.gov/ITG.hm.pg.docs/dissect/
info.html

FROGGY Page
http://www.cs.yale.edu/HTML/YALE/CS/
HyPlans/loosemore-sandra/froggy.html

Fujita Health Univ.
http://pathy.fujita-hu.ac.jp/pathy.html

Fungal Genetics Stock Ctr.
http://kufacts.cc.ukans.edu/cwis/units/fgsc/
main.html

G protein-Coupled Receptor Database
(GCRDb)
http://receptor.mgh.harvard.edu/
GCRDBHOME.html

G.M. Church Lab
http://twod.med.harvard.edu/

Ganglion - Medical Ctr.
http://ganglion.anes.med.umich.edu/

GasNet Anaesthesiology Server
http://gasnet.med.nyu.edu/HomePage.html

GENETHON - Human Genome Centre
http://www.genethon.fr/genethon_en.html

Genetics at Univ. Naples, Italy
http://biol.dgbm.unina.it:8080/

Genetics Biopages
http://golgi.harvard.edu/biopages/
genetics.html

GenoBase Server
http://specter.dcrt.nih.gov:8004/

Genome Machine
http://www.pathology.washington.edu/
GDB_select_chromosome.html

Genome Therapeutics Corporation
http://www.cric.com/

GenomeNet
http://www.genome.ad.jp/

Genosys Biotechnologies, Inc.
http://www.genosys.com/

Geographic Information Systems Lab.
http://ice.gis.uiuc.edu/

Georgia Tech Medical Informatics
http://www.cc.gatech.edu/gvu/
medical_informatics/
medinfo_home_page.html

Globewide Network Academy
http://uu-gna.mit.edu:8001/uu-gna/

Globin gene server
http://globin.cse.psu.edu/

Glucoamylase
http://www.public.iastate.edu/~pedro/glase/
glase.html

Good Medicine Magazine
http://none.coolware.com/health/good_med/
ThisIssue.html

Gordon Conference Information
http://hackberry.chem.niu.edu:70/1/
ConferenceListings/GordonConferences

Guide to Public Health
http://128.196.106.42/ph-hp.html

GUIs in Bioinformatics Workshop
http://nimsn41.nimr.mrc.ac.uk/mathbio/t-
flores/GUI-Bioinform/meeting.html

Habitat Ecology
http://biome.bio.ns.ca/

Harvard Biochemistry, Molecular Biology,
and Biophysics
http://golgi.harvard.edu/biopages/

Harvard Bioinformatics
http://golgi.harvard.edu/gilbert-bi.html

Harvard Biolabs
http://golgi.harvard.edu/biopages/all.html

Harvard Biological Labs.
http://golgi.harvard.edu/homepage.genome

Harvard Biostatistics
http://biosun1.harvard.edu/

Harvard College of Pharmacy
http://golgi.harvard.edu/biopages/
kerouac.pharm.uky.edu/Default.html

Harvard Ctr. for Imaging and Pharmaceutical Research
http://cipr-diva.mgh.harvard.edu/

Harvard Radiology
http://count51.med.harvard.edu/BWH/
BWHRad.html

Harvard Evolution
http://golgi.harvard.edu/biopages/
evolution.html

Harvard Medical Ctr.
http://golgi.harvard.edu/www-
med.stanford.edu/MedCenter/welcome.html

Harvard Microbiology & Virology
http://golgi.harvard.edu/biopages/micro.html

Harvard Neurobiology
http://golgi.harvard.edu/biopages/neuro.html

Harvard Plant Biology
http://golgi.harvard.edu/biopages/botany.html

Hawkes Nest
http://www.ucalgary.ca/~rhawkes/

HBPLUS - Hydrogen Bond Calculator
http://128.40.46.10/pub/hbplus/home.html

Health & Medicine
http://nearnet.gnn.com/wic/med.toc.html

Health Resources
http://alpha.acast.nova.edu/medicine.html

HealthNet
http://debra.dgbt.doc.ca/~mike/home.html

HealthWeb
http://www.ghsl.nwu.edu/healthweb/

Herpetology Resources
http://xtal200.harvard.edu:8000/herp/

Historical Ctr. for the Health Sciences
http://http2.sils.umich.edu/HCHS/

History of Medicine Exhibits
http://www.nlm.nih.gov/hmd.dir/hmd.html

History of Science, Technology and
Medicine
http://coombs.anu.edu/SpecialProj/ASAP/
WWWVL-HSTM.html

HIV/AIDS information
http://vector.casti.com/QRD/.html/AIDS.html

Hopkins Bio-Informatics Home Page
http://www.gdb.org/hopkins.html

Human Genome Ctr. at LBL
http://www-hgc.lbl.gov/GenomeHome.html

Human Genome Ctr. at the Univ. of
Michigan
http://mendel.hgp.med.umich.edu/Home.html

Human Genome Map Search
http://www.cis.upenn.edu/~khart/form1.html

Human Genome Mapping Project
http://www.hgmp.mrc.ac.uk/

Human Genome Project Resources and
Meetings
http://gdbwww.gdb.org/gdbdoc/
genomic_links.html

Human Life
http://www.cen.uiuc.edu/~jj9544/4.html

ICGEB
http://base.icgeb.trieste.it/

Idaho State Univ. College of Pharmacy
http://pharmacy.isu.edu/welcome.html

IEHS Lab. of Molecular Biophysics
http://epr0.niehs.nih.gov/

Illinois Natural History Survey
http://www.inhs.uiuc.edu:70/

Image Processing and Analysis Group
http://noodle.med.yale.edu/

Information Ctr. for the Environment
http://ice.ucdavis.edu/

Insect Collection
http://iris.biosci.ohio-state.edu/inscoll.html

Institut fuer Molekulare Biotechnologie
http://www.imb-jena.de/

Institut fuer Pharmazeutische Technologie
http://www.tu-bs.de/pharmtech/pht.html

Institute for Health Informatics
http://www.ihi.aber.ac.uk/index.html

Institute of Biodiversity
http://www.inbio.ac.cr/

Integrated Botanical Information System
http://155.187.10.12/ibis/ibis-home.html

Integrated Genome Database
http://moulon.inra.fr:8001/acedb/igd.html

Interactive Frog Dissection
http://curry.edschool.virginia.edu/~insttech/
frog/

Internet/Bitnet Health Science Resources
http://kufacts.cc.ukans.edu/cwis/units/
medcntr/menu.html

Intl. Centre for Genetic Engineering and
Biotechnology
http://www.icgeb.trieste.it/

Intl. Institute of Genetics and Biophysics
http://sun01.iigb.na.cnr.it/

Intl. Organisation of Palaeobotany
http://sunrae.uel.ac.uk/palaeo/index.html

Intl. Organization for Plant Information
http://life.anu.edu.au/biodiversity/iopi/iopi.html

Introduction to ACEDB
http://www.caos.kun.nl/genomics/ACeDB.tut/
TOC.html

Iowa Entomology Server
http://www.public.iastate.edu/~entomology/

Iowa State College of Veterinary Medicine
http://www.iastate.edu/colleges/vetmed/
index.html

Jackson Lab.
http://www.jax.org/

Japan Animal Genome Database
http://ws4.niai.affrc.go.jp/jgbase2.html

Japanese Dairy Cattle Improvement
Program
http://ws4.niai.affrc.go.jp/dairy/dairy.html

JASON Project
http://seawifs.gsfc.nasa.gov/JASON/
JASON.html

Joel's Hierarchical Subject Index
http://www.cen.uiuc.edu/~jj9544/index.html

Johns Hopkins Univ. Bioinformatics
http://www.gdb.org/hopkins.html

Journal of Biomedical Optics
http://www.spie.org/web/journals/
webbiomed.html

La Jolla Cancer Research Foundation
http://192.231.106.66/

Lab. for Biological Informatics and
Theoretical Medicine
http://bitmed.ucsd.edu/

Landscape Ecology & Biogeography
http://life.anu.edu.au/landscape_ecology/
landscape.html

LANL Medical Data Analysis Projects
http://www.c3.lanl.gov/cic3/projects/Medical/
main.html

Larg*net
http://johns.largnet.uwo.ca/

Lateiner Dataspace
http://www.dataspace.com/

Lawrence Berkeley Lab.
http://www.lbl.gov/LBL.html

Leeds Dept. of Biochemistry and Molecular Biology
http://gps.leeds.ac.uk/bmb.html

Life Science Computing
http://ftp.cognet.ucla.edu/

LLNL Biology and Biotechnology Research Program
http://www-bio.llnl.gov/bbrp/
bbrp.homepage.html

Lynn Cooley Lab
http://info.med.yale.edu/cooley/index.html

Macquarie Univ.
http://www.bio.mq.edu.au/

Magnetic Resonance Imaging Group
http://www-mri.uta.edu/

Magnetic Resonance Technology for Basic Biological Research
http://bmrl.med.uiuc.edu:8080/

Maize Genome Project
http://teosinte.agron.missouri.edu/top.html

Major Histocompatibility Complex page
http://histo.cryst.bbk.ac.uk/

Manatee Information
http://www.satelnet.org/manatee/

Marine Biological Lab.
http://www.mbl.edu/

Markus Meister Lab
http://rhino.harvard.edu/

Mass Extinction Simulation
http://www.lassp.cornell.edu/newmme/
extinction.html

Massachusetts General Hospital
http://golgi.harvard.edu/biopages/
all.html#HMS

Master Gardener Information
http://leviathan.tamu.edu:70/1s/mg

Mathematical Biology Lab
http://www.ncifcrf.gov:2001/

Mayo Foundation Biomedical Imaging Resource
http://autobahn.mayo.edu/BIR_Welcome.html

McNally Lab at Washington University
http://tyrone.wustl.edu/~keith/intro.html

Meat Animal Research Ctr.
http://sol.marc.usda.gov/

Mechanistic Biology and Biotechnology Ctr.
http://www.anl.gov/CMB/cmb_welcome-
revs.html

Medical Imaging Links
http://agora.leeds.ac.uk/comir/resources/
links.html

Medical Physics
http://info.biomed.abdn.ac.uk/

MedLink
http://www.ls.se/medlink/

MedSearch America
http://www.medsearch.com:9001/

MEERC - Multiscale Experimental Ecosystem Research Ctr.
http://kabir.umd.edu/Welcome.html

Mendelian Inheritance in Man
http://gdbwww.gdb.org/omimdoc/
omimtop.html

Metabolic Pathways Charts
http://www.mcs.anl.gov/home/towell/
metabhome.html

Michigan State Entomology
http://esalsun10.ent.msu.edu/dept/main.html

Midwifery
http://www.csv.warwick.ac.uk:8000/
midwifery.html

Millipore On-line Catalog
http://www.gdb.org/Dan/catal/milli-intro.html

Miscellaneous Biomedical Information Archives
http://www.nlm.nih.gov/current_news.dir/
biomed.html

Mississippi State Univ. College of Veterinary Medicine
http://pegasus.cvm.msstate.edu/

Missouri Botanical Garden
http://straylight.tamu.edu/MoBot/
welcome.html

MIT Ctr. for Biological and Computational Learning
http://www.ai.mit.edu/projects/cbcl/web-homepage/web-homepage.html

MIT Ctr. for Genome Research at the Whitehead Institute
http://www-genome.wi.mit.edu/

Molecular Biophysics Lab
http://biop.ox.ac.uk/

Molecular Simulations
http://www.msi.com/

Molecular Virology
http://www.bocklabs.wisc.edu/

Molybdoenzyme Research Lab
http://www.nick.med.usf.edu/

Monash Medical Informatics
http://adrian.med.monash.edu.au/

Mouse Genome Database
http://www.informatics.jax.org/mgd.html

Mouse Locus Catalog
http://www.gdb.org/Dan/mouse/mlc.html

MultiMedia Medical Biochemistry Server
http://ubu.hahnemann.edu/

Multimedia Medical Textbooks
http://indy.radiology.uiowa.edu/
MultimediaTextbooks.html

Museum of Paleontology, Berkeley
http://ucmp1.berkeley.edu/

MycDB
http://kiev.physchem.kth.se/MycDB.html

Mycoplasma capricolum Genome Project
http://uranus.nchgr.nih.gov/myc.html

Nagoshi Lab
http://fly2.biology.uiowa.edu/

Nagoya Univ. School of Medicine
http://www.med.nagoya-u.ac.jp/

NASA Ames Biocomputation Ctr.
http://biocomp.arc.nasa.gov/

National Cancer Ctr.
http://www.ncc.go.jp/

National Ctr. for Biotechnology Information
http://www.ncbi.nlm.nih.gov/

National Ctr. for Genome Resources
http://www.ncgr.org/

National Environmental Information Service
http://www.cais.com/tne/neis/default.html

National Institute for Basic Biology
http://nibb1.nibb.ac.jp/

National Institute of Animal Industry
http://ws4.niai.affrc.go.jp/niai/NIAI.html

National Institute of Biodiversity
http://www.inbio.ac.cr/

National Institute of Environmental Health Sciences
http://www.niehs.nih.gov/Home.html

National Institute of Standards and Technology
http://www.nist.gov/

National Institutes of Health
http://www.nih.gov/

National Integrated Pest Mgmt. Information System
http://ipm_www.ncsu.edu/

National Library of Medicine (NLM)
http://www.nlm.nih.gov/

National Marine Fisheries Service
http://kingfish.ssp.nmfs.gov/home-page.html

National Science Foundation
http://www.nsf.gov/

National Toxicology Program
http://www.niehs.nih.gov/ntp/ntp.html

National Univ. of Singapore Biocomputing
http://biomed.nus.sg/

Natural History Museum
http://www.nhm.ac.uk/

NCSU College of Veterinary Medicine
http://www2.ncsu.edu/ncsu/cvm/
cvmhome.html

NCSU Entomology
http://ent2.ent.ncsu.edu/

NetBiochem
http://www.hahnemann.edu/Heme-Iron/
NetWelcome.html

NetVet — Veterinary Medicine
http://netvet.wustl.edu/

Neural Networks
http://www.cs.utexas.edu/~sirosh/nn.html

Neuro-Implant Program
http://he1.uns.tju.edu/~doctorb/bppp.html

Neuroscience Internet Resource Guide
http://http2.sils.umich.edu/Public/nirg/nirg1.html

NeuroScience Web Search
http://www.acsiom.org/nsr/neuro.html

NeuroWeb
http://salk.edu/

New England Biolabs
http://www.neb.com/

NIH Biomedical Resources
http://www.nlm.nih.gov/current_news.dir/biomed.html

NIH GenoBase Server
http://specter.dcrt.nih.gov:8004/

NIH Guide to Grants and Contracts
http://www.med.nyu.edu/nih-guide.html

NIH Health and Clinical Topics
http://www.nih.gov/health

NIH Molecular Biology Databases
http://www.nih.gov/molbio

NIH Molecular Modeling
http://www.nih.gov/molecular_modeling/mmhome.html

Northwest Fisheries Science Ctr.
http://listeria.nwfsc.noaa.gov/

Nottingham Arabidopsis Stock Centre
http://nasc.nott.ac.uk/

Nova Scotia Agricultural College
http://www.nsac.ns.ca/

Nova-Links
http://alpha.acast.nova.edu/start.html

NRL-3D
http://www.gdb.org/Dan/proteins/nrl3d.html

NYU Anesthesiology
http://gasnet.med.nyu.edu/index.html

NYU Biochemistry
http://www.med.nyu.edu/Biochem/HomePage.html

NYU Medical Ctr.
http://www.med.nyu.edu/HomePage.html

NYU Neurological Surgery
http://www.med.nyu.edu/NeuroSurgery/HomePage.html

Oak Ridge National Labs., Environmental Science
http://jupiter.esd.ornl.gov/

Ohio State College of Biological Sciences
http://hagar.biosci.ohio-state.edu/

Oklahoma State Univ. College of Veterinary Medicine
http://www.cvm.okstate.edu/

Oncogene Database
http://mbcr.bcm.tmc.edu:8080/oncogene.html

OncoLink
http://cancer.med.upenn.edu/

Organelle Genome Megasequencing Project
http://megasun.bch.umontreal.ca/welcome.html

OWL non-redundant protein sequence database
http://www.gdb.org/Dan/proteins/owl.html

Oxford Univ. Centre for Molecular Sciences
http://nmra.ocms.ox.ac.uk/

Oxford Univ. Lab. of Molecular Biology
http://biop.ox.ac.uk/

Oxford Univ. Plant Sciences
http://ifs.plants.ox.ac.uk/

P450 Containing Systems
http://www.icgeb.trieste.it/p450/

Pacific Northwest Lab. Medical Technology and Systems
http://www.emsl.pnl.gov:2080/docs/cie/MTS.html

Pacific Rim Biodiversity Catalog
http://ucmp1.berkeley.edu/pacrim.html

Palaeontology
http://nearnet.gnn.com/wic/palaeon.toc.html

Palo Alto Medical Foundation
http://www.service.com/PAMF/home.html

Palynology & palaeoclimatology
http://life.anu.edu.au/landscape_ecology/pollen.html

Pathology WWW Server
http://www.pathology.washington.edu/

Pathy for medical information
http://www.med.nagoya-u.ac.jp/pathy/
pathy.html

PCR Guide
http://bioinformatics.weizmann.ac.il:70/1s/
bioguide

Periodic Table of the Elements
http://143.167.43.25/chemistry/web-elements/
periodic-table.html

Periodical references to journals in the area
of molecular biology
http://nxoc01.cern.ch:8001/net.bio.net/
biology-journal-contents?

Pharmacy Server
http://157.142.72.77/

PHYLIP Documentation
http://www2.pasteur.fr/~tekaia/phylip.doc.html

Phylogenetic Tree Construction
http://www.mcs.anl.gov/summaries/
overbeek93/overbeek93.html

Physical Map of the Human Genome
http://ceph-genethon-map.genethon.fr/ceph-
genethon-map.html

Plant Disease Handbook
http://cygnus.tamu.edu/Texlab/tpdh.html

Plant Genome
http://probe.nalusda.gov:8000/plant/
index.html

Plant Genome WWW Server
http://probe.nalusda.gov:8000/index.html

Plant Pathology
http://resc9.res.bbsrc.ac.uk/plantpath/molbio/

Plant Pathology Dept. at Rothamsted
Experimental Station
http://resc9.res.bbsrc.ac.uk/plantpath/

Poisons Information Database
http://biomed.nus.sg/PID/PID.html

Polio and Post-Polio Resources
http://www.eskimo.com/~dempt/polio.html

Pollen Data
http://www.unlv.edu/CCHD/pollen/

Polyfiltronics - Microplate News
http://www.polyfiltronics.com/

Portable Dictionary of the Mouse Genome
http://mickey.utmem.edu/front.html

Positron Emission Tomography
http://pss023.psi.ch/

Primer on Molecular Genetics
http://www.gdb.org/Dan/DOE/intro.html

Principia Cybernetica
http://pespmc1.vub.ac.be/

Principles of Protein Structure
http://seqnet.dl.ac.uk:8000/vsns-pps/

PRODOM Protein Domain Server
http://www.sanger.ac.uk/~esr/prodom.html

Programs for Comparison and Recognition of Protein Structures
http://www-lmmb.ncifcrf.gov/~nicka/info.html

PROSITE protein pattern searches
http://www.embl-heidelberg.de/searches/
prosite.html

Protein Identification Resource
http://www.gdb.org/Dan/proteins/pir.html

Protein Science (peer-reviewed journal)
and the Proteins Society
http://www.prosci.uci.edu/

Protein Structure Group
http://www.yorvic.york.ac.uk/

Protist Image and Data Collection
http://megasun.bch.umontreal.ca/protists/
protists.html

Purdue Univ. Indianapolis Biology
http://www.biology.iupui.edu/

Queen's Univ.
http://biology.queensu.ca/

Quest 2D Protein Database
http://siva.cshl.org/index.html

Radiology Imaging Ctr.
http://visual-ra.swmed.edu/

Radiology Webserver
http://www.rad.washington.edu/

REBASE - restriction enzymes
http://nxoc01.cern.ch:8001/bio.vu.nl:9000/
rebase

Recherche en Sciences de la Vie et de la
Santé
http://www.rsvs.ulaval.ca/

Reference Library DataBase
http://gea.lif.icnet.uk/

Representation Models in Molecular
Graphics
http://scsg9.unige.ch/eng/toc.html

Rethinking AIDS
http://enuxsa.eas.asu.edu/~jvagner/

Rice Univ. Biochemistry and Cell Biology
http://helix.rice.edu/Bioch_info/

Rice Univ. Institute of Biosciences and Bioengineering
http://helix.rice.edu/Institute/

Rothamsted Experimental Station
http://resc9.res.bbsrc.ac.uk/

Royal (Dick) School of Veterinary Studies
http://www.vet.ed.ac.uk/

Royal Botanic Gardens
http://www.rbgkew.org.uk/

Royal Free Hospital of Medicine
http://www.rfhsm.ac.uk/

Royal Postgraduate Medical School
http://mpcc3.rpms.ac.uk/rpms_home.html

Saccharomyces (Yeast) Genome
http://genome-gopher.stanford.edu/

Salk Institute
http://salk.edu/

San Diego State Computational Biology
http://www.sdsc.edu/1/SDSC/Research/Comp_Bio

Sanger Centre
http://www.sanger.ac.uk/

Sci. Bio.Evolution Home Page
http://www.cqs.washington.edu/~evolution/

Science & Math Resources for Education
http://life.anu.edu.au/education.html

Science, Medicine, and Health Web Resources
http://www.main.com/dms/science-page.html

Scripps Research Institute
http://www.scripps.edu/

Selected Topics in General Virology
http://www.bocklabs.wisc.edu/Tutorial.html

SeqAnalRef
http://expasy.hcuge.ch/

SEQNET
http://www.dl.ac.uk/SEQNET/home.html

Sequence Annotation Server
http://dot.imgen.bcm.tmc.edu:9331/seq-annot/home.html

Smoky Mountain Field Station
http://www.ce.utk.edu/smokey.html

Society for Applied Spectroscopy
http://esther.la.asu.edu/sas/

Soil Science Web Server
http://saturn.soils.umn.edu/

South Florida Environmental Reader
http://envirolink.org/florida/

Southeastern Biological Science Ctr.
http://www.nfrcg.gov/

Stanford Medical Media and Information Technologies
summit.stanford.edu/welcome.html

Stanford Univ. Ctr. for Advanced Medical Informatics
http://camis.Stanford.EDU/

Sumeria
http://werple.apana.org.au/sumeria/

Swiss-2DPAGE
http://expasy.hcuge.ch/ch2d/ch2d-top.html

Swiss-3DIMAGE
http://expasy.hcuge.ch/pub/Graphics

SWISS-PROT Protein Sequence Database
http://www.ebi.ac.uk/ebi_docs/swissprot_db/swissprot.html

SwissProt
http://expasy.hcuge.ch/sprot/sprot-top.html

Symposium on Computer Aided Chemistry and Bioinformatics
http://www.caos.kun.nl/symposium/

TALARIA: Clinical Practice Guidelines for Cancer Pain
http://www.stat.washington.edu/

Tasmanian Parks & Wildlife Service
http://www.parks.tas.gov.au/tpws.html

Temple Univ.
http://astro.ocis.temple.edu/~myers

Temple Univ. Dept. of Physiology
http://astro.ocis.temple.edu/~roy/physio.html

Texas A&M Univ. Biology Herbarium
http://straylight.tamu.edu/tamu/biology/biology_herbarium.html

Texas A&M University - Biology Department
http://bio-www.tamu.edu/

Texas Extension Plant Pathologists
http://cygnus.tamu.edu/Texlab/people.html

Theoretical Biophysics Group
http://www.ks.uiuc.edu:1250/

Thomas Jefferson Univ.
http://www.tju.edu/

3D Image Reconstruction Information
http://biocomp.arc.nasa.gov/3dreconstruction

Timelines and Scales of Measurement List
http://cast0.ast.cam.ac.uk/Xray_www/niel/
scales.html

TraumAID
http://www.cis.upenn.edu/~traumaid/
home.html

Tree Physiology
http://sol.uvic.ca/treephys/

Tulane Medical Ctr.
http://www.mcl.tulane.edu/

Type Specimen and Other Catalogs
http://ucmp1.berkeley.edu/catalogs.html

U.S. Dept. of Health and Human Services
http://www.os.dhhs.gov/

U.S. National Science Foundation
http://stis.nsf.gov/

UC Davis College of Veterinary Medicine
http://vmgopher.ucdavis.edu/

UCLA Anesthesiology
http://hypnos.anes.ucla.edu/index.html

UCLA Biology
http://www.lifesci.ucla.edu/bio/

UCLA Biology Repository
http://lifesci.ucla.edu/repository/biology/

UCLA Chemistry and Biochemistry
http://www.chem.ucla.edu/dept/
Chemistry.html

UCLA Life Sciences
http://lifesci.ucla.edu/

UCSD Chemistry and Biochemistry
http://checfs1.ucsd.edu/

UFL Dept. of Anesthesiology
http://www.anest.ufl.edu/

UIUC School of Life Sciences
http://www.life.uiuc.edu/

UMDS
http://www.umds.ac.uk/

UMDS Medical Image Processing Group
http://nothung.umds.ac.uk/

UMich Genome Ctr.
http://www.hgp.med.umich.edu/Home.html

United States Geological Survey
http://info.er.usgs.gov/network/science/
biology/index.html

Univ. Berlin, Institut fuer Biochemie
http://www.chemie.fu-berlin.de/fb_chemie/ibc/
ibc_ag.html

Univ. of Bonn Medical Ctr.
http://imsdd.meb.uni-bonn.de/

Univ. of Cambridge School of Biological
Sciences
http://www.bio.cam.ac.uk/

Univ. of Colorado, Institute for Behavioral
Genetics
http://ibgwww.colorado.edu/

Univ. of Delaware
http://www.udel.edu/

Univ. of Florida Ctr. for Structural Biology
and Ctr. for Mammalian Genetics
http://ufthm.health.ufl.edu/

Univ of Florida Center for Structural
Biology
http://csbnmr.health.ufl.edu/

Univ. of Florida Microbiology and Cell
Science
http://micro.ifas.ufl.edu/

Univ. of Geneva (ExPASy)
http://expasy.hcuge.ch/

Univ. of Genoa, Ctr. for Biomedical and
Biophysical Technologies
http://citbb.unige.it/

Univ. of Georgia Dept. of Botany
http://dogwood.botany.uga.edu/

Univ. of Illinois College of Medicine
http://www.med.uiuc.edu/

Univ. of Indiana Ctr. for Innovative
Computer Applications
http://www.cica.indiana.edu/projects/Biology/
index.html

Univ. of Iowa
http://indy.radiology.uiowa.edu/

Univ. of Iowa, Radiation and Free Radical Biology
http://everest.radiology.uiowa.edu/~rad/radhome.html

Univ. of Kansas Medical Ctr.
http://kufacts.cc.ukans.edu/cwis/units/medcntr/library.html

Univ. of Minnesota Biomedical Engineering
http://pro.med.umn.edu/bmec/bmec.html

Univ. of Minnesota Medical School
http://lenti.med.umn.edu/

Univ. of Montreal
http://merck.bch.umontreal.ca/homepages/bchnet.html

Univ. of Nijmegen Laboratory for Biomaterials
http://www.kun.nl/biomat

Univ. of Oregon Biology Resources
http://darkwing.uoregon.edu/~tklassen/biohome/bio.html

Univ. of Pennsylvania
http://www.upenn.edu/

Univ. of Pennsylvania Bioengineering
http://www.seas.upenne.edu/be/behome.html

Univ. of Rochester Biophysics
http://www.urmc.rochester.edu/smd/biophys/index.htm

Univ. of Sheffield
http://143.167.43.25/

Univ. of Southampton Biomedical server
http://medstats.soton.ac.uk/

Univ. of Tennessee Biomedical Engineering
http://www.mecca.org/BME/bme-home.html

Univ. of Texas Southwestern Medical Ctr.
http://www.swmed.edu/

Univ. of Texas/Houston Dept. of Pathology
http://hyrax.med.uth.tmc.edu/

Univ. of Texas/Houston School of Public Health
http://utsph.sph.uth.tmc.edu/

Univ. of Vermont
http://www.uvm.edu/

Univ. of Washington Pathology
http://www.pathology.washington.edu/

Univ. of Washington Physiology/Biophysics
http://www.physiol.washington.edu/pbio/homepage.htm

Univ. of Wisconsin Computational Biology
http://www.cs.wisc.edu/~shavlik/uwcompbio.html

Univ. of Zürich Biocomputing and Modeling
http://www-bio.unizh.ch/xmosaic.home

Univ. Salzburg, Molekular Biology
http://www.gen.sbg.ac.at/info/internet/start.html

UPENN Chr22DB
http://www.cis.upenn.edu/~cbil/chr22db/chr22dbhome.html

UPENN Computational Biology and Informatics Lab.
http://www.cis.upenn.edu/~cbil/home.html

UPenn Medical Image Processing Group
http://mipgsun.mipg.upenn.edu/

USGS Biology
http://info.er.usgs.gov/network/science/biology/index.html

Utah State Dept. of Biology
http://www.biology.usu.edu/index.html

Vermont Entomology
http://nut.ento.vt.edu/

Victoria State Emergency Service
http://www.citri.edu.au/~jck/vicses/vicses.html

Victorian (Australia) Institute of Forensic Pathology
http://www.vifp.monash.edu.au/

Virginia Tech/Univ. of Maryland College of Veterinary Medicine
http://www.vetmed.vt.edu/

Virology
http://www.bocklabs.wisc.edu/Welcome.html

Virology — Big List of Links
http://www.tulane.edu/~dmsander/garryfavweb.html

Virtual Genome Ctr.
http://alces.med.umn.edu/VGC.html

Virtual Hospital
http://vh.radiology.uiowa.edu/

Virtual School of Natural Sciences
http://uu-gna.mit.edu:8001/uu-gna/schools/
vsns/index.html

Viruses
http://life.anu.edu.au/./viruses/virus.html

VISBL Laboratory, University of Chicago
http://http.bsd.uchicago.edu/visbl/

Vision & Robotics Group
http://www.cs.yale.edu/HTML/YALE/VISION/
GroupPR.html

Vrije Universiteit Brussel
http://dinf.vub.ac.be/sciences/dbio/
dbiohome.html

W.J. Freeman Lab
http://sulcus.berkeley.edu/

W.M. Keck Ctr. for Genome Informatics
http://keck.tamu.edu/ibt.html

Wageningen Agricultural Univ.
http://www.wau.nl/welcome.html

Walter Gilbert Lab
http://golgi.harvard.edu/gilbert.html

Warwick Dept. of Nursing
http://www.csv.warwick.ac.uk:8000/
default.html/

Washington U (St. Louis) Biomedical
Engineering
http://ibc.wustl.edu/

Washington Univ.
http://biogopher.wustl.edu/

Washington Univ. Institute for Biomedical
Computing
http://ibc.wustl.edu/

Webb Miller Lab Globin Server
http://globin.cse.psu.edu/

Weizmann Institute Bioinformatics
http://bioinformatics.weizmann.ac.il:70/

Welch Medical Library
http://www.welch.jhu.edu/

West Virginia School of Medicine
http://musom.mu.wvnet.edu/

Whitehead Institute for Biomedical
Research and MIT Ctr. for Genome
Research
http://www-genome.wi.mit.edu/

Whole Internet Catalog
http://nearnet.gnn.com/wic/
newrescat.toc.html

Wildlife & Fisheries Biology Dept.
http://www-wfb.ucdavis.edu/

Wisconsin Regional Primate Ctr. Research
Ctr.
http://www.primate.wisc.edu/

Worcester Foundation for Experimental
Biology
http://sci.wfeb.edu/

World Health Organization (WHO)
http://www.who.ch/

World Wide Web Journal of Biology
http://epress.com/w3jbio/

WWW in Biology
http://www.ch.embnet.org/bio-www/info.html

WWW Virtual Library of Biosciences
http://golgi.harvard.edu/biopages.html

Xenopus laevis page
http://timpwrmac.clh.icnet.uk/
xenopusintro.html

Yahoo Medicine Index
http://www.yahoo.com/Health/Medicine/

Yale Univ.
http://www.yale.edu/

Yale Univ. Ctr. for Medical Informatics
http://paella.med.yale.edu/

Yale Univ. Ctr. for Theoretical and Applied
Neuroscience
http://www.cs.yale.edu/HTML/YALE/CTAN/
FrontDoor.html

Young Scholars Page
http://davinci.vancouver.wsu.edu/omsi/
OMSIYS.html

Zebrafish Information Server
http://zebra.scarolina.edu/

Zebrafish Server
http://zfish.uoregon.edu/

Zimmer-Faust Lab
http://tbone.biol.scarolina.edu/

Molecular Biology

ALSBYTE Biotech Products
http://www.alsbyte.com/bio/

Australian National University - Molecular Biology
http://life.anu.edu.au/molbio.html

Biochemistry, Biophysics, and Molecular Biology Virtual Library
http://golgi.harvard.edu/biopages/biochem.html

BioMolecular Engineering Research Center
http://bmerc-www.bu.edu/

Biomolecular Engineering and Structural Biology
http://www.cryst.bbk.ac.uk/CEC/eupage.html

Cell Mechanics and Cellular Engineering
http://msrbsgi1.mc.duke.edu/~farsh/cv/cellmech.html

European Molecular Biology Laboratory (EMBL)
http://www.embl-heidelberg.de/

Göteborg Univ.
http://www.lundberg.gu.se/mol/mol-top.html

GTF-LAB
http://www.algonet.se/~gtflab/

Hopkins Bio-Informatics Home Page
http://www.gdb.org/hopkins.html

Macromolecular Biology Project at CRS4
http://www.crs4.it/~enzo/group_mbp.html

Mass General Hospital Molecular Biology
http://xanadu.mgh.harvard.edu/DMB_Home_Page.html

Meeting on Interconnection of Molecular Biology Databases
http://www.ai.sri.com/people/pkarp/mimbd.html

Molecular Biology Core Facilities / Dana-Farber Cancer Institute
http://mbcf.dfci.harvard.edu/

Molecular Biology Software Guide
http://www.public.iastate.edu/~pedro/research_tools.html

Molecular Biology Vector Sequence Database
http://biology.queensu.ca/~miseners/vector.html

Molecular Biology WWW Servers
http://www.genome.ad.jp/other_servers/other_servers.html

MWG-Biotech
http://www.mwgdna.com/biotech/

NIH Molecular Modeling
http://www.nih.gov/molecular_modeling/mmhome.html

Standards and definitions for molecular biology software
http://ibc.wustl.edu/standards/

Starting Points for Molecular Biology Scientists
http://www.gen.sbg.ac.at/info/internet/start.html

Univ. of Oregon Institute of Molecular Biology
http://darkwing.uoregon.edu/~jhaack/

Biochemistry

Aberdeen Univ, Biochemistry Graphics Room
http://www.biochem.abdn.ac.uk/

Biochemistry Bits
http://biop.ox.ac.uk/www/biochem.html

Biochemistry Lab. at KAIST
http://biochem.kaist.ac.kr/

Computational Biochemistry Research Group
http://cbrg.inf.ethz.ch/

Molecular Biophysics and Biochemistry
http://bmb.wustl.edu/

Purdue University department of Biochemistry
http://www.biochem.purdue.edu/

Royal Institute of Technology, Sweden
http://kiev.physchem.kth.se/

Synthetic Genetics
http://inetsol.com/syngen/

UCHC Molecular Biology and Biochemistry
http://panda.uchc.edu/~mbb/mbb.html

Univ. of Leeds
http://gps.leeds.ac.uk/bmb.html

Univ. of Toronto Biochemistry
http://bioinfo.med.utoronto.ca/biochemistry.html

Biology Publications Online

Annual Reviews Inc. Index
   http://www.ncifcrf.gov:2001/annRev.html

BINARY: Computing in Microbiology
   http://www.ftpt.br/cgi-bin/bioline/bi/

Biocomputing News
   http://beta.embnet.unibas.ch/basel/bcnews/
   default.html

Bioline Publications
   http://www.ftpt.br/cgi-bin/bioline/bioline

Biology & Medicine
   http://golgi.harvard.edu/biopages.html

Bionic
   http://nearnet.gnn.com/wic/molbio.05.html

Cold Spring Harbor Lab. Press
   http://www.cshl.org/about_cshl_press.html

Complexity Intl.
   http://life.anu.edu.au/ci/ci.html

Conservation Ecology
   http://journal.biology.carleton.ca/Jrnl./
   Overview.html

Drosophila Information Newsletter
   http://gopher.cic.net/11/e-serials/alphabetic/d/
   drosophila

Human Genome Newsletter (U.S. DOE)
   http://gopher.gdb.org/11/Genome/hgnews

More information on electronic journals
   http://journal.biology.carleton.ca/Jrnl./
   background/HotArticles.html

National Animal Genome Research
Program Newsletter
   http://probe.nalusda.gov:8000/animal/
   NAGRPnews/index.html

The Scientist
   http://ds.internic.net/11/pub/the-scientist

Tree Physiology
   http://sol.uvic.ca/treephys/Tree

World Health Organization Library Digest
   http://gopher.who.ch/11/.hlt/.digest

Chemistry

See also Biology & Biotechnology, Electronics & Electrical Engineering, Engineering, Energy, Medicine, Physics

Aberdeen Univ.
http://www.abdn.ac.uk/~che210/

Academia Sinica, Inst. of Chemistry
http://www.ch.sinica.edu.tw/

Akron Univ.
http://atlas.chemistry.uakron.edu:8080/

Alchemist's Den - Internet Resources for Organic Chemist
http://gpu.srv.ualberta.ca/~psgarbi/
psgarbi.html

American Chemical Society
http://www.acs.org/

American Peptide Society
http://www.chem.umn.edu/orgs/ampepsoc/
apshome.html

Applied Molecular Science (SOUKAN), IMS
http://solaris.ims.ac.jp/soukan.html

Aquapal
http://www.i-way.co.uk/~janthony/
aquapal.html

ARSoftware's Online Internet Catalog
http://arsoftware.arclch.com/

ASD
http://pluto.njcc.com/~bpapp/chempoin.html

Auburn Univ.
http://www.duc.auburn.edu/chemistry/
faculty_interests.html

Australian Chemicals Resources
http://www.vianet.net.au/~acted/

Beckman Instruments, Inc.
http://www.beckman.com/

Beilstein Info. System
http://www.beilstein.com/

BioChemNet
http://schmidel.com/teaching.htm

BioInorganic Chemistry Server
http://chemserv.bc.edu/Bioinorganic/
BioInorganic.html

Bioinorganic Chemistry Server
http://sbchm1.sunysb.edu/koch/biic.html

Biomolecular and Biosequence Databases
http://golgi.harvard.edu/sequences.html

BioSupplyNet
http://www.biosupplynet.com/bsn/

Biosym Technologies
http://www.biosym.com/

Birkbeck College, Univ. of London
http://www.bbk.ac.uk/

Birmingham Univ. School of Chemistry
http://chemwww.bham.ac.uk/
Chemistry_home.html

Boston College, Merkert Chemistry Center
http://chemserv.bc.edu/

Boston Univ.
http://chem.bu.edu/

Brazilian Chemical Society
http://www.sbq.org.br/

Brigham Young Univ.
http://nmra.byu.edu/welcome.html

Bristol Univ.
http://www.bristol.ac.uk/

Brookhaven National Lab
http://www.chemistry.bnl.gov/chemistry.html

Brown Univ.
http://www.chem.brown.edu/index.html

Bruker Analytische Messtechnik GmbH
http://www.bruker.de/Bruker.html

Budapest Univ. of Technology
http://www.fsz.bme.hu/bme/chemical/

Bullfrog
http://www-leland.stanford.edu/~lefig/index.html

Butler Univ.
http://www.butler.edu/www/chemistry

California State Univ. Fresno
http://129.8.104.30:8080/

California State Univ. Stanislaus
http://wwwchem.csustan.edu/

Caltech
http://www.caltech.edu/caltech/Chemistry.html

Calvin College Biochemistry
http://www.calvin.edu/~grayt/Chemistry_at_Calvin.html

Cambridge Crystallographic Data Centre
http://csdvx2.ccdc.cam.ac.uk/

Cambridge Scientific Computing, Inc.
http://www.camsci.com/

Cambridge Univ.
http://www.ch.cam.ac.uk/

CambridgeSoft Corp.
http://www.camsci.com/

Campinas State Univ.
http://www.iqm.unicamp.br/iqm.html

Canadian Society for Chemistry Organic Chemistry
http://www.chemistry.mcmaster.ca/csc/orgdiv/orgdiv.html

Canadian Society for Chemistry Surface Science Division
http://www.inrs-ener.uquebec.ca/surfsci/index.html

Carnegie Mellon Univ.
http://www.chem.cmu.edu/

Case Western Reserve Univ.
http://chemwww.cwru.edu/

Center for Molecular Design
http://wucmd.wustl.edu/

Center for Scientific Computing
http://www.csc.fi/lul/csc_chem.html

Chalmers Univ.
http://www.che.chalmers.se/

ChemFinder Searching
http://chemfinder.camsoft.com/

Chemical Abstracts Service
http://info.cas.org/welcome.html

Chemical Education Resources
http://www.cerlabs.com/chemlabs

Chemical Engineering Index
http://www.che.ufl.edu/WWW-CHE/index.html

Chemical Heritage Foundation
http://beckman1.sas.upenn.edu/index.htm

Chemical Industry Inst. of Toxicology
http://www.ciit.org/HOMEP/ciit.html

Chemical Marketing Online
http://www.chemon.com/

Chemical MIME Pro
http://chem.leeds.ac.uk/Project/MIME.html

Chemical On-line Presentations, Talks, and Workshops
http://www.ch.ic.ac.uk/talks/

Chemical Physics Preprint Database
http://www.chem.brown.edu/chem-ph.html

Chemical Reactions, Kinetics, and Dynamics Group
http://www-cst6.lanl.gov/

Chemical Resources in Italy
http://chpc06.ch.unito.it/chempointers_it.html

Chemical Society of Japan
http://www.syp.toppan.co.jp:8082/bcsjstart.html

Chemist's Art Gallery
http://www.csc.fi/lul/chem/graphics.html

Chemistry Associates
http://www.vicnet.net.au/~chemas/education.htm

Chemistry Hypermedia Project
http://www.chem.vt.edu/chem-ed/vt-chem-ed.html

Chemistry Principles
http://www.unm.edu/~dmclaugh/Principles.html

Chemistry Textbook Archive
http://www.umsl.edu/divisions/artscience/chemistry/books/welcome.html

Chemistry UK Internet resource Index from U-NET Limited
http://www.u-net.com/ukchem/

Chemistry WWW Virtual Library
http://www.chem.ucla.edu/chempointers.html

Chemists Address/Phone Book
http://hackberry.chem.niu.edu:70/0/ChemDir/index.html

ChemSearch Corp.
http://www.sonic.net/chemsearch

ChemSource
http://www.chemsource.com/

CNRS, Departement deSciences Chimiques
http://www.cpma.u-psud.fr/

Coatings Industry Alliance
http://www.coatings.org/cia/

Columbia Univ.
http://www.cc.columbia.edu/~chempub/

Computational Chemistry Center
http://derioc1.organik.uni-erlangen.de/

Computational Medicinal Chemistry Group
http://cmcind.far.ruu.nl/

Computer Ctr. Institute for Molecular Science (CCIMS)
http://ccinfo.ims.ac.jp/

Cornell Univ.
http://www.chem.cornell.edu/

Crystallography
http://www.unige.ch/crystal/crystal_index.html

CSIRO — Division of Chemicals & Polymers
http://www.chem.csiro.au/chempol.htm

Ctr. for Scientific Computing, Chemistry Server
http://www.csc.fi/lul/csc_chem.html

Czech Academy of Sciences, Inst. of Chemical Process Fundamentals
http://www.icpf.cas.cz/

Danish Chemical Society
http://www.ruc.dk/dis/chem/kemfor/kemfor.htm

Database of Conjugated Polymers
http://www.imc.uni-hannover.de/elektro/database-engl.html

Diamond Growth Research Group
http://www.hw.ac.uk/cheWWW/DIAMOND/group.html

Electrochemical Society, Inc.
http://www.electrochem.org/

Electronic Publishing and Chemical MIME
http://kaupp.chemie.uni-oldenburg.de/~haak/hyper/hypermoleculs.html

Enke Research Laboratory, Mass Spectrometry
http://enke.unm.edu/

European Chemical Society
http://ecs.tu-bs.de/ecs

European Federation for Medicinal Chemistry (EFMC)
http://sgich1.unifr.ch/EFMC.html

European Photochemistry Society
http://www.chemres.hu/EPA/homepage.html

Fisher Scientific, Internet Catalog
http://www.fisher1.com/

Geopolymer Institute
http://www.insset.u-picardie.fr/geopolymer/

German Virtual Library - Chemie
http://www.rz.uni-karlsruhe.de/Outerspace/VirtualLibrary/54.html

Global Instructional Chemistry Forum
http://www.ch.ic.ac.uk/GIC/

Hyperactive Molecules (Chemical MIME in action)
http://www.ch.ic.ac.uk/chemical_mime.html

Imperial College
http://www.ch.ic.ac.uk/

Indiana Univ. Purdue Univ. Indianapolis
http://chem.iupui.edu/homepage.html

Institute of Heavy Organic Synthesis (ICSO Poland)
http://193.59.2.1/

Institute of Physical and Theoretical Chemistry
http://pctc.chemie.uni-erlangen.de/

International Society of Heterocyclic Chemistry
http://euch6f.chem.emory.edu/ishc.html

Iowa General Chemistry Network: A FIPSE Project
http://www.public.iastate.edu/~fipse-chem/homepage.html

Journal of Biological Chemistry
http://www-jbc.stanford.edu/jbc/

Journal of Chemical Education:Software
http://jchemed.chem.wisc.edu/cheds.html

Katholieke Universiteit Leuven, Center for Surface Chemistry and Catalysis
http://134.58.73.250/ifc/interph.htm

Laboratory Equipment Exchange
http://www.magic.mb.ca/~econolab/

Laboratory for Magnetic Resonance
http://hawserv80.tamu.edu/hawhomepage/Haw1.html

LANL Inorganic Elemental Analysis Group
http://mwanal.lanl.gov/Group_Homepages/CST-8

Louisiana State Univ.
http://chrs1.chem.lsu.edu/

M A G N E T: Magnetic Resonance
http://atlas.chemistry.uakron.edu:8080/cdept.docs/nmrsites.html

Macquarie Univ
http://www.chem.mq.edu.au/

MacroModel Home Page
http://www.cc.columbia.edu/~chempub/mmod/mmod.html

Mass Spectrometry Laboratories
http://www.nd.edu/~dgriffit/MassSpec/masspec.html

Michigan Molecular Institute
http://www.miep.org/mmi/

Millipore On-Line Catalog
http://www.millipore.com/

MOLGEN
http://btm2xd.mat.uni-bayreuth.de/molgen/mghome.html

Multimedia Journal of Chemical Education
http://chemistry.uca.edu/mjce/

Nanotechnology on the WWW
http://www.arc.ab.ca/~morgan/Nano.html

Nanotechnology Page from Xerox PARC
http://nano.xerox.com/nano/

National Center for Supercomputing Applications, NCSA ChemViz Group
http://eads.ncsa.uiuc.edu/~datkins/

National Inst. of Chemistry in Ljubljana
http://www.ki.si/

National Institute of Health, Molecular Modeling Page
http://www.nih.gov/molecular_modeling/mmhome.html

National Inst. of Materials and Chemical Research
http://www.aist.go.jp/NIMC/

National Instruments (LabVIEW)
http://www.natinst.com/

NIST Chemistry WebBook
http://webbook.nist.gov/

North American Catalysis Society
http://www.dupont.com/nacs/

Ohio Supercomputer Ctr., Computational Chemistry List
http://www.osc.edu/chemistry.html

Oxford Molecular Group
http://www.oxmol.co.uk/

Pacific Northwest Laboratories, Environmental and Molecular Sciences Lab
http://www.emsl.pnl.gov:2080/

Polish Chemical Society
http://python.chem.uw.edu.pl/

Poly-Links
http://www.polymers.com/

PolyNet
http://www.cilea.it/polynet/

Process Associates of America
http://www.ProcessAssociates.com/

Radiation Research Journal
http://www.whitlock.com/kcj/science/radres/default.htm

Rensselaer Polytechnic Institute
http://www.rpi.edu/dept/chem/cheminfo/chemres.html

Representation of Molecular Models and Rendering Techniques
http://scsg9.unige.ch/eng/toc.html

Research Organics
http://resorg.com/

Rockefeller Univ. Physical Biochemistry
http://mriris.rockefeller.edu/

Royal Society of Chemistry
http://chemistry.rsc.org/rsc/

Scientific Instrument Services (SIS)
http://www.sisweb.com/

Sonochemistry Network page (Ultrasound in Chemistry)
http://www.dechema.de/englisch/fue/sonochem/pages/sono1.htm

Technical Ceramics References
http://www.ikts.fhg.de/ceramics.html

Technical Research Centre of Finland
http://www.vtt.fi/ket/kethome.html

Technical Univ. Dresden, Germany,
http://ctch03.chm.tu-dresden.de/

Tel Aviv Univ.
http://www.tau.ac.il/chemistry/

Theoretical Chemistry Postdoctoral Clearinghouse
http://www.chem.emory.edu/1/cheminfo

U. S. Occupational Safety and Health Administration
http://www.osha.gov/

Univ. College (UNSW) in Canberra
http://apamac.ch.adfa.oz.au/

Univ. of California Berkeley
http://www.cchem.berkeley.edu/index.html

Univ. of California Davis
http://www-chem.ucdavis.edu/

Univ. of California San Diego
http://checfs1.ucsd.edu/

Univ. of Durham
http://www.dur.ac.uk/~dch0www/index.html

Univ. of Groningen
http://www.chem.rug.nl/

Univ. of Korea
http://jschem.korea.ac.kr/

Univ. of Liverpool, Computers in Teaching Initiative (CTI) Centre for Chemistry
http://www.liv.ac.uk/ctichem.html

Univ. of Rhode Island
http://www.chm.uri.edu/index.html

Univ. of Sheffield
http://www2.shef.ac.uk/chemistry/chemistry-home.html

Univ. of Southern Mississippi, Polymer Science Research Ctr.
http://www.usm.edu/psrc/dps-menu.html

Univ. of Sussex
http://tcibm.mols.sussex.ac.uk/

Univ. of Zürich, Biocomputing and Molecular Modeling
http://www-bio.unizh.ch/xmosaic.html

Vienna Univ. of Technology, Institute of Analytical Chemistry
http://www.iac.tuwien.ac.at/

Virginia Tech
http://www.chem.vt.edu/

Water Resources
http://www.wco.com/~rteeter/waterlib.html

Web Chemistry Master Index
http://www.latrobe.edu.au/chejs/chem.html

WebElements Home Page
http://www.shef.ac.uk/uni/academic/A-C/chem/web-elements/web-elements-home.html

World Association of Theoretical Organic Chemists
http://www.ch.ic.ac.uk/watoc.html

World Wide Chemnet, Inc.
http://www.galstar.com/~chemnet/index.html

WWW Chemicals
http://soho.ios.com/~ilyak

X-ray and Mass Spectrometry
http://laue.chem.ncsu.edu/web/xray.welcome.html

Computer Science

See also Artificial Intelligence, Electronics & Electrical Engineering, Engineering, Imaging Technologies, Linguistics & Natural Language, Mathematics, Optics, Physics, Security, and Virtual Reality

ACM SIGGRAPH Online Bibliography Project
http://www.tu-graz.ac.at:2900/Csiggraphbib

ACM SIGMOD Information Server
http://bunny.cs.uiuc.edu/README.html

Ada Project - Resources for Women in Computing
http://www.cs.yale.edu/HTML/YALE/CS/HyPlans/tap/

Advanced Research Corp
http://info.arc.com/

AHPCRC
http://www.arc.umn.edu/html/ahpcrc.html

Alpha 7
http://www.ife.ee.ethz.ch/music/alpha/alpha.html

American Computer Scientists Association Inc. (ACSA)
http://www.acsa2000.net/

American Electronics Association
http://www.aeanet.org/

Aminet Amiga Archive
http://ftp.wustl.edu/~aminet/

Apple Computers
http://www.apple.com/

Apple Network
http://www.hsas.washington.edu/ANMA/ANMA.html

ARPA - Advanced Research Projects Agency
http://ftp.arpa.mil/

Association for Computational Linguistics (ACL)
http://www.cs.columbia.edu/~acl/HOME.HTML

Association for Computing Machinery - ACM
http://www.acm.org/

Association for Systems Management
http://www.infoanalytic.com/asm/

Association for Women in Computing
http://www.halcyon.com/monih/awc.html

Australian Computer Science Academics Database (ACSADB)
http://coral.cs.jcu.edu.au/acsadb/

Bar Ilan Univ.
http://www.cs.biu.ac.il8080/

Berkeley Systems Design, INC (BSD).
http://www.bsdi.com/

Berlin and Brandenburg CS Depts.
http://www.cs.tu-berlin.de/inf-bb/index.html

Bibliographies in BibTeX Format
http://www.ira.uka.de/ftp/ira/bibliography/index.html

Bilkent Univ.
http://www.cs.bilkent.edu.tr/

Boston Univ. Center
http://conx.bu.edu/CCS/ccs-home-page.html

Brigham Young Univ.
http://www.cs.byu.edu/homepage.html

British Computer Society
http://www.bcs.org.uk/

Brown Univ.
http://www.cs.brown.edu:8001/home-page.html

BSDI Europe
http://www.hillside.co.uk/

C++ Tutorial Textbook
http://info.desy.de/gna/html/cc/text/index.html

CalPoly
http://www.calpoly.edu/~acs/

CalTech College of Computing
http://www.ccsf.caltech.edu/ccsf.html

CalTech Computation and Neural Systems
http://www.cns.caltech.edu/

Carleton Univ.
http://www.sce.carleton.ca/

Carnegie-Mellon Software
http://www.sei.cmu.edu/FrontDoor.html

CCAE-Lisbon
http://www.inesc.pt/inesc/centros/ccae.html

CCD-Brookhaven
http://docserver.bnl.gov/com/www/
default.html

CCRC-Washington Univ.
http://dworkin.wustl.edu/

CCSR-Beckman
http://www.ccsr.uiuc.edu/CCSRHome.html

Center for Innovative Computer Applications
http://www.cica.indiana.edu/news/campus/
index.html

Center for Scientific Computing, Finland
http://www.csc.fi/

Center for Software Development
http://www.center.org/csd/home.html

Centre Universitaire d'Informatique
http://cui_www.unige.ch/

CERN
http://www1.cern.ch/

CERN Software Technology Interest Group
http://dxsting.cern.ch/sting/sting.html

Clemson Univ.
http://diogenes.cs.clemson.edu/CSE/.html

Colorado Center for Applied Parallel Processing
http://www.cs.colorado.edu/home/capp/
demo.html

Colorado Internet Cooperative Association
http://plaza.xor.com/coop/index.html

Colorado State Univ.
http://www.cs.colostate.edu/

Columbia Univ.
http://www.cs.columbia.edu/

Commodore 64 and 128
http://www.warwick.ac.uk/~stuce/c64.html

Computer Networks and Distributed Systems Research Lab
http://netweb.usc.edu/

Computer Science Bibliography Collection
http://liinwww.ira.uka.de/bibliography/
index.html

Computer Software Management and Information Ctr.
http://www.cosmic.uga.edu/

Computer Wave Newspaper E-Zine
http://computerwave.com/

Computer-Mediated Communications Archive
http://www.rpi.edu/~decemj/cmc/center.html

Concurrent Systems Lab
http://www.comlab.ox.ac.uk/archive/
concurrent.html

Cornell Univ.
http://www.cs.cornell.edu/

COSMIC Information
http://www.cosmic.uga.edu/

CPSR
http://www.cpsr.org/home

CPU Info Center
http://www.ncsa.uiuc.edu/General/
MetaCenter/MetaCenterHome.html

Cray Research
http://www.cray.com/

CREMISI
http://cremisi.rob.csata.it/

CRL-Japan
http://www.crl.go.jp/

CSHC-U of MD
http://wais.isr.umd.edu/CCDS/homepage.html

CSIRO / Flinders Joint Research Centre in Information
http://www.jrc.flinders.edu.au/

CSL-SRI
http://www.csl.sri.com/

CSP, Italy
http://services.csp.it/welcome.html

CWI
http://www.cwi.nl/default.html

Dartmouth College
http://www.cs.dartmouth.edu/

De Montfort Univ., Leicester, UK
http://www.cms.dmu.ac.uk/Research/

DoD HPC User's Group
http://www.fim.wpafb.af.mil/hpcug/hpcug.html

Duke Univ.
http://www.cs.duke.edu/home-page.html

ECRC GmbH, Germany.
http://www.ecrc.de/

ERCIM
http://www-ercim.inria.fr/

ERG-Aberdeen
http://www.erg.abdn.ac.uk/misc/personnel.html

Ethernet Homepage at U. Texas
http://mojo.ots.utexas.edu/ethernet/ethernet-home.html

European Computer-Industry Research
http://www.ecrc.de/

EWB: The Environment WorkBench
http://satori2.lerc.nasa.gov/DOC/EWB/ewbhome.html

Exeter Univ.
http://www.dcs.exeter.ac.uk/

EXUG
http://www.informatik.uni-dortmund.de/EXUG/EXUG.html

FIZ Karlsruhe
http://www.zblmath.fiz-karlsruhe.de/

Florida State Univ.
http://www.cs.fsu.edu/

Formal Methods Lab
http://www.comlab.ox.ac.uk/archive/formal-methods.html

Fortran 90 Repository
http://www.nag.co.uk/1/nagware/Examples

Fortran 90 Tutorials
http://asis01.cern.ch/CN/CNTUT/f90/Overview.html

Free On-line Dictionary of Computing
http://wombat.doc.ic.ac.uk/

Front Range UNIX Users' Group
http://plaza.xor.com/fruug/index.html

Georgia Tech Graphics, Visualization, and Usability Center
http://www.gatech.edu/gvu/gvutop.html

German National Research Center for Computer Science (GMD)
http://www.gmd.de/

"Grex" Open Computer Conference System.
http://pubweb.parc.xerox.com/

Harvard Univ.
http://das-www.harvard.edu/

HCRC-Edinburgh
http://www.cogsci.ed.ac.uk/hcrc/home.html

Helsinki Univ.
http://www.hut.fi/d_cs.html

High Performance Computing Sites and Resources Worldwide
http://www.nas.nasa.gov/RNR/Parallel/HPC-sites.html

ICBL-Edinburgh
http://www.icbl.hw.ac.uk/

IEE - Institution of Electrical Engineers
http://www.iee.org.uk/

IEEE - Institute of Electrical and Electronics Engineers
http://www.ieee.org/

IEEE Electromagnetic Compatibility Society
http://www.emclab.umr.edu/ieee_emc/

IHNS-Japan
http://www.glocom.ac.jp/IHNS/intro.html

IIASA-Austria
http://www.iiasa.ac.at/welcome.html

Index to Multimedia Information Sources
http://cui_www.unige.ch/OSG/MultimediaInfo/index.html

Indiana Univ.
http://www.cs.indiana.edu/

Info-Mac Hyperarchive
http://hyperarchive.lcs.mit.edu/HyperArchive.html

Information and Computation
http://theory.lcs.mit.edu/~iandc/

Information Science Research Inst.
http://www.isri.unlv.edu/

Institute for Advanced Computer Studies.
http://www.umiacs.umd.edu/

Integrated Computer Solutions
http://www.ics.com/

Intergraph Online
http://www.intergraph.com/

Internet Computer Index (ICI)
http://ici.proper.com/

Internet DTP Jumplist
http://www.cs.purdue.edu/homes/gwp/dtp/dtp.html

Iowa State Univ.
http://www.cs.iastate.edu/

IRIS-Brown
http://www.iris.brown.edu/iris

ISI-USC
http://www.isi.edu/

ISR
http://www.isr.umd.edu/

ISRI-UNLV
http://www.isri.unlv.edu/

ISS-Singapore
http://www.iss.nus.sg/

Johns Hopkins Univ.
http://www.cs.jhu.edu/

Kaman Sciences Data and Analysis Center
http://www.utica.kaman.com:8001/

Khoral Research Home
http://www.khoros.unm.edu/

Khoros Informatics
http://www.infc.ulst.ac.uk/local/khoros/

Khoros Model
http://cornea.mbvlab.wpafb.af.mil/khoros.html

Khoros Toolbox Development
http://www.c3.lanl.gov:1331/c3/projects/Khoros/main.html

KSL NRC, Canada.
http://ai.iit.nrc.ca/home_page.html

Lateiner Dataspace, USA.
http://www.dataspace.com/

Leiden Univ. - CS Department
http://www.wi.leidenuniv.nl/

Linux Documentation Project
http://sunsite.unc.edu/mdw/linux.html

LIT-Switzerland
http://litsun.epfl.ch/

LLNL
http://www-atp.llnl.gov/

Logic Programming
http://www.comlab.ox.ac.uk/archive/logic-prog.html

Lund Institute of Technology, Sweden
http://www.dna.lth.se/

Macintosh FAQs
http://www.astro.nwu.edu/lentz/mac/faqs/home-faqs.html

Mathematica World
http://www.vut.edu.au/MW/

MathSource - Resource for Mathematica
http://mathsource.wri.com/

Mathworks Home Page
http://www.mathworks.com/

Maui High Performance Computing Center
http://www.mhpcc.edu/mhpcc.html

McDonnell Douglas Aerospace
http://pat.mdc.com/

Microsoft Advanced Technology Div.
http://www.research.microsoft.com/

Mississippi State Univ.
http://www.cs.msstate.edu/dist_computing/mpi.html

Mississippi Univ.
http://www.mcsr.olemiss.edu/

MIT Laboratory for Computer Science
http://www.lcs.mit.edu/

MIT Telemedia, Networks and Systems Group
http://www.tns.lcs.mit.edu/tns-www-home.html

Mobile and Wireless Computing
http://snapple.cs.washington.edu:600/mobile/mobile_www.html

Monash Univ.
http://www.cs.monash.edu.au/

Multimedia Communications Research Lab
http://mango.genie.uottawa.ca/

NASA Ctr. for Computational Sciences
http://farside.gsfc.nasa.gov:80/NCCS/

NASA Digital Library Technology
http://farside.gsfc.nasa.gov:80/ISTO/DLT/

National Energy Research Supercomputer Center
http://www.nersc.gov/

National Institute for Management Technology (NIMT), Ireland.
http://www.nimt.rtc-cork.ie/nimt.htm

NCSA - National Center for Supercomputing Applications
http://www.ncsa.uiuc.edu/General/NCSAHome.html

NECTEC-Thailand
http://www.nectec.or.th/nectec.html

Net Guru Technologies Inc.
http://www.internet-is.com/netguru/

Netlib
http://www.netlib.org/

Network Computing Devices, Inc. (NCD)
http://www.ncd.com/

Newton Info Page
http://www.uth.tmc.edu/newton_info/

NeXT news and information
http://www1.cern.ch/CENeXT/Overview.html

North Carolina State Univ. ACS
http://www.acs.ncsu.edu/Sybase/Archive.html

Northeast Parallel Architectures Center (NPAC)
http://www.npac.syr.edu/

Novell European Support Center
http://ftp.novell.de/default.html

Novell Online Services
http://www.novell.com/

NPAC-Syracuse
http://minerva.npac.syr.edu/home.html

NRL-AITB
http://www.ait.nrl.navy.mil/home.html

Numerical Algorithms Group Ltd (NAG), UK
http://www.nag.co.uk/

Object-oriented Programming
http://www.clark.net/pub/howie/OO/oo_home.html

Ohio Supercomputer Center
http://www.osc.edu/welcome.html

Old Dominion Univ.
http://www.cs.odu.edu/index.html

OPTICS.ORG - The Photonics Resource Center
http://www.optics.org/

Oregon Graduate Institute
http://www.cse.ogi.edu/

Oxford Univ.
http://www.comlab.ox.ac.uk/

Paradigm Software
http://192.246.168.15/Paradigm.html

Paragon Manuals
http://www.ccsf.caltech.edu/paragon/man.html

Parallel Computing Meta FAQ
http://ivory.nosc.mil/~trancv/ppdir/PP-mFAQ.new.html

Parallel Tools Consortium
http://www.llnl.gov/ptools/ptools.html

Partnership in Advanced Computing Technologies (PACT), Bristol, UK.
http://www.pact.srf.ac.uk/

PERL - Practical Extraction and Report Language
http://www.cs.cmu.edu:8001/htbin/perl-man

Pitt SCC
http://pscinfo.psc.edu/

PowerPC News
http://power.globalnews.com:8000/

Princeton Univ.
http://www.cs.princeton.edu/

Programming Languages
http://src.doc.ic.ac.uk/bySubject/Computing/Languages.html

Programming Technology Lab
http://progwww.vub.ac.be/prog/home.html

Purdue Univ.
http://www.cs.purdue.edu/

QMS, Inc.
http://www.qms.com/

Quadralay
http://www.quadralay.com/home.html

RAND
http://www.rand.org/

RENATER-Paris
http://www.urec.fr/Renater/

Research Institute for Computing and
Information Systems
http://ricis.cl.uh.edu/

RICIS-Houston
http://rbse.jsc.nasa.gov/

Robert Lentz's Macintosh Resources
http://www.astro.nwu.edu/lentz/mac/home-
mac.html

Rochester Institute of Technology
http://www.cs.rochester.edu/

Rocky Mountain Internet Users' Group
http://plaza.xor.com/rmiug/index.html

Royal Institute of Technology, Stockholm
http://www.nada.kth.se/index-en.html

Rutherford Appleton Laboratory
http://web.inf.rl.ac.uk/

Safety-Critical Systems
http://www.comlab.ox.ac.uk/archive/
safety.html

San Diego Supercomputer Center
http://www.sdsc.edu/

Sandia National Lab
http://www.sandia.gov/

Scandal Supercomputing Project
http://parallel.scandal.cs.cmu.edu/www/

SCO Open Systems Software
http://www.uniforum.org/

Silicon Graphics (SGI).
http://www.sgi.com/

Society for Information Display
http://www.display.org/sid/

Software for MIMD Parallel Computers
http://www.ccsf.caltech.edu/software.html

SRC-Digital
http://www.research.digital.com/SRC/
home.html

SRI
http://www.csl.sri.com/

Stanford Center for Design Research
(CDR).
http://gummo.stanford.edu/

Stanford Center for Information
http://logic.stanford.edu/cit/cit.html

Stanford Univ. Knowledge Systems
http://www-ksl.stanford.edu/

SUN Microsystems
http://www.sun.com/

Sunergy
http://www.sun.com/sunergy/

Sunsite Northern Europe
http://src.doc.ic.ac.uk/public/aminet/info/www/
home-src.doc.html

Supercomputer Computations Research
Institute (SCRI), Florida, USA.
http://www.scri.fsu.edu/

Swarthmore College Computer Society
http://sccs.swarthmore.edu/

SymbolicNet
http://symbolicnet.mcs.kent.edu/

SYNERGY Project
http://argo.cis.temple.edu:4000/

Tandem Computers
http://www.tandem.com/

Technical Reports Master archive site
http://www.cs.indiana.edu/ucstri/sitelist.html

Technology Board of Trade (reusable
software)
http://www.service.com/tbot/

Technology Review
http://www.mit.edu:8001/afs/athena/org/t/
techreview/www/tr.html

TeX documentation
http://noa.huji.ac.il/tex/www/top.html

UMTK
http://www.cs.usm.my/utmk/utmkhome.htm

Unified Computer Science TR Index
http://cs.indiana.edu/cstr/search

United Technologies Research Center
http://utrcwww.utc.com/UTRC/General/
UTRCGen.html

Univ. of British Columbia
http://www.cs.ubc.ca/home

Univ. of California - Berkeley
http://http.cs.berkeley.edu/

Univ. of California - Santa Barbara
http://www.ece.ucsb.edu/

Univ. of Chile
http://www.dcc.uchile.cl/

Univ. of Colorado
http://www.cs.colorado.edu/

Univ. of Florida
http://www.cis.ufl.edu/

Univ. of Helsinki
http://www.cs.helsinki.fi/

Univ. of Illinois at Chicago
http://www.eecs.uic.edu/

Univ. of Illinois at Urbana-Champaign
http://www.cs.uiuc.edu/

Univ. of Iowa
http://www.cs.uiowa.edu/

Univ. of Iowa COMPS Lab
http://caesar.cs.uiowa.edu/

Univ. of Limerick
http://itdsrv1.ul.ie/CSIS/computer-science-info.html

Univ. of Manchester
http://www.cs.man.ac.uk/

Univ. of Manitoba
http://ftp.cs.umanitoba.ca/

Univ. of Maryland
http://gimble.cs.umd.edu/

Univ. of Maryland Baltimore County
http://www.cs.umbc.edu/

Univ. of Massachusetts Dartmouth
http://ciswww.cogsci.umassd.edu/welcome.html

Univ. of Missouri - Rolla
http://www.cs.umr.edu/

Univ. de Montréal (DIRO)
http://www.iro.umontreal.ca/

Univ. of Newcastle
http://catless.ncl.ac.uk/

Univ. of Nottingham
http://web.cs.nott.ac.uk/Papers/index.html

Univ. of Pisa
http://www.di.unipi.it/welcome.html

Univ. of S. Louisiana CACS
http://www.cacs.usl.edu/Departments/CACS/

Univ. of Salzburg
http://www.cosy.sbg.ac.at/welcome.html

Univ. of Saskatoon
http://alf.usask.ca/Home.html

Univ. of Southern California, Information Sciences Institute
http://www.isi.edu/

Univ. of Sydney, Basser
http://www.cs.su.oz.au/

Univ. of Tennessee
http://www.utcc.utk.edu/

Univ. of Texas - Austin
http://www.cs.utexas.edu/

Univ. of Texas - Neural Nets
http://www.cs.utexas.edu/~nn/

Univ. of Toronto
http://www.cdf.utoronto.ca/

Univ. of Tromso, Norway
http://www.cs.uit.no/en/

Univ. of Washington
http://www.cs.washington.edu/

Unix HENSA Archive (U. of Kent)
http://www.hensa.ac.uk/

Uppsala Univ., Sweden
http://www.csd.uu.se/

USENIX Association
http://www.usenix.org/

Virtual Software Library and Search Engine
http://www.fagg.uni-lj.si/cgi-bin/vsl-front

Women and Computer Science
http://www.ai.mit.edu/people/ellens/gender.html

Worcester Polytechnic
http://cs.wpi.edu/

X Consortium
http://www.x.org/

Xerox PARC
http://pubweb.parc.xerox.com/

Yahoo Computing Resources
http://www.yahoo.com/Science/Computer_Science/

Electronics & Electrical Engineering

See also Chemistry, Computer Science, Energy, Engineering, Imaging Technologies, Physics

Aalborg Univ.
http://www-i8.auc.dk

Aberdeen Univ.
http://www.erg.abdn.ac.uk/

AESF - American Electroplaters and Surface Finishers
http://www.finishing.com/AESF/index.html

(Almost) All Electrical Engineering Department Home Pages
http://www.ee.umr.edu/schools/ee_programs.html

American Chemical Society
http://www.acs.org

American Electronics Association
http://www.aeanet.org/

American Institute of Physics
http://aip.org/

American Physical Society
http://aps.org/

American Solar Energy Society
http://www.engr.wisc.edu/centers/sel/ases/ases2.html

American Vacuum Society
http://www.vacuum.org/

Argonne National Lab.
http://epics.aps.anl.gov/argonne.html

Arizona State Univ.
http://www.eas.asu.edu:7001/

APICS - The American Production and Inventory Control Society
http://www.industry.net/gif/o/prof-org/homeapic.htm

ARPA STARS Program
http://www.stars.ballston.paramax.com/index.html

Association for Computing Machinery
http://info.acm.org/

Association for Computing Machinery at UIUC
http://www.acm.uiuc.edu/

Aston Univ.
http://www.eeap.aston.ac.uk/home.html

AT&T Bell Labs. Research
http://www.research.att.com/

Audio Engineering Society
http://www.cudenver.edu/aes/index.html

BCS - British Computer Society
http://www.gold.net/bcs/

Bel Canto
http://math-www.uio.no/bel-canto/

Bilkent Univ. - EEE
http://manisa.ee.bilkent.edu.tr:2222/

Biofuels Information Network
http://www.esd.ornl.gov/BFDP/BFDPMOSAIC/binmenu.html

Bogazici Univ.
http://dec002.cmpe.boun.edu.tr/

Bottom Line Archive
http://www.oulu.fi/tbl.html

Bradley Univ.
http://cegt201.bradley.edu/

British Electrophoresis Society
http://sunspot.bioc.cam.ac.uk/BES.html

Broker at USC/ISI
http://drax.isi.edu:70/

Brookhaven National Lab.
http://suntid.bnl.gov:8080/bnl.html

BYU
http://www.ee.byu.edu/

California Polytechnic State Univ.
http://www.elee.calpoly.edu/

Caltech
http://www.micro.caltech.edu

Canadian Association of Physics
http://www.inrs-ener.uquebec.ca/surfsci/
index.html

Carleton Univ.
http://www.sce.carleton.ca/

Carnagie Mellon Univ.
http://www.ece.cmu.edu/

Catania Systems and Control Group
http://imdes02.dees.unict.it

CCDs for Material Scientists
http://zebu.uoregon.edu/ccd.html

Centro de Pesquisa e Desenvolvimento em
Engenharia Eletrica
http://www.cpdee.ufmg.br/

Chalmers Univ.
http://www.ce.chalmers.se/

Circuit Cellar INK
http://www.circellar.com/

Circuits and Systems Society
http://www.ee.gatech.edu/orgs/cas/

Circuit Theory Laboratory - HUT
http://picea.hut.fi

Clemson Univ.
http://www.eng.clemson.edu/~ECE/

Colorado State Univ.
http://www.lance.colostate.edu/ee/

Columbia CTR WWW
http://www.ctr.columbia.edu/
CUCTR_Home.html

Common LISP Hypermedia Server
http://www.ai.mit.edu/projects/iiip/doc/cl-http/
server.html

Community Computer Network Surveys
http://www.cs.washington.edu/research/
community-networks/

Components Packaging and Manufacturing
Technology
http://naftalab.bus.utexas.edu/ieee

Computer and Communication Companies
http://www-atp.llnl.gov/atp/companies.html

Computer and Network Security Index
http://www.tansu.com.au/Info/security.html

Computer Integrated Manufacturing at
Maryland
http://gimble.cs.umd.edu/cim/cim.html

Computer Sciences Tech Report Index (U.
Indiana)
http://cs.indiana.edu/cstr/search

Computer Security FAQ
http://www.cis.ohio-state.edu/hypertext/faq/
usenet/security-faq/faq.html

Computer Systems Lab, NTU, Taiwan
http://earth.csie.ntu.edu.tw/

Concordia Univ.
http://www.ece.concordia.ca/

Cornell Nanofabrication Facility (CNF)
http://www.nnf.cornell.edu/

Consulting-Specifying Engineer magazine
http://www.csemag.com/

Continuous Electron Beam Accelerator
Facility
http://www.cebaf.gov:3000/cebaf.html

Ctr. for Compound Semiconductor
Microelectronics
http://www.ccsm.uiuc.edu/micro/

Ctr. for Display Technology & Manufacturing
http://dtm.eecs.umich.edu/

Ctr. for Information Technology
http://logic.stanford.edu/cit/cit.html

Ctr. for Integrated Electronics - Rensselaer
Polytechnic Institute
http://hbt.cie.rpi.edu:1800/

Delft Univ. of Technology
http://www.twi.tudelft.nl/welcome.html

DesignNet
http://cdr.stanford.edu/html/SHARE/
DesignNet.html

Distributed ELectronic Telecommunications Archive (DELTA)
http://gozer.idbsu.edu/business/nethome.html

Distributed Multimedia Survey: Standards
http://cui_www.unige.ch/OSG/MultimediaInfo/
mmsurvey/standards.html

Duisburg Univ., Optoelectronics
http://optorisc.uni-duisburg.de/

Duke
http://www.ee.duke.edu/

ECCI
http://sass577.endo.sandia.gov/ecci/
white_paper.html

Edinburgh Univ.
http://www.ee.ed.ac.uk/

Edupage Newsletter
http://www.ee.surrey.ac.uk/edupage/

EE/CS Mother Site
http://www-soe.stanford.edu/soe/ieee/
eesites.html

EEB Home Page
http://www.eeb.ele.tue.nl/index.html

EE Circuits Archive
http://www.ee.washington.edu/eeca

EE Network Sites
http://engr-www.unl.edu/ee/eeshop/
netsites.html

Electric Power Research Institute
http://www.epri.com/

Electric Press, Inc.
http://www.elpress.com/homepage.html

Electrical Engineering Circuits Archive
http://weber.u.washington.edu/~pfloyd/ee/
index.html

Electrical Engineering on the WWW
http://www.e2w3.com/

Electrical Engineering Virtual Library
http://arioch.gsfc.nasa.gov/wwwvl/ee.html

Electricity Association
http://www.cityscape.co.uk/users/bm27/
index.htm

Electrochemical Society
http://www.electrochem.org/

Electronic Design Automation (EDA)
Standards Roadmap
http://www.cfi.org/roadmap/
roadmapHomePage.html

Electron Devices Society (EDS)
http://www.ece.neu.edu/eds/EDShome.html

Electronic Circuit Consulting and Design
http://www.mcnc.org/HTML/ETD/eccd.html

Electronic Circuit Design Group (EEB)
http://www.eeb.ele.tue.nl/

Electronic Design Magazine
http://www.ima.org/members/eee05.html

Electronic Engineering Times
http://techweb.cmp.com/eet

Electronic Industries Association
http://www.eia.org/norm.htm

Electronics Manufacturing Guide
http://www.circuitworld.com/

Electronic Materials Research
http://weber.u.washington.edu/~pearsall/

Electronic Resources Index
http://pasture.ecn.purdue.edu/~laird/
Electronics/index.html

Electronic Virtual Trade Show
http://www.vts.com

ElectroScience Lab.
http://hertz.eng.ohio-state.edu/

Electrotechnik
http://www.rz.uni-karlsruhe.de/Outerspace/
VirtualLibrary/621.3.html

EMC Gateway at SETH Corp.
http://www.sethcorp.com/

Employment in Engineering
http://www.wpi.edu/Academics/IMS/Library/
jobguide/engin.html

EMS Technologies, Inc.
http://www.elmg.com/

Energy Sciences Network
http://www.es.net/

Environmental Research Institute of
Michigan (ERIM)
http://www.erim.org/

European Circuit Society
http://www.it.dtu.dk/ecs/

FAQs for Electrical Engineering
http://www.e2w3.com/bin/gen_cat_idx.cgi/150

FAQ Link In List
http://www.paranoia.com/~filipg/HTML/LINK/
Fils_FAQ.html

Fermi National Accelerator Ctr.
http://fnnews.fnal.gov/

Finnish WWW servers
http://www.cs.hut.fi/finland.html

Fintronic Linux Systems Catalog
http://www.fintronic.com/linux/catalog.html

Florida State Univ.
http://ealpha1.eng.fsu.edu/ee.html

Formal Methods
http://www.comlab.ox.ac.uk/archive/formal-methods.html

Free Compilers List
http://cui_www.unige.ch/OSG/Langlist/Free/free-toc.html

Free Univ. of Brussels
http://pespmc1.vub.ac.be/VUBULB.html

George Mason Univ.
http://bass.gmu.edu/

Georgia Tech
http://www.ee.gatech.edu/

HCI Resources Page
http://www.ida.liu.se/labs/aslab/groups/um/hci/

Helsinki Univ. of Technology
http://www.hut.fi/d_ee.html

Helsinki Univ. of Technology Circuit Theory Lab
http://picea.hut.fi/

Heriot-Watt Univ.
http://www.cee.hw.ac.uk/

High Frequency Sites - All Over the World
http://www.hfs.e-technik.tu-muenchen.de/ext/d07/hf-sites.html

HobokenX
http://www.stevens-tech.edu/hobokenx/

HUT Circuit Theory Lab.
http://picea.hut.fi/

IEE - Institution of Electrical Engineers
http://www.iee.org.uk/

IEEE Aerospace and Electronic Systems Society
http://rsd1000.gatech.edu/public_html/bobt/AESS_Home_Page.html

IEEE - Institute of Electrical and Electronics Engineers
http://www.ieee.org/

IEEE Circuits and Systems Society
http://www.ee.gatech.edu/orgs/cas/

IEEE Consumer Electronics Society
http://www.ieee.org/ce/

IEEE Dielectrics and Electrical Insulation Society
http://www.eng.rpi.edu/dept/epe/WWW/DEIS

IEEE Electromagnetic Compatibility Society
http://www.emclab.umr.edu/ieee_emc/

IEEE Electron Devices Society
http://www.ieee.org/society/eds/

IEEE Instrumentation and Measurement Society
http://www.ieee.org/im/www-3s.htm

IEEE Power Electronics Society
http://www.ieee.org/society/pels

IEEE Solid-State Circuits Council/Society
http://www_sscc.eecg.toronto.edu/info/

IEEE Spectrum
http://www.spectrum.ieee.org/

IEEE Ultrasonics, Ferroelectrics and Frequency Control Society
http://www.ieee.org/society/uffc/

IKEDA lab.Chiba
http://www.hike.te.chiba-u.ac.jp/

Illinois Institute of Technology
http://www.ece.iit.edu/

Imperial College, London
http://www.ee.ic.ac.uk/

IDA - The Industrial Distribution Association
http://www.industry.net/gif/o/pmt-org/home-ida.htm

Information Processing Science
http://rieska.oulu.fi/

Information Systems in Austria
http://www.cosy.sbg.ac.at/directories/austria.html

Innovatronix Inc. Home Page
http://www.globe.com.ph/~tronix/

IPC - The Institute for Interconnecting and Packaging Electronic Circuits
http://www.ipc.org/

Institute for Technology Development
http://www.aue.com/ITD_info.html

Institute of Physics
http://www.iop.org/

ISO - International Standards Organization
http://www.iso.ch/welcome.html

Institute of Technology, Lund, Sweden.
http://www.elmat.lth.se/

Instituto de Engenharia de Sistemas
http://albertina.inesc.pt/

Intl. Commission on Illumination (CIE)
http://www.hike.te.chiba-u.ac.jp/ikeda/CIE/home.html

Intl. Computer Science Institute
http://http.icsi.berkeley.edu/

Intl. Electronics Reliability Institute
http://info.lut.ac.uk/departments/el/research/ieri/index.html

Intl. Electrotechnical Commission (IEC)
http://www.iec.ch/

Intl. Microwave Power Institute
http://www.impiweb.org

International Standards Organization (ISO)
http://www.iso.ch/

Intl. Teletimes — Biographies
http://www.wimsey.com/teletimes.root/biography.html

IRC in Polymer Science and Technology (Leeds)
http://irc.leeds.ac.uk/

ISDN Page
http://alumni.caltech.edu/~dank/isdn/

ISHM — The Microelectronics Society
http://www.ishm.ee.vt.edu/

ISU Computing and Information Services
http://www.ilstu.edu/

ITEA Southern Cross Chapter Home Page
http://130.220.64.152/iteahome.htm

Johns Hopkins Univ. Sensory Communications and Analog VLSI Laboratories
http://olympus.ece.jhu.edu/

JVC Service & Engineering
http://www.jvc-us.com/

KAIST
http://ee.kaist.ac.kr/

Kansas State Univ.
http://www.eece.ksu.edu/

King's College London
http://www.eee.kcl.ac.uk/

KTH Sweden
http://www.e.kth.se/home/elektro-home-eng.html

KU Leuven
http://www.esat.kuleuven.ac.be/

Kuhnke GmbH
http://www.cls.de/kuhnke/Welcome.html

Kuwait Univ.
http://burgan.eng.kuniv.edu.kw:8080/

Kyoto Univ. Info Science Lab
http://www.lab1.kuis.kyoto-u.ac.jp/

Kyushu Univ., Japan
http://www.ee.kyushu-u.ac.jp/index.html

Laboratory for EM Fields and Microwave
http://www.ifh.ee.ethz.ch/

Lamont-Doherty Earth Observatory Mosaic
http://www.ldeo.columbia.edu/

LANL Advanced Computing Lab.
http://www.acl.lanl.gov/Home.html

Laser WWW Information Server
http://www.law.indiana.edu/misc/laser.html

Launch Pad for UK Electronic Engineers
http://www.ibmpcug.co.uk/~sunrise/index.htm

Lawrence Berkeley Lab.
http://www.lbl.gov/LBL.html

Lawrence Livermore National Lab.
http://www.llnl.gov/

LESO-PB: Laboratoire d'Énergie Solaire et de Physique du Bâtiment
http://lesowww.epfl.ch/index.html

Lexicon of Semiconductor Terms
http://rel.semi.harris.com/docs/lexicon/

LLNL High Energy Physics Group
http://gem1.llnl.gov/

Lober & Walsh Engineering
http://www.lober-and-walsh.com/

Lockheed
http://hitchhiker.space.lockheed.com/aic/README.html

Los Alamos National Lab.
http://www.lanl.gov/

Lublin Technical Univ., Poland
http://volt.pol.lublin.pl/

Massana Ltd., Dublin, Ireland - ASIC design for DSP applications
http://www.massana.ie/

Materials Research Society (MRS)
http://www.mrs.org/

MBONE - an overview
http://www.cs.ucl.ac.uk/mice/mbone_review.html

MCC
http://epims1.gsfc.nasa.gov/MCC/MCC.html

McCann Electronics
http://www.mccann1.com/

McDonald Distributors
http://www.mcdonald.com/mcdonald/

MCNC Transfers Technolgy to Interpath
http://www.interpath.net/INTERPATH/Interpath.html

MDA - Houston
http://pat.mdc.com/

Measurement Science & Technology, NASA Langley Research
http://ndb1.larc.nasa.gov/

Michigan Technological Univ.
http://www.ee.mtu.edu/

Microelectronics Research Ctr.
http://www.mrc.uidaho.edu/

Microsensor & Actuator Technology (MAT) Berlin
http://www-mat.ee.tu-berlin.de/

Microwave Journal
http://www.mwjournal.com/mwj.html

Mississippi State Univ.
http://www.ee.msstate.edu/

MIT - Research Laboratory of Electronics
http://rleweb.mit.edu/

Monash Univ.
http://www.cs.monash.edu.au/

MTL Instruments Group plc
http://www.mtl-inst.com/

Multimedia Information Sources Index
http://cui_www.unige.ch/OSG/MultimediaInfo/index.html

NASA EEE Links
http://arioch.gsfc.nasa.gov/eee_links/eeeintro.html

Newton's International Electrical Journal
http://www.polarnet.com/users/GNewton/newt.htm

N.R.C. Canada Autonomous Systems Lab
http://autsrv.iitsg.nrc.ca/choice.html

Nagoya Univ. - Bio-Electronics Lab
http://www.bioele.nuee.nagoya-u.ac.jp/

Nanoelectronics Lab, Univ. of Cincinnati
http://www.eng.uc.edu/nano/nanohome.html

Nanotechnology TechnoLinks
http://kappa.iis.u-tokyo.ac.jp/~fasol/qutechnolinks.html

NASA/Goddard Space Flight Ctr.
http://hypatia.gsfc.nasa.gov/GSFC_homepage.html

National Microelectronics Research Centre
http://nmrc.ucc.ie/

National Nanofabrication Users' Network
http://www.ece.ucsb.edu/department/centers/nnun.html

National Technical Univ. of Athens
http://www.ntua.gr/

NAVE Navigating and Acting in Virtual Environments (virtual reality, spatial sound, CU Boulder)
http://www.cs.colorado.edu/homes/cboyd/public_html/Home.html

Network Nation Revisited
http://www.stevens-tech.edu/~dbelson/thesis/thesis.html

New Mexico State Univ.
http://pslwww.nmsu.edu/Welcome.html

New Mexico Tech - EE/Physics
http://www.ee.nmt.edu/

North Carolina State Univ.
http://www.ece.ncsu.edu/

Northwestern Univ.
http://www.eecs.nwu.edu/

NSF SUCCEED Engineering Visual Database
http://succeed.edtech.vt.edu/

NTUA WWW Server - SoftLab
http://www.ntua.gr/

Numerix - DSP Solutions
http://www.compulink.co.uk/~numerix/

Oak Ridge National Lab.
http://jupiter.esd.ornl.gov/

OCEAN Users Manual
http://olt.et.tudelft.nl/usr1/patrick/public_html/
docs/wwman/wwman.html

Ocean Sea-of-Gates Design System
http://olt.et.tudelft.nl/ocean/ocean.html

Ohio State ElectroScience Laboratory
http://hertz.eng.ohio-state.edu/

OPTICS.ORG - The Photonics Resource
Center
http://www.optics.org/

Oregon State Univ.
http://www.ece.orst.edu/

Pacific Northwest Lab.
http://romana.crystal.pnl.gov/pnl.html

Parallel Computing Archive at HENSA/
Unix
http://www.hensa.ac.uk/parallel/

Philadelphia IEEE Consultants' Network
http://www.ece.vill.edu:80/conet/

Pioneer Global Home Page
http://www.pn.com/

PNL Medical Technology and Systems
Initiative
http://www.emsl.pnl.gov:2080/docs/cie/
MTS.html

Politechnika Gdanska - Electronics
http://www.gumbeers.elka.pg.gda.pl/

Project Mgmt Software Reviews
http://www.wst.com/projplan/proj-
plan.reviews.html

Purdue Univ.
http://dynamo.ecn.purdue.edu/

Quadralay Cryptography Archive
http://www.quadralay.com/www/Crypt/
Crypt.html

Radiology Imaging Research Ctr., UT
Southwestern
http://visual-ra.swmed.edu/

Raven Systems Home Page
http://eskinews.eskimo.com/~ravensys/

Reliability Engineering
http://rel.semi.harris.com/

Rensselaer Polytechnic Univ.
http://ecse.rpi.edu/

Risk-Related research at LBL
http://www.lbl.gov/LBL-Programs/Risk-
Research.html

Robotech HazHandler
http://www.arc.ab.ca/robotech/

Rockwell Network Systems
http://www.rns.com/rockwell/about.html

Royal Institute of Technology, Kista,
Sweden, Teleinformatics
http://www.it.kth.se/

RSNA Electrical Journal
http://ej.rsna.org/

Ruhr-Universitaet Bochum Elektrische
Steuerung und Regelung
http://www.esr.ruhr-uni-bochum.de/

Russian and East European Studies
Resources
http://www.pitt.edu/~cjp/rstech.html

Safety-Critical Systems
http://www.comlab.ox.ac.uk/archive/
safety.html

Sandia National Lab.
http://www.cs.sandia.gov/pub/WWW/
Sandia_home_page.html

Santa Clara Univ.
http://pcsel10.scu.edu/coen

SEAS
http://www.cc.saga-u.ac.jp/saga-u/riko/ee/
ee.html

SEMATECH
http://www.sematech.org/

Semiconductor Equipment and Materials
International (SEMI)
http://www.semi.org

Semiconductor Subway
http://www-mtl.mit.edu/semisubway.html

SemiWeb
http://www.semiweb.com

Sendai Univ. Information Engineering
http://infodm.info.sendai-ct.ac.jp/

Signal Processing Information Base (SPIB)
http://spib.rice.edu/spib.html

SMTA - Surface Mount Technology Association

http://www.smta.org

Society for Information Display (SID)
http://www.display.org/sid/

Solid-State Technology Magazine
http://www.solid-state.com/

SonicPRO Home Page
http://www.human.com/sonic/sonic.html

Southern Methodist Univ.
http://www.seas.smu.edu/ee.html

Space Electronics Research Group
http://www.vuse.vanderbilt.edu/~pagey/serg/serg.html

Space Environment Effects Branch
http://satori2.lerc.nasa.gov/

SPIE — The Intl. Society for Optical Engineering
http://www.spie.org/

SRI-CSL-FM
http://www.csl.sri.com/sri-csl-fm.html

SSC Home Page
http://pdsppi.igpp.ucla.edu/ssc/Welcome.html

St. Cloud State Univ.
http://condor.stcloud.msus.edu/ee/index.html

Stanford Linear Accelerator Ctr.
http://slacvm.slac.stanford.edu/FIND/SLAC.HTML

Stanford Univ.
http://www.stanford.edu/

Stanford Univ. Information Systems Laboratory
http://www-isl.stanford.edu/

STO's Internet Patent Search System
http://sunsite.unc.edu/patents/intropat.html

Stony Brook
http://www.sunysb.edu/

Subjective Electronic Information Repository
http://cbl.leeds.ac.uk/nikos/doc/repository.html

Superconducting Super Collider
http://www.ssc.gov/

Swansea
http://faith.swan.ac.uk/chris.html/DeptEEE/eeehome.html

Swiss Federal Institute of Technology, Zurich - Electrical Engineering
http://www.ee.ethz.ch/

TCAD
http://www-ee.stanford.edu/tcad.html

Technical Data Services Searchable Database
http://www.tds-net.com

Technical Reports, Preprints and Abstracts - NASA LaRC Technical Library
http://www.larc.nasa.gov/org/library/abs-tr.html

Technical Univ. of Berlin - High Voltage and Power Engineering
http://IHS.ee.TU-Berlin.DE/

Technical Univ. of Budapest
http://www.fsz.bme.hu/bme/bme.html

Technical Univ. of Delft, Netherlands
http://muresh.et.tudelft.nl/

Technical Univ. of Dresden
http://eietu2.et.tu-dresden.de/ET-en.html

Technical Univ. of Szczecin, Poland
http://www.tuniv.szczecin.pl/electric.html

Telecommunications Library
http://www.wiltel.com/library/library.html

Telemedia, Networks, and Systems
http://tns-www.lcs.mit.edu/tns-www-home.html

Temple Univ.
http://opus.eng.temple.edu/

Texas A&M Energy Systems Lab
http://www-esl.tamu.edu/

Texas A&M Univ.
http://eesun1.tamu.edu/

Thant's Animations Index
http://mambo.ucsc.edu/psl/thant/thant.html

Therma-Wave, Inc.
http://www.thermawave.com/

Trinity College Dublin
http://www.tcd.ie/

Tufts Univ.
http://www.cs.tufts.edu/

UC Berkeley
http://www.ece.ucsb.edu/

UC Davis
http://www.ece.ucdavis.edu/

UC Los Angeles
http://www.ee.ucla.edu/

UC San Diego
http://ece.ucsd.edu/

UC Santa Barbara
http://www.ece.ucsb.edu/

UCL - Microelectronics Laboratory
http://www.dice.ucl.ac.be/lab.html

UIUC EE
http://www.ece.uiuc.edu/

UIUC Photonic Systems Group
http://www.phs.uiuc.edu/

UK Solar Energy Society
http://sun1.bham.ac.uk/thorntme/

UMR
http://www.ee.umr.edu/

Union College
http://dragon.union.edu/

United Technologies Research Ctr.
http://utrcwww.utc.com/UTRC/General/
UTRCGen.html

Univ.of Arizona
http://www.ece.arizona.edu/

Univ. of Adelaide
http://www.eleceng.adelaide.edu.au/

Univ. of Alabama at Huntsville
http://eb-p5.eb.uah.edu/ece/ecehome.html

Univ. of Alberta
http://nyquist.ee.ualberta.ca/

Univ. of California Society of Electrical
Engineers
http://ucsee.EECS.Berkeley.EDU/index.html

Univ. of Calgary
http://www.enel.ucalgary.ca/Welcome.html

Univ. of Cape Town
http://www.ee.uct.ac.za/

Univ. of Cincinnati
http://www.cas.uc.edu/

Univ. of Cincinnati Nanolab
http://uceng.uc.edu/ece/Nano/
Nanohome.html

Univ. of Connecticut
http://www.eng2.uconn.edu/ese/

Univ. College Cork
http://www.ucc.ie/ucc/depts/elec/elec-
home.html

Univ. of Evansville
http://uenics.evansville.edu/eecs.html

Univ. of Florida
http://www.eel.ufl.edu/

Univ. of Ghent
http://www.elis.rug.ac.be/

Univ. of Hawaii
http://www.eng.hawaii.edu/UHCOEhome.html

Univ. of Hawaii at Manoa
http://spectra.eng.hawaii.edu/

Univ. of Iowa Virtual Hospital
http://indy.radiology.uiowa.edu/
VirtualHospital.html

Univ. Kaiserslautern
http://www.uni-kl.de/

Univ. of Kansas
http://www.tisl.ukans.edu/EECS/EECS.html

Univ. of Kansas TISL
http://www.tisl.ukans.edu/TISL-Home.html

Univ. of Karlsruhe Institute of Computer
Design and Fault Tolerance
http://goethe.ira.uka.de/

Univ. of Laval
http://www.gel.ulaval.ca/

Univ. of Manitoba
http://www.ee.umanitoba.ca/

Univ. of Manitoba - High Voltage Power
Transmission Research Laboratory
http://www.ee.umanitoba.ca/Groups/
highvolt.html

Univ. of Maribor, Slovenia
http://www.uni-mb.si/

Univ. of Maryland at College Park
http://www.ee.umd.edu/

Univ. of Maryland Baltimore County
http://www.engr.umbc.edu/~itl/ee.html

Univ. of Maryland Baltimore County
http://www.engr.umbc.edu/~itl/ee.html

Univ. of Massachusetts - Lowell
http://www.uml.edu/Dept/EE/

Univ. of Massachusetts Lab. for Perceptual Robotics
http://piglet.cs.umass.edu:4321/lpr.html

Univ. of Memphis
http://lear.csp.ee.memphis.edu/

Univ. of Michigan
http://www.eecs.umich.edu/

Univ. de Nantes - IRESTE
http://ireste.ireste.fr/

Univ. of Nebraska
http://engr-www.unl.edu/ee/

Univ. of Nebraska-Lincoln
http://www.engr.unl.edu/ee/

Univ. of Neuchatel Institute of Microtechnology
http://www-imt.unine.ch/

Univ. of New Hampshire
http://www.ece.unh.edu/

Univ. of Nottingham
http://www.nott.ac.uk/

Univ. of Oulu, Finland
http://ee.oulu.fi/EE/
Electrical.Engineering.html

Univ. of Padova
http://www.dei.unipd.it/

Univ. of Reading
http://www.elec.rdg.ac.uk/

Univ. of Rhode Island
http://www.ele.uri.edu/

Univ. College Salford
http://www.ucsalf.ac.uk/~bens/eleclink.htm

Univ. of South Carolina
http://www.ece.sc.edu/

Univ. of Southern California
http://www.engr.scarolina.edu/

Univ. of Surrey
http://www.ee.surrey.ac.uk/

Univ. of Technology, Sydney
http://www.ee.uts.edu.au/eeo/eeo.html

Univ. of Texas at Arlington
http://www-ee.uta.edu/

Univ. of Texas El Paso
http://cs.utep.edu/csdept/../engg/eeeng.html

Univ. of the Witwatersrand, Johannesburg
http://www-eng.wits.ac.za/elec/elec.html

Univ. of Tokyo
http://www.ee.t.u-tokyo.ac.jp/

Univ. of Toronto
http://www.eecg.toronto.edu/

Univ. of Twente
http://utelicehp4.el.utwente.nl/

Univ. del Valle
http://maxwell.univalle.edu.co/

Univ. of Victoria
http://www-ece.uvic.ca/

Univ. of Virginia
http://www.ee.virginia.edu/

Univ. of Washington
http://www.ee.washington.edu/

Univ. of Westminster
http://www.wmin.ac.uk/CMSA/welcome.html

Univ. of Wisconsin - Madison ANS Student Chapter
http://trans4.neep.wisc.edu/ANS/

Univ. of Wyoming
http://wwweng.uwyo.edu/

User Society for Electronic Design Automation
http://www.useda.org/useda/

UTS
http://www.uts.edu.au/home.html

Vanderbilt - Space Electronics Research Group
http://www.vuse.vanderbilt.edu/~pagey/serg/serg.html

VLSI at UC Florida
http://www.tcad.ee.ufl.edu/

VLSI at Univ. Laval
http://www.gel.ulaval.ca/~vision/vlsi/vlsi.html

VLSI Design Lab
http://www.vlsi.concordia.ca/

VLSI at Harvard
http://atlantis.harvard.edu/

VLSI Systems Lab — KAIST
http://pansori.kaist.ac.kr/

W3EAX - Univ. of Maryland
http://w3eax.umd.edu/w3eax.html

Warsaw Univ. of Technology
http://www.iem.pw.edu.pl/

Washington State Univ.
http://www.eecs.wsu.edu/

Weather & global monitoring
http://life.anu.edu.au/weather.html

West Virginia Univ. - Concurrent Engineering Research Ctr.
http://www.cerc.wvu.edu/

WilTel
http://www.wiltel.com/

Yahoo Electrical Engineering Index
http://www.yahoo.com/Science/Engineering/Electrical_Engineering/

Yale Univ. Image Processing and Analysis
http://noodle.med.yale.edu/

Energy

See also Chemistry, Electronics &
Electrical Engineering, Engineering, Physics

Advanced Research Projects Agency -
Electric & Hybrid Vehicle Data Center
http://www.ev.hawaii.edu/

AE-Guide
http://solstice.crest.org/online/aeguide/
aehome.html

Aerometric Information Retrieval System
http://www.epa.gov/docs/airs/airs.html

Air Infiltration and Ventilation Center
http://www.demon.co.uk/aivc

Air Resources Board
http://www.cahwnet.gov/epa/arb.htm

Alan Glennon's Geyser Page
http://www.wku.edu:80/~glennja/pages/
geyser.html

Alternative Fuels Data Center
http://www.afdc.nrel.gov

American Council for an Energy Efficient
Economy
http://solstice.crest.org:80/efficiency/aceee/
index.html

American Nuclear Society
http://www.ans.org

American Society of Engineering Technology
http://pegasus.cc.ucf.edu/~aset/

American Solar Energy Society
http://www.engr.wisc.edu/centers/sel/ases/
ases2.html

American Wind Energy Association
(AWEA)
http://www.igc.apc.org/awea/

Argonne National Laboratory
http://www.anl.gov

ARI's CoolNet — Air-Conditioning and
Refrigeration Inst.
http://www.ari.org

Army Profiler Research Facility, White
Sands Missile Range
http://aprf.arl.mil/aprf.html

Association of Energy Services Professionals
http://www.dnai.com:80/AESP/

Biofuels Information Network
http://www.esd.ornl.gov/BFDP/
BFDPMOSAIC/binmenu.html

Biomass Archive, NCSR, Greece
http://www.ariadne-t.gr/phaethon/biomass/
bresource.html

Biomass Energy Alliance
http://www.biomass.org/biomass/

Biomass Resource Information Clearinghouse
http://asd.nrel.gov/projects/rredc/data/
biomass

BioTools — Useful sites for Biomass and
Biomass Energy compiled by T.R. Miles,
Consulting Engineer
http://www.teleport.com/~tmiles/biotools.htm

Bonneville Power Administration
http://www.bpa.gov/

BRIDGE — British Mid Ocean Ridge
Initiative
http://www.nwo.ac.uk/iosdl/Rennell/Bridge/

Brookhaven National Laboratory
http://www.bnl.gov/bnl.html

Building Industry Exchange Foundation
http://www.building.com/bix/

CADDET — Centre for the Analysis and
Dissemination of Demonstrated Energy
Technologies
http://www.ornl.gov/CADDET/caddet.html

California Energy Commission
http://www.energy.ca.gov/energy/
homepage.html

California Energy Commission's Agricultural Energy Assistance Program
http://www.sarep.ucdavis.edu/aeap

California Environmental Resources Evaluation System
http://www.ceres.ca.gov/

California Inst. for Energy Efficiency
http://eande.lbl.gov/CIEE/ciee_homepage.html

California's Natural Resources
http://www.ceres.ca.gov/ceres/calweb/Natural_Resources.html

CALSTART — California's Advanced Transportation Consortium
http://www.dnai.com/~jandro/calstart.html

Canada's Dept. of Natural Resources Energy Sector
http://es1.es.emr.ca/

Centre for Alternative Technology - Wales, U.K.
http://www.foe.co.uk:80/CAT/

Centre for Alternative Transportation Fuels — BC Research Inc.
http://www.bcr.bc.ca/catf/default.htm

Centre d'Energetique
http://www-cenerg.cma.fr/

Center for Renewable Energy and Sustainable Technology
http://solstice.crest.org/

Central European Environmental Expert Database
http://www.cedar.univie.ac.at/data/ceed/

Chrysler Corporation - Info on Alternative Fuels
http://www.chryslercorp.com/environment/alternative_fuels.html

Clean Vehicles and Fuels for British Columbia
http://www.env.gov.bc.ca/~cvf/

ClimateStudies
http://info.cern.ch/hypertext/DataSources/bySubject/Overview.html#ove2

Coal Research at Univ. of Texas
http://www.utexas.edu/research/beg/coal.html

Coalition for Safer Cleaner Vehicles
http://www.access.digex.net/~drmemory/cscv.html

Coso Geothermal Project
http://www1.chinalake.navy.mil/Geothermal.html

DIII-D Fusion Home Page
http://FusionEd.gat.com/

Directory of Energy-Related Graduate Programs in U.S. Universities
http://solstice.crest.org/social/grad/index.html

DOE's Energy Partnerships for a Strong Economy
http://www.eren.doe.gov/ee-cgi-bin/ccap.pl

DOE Office of Scientific and Technical Information
http://www.doe.gov/html/osti/

DOE Univ. of California
http://labs.ucop.edu/

Dual-Mode Electric Vehicle System: the RUF System
http://weber.u.washington.edu:80/~jbs/PRT/RUF_Concept.html

Earth Sciences Catalogue and Search Facility
http://www.einet.net/galaxy/Science/Geosciences.html

Eco-Motion Electric Cars
http://www.cyberzine.org/html/Electric/ecomotion.html

EcoElectric Corporation
http://www.primenet.com/~ecoelec/

Electric and Hybrid Vehicles
http://www.csv.warwick.ac.uk/~esrjo/ev_hp.html

Electric Power Research Inst.
http://www.epri.com/

Energy Efficiency and Renewable Energy Clearinghouse
http://nrelinfo.nrel.gov/web_info/documents/erec_fact_sheets/erec.html

Energy Efficiency Office
http://www.bre.co.uk/bre/otherprg/eeobp

Energy Efficient Housing in Canada
http://web.cs.ualberta.ca/~art/house/

Energy Federation Inc.
http://www.efi.org/biz/efi/home.html

Energy Ideas
http://www.rl.ac.uk/Dept.s/tec/erunrg.html

Energy Quest — Energy Education from the California Energy Commission
http://www.energy.ca.gov/energy/education/eduhome.html

Energy WWW Virtual Library
http://solstice.crest.org/online/virtual-library/VLib-energy.html

Energy Yellow Pages
http://www.ccnet.com/~nep/yellow.htm

EnviroLink Network
http://envirolink.org/issues/energy.html

Environment Canada's National Pollutant Release Inventory
http://ellesmere.ccm.emr.ca/npri/clone/npri_ec.html

Environmental and Engineering Geophysical Society (EEGS)
http://www.esd.ornl.gov:80/EEGS/

Environmental Measurements Laboratory
http://www.eml.doe.gov/

Environmental Network
http://envirolink.org/enviroed/

Ex-USSR Nuclear Technology and The World
http://www.ida.net/users/pbmck/xsovnuc/exs_top.htm

Federal Emergency Management Agency
http://www.fema.gov/

Ford Motor Company — Exploring the Alternatives to Gasoline
http://www.ford.com/corporate-info/environment/GasAlt.html

Fourth International Meeting on Heat Flow and the Structure of the GeoSphere (1996)
http://www.eps.mcgill.ca/~hugo/heat.html

Franklin Inst. Science Museum — Future Energy Exhibit
http://sln.fi.edu/tfi/exhibits/f-energy.html

Franklin Inst. Science Museum — Wind Study Unit
http://sln.fi.edu/tfi/units/energy/wind.html

Fusion Research Index
http://fusioned.gat.com/webstuff/FusionInfo.html

Gaining Ground — Sustainable Energy
http://www.nceet.snre.umich.edu/GAIN/GG.W95.html

Geothermal Energy in Iceland
http://www.os.is/os-eng/geo-div.html

Geothermal Exploration in Korea
http://www.kigam.re.kr/env-geology.html

Geothermal Heat Pump Consortium
http://www.ghpc.org/index.html

Geothermal Heat Pump Initiative in the U.S.
http://www.eren.doe.gov/ee-cgi-bin/cc_heatpump.pl

Geothermal Resources Council Library & Information
http://grclib.html

Geothermal Sciences
http://solstice.crest.org/renewables/geothermal/grc/index.html

Green Wheels Electric Car Company
http://northshore.shore.net/~kester/

Greenpeace — Climate Crisis Homepage
http://www.greenpeace.org/~climate/

GREENTIE — Greenhouse Gas Technology Information Exchange
http://www.greentie.org/greentie

Home Energy Magazine On Line
http://www.eren.doe.gov/ee-cgi-bin/hem.pl

Home Systems Network — Home automation
http://www.ionet.net/mall/hsn/index.htm

HVAC Contract Services Canada
http://www.wchat.on.ca/hvacr/index.htm

Hybrid Electric Vehicle Program
http://info.nrel.gov/research/hev/resources/hybrid1.html

Idaho National Engineering Laboratory
http://www.inel.gov/

IEA Solar Heating and Cooling
http://www-iea.vuw.ac.nz:90/

IEEE Power Engineering Society
http://www.ieee.org/power/power.html

Institute of Nuclear Physics, Cracow, Poland
http://www.ifj.edu.pl/

International Association for Solar Energy Education
http://www.hrz.uni-oldenburg.de/~kblum/iasee.html

International Directory of Energy Efficiency Institutions
http://www.weea.org/online/direct/country/start.htm

International Geothermal Association
http://www.demon.co.uk/geosci/igahome.html

International Radiation Protection Association
http://www.tue.nl/sbd/irpa/irpahome.htm

Joint Ctr. for Energy Mgmt.
http://bechtel.colorado.edu/ceae/Centers/Jcem/jcemmain.html

K-12 Environmental Resources on the Internet for Teachers
http://www.envirolink.org/enviroed/envirok12.html

Lawrence Berkeley Laboratories' Energy and Environment department
http://eande.lbl.gov/EE.html

LBL's Center for Building Science
http://eande.lbl.gov/CBS.html

Lawrence Livermore National Laboratory Energy Page
http://www-energy.llnl.gov/

LPG as an Automotive Fuel
http://wps.com/LPG/index.html

Lockheed Martin Energy Systems, Inc.
http://www.ornl.gov/mmes.html

Magnetic Fusion Energy Database (MFEDB)
http://hagar.ph.utexas.edu:1080/

MIT Plasma Fusion Center WWW Server
http://cmod2.pfc.mit.edu/

National Center for Vehicle Emissions Control and Safety
http://www.colostate.edu/Depts/NCVECS/ncvecs.html

National Energy Foundation
http://www.xmission.com/~nef/

National Energy Information Center Energy Education Guide
http://solstice.crest.org/social/eerg/index.html

National Renewable Energy Laboratory
http://info.nrel.gov/

New Brunswick Dept. of Environment— Air Quality Section
http://www.gov.nb.ca/environm/operatin/air/air_1.html

NOAA's Air Resources Laboratory
http://www.cdc.noaa.gov/PandP/ARL.html

Oak Ridge National laboratory — Energy Efficiency & Renewable Energy
http://www.ornl.gov/ORNL/Energy_Eff/Energy_Eff.html

Office of Surface Mining - U.S. Dept. of the Interior
http://info.er.usgs.gov/doi/office-of-surface-mining.html

Oil Online
http://www.oilonline.com

Pacific Northwest National Laboratory
http://www.pnl.gov:2080/

Pacific Rim Consortium in Energy, Combustion, and the Environment Participants
http://parcon.eng.uci.edu/participants.html

Pantex Nuclear Weapons Plant
http://www.pantex.com/PX/about.htm

Partnership for a New Generation of Vehicles
http://picard.aero.hq.nasa.gov/index.html

Planet Earth's Energy Listings on Web
http://godric.nosc.mil/planet_earth/energy.html

Power Electronic Building Blocks
http://www.pebb.dt.navy.mil

Power Engineering Notes
http://home.earthlink.net/~abisamra/index.html

Power Plant Training Simulators
http://www.albany.net/~dmills/simulators.html

Princeton Plasma Physics Laboratory
http://www.pppl.gov/

Renaissance Cars
http://www.qualcomm.com/users/sck/ev/renaissance.html

Renewable Energy Education Module
http://solstice.crest.org/renewables/re-kiosk/index.shtml

Retro-Vision Magazine — Residential
Energy Efficiency
http://es1.es.emr.ca/retro/retro.html

Rocky Mountain Inst.
http://solstice.crest.org/efficiency/rmi/
index.html

Rotorua, New Zealand, Geothermal Areas
http://www.akiko.lm.com/NZ/NZTour/Rotorua/
Geothermal.html

Sacramento Electric Vehicle Association
http://www.calweb.com/~tonyc/
sevahome.html

Santa Barbara County Air Pollution
Control District
http://rain.org/~sbcapcd/sbcapcd.html

Solar and Renewable Energy Conferences
Calendar
http://nrelinfo.nrel.gov:70/1m/hot-stuff/
calendar.html

Solar Energy and Building Physics Lab.
http://lesowww.epfl.ch/index.html

Stanford Univ. Geothermal Program
http://ekofisk.stanford.edu/geotherm.html

T-2 Nuclear Information Service
http://t2.lanl.gov/

Texas A&M's Energy Science Lab.
http://www-esl.tamu.edu/

Transportation and the Economy
http://sunsite.unc.edu/darlene/tech/
report9.html

UK Solar Energy Society
http://sun1.bham.ac.uk/thorntme/

Univ. of Illinois Energy Resources Center
http://www.erc.uic.edu/

Univ. of Oregon Energy and Environment
http://zebu.uoregon.edu/energy.html

Univ. of Strathclyde Energy Systems
Research Unit
http://www.strath.ac.uk/Dept.s/ESRU/
esru.html

U.S. Dept. of Energy
http://www.doe.gov/

U.S. Environmental Protection Agency
http://www.epa.gov/

US Fusion Energy Sciences Program
http://wwwofe.er.doe.gov/

Utility Biomass Energy Commercialization
Association
http://www.paltech.com/ttc/ubeca/index.htm

Utility Photovoltaic Group
http://www.paltech.com/ttc/upvg/index.htm

Washington Univ.'s Center for Air
Pollution Impact and Trend Analysis
http://capita.wustl.edu

WWW Virtual Library: Energy
http://solstice.crest.org/online/virtual-library/
VLib-energy.html

Zero Energy Building Project
http://www.ncsa.uiuc.edu/evl/science/zero/
zero.html

Engineering

See also Aeronautics & Aerospace, Chemistry, Computer Science, Electronics & Electrical Engineering, Energy, Imaging Technologies, Optics, Physics

Acoustical Society of America
http://asa.aip.org

Acoustics and Vibration Virtual Library
http://web.mit.edu/org/a/avlab/www/
vl.home.html

Advanced Computational Engineering
Lab, Univ. of Texas, Austin
http://diana.ae.utexas.edu/

Aeronautics and Aeronautical Engineering
Virtual Library
http://macwww.db.erau.edu/www_virtual_lib/
aeronautics.html

Aerospace Engineering Virtual Library
http://macwww.db.erau.edu/www_virtual_lib/
aerospace.html

American Ceramic Society
http://www.smartpages.com/acers/

American Electronics Association
http://www.aeanet.org/

American Institute of Physics
http://aip.org/

American Mathematical Society
http://www.ams.org

American Nuclear Society
http://www.ans.org

American Society for Engineering Education
http://www.asee.org/

American Society of Heating, Refrigerating and Air-Conditioning Engineers, Inc. (ASHRAE)
http://www.ashrae.org/

American Society of Mechanical Engineers (ASME)
http://www.asme.org

American Vacuum Society
http://www.vacuum.org/

American Water Works Association
http://www.awwa.org

Applied Research Lab at Penn
http://www.arl.psu.edu/

Archtecture, Land. Archtecture Virtual Library
http://www.clr.toronto.edu:1080/VIRTUALLIB/
archGALAXY.html

Arizona State Univ. MAE Design Automation Lab
http://asudesign.eas.asu.edu/

Army Construction Engineering Research Labs.
http://www.cecer.army.mil/

ARPA iMEMS (integrated MicroElectroMechanical Systems) Program
http://nitride.eecs.berkeley.edu:8001/

Association for Computing Machinery
http://info.acm.org/

ASU Design Automation Lab
http://ASUdesign.eas.asu.edu/

Audio Engineering Society
http://www.cudenver.edu/aes/index.html

BMEnet - Biomedical Engineering
http://bme.www.ecn.purdue.edu/bme

Bridge Engineering
http://www.best.com/~solvers/bridge.html

Brigham Young Univ. ADCATS
http://vince.et.byu.edu/

Brown Univ. Fluid Mechanics
http://www.cfm.brown.edu/

Caltech Mechanical Engineering Ctr.
http://avalon.caltech.edu/me/

Cambridge Univ.
http://www.eng.cam.ac.uk

Canadian Society for Mechanical Engineering
http://home.istar.ca/~csocme/index.htm

Carleton Systems and Computer Engineering
http://www.sce.carleton.ca/

Carnegie Mellon Software Engineering Institute
http://www.sei.cmu.edu/FrontDoor.html

Carnegie Mellon Univ. E&CE
http://www.ece.cmu.edu/Home-Page.html

Center for Research on Computation and Applications
http://www.cerca.umontreal.ca/

CESR
http://pdsppi.igpp.ucla.edu/cesr/Welcome.html

Chemical Engineering Virtual Library
http://www.che.ufl.edu/WWW-CHE/index.html

CIM Systems Research Ctr. at Arizona State Univ.
http://enws324.eas.asu.edu/

Civil Engineering at Christian Brothers Univ.
http://www.cbu.edu/engineering/ce/cehome.htm

Civil Engineering Virtual Library
http://howe.ce.gatech.edu/WWW-CE/home.html

Clarkson Univ. Materials Engineering
http://m_struct.mie.clarkson.edu/VLmae.html

Clemson Univ. Design
http://www.eng.clemson.edu/dmg/DMG.html

Clemson Univ. Mechanical Engineering
http://macmosaic.eng.clemson.edu/Academic.Depts/ME/ME.html

Colorado School of Mines
http://www.mines.colorado.edu/

Computer and Communication Companies
http://www-atp.llnl.gov/atp/companies.html

Computer and Network Security Reference Index
http://www.tansu.com.au/Info/security.html

Computer Assisted Mechanics and Engineering Sciences (CAMES) Journal
http://www.ippt.gov.pl/zmit/www/CAMES.html

Computer Integrated Manufacturing at Maryland
http://gimble.cs.umd.edu/cim/cim.html

Computational Fluid Dynamics Resources at Chalmers
http://www.tfd.chalmers.se/CFD_Online/

Computational Fluid Dynamics Review
http://mae.engr.ucdavis.edu/CFD/dbanks/CFDREV/

Computational Fluid Dynamics, Univ. of Texas at Austin
http://diana.ae.utexas.edu/

Consortium on Green Design and Manufacturing server
http://euler.berkeley.edu/green/cgdm.html

Control Engineering Virtual Library
http://www-control.eng.cam.ac.uk/extras/Virtual_Library/Control_VL.html

Cornell Univ. Chemical Engineering
http://latoso.cheme.cornell.edu/

Cornell Univ. Engineering M&AE
http://www.tc.cornell.edu/~maxfield/mae/

Cranfield Univ.
http://www.cranfield.ac.uk

Ctr. for Case Studies in Engineering
http://www.civeng.carleton.ca/ECL/about.html

Curtin Univ., Perth, Western Australia
http://guri.cage.curtin.edu.au/~fish/home.html

Delft Univ. of Technology
http://www.twi.tudelft.nl/welcome.html

DesignNet Directory of Mechatronic and Engineering Services
http://cdr.stanford.edu/html/SHARE/DesignNet.html

Earthquake Engineering, UC Berkeley
http://nisee.ce.berkeley.edu/

ECSEL Coalition
http://echo.umd.edu/

ECSEL Program (Penn State)
http://albatross.psu.edu/

Edinburgh Chemical Engineering
http://www.chemeng.ed.ac.uk/

Electrical Engineering Virtual Library
http://www.ece.iit.edu/~power/power.html

Electromagnetics Library
http://emlib.jpl.nasa.gov/

Electronic & Manufacturing Engineering
http://www.wmin.ac.uk/CMSA/welcome.html

Energy Systems Lab. - Texas A&M Univ.
http://www-esl.tamu.edu/

Engineering & Technology at EINet Galaxy
http://galaxy.einet.net/galaxy/./Engineering-and-Technology.html

Engineering Council
http://www.engc.org.uk/

Engineering Employment EXPO
http://stimpy.cen.uiuc.edu/comm/expo/

Engineering Software Exchange
http://www.engineers.com/ese/ese.html

Engineering Virtual Library
http://arioch.gsfc.nasa.gov/wwwvl/engineering.html

Environmental Engineering
http://www.nmt.edu/~jjenks/engineering.html

ERIM - Environmental Research Institute of Michigan
http://www.erim.org/

Formal Methods Virtual Library
http://www.comlab.ox.ac.uk/archive/formal-methods.html

Fraunhofer Institute of Ceramic Technologies and Sintered Materials
http://www.ikts.fhg.de/ikts.engl.html

Gas Dynamics Lab, Princeton Univ.
http://ncd1901.cfd.princeton.edu/

Geometry Ctr. at the Univ. of Minnesota
http://freeabel.geom.umn.edu/

Georgia Tech Civil Engineering
http://howe.ce.gatech.edu/WWW-CE/home.html

Geotechnical Engineering Virtual Library
http://geotech.civen.okstate.edu/wwwVL/index.html

HCI Resources
http://www.ida.liu.se/labs/aslab/groups/um/hci/

HCRL Home Page at The Open Univ., UK
http://hcrl.open.ac.uk/

Houston Internet Connection
http://www.jsc.nasa.gov/houston/HoustonInternet.html

Hydromechanics
http://www50.dt.navy.mil/

ICARIS - CIC research network
http://audrey.fagg.uni-lj.si/ICARIS/index.html

IEE - Institution of Electrical Engineers
http://www.iee.org.uk/

IEEE - Institute of Electrical and Electronics Engineers
http://www.ieee.org/

IKEDA lab. Chiba
http://www.hike.te.chiba-u.ac.jp/

Industrial Engineering Virtual Library
http://isye.gatech.edu/www-ie/

IndustryNET
http://www.industry.net/

Institute of Fluid Science
http://hh.ifs.tohoku.ac.jp/

Institute of Physics
http://www.iop.org/

International Centre for Heat and Mass Transfer
http://www.metu.edu.tr:80/~hersoy/index.html

International Council on Systems Engineering
http://usw.interact.net/incose/

International Society for Measurement and Control (ISA)
http://www.isa.org/

International Union of Materials Research Societies
http://mrcemis.ms.nwu.edu/iumrs/index.html

Intl. Centre For Heat and Mass Transfer (ICHMT)
http://www.metu.edu.tr/~hersoy/index.html

ISA - The International Society for Measurement and Control
http://www.isa.org/

ISSI Biography
http://www.issi.com/issi/issi-bio.html

Journal of Fluids Engineering
http://borg.lib.vt.edu/ejournals/JFE/jfe.html

Journal of Mechanical Design
http://www-jmd.engr.ucdavis.edu/jmd/

Kansas State Univ. College of Engineering
http://www.engg.ksu.edu/home.html

Kyushu Univ., Japan
http://www.ee.kyushu-u.ac.jp/index.html

Lulea Univ., Div. of Energy Engineering
http://www.luth.se/depts/mt/ene/

Manhattan College School of Engineering
http://www.mancol.edu/engineer/engrpage.html

Materials Engineering Virtual Library
http://m_struct.mie.clarkson.edu/VLmae.html

Materials Research Society
http://dns.mrs.org/

Mechanical Engineering Software
ftp://ftp.mecheng.asme.org/pub

Mechanical Engineering Virtual Library
http://cdr.stanford.edu/html/WWW-ME/home.html

Microelectromechanical Systems at MIT
http://arsenio.mit.edu/MEMSatMIT.html

MEMS Technology Applications Center at MCNC
http://www.mcnc.org/HTML/ETD/MEMS/memshome.html

Mississippi State Univ.
http://www.msstate.edu/

Moscow State University - Institute Of Mechanics
http://jan.inmech.msu.su/

Nanotechnology on the WWW
http://www.arc.ab.ca/~morgan/Nano.html

NASA Johnson Space Flight Ctr. Software Engineering
http://rbse.jsc.nasa.gov/virt-lib/soft-eng.html

NASA Langley Research Ctr.
http://www.larc.nasa.gov/larc.html

NASA Technical Report Server (NTRS)
http://techreports.larc.nasa.gov/cgi-bin/NTRS

National Physical Laboratory — UK
http://www.npl.co.uk/

Naval Architecture and Ocean Engineering Virtual Library
http://arioch.gsfc.nasa.gov/wwwvl/engineering.html#naval

NCCOSC Home Page
http://www.nosc.mil/NCCOSCMosaicHome.html

NCSU College of Engineering Home Page
http://www.eos.ncsu.edu/coe/coe.html

NIST Manufacturing Engineering Lab.
http://www.nist.gov/mel/melhome.html

Nonlinear Dynamics Lab, Saratov, Russia
http://chaos.ssu.runnet.ru/

Northwestern Univ.
http://voltaire.mech.nwu.edu/

Notre Dame Aerospace and Mechanical Engineering
http://www.nd.edu/Departments/EN/AME/HomePage.html

NSF SUCCEED Engineering Visual Database
http://succeed.edtech.vt.edu/

Nuclear Engineering Virtual Library
http://neutrino.nuc.berkeley.edu/NEadm.html

On-line Catalog at the Technical Univ. of Darmstadt
http://venus.muk.maschinenbau.th-darmstadt.de/rth/rk/rkhome.html

Optical Engineering Virtual Library
http://www.spie.org/wwwvl_optics.html

OPTICS.ORG - The Photonics Resource Center
http://optics.org/

Patent Information
http://sunsite.unc.edu/patents/intropat.html

Penn State
http://www.esm.psu.edu

Pohang Univ. of Science and Technology (Postech), Korea:
http://firefox.postech.ac.kr/

Power Engineering Virtual Library
http://www.analysys.co.uk/commslib.htm

Production and Design Engineering Lab.
http://utwpue.wb.utwente.nl/

Project Mgmt. Software FAQ
http://www.wst.com/projplan/proj-plan.FAQ.html

PSU College of Earth and Mineral Sciences
http://www.ems.psu.edu/

Queens University Engineering Society
http://engsoc.queensu.ca

Rapid Prototyping Virtual Library
http://arioch.gsfc.nasa.gov/wwwvl/engineering.html#proto

RBSE Program
http://rbse.jsc.nasa.gov/eichmann/rbse.html

Robotech HazHandler
http://www.arc.ab.ca/robotech/

Robotics Internet Resources Page
http://piglet.cs.umass.edu:4321/robotics.html

Robotics Internet Resources Compendium
http://www.eg.bucknell.edu/~robotics/rirc.html

Robotics Jump Page
http://www.sm.luth.se/csee/er/sm-roa/
Robotics/RobotJump.html

RUL Mathematics & Computer Science -
Software Engineering and IS
http://www.wi.leidenuniv.nl/CS/SEIS/
summary.html

Russian and East European Studies Net
Resources
http://www.pitt.edu/~cjp/rstech.html

Russian and East European Studies Virtual
Library
http://www.pitt.edu/~cjp/rees.html

Safety-Critical Systems Virtual Library
http://www.comlab.ox.ac.uk/archive/
safety.html

SHARE DesignNet Page
http://cdr.stanford.edu/html/SHARE/
DesignNet.html

Sheffield Dept of Automatic Control &
Systems Engineering
http://www2.shef.ac.uk/acse/ACSE.html

Shock & Vibration Information Analysis
Ctr. (SAVIAC)
http://saviac.usae.bah.com/

Society for Applied Spectroscopy
http://esther.la.asu.edu:80/sas/

Society for Experimental Mechanics
http://www.sem.bethel.ct.us/

Society of Automotive Engineers
http://www.sae.org/

Society of Manufacturing Engineers
http://www.sme.org/

Software Engineering Virtual Library
http://www-control.eng.cam.ac.uk/extras/
Virtual_Library/Control_VL.html

Software Technology for Fluid Mechanics
http://www.ts.go.dlr.de/sm-sk_info/STinfo/
STgroup.html

Solid Mechanics, Chalmers Univ. of
Technology, Sweden
http://www.solid.chalmers.se/

Space Shuttle News Reference Manual
http://www.ksc.nasa.gov/shuttle/technology/
sts-newsref/stsref-toc.html

SPIE-The Intl. Society for Optical Engineering
http://www.spie.org/

Stanford Knowledge Systems Lab.
http://www-ksl.stanford.edu/

Stanford Univ.
http://CDR.stanford.edu/html/WWW-ME/
home.html

Stanford Univ. Ctr. for Design Research
http://gummo.stanford.edu/

STO's Internet Patent Search System
http://sunsite.unc.edu/patents/intropat.html

Structural Engineering Virtual Library
http://touchstone.power.net/seaoc/
sevhmpg1.htm

Subjective Electronic Information Repository
http://cbl.leeds.ac.uk/nikos/doc/
repository.html

Swarthmore College
http://www.engin.swarthmore.edu/

Switzerland - Information servers
http://heiwww.unige.ch/switzerland/

Systems and Control Engineering Virtual
Library
http://src.doc.ic.ac.uk/bySubject/Computing/
Overview.html

Technical Univ. of Budapest
http://www.fsz.bme.hu/bme/bme.html

Technical Univ. of Darmstadt
http://venus.muk.maschinenbau.th-
darmstadt.de/

Technical Univ. of Nova Scotia
http://www.tuns.ca/

Texas A&M Univ.
http://www.tamu.edu/default.html

Thermal Design and Analysis
http://www.kkassoc.com:80/~takinfo/

Thermal Engineering Resource
http://stecwww.fpms.ac.be/htmls/HotList/

Turbulence Links Around the WWW
http://stimpy.ame.nd.edu/gross/fluids/
turbulence.html

UALR Biologic Fluid Dynamics
http://giles.ualr.edu/

UC Berkeley
http://www.Berkeley.EDU/

UCSD Science & Engineering Library
http://scilib.ucsd.edu

UIUC Engineering
http://stimpy.cen.uiuc.edu/comm/eoh

UNCC Mechanical Engineering & Engineering Science
http://www.coe.uncc.edu/~ksriram/me_home_pg.html

Univ. of Alabama in Huntsville
http://www.uah.edu/colleges/engineering/engineering.html

Univ. of Alberta EE
http://nyquist.ee.ualberta.ca/index.html

Univ. of Alberta Water Resources Engineering
http://maligne.civil.ualberta.ca/home.html

Univ. of Bradford - Engineering in Astronomy Group
http://www.eia.brad.ac.uk/eia.html

Univ. of Bristol, UK
http://www.fen.bris.ac.uk/welcome.html

Univ. of Calgary Micronet Multidimensional Signal Processing Research Group
http://www-mddsp.enel.ucalgary.ca/

Univ. of Edinburgh
http://ouse.mech.ed.ac.uk/

Univ. of Evansville
http://www-cecs.evansville.edu/

Univ. of Florida Chemical Engineering
http://www.che.ufl.edu/WWW-CHE/index.html

Univ. of Florida Process Improvement Lab.
http://www.che.ufl.edu/

Univ. of Hawaii
http://www.eng.hawaii.edu/

Univ. of Illinois at Urbana-Champaign - Theoretical and Applied Mechanics
http://www.tam.uiuc.edu/

Univ. of Ljubljana, FAGG
http://www.fagg.uni-lj.si/index.html

Univ. of Manitoba Civil and Geological Engineering
http://www.ce.umanitoba.ca/homepage.html

Univ. of Maryland Institute for Systems Research
http://gimble.cs.umd.edu/cim/cim.html

Univ. of Michigan
http://www.engin.umich.edu/college/

Univ. of Minnesota Biomedical Engineering
http://pro.med.umn.edu/bmec/bmec.html

Univ. of Minnesota Geometry Ctr.
http://freeabel.geom.umn.edu/

Univ. of New Hampshire Robotics
http://www.ece.unh.edu/robots/rbt_home.htm

Univ. of Portland
http://www.up.edu/

Univ. of Queensland, Computational Fluid Dynamics
http://www.uq.edu.au/~e4ppetri/CFD.html

Univ. of South Carolina Engineering
http://www.engr.scarolina.edu/

Univ. of Tennessee Biomedical Engineering
http://www.mecca.org/BME/bme-home.html

Univ. of Twente Lab. of Production & Design Engineering
http://utwpue.wb.utwente.nl/

Univ. of Virginia Engineering Physics
http://bohr.ms.virginia.edu/ep/

Univ. of Washington Computer Science & Engineering
http://www.cs.washington.edu/

Univ. of Wyoming
http://wwweng.uwyo.edu/

US Army Advanced Simulation and Software Engineering Technology
http://lincoln.cecer.army.mil/asset.html

US Patents Searchable Archive
http://town.hall.org/patent/patent.html

Wastewater Engineering Virtual Library
http://www.halcyon.com/cleanh2o/ww/welcome.html

Welding Engineering Virtual Library
http://www.bath.ac.uk/Centres/AWJU/wwwvl3.html

Yahoo Mechanical Engineering Resources
http://www.yahoo.com/Science/Engineering/Mechanical_Engineering/

Geology & Geophysics

See also Meteorology, Oceanography

Aberdeen Univ.
http://hutton.geol.abdn.ac.uk/

ADEPT - Aquifer Data Evaluation
http://www.us.net/adept/welcome.html

Agency for Toxic Substances and Disease
Registry
http://atsdr1.atsdr.cdc.gov:8080/
atsdrhome.html

AGSO - Australian Geological Survey
Organisation
http://garnet.bmr.gov.au/

Alaska Volcano Observatory
http://www.avo.alaska.edu

American Crystallographic Association
http://nexus.mfb.buffalo.edu/ACA/

American Geological Institute
http://jei.umd.edu/agi/agi.html

American Geophysical Union
http://earth.agu.org/kosmos/homepage.html

American Rescue Team
http://www.Acosta.com/AmerRescue.html

American Rock Mechanics Association
http://sair019.energylan.sandia.gov:70/0/
RockNet/rocknet.html

Analytical Spectral Devices, Inc.
http://www.asdi.com/asd/

Arctic and Antarctic Research Center at
UC San Diego
http://arcane2.ucsd.edu/

Arctic Studies Center — Smithsonian
Institution
http://nmnhwww.si.edu/arctic/

Arizona Geographic Information Council
http://www.state.az.us/gis3/agic/
agichome.html

Association of Petroleum Geochemical
Explorationists (APGE)
http://www.csn.net/~jamesf/apge.htm

Atlantic Marine Geology
http://bramble.er.usgs.gov

Australian Environmental Resources
Information Network
http://kaos.erin.gov.au/erin.html

Australian Geological Survey
Organisation
http://www.agso.gov.au/

Australian Institute of Geoscientists
http://www.civgeo.rmit.edu.au/aig/aig.html

Bay Area Digital Geo-Resource
http://www.svi.org/badger.html

British Crystallographic Association
http://www.cryst.bbk.ac.uk/BCA/index.html

British Geological Survey (BGS)
http://www.nkw.ac.uk/bgs/

Brown Univ.
http://www-geo.het.brown.edu/geo/

Bureau of Indian Affairs - Div. of Energy
and Mineral Resources
http://snake2.cr.usgs.gov/

Bureau of Land Management Geospatial
http://www.blm.gov/gis/gishome.html

Byrd Polar Research Center - Ohio State
University
http://www-bprc.mps.ohio-state.edu/

California Cooperative Snow Surveys
http://snow.water.ca.gov/

California State Univ., Chico
http://rigel.csuchico.edu/

Caltech Division of Geological and
Planetary Science
http://www.gps.caltech.edu/

Cambridge Earth Sciences
http://rock.esc.cam.ac.uk/main.html

Canada Centre for Mapping
http://www.geocan.nrcan.gc.ca/

Canadian National Net Combined U.S. Catalog
http://www.geophys.washington.edu/cnss.cat.html

Carolina Geological Soc.
http://www.geo.duke.edu/cgsinfo.htm

Cascades Volcano Observatory
http://vulcan.wr.usgs.gov

Center for Clean Technology
http://cct.seas.ucla.edu

Center for Earthquake Research and Information
http://www.ceri.memphis.edu/

Center for Remote Sensing and Spatial Analysis
http://deathstar.rutgers.edu/welcome.html

Centre for Technical Geoscience in Delft, the Netherlands
http://wwwak.tn.tudelft.nl/CTG/Overview.html

CIESIN Information for a Changing World
http://www.ciesin.org

Coastal Ocean Modeling
http://crusty.er.usgs.gov

Colorado School of Mines
http://gn.mines.colorado.edu/

CREWES Project (Consortium for Research in Elastic Wave Exploration Seismology)
http://www-crewes.geo.ucalgary.ca/

Ctr. for Earth Observation
http://stormy.geology.yale.edu/ceo.html

CWP - Ctr. for Wave Phenomena
http://cwp.mines.colorado.edu:3852/

Dalhousie Univ.
http://www.dal.ca/www_root_es/es-home.html

DeLORME Mapping
http://www.delorme.com/

Desert Research Inst.
http://www.dri.edu

Digital Relief Map of USA
http://ageninfo.tamu.edu/apl-us/

Duke Univ.
http://www.geo.duke.edu/

Earth Observing System Information Server
http://eos.nasa.gov/

Earth Sciences and Resources Inst. - Univ. of Utah
http://www.esri.utah.edu/

Earthquake and Landslide Hazards
http://gldage.cr.usgs.gov

EcoNet - League of Conservation Voters
http://www.econet.org/lcv/

Edinburgh Dept. of Geology and Geophysics
http://www.glg.ed.ac.uk/

EE-LINK - Environmental Education on the Internet
http://www.nceet.snre.umich.edu/index.html

Energy Research Clearing House
http://www.main.com:80/~ERCH/

Energy Resource Surveys Program
http://sedwww.cr.usgs.gov:8080

EnviroLink Network
http://envirolink.org/about.html

Environment Canada's Green Lane in Atlantic Canada
http://www.ns.doe.ca/how.html

Environmental Design College at the Univ. of California, Berkeley
http://www.ced.berkeley.edu/

Environmental Industry Web Site
http://www.enviroindustry.com/

Environmental Information Services
http://www.esdim.noaa.gov/

Environmental Professional's Homepage
http://www.clay.net

EnviroSense
http://wastenot.inel.gov/envirosense

EnviroWeb
http://envirolink.org/

EROS Data Center
http://sun1.cr.usgs.gov/eros-home.html

European Association of Geoscientists & Engineers
http://www.ruu.nl/eage/

Explorer from the Univ. of Kansas
http://unite.tisl.ukans.edu/xmintro.html

Federal Emergency Management Agency
http://www.fema.gov/

Federal Geographic Data Committee
http://fgdc.er.usgs.gov

Flagstaff Field Center
http://wwwflag.wr.usgs.gov

Fossil Fuels & Environmental Geochemistry
http://borg.ncl.ac.uk/

Gemology & Lapidary Resources
http://www.teleport.com/~raylc/gems/index.html

Geneva Univ. - Crystallography
http://www.unige.ch/

GEOBYTE—sponsored by the American Association of Petroleum Geology
http://www.NeoSoft.com:80/aapg/

Geochemical Institute of Goettingen, Germany
http://www.uni-geochem.gwdg.de/docs/home.htm

Geochemical Society
http://www.ciw.edu/geochemical_society/

Geodetic Survey of Canada
http://www.geod.emr.ca/

GeoForschungsZentrum Potsdam
http://www.gfz-potsdam.de/

Geographic Information Systems - GIS
http://www.usgs.gov/research/gis/title.html

Geographic Resources Analysis Support System
http://www.cecer.army.mil/grass/GRASS.main.html\

Geological Society of Denmark
http://home4.inet.tele.dk/dgfth/dgfpage.htm

Geological Society of the UK
http://www.geolsoc.org.uk/homepage.htm

Geological Survey of Canada
http://agcwww.bio.ns.ca/

Geological Survey of Finland
http://www.gsf.fi/

Geological Survey of Japan
http://www.aist.go.jp/GSJ/

Geomagnetism Group
http://ub.nmh.ac.uk/

Geophysics in Germany
http://www.ciw.edu/rumpker/geolinks.html/

Geophysics WWW Virtual Library
http://www-crewes.geo.ucalgary.ca/VL-Geophysics.html

Geoscience, Erlangen/Germany
http://www.rrze.uni-erlangen.de/docs/FAU/fakultaet/natlll/geo_min/

GeoWeb
http://www.pacificnet.net/~gimills/main.html

GIS FAQ
http://www.census.gov/geo/gis/faq-index.html

GIS User Guide to Internet Tools
http://jupiter.qub.ac.uk/GIS/GIS.html

Glaciology at the Univ. of British Columbia
http://www.geop.ubc.ca/Glaciology/glaciol.html

Global Change Research Program
http://geochange.er.usgs.gov

Global Environmental Network for Information Exchange
http://www-genie.mrrl.lut.ac.uk/

Global Land Cover Test Sites Project
http://dia.maxey.dri.edu:80/glcts/

Global Land Information System
http://sun1.cr.usgs.gov/glis/glis.html

Great Lakes Information Network
http://www.great-lakes.net:2200/0/glinhome.html

Great Lakes Regional Environmental Information System
http://epawww.ciesin.org

Groundwater Remediation Project
http://gwrp.cciw.ca/

HPCC Earth and Space Science Applications Project
http://nccsinfo.gsfc.nasa.gov:80/ESS/

Hydrologic Information Center
http://www.nohrsc.nws.gov/~hic

Illinois State Geological Survey
http://www.isgs.uiuc.edu/isgshome.html

Incorporated Research Institutions for Seismology
http://www.iris.washington.edu/

Indonesian Association of Geologists
http://www.geocities.com/TheTropics/3581/

INFO-MINE - Mining Information Online
http://www.info-mine.com/

Initiatives in Environmental Technology Investment
http://web.wpi.org/uetc/

Inst. for Geology and Palaeontology, Technical Univ. of Clausthal, Germany
http://www.inggeo.tu-clausthal.de/english/Welcome-e.html

Inst. for Mineralogy, Technical Univ. of Clausthal, Germany
http://www.immr.tu-clausthal.de/

Inst. for Technology Development/Space Remote Sensing Center
http://ma.itd.com/welcome.html

Inst. of Mineralogy at the Freiberg Univ. of Mining and Technology
http://www.mineral.ba-freiberg.de/index_en.html

Inst. of Seismology, Univ. of Helsinki
http://smo1.helsinki.fi:2001/HOME/1.html

Inst. of Soil Science
http://134.76.143.27/soil-hmp.htm

Institute of Geology and Palaeontology of the Technical Univ. of Clausthal
http://www.inggeo.tu-clausthal.de/

Institute of Geophysics and Planetary Physics at Scripps
http://igpp.ucsd.edu/

International Association for Environmental Hydrology
http://www.hydroweb.com

International Centre for Antarctic Information and Research
http://icair.iac.org.nz/

International Union of Crystallography
http://www.iucr.ac.uk/welcome.html

International Union of Geodesy and Geophysics
http://earth.agu.org/iugg/internat.html

Ionospheric Physics Group
http://ion.le.ac.uk/index.html

Iowa Geological Survey Bureau
http://www.igsb.uiowa.edu

Istituto Internazionale di Vulcanologia
http://www.iiv.ct.cnr.it/index.html

JASON Project Voyages I-VII
http://seawifs.gsfc.nasa.gov/JASON/JASON.html

Joint Education Initiative at the Univ. of Maryland at College Park
http://jei.umd.edu/jei/jei.html

La Trobe Univ. School of Earth Sciences, Australia
http://www.latrobe.edu.au/WWW/Earth/earth.html

Lamont Doherty Earth Observatory of Columbia Univ.
http://lamont.ldgo.columbia.edu/

Lawrence Livermore National Laboratory
http://www-ep.es.llnl.gov/www-ep/igpp.html

LSU Geology
http://gbyerly.geol.lsu.edu/geology/geology.html

Magnetic Field Monitoring & Charting Program
http://wwwgeomag.cr.usgs.gov/geomag

Manchester Geology Dept.
http://info.mcc.ac.uk/Geology/home-page.html

Mapping Applications Center
http://www-nmd.usgs.gov/mac

McGill Univ.
http://stoner.eps.mcgill.ca/

MERLIN - Mutlisource Environmental Data Display for Internet Archives
http://www.ssec.wisc.edu/software/merlin.html

Michigan Technological Univ.
http://www.geo.mtu.edu/

Michigan Technological Univ. Volcanoes
http://www.geo.mtu.edu/volcanoes/

Mineralogical Society of America
http://geology.smith.edu/msa/msa.html

Minerals, Metals & Materials Society
http://www.tms.org/

Minnesota Geological Survey
http://geolab.geo.umn.edu:80/mgs/

MIT's Earth Resources Lab.
http://www-erl.mit.edu/

MODIS Airborne Simulator
http://ltpwww.gsfc.nasa.gov/MODIS/MAS/Home.html

Museum of Palentology, Univ. of California - Berkeley
http://ucmp1.berkeley.edu/

NAISMap WWW-GIS
http://ellesmere.ccm.emr.ca/naismap/
naismap.html

NASA EOS IDS Volcanology Team
http://www.geo.mtu.edu:80/eos/

NASA HPCC Earth and Space Science Applications Project
http://hypatia.gsfc.nasa.gov/
NASA_homepage.html

National Biological Survey - Environmental Management Technical Center
http://www.emtc.nbs.gov/

National Center for Geographic Information and Analysis
http://www.ncgia.ucsb.edu/

National Earthquake Information Center
http://www.usgs.gov/data/geologic/neic/
index.html

National Geophysical Data Center
http://meridian.ngdc.noaa.gov/ngdc.html

National Mapping Information
http://www-nmd.usgs.gov

National Marine and Coastal Geology Program
http://marine.usgs.gov

National Snow and Ice Data Center
http://www-nsidc.colorado.edu/

National Supercomputing Center for Energy and the Environment
http://www.nscee.edu/nscee/

Natural Environment Research Council
http://www.nerc.ac.uk/

Natural Resources Canada
http://www.emr.ca/

Netherland Organization for Applied Scientific Research-TNO
http://www.tno.nl

New Mexico GISAC
http://www.state.nm.us/gisac/
gisac_home.html

New South Polar Times Project
http://xalph.ast.cam.ac.uk/public/niel/
scales.html

Niel's Timelines and Scales of Measurement List
http://cast0.ast.cam.ac.uk/Xray_www/niel/
scales.html

NOAA - National Oceanic and Atmospheric Administration
http://www.noaa.gov/

NOHRSC Snow Maps
http://www.nohrsc.nws.gov/

Northeast River Forecast Center
http://mohawk.ll.mit.edu

NSDI MetaData and WWW Mapping Sites
http://www.blm.gov/gis/nsdi.html

NSF Geosciences UNIDATA Integrated Earth Information Server
http://atm.geo.nsf.gov/

Ocean Bottom Seismometer Program
http://obs.er.usgs.gov

Oklahoma Univ.
http://geowww.gcn.uoknor.edu/www/Geol/
Geol.html

Online Resources for Earth Scientists
http://www.csn.net/~bthoen/ores

Pacific Forestry Centre
http://www.pfc.forestry.ca/

Pacific Marine Geology
http://walrus.wr.usgs.gov

Pacific Northwest Laboratory
http://terrassa.pnl.gov:2080/

Palaeobotany International Organisation
http://sunrae.uel.ac.uk/palaeo/index.html

Paleomap Foundation
http://www.paleomap.com/

Pasadena Field Office of the U.S. Geological Survey
http://aladdin.gps.caltech.edu/usgs-pas.html

Pennsylvania State Univ. — College of Earth & Mineral Sciences
http://www.ems.psu.edu/

Pennsylvania State Univ. — Earth System Science Center
http://www.essc.psu.edu/

Petroleum Science and Technology Institute (PSTI)
http://www.psti.co.uk/psti.html

Polar Science Center — Univ. of Washington
http://psc.apl.washington.edu/

Princeton Geological & Geophysical Sciences
http://wombat.princeton.edu/

Quaternary Research Association
http://www2.tcd.ie/~pcoxon/qra.html

Regional Environmental Center for Central and Eastern Europe
http://www.rec.hu/

Research Program in Environmental Planning & Geographic Information Systems
http://www.regis.berkeley.edu/

Rice Univ.
http://zephyr.rice.edu/Dept./dept_intro.html

Rocky Mountain Mapping Center
http://rmmcweb.cr.usgs.gov

RVARES Group, Reston, VA
http://wwwrvares.er.usgs.gov

San Francisco Bay Area Regional Database
http://bard.wr.usgs.gov

Sandia National Labs Geoscience & Geotechnology Center
http://sair019.energylan.sandia.gov:70/0/Sandia_Geosciences/center.html

Seismological Laboratory at Caltech
http://www.gps.caltech.edu/seismo/seismo.page.html

Sevilleta Long-Term Ecological Research Project
http://sevilleta.unm.edu/

Society for Sedimentary Geology
http://dc.smu.edu/semp_sp/home.html

Society of Exploration Geophysicists
http://www.seg.org/

Society of Petroleum Engineers
http://www.spe.org/

Soil and Water Conservation Soc.
http://www.netins.net/showcase/swcs

South Florida Ecosystem Program
http://fl-h2o.usgs.gov/sfei.html

Southeastern Geology Journal
http://geo.duke.edu/seglgy.htm

Southern Arizona Seismological Observatory
http://www.geo.arizona.edu/saso/

Southern California Earthquake Center Data Center
http://scec.gps.caltech.edu/

South Pole Observatory
http://www.cmdl.noaa.gov/spo/spo.html

Speleology Information Server
http://speleology.cs.yale.edu

Stanford Exploration Project
http://sepwww.stanford.edu/

State of California-Teale data center
http://www.gislab.teale.ca.gov

State Univ. of New York (SUNY) at Stony Brook
http://sbast3.ess.sunysb.edu/home.html

Surfing the InterNet for Earthquake Data
http://www.geophys.washington.edu/seismosurfing.html

Texas WaterNet
http://ageninfo.tamu.edu/twri

U.S. Army Corps of Engineers - Construction Engineering Research Laboratories
http://www.cecer.army.mil/welcome.html

UNAVCO, the Univ. NAVSTAR Consortium
http://www.unavco.ucar.edu/

Union College
http://zircon.geology.union.edu/

United States Geological Survey
http://www.usgs.gov/

Univ. at Buffalo
http://www.geog.buffalo.edu/

Univ. of Arizona
http://www.geo.arizona.edu/

Univ. of Bristol
http://www.gly.bris.ac.uk/

Univ. of Calgary, Dept. of Geology and Geophysics
http://www.geo.ucalgary.ca/

Univ. of California - Berkeley Museum of Palentology
http://ucmp1.berkeley.edu/

Univ. of California, Davis, Information Center for the Environment
http://ice.ucdavis.edu/

Univ. of Chicago
http://geosci.uchicago.edu/

Univ. of Erlangen - Geosciences Departments
http://www.rrze.uni-erlangen.de/tree/FAU/fakultaet/natlll/geo_min

Univ. of Hawaii at Manoa
http://www.soest.hawaii.edu/

Univ. of Idaho Library - Electronic Green Journal
http://www.lib.uidaho.edu:70/docs/egj.html

Univ. of Illinois - The Daily Planet
http://www.atmos.uiuc.edu/

Univ. of Kansas - Explorer
http://unite.ukans.edu/xmintro.html

Univ. of Kassel Ecological Modelling
http://dino.wiz.uni-kassel.de/ecobas.html

Univ. of Manchester
http://info.mcc.ac.uk/Geology/home-page.html

Univ. of Oxford - Dept. of Earth Sciences
http://www.earth.ox.ac.uk/

Univ. of Texas
http://www.utexas.edu/cons/geo

Univ. of Virginia, Environment
http://ecosys.drdr.virginia.edu/Environment.html

USDA-ARS National Soil Erosion Laboratory
http://purgatory.ecn.purdue.edu:20002/NSERL/nserl.html

Virtual Geomorphology
http://hum.amu.edu.pl/~sgp/gw/gw.htm

Volcano Images from the Space Shuttle's Radar
http://southport.jpl.nasa.gov/volcanopic.html

Volcano Systems Center, Univ. of Washington
http://vsc.washington.edu/

Washington Univ.
http://www.geophys.washington.edu/

Water Resources of the United States
http://h2o.er.usgs.gov

Western Region Geologic Information Server
http://wrgis.wr.usgs.gov

World Data Center for Marine Geology & Geophysics
http://www.ngdc.noaa.gov/mgg/aboutmgg/wdcamgg.html

WWW Virtual Library: Environment
http://ecosys.drdr.virginia.edu/Environment.html

Xroads Western Region Center
http://xroads.wr.usgs.gov

Imaging Technologies

See also Computer Science, Electronics & Electrical Engineering, Engineering, Medicine, Optics, Physics, Virtual Reality

Aalborg Univ. Laboratory of Image
Analysis
http://www.vision.auc.dk/~hic/auc-head.html

Advanced Liquid Crystalline Optical
Materials, Kent State Univ.
http://alcom.kent.edu/ALCOM/ALCOM.html

AIG-Manchester Advanced Interfaces
Group
http://www.cs.man.ac.uk/aig/aig.html

Algorithm Image Gallery
http://axpba1.ba.infn.it:8080/

Amerinex Artificial Intelligence, Inc.
http://www.aai.com/

Arizona State Univ., MAE Design Automation Lab
http://asudesign.eas.asu.edu/

ARPA Display Technology Programs
http://esto.sysplan.com/ESTO/Displays//

Asia Technical Information Progam Flat
Panel Display Project
http://www.atip.or.jp/fpd.html

Association for Computing Machinery
http://info.acm.org/

AT&T Bell Laboratories
http://www.research.att.com/

Australian National University, Centre for
Visual Sciences
http://cvs.anu.edu.au/CVS.html

Beckman Institute Visualization Facility
http://delphi.beckman.uiuc.edu:80/

CAD Centre, Univ. of Strathclyde,
Glasgow, Scotland
http://www.cad.strath.ac.uk/Home.html

Cadence Design Systems
http://www.cadence.com/

Caltech Interactive Volume Browser
http://www.scp.caltech.edu:80/~mep/ivb.html

Cambridge Univ. Rainbow Research
Group
http://www.cl.cam.ac.uk/Research/Rainbow/

Cardiff's VR Page
http://www.cm.cf.ac.uk/User/Andrew.Wilson/
VR/

Carlson Center for Imaging Science at RIT
http://www.cis.rit.edu

Carnegie Mellon Computer Vision
http://www.cs.cmu.edu:8001/afs/cs/project/cil/
ftp/html/vision.html

Carnegie Mellon Univ. 3D-Stereoscopic
Video Display
http://www.cs.cmu.edu/afs/cs/project/sensor-
9/ftp/www/homepage.html

CERN Computer Aided Detector Design
http://cadd.cern.ch/welcome.html

CGU-Manchester—The Computer
Graphics Unit Research
http://info.mcc.ac.uk/CGU/CGU-
research.html

CIDTECH
http://www.cidtec.com

CIE - International Commission on
Illumination
http://www.hike.te.chiba-u.ac.jp/ikeda/CIE/
home.html

Colour Technology Forum
http://www.hike.te.chiba-u.ac.jp/ikeda/Color/
home.html

Coreco
http://www.dspnet.com/dspnet/coreco/
coreh.html

Crew Systems Ergonomics Information
Analysis Ctr.
http://www.dtic.dla.mil/iac/cseriac/cseriac.html

Ctr. for Display Manufacturing and
Technology, Univ. of Michigan
http://dtm.eecs.umich.edu

Ctr. for In Vivo Microscopy
http://wwwcivm.mc.duke.edu/

Ctr. for Information Enhanced Medicine
(CIeMed)
http://ciemed.iss.nus.sg/ciemed.html

Ctr. for Microelectronics and Optoelectronics
http://www-phys.llnl.gov/H_Div/CMO/
cmo.html

Ctr. for Scientific Computing Graphics
Group (Finland)
http://www.csc.fi:80/visualization/
graphics_group.html

Curt Deckert Associates
http://www.deltanet.com/cda

Cybernetic Vision Research Group,
Universidade de Sao Paulo
http://scorpions.ifqsc.sc.usp.br/ifsc/ffi/grupos/
instrum/visao/cybervision.htm

Data Translation
http://www.datx.com

DataCube
http://www.cera.com/datawwwx.htm

David Sarnoff Research Ctr.
http://www.sarnoff.com//

Directed Perception Inc.
http://www.DPerception.com

Displaytech
http://www.displaytech.com/

Diversity Univ. MOO
http://pass.wayne.edu/DU.html

DSPNET - DSP Technology On-line
http://dspnet.com/

DVC
dvc.html

Electronic Engineering Times (EE Times)
http://techweb.cmp.com:2090/techweb/eet/
current/

Environmental Research Institute of
Michigan (ERIM)
http://www.erim.org

Frank DeFreitas Holography Studio
http://www.enter.net/~holostudio/

Frederik Philips Magnetic Resonance
Research Ctr.
http://www.emory.edu/RADIOLOGY/MRI/
FPMRRCb.html

Gamma and Color FAQ
http://www.inforamp.net/~poynton/Poynton-
colour.html

General Imaging Corp.
http://www.gicorp.com

Georgia Institute of Technology's Graphics, Visualization, and Usability Ctr.
http://www.gatech.edu/gvu/gvutop.htm

Georgia Tech Multimedia Technology Lab
http://www.oip.gatech.edu/mmtltop.html

Graduate Hospital Imaging Ctr.
http://www.netaxs.com/~gradimag/

Guy's and St. Thomas' Hospitals Medical
Image Processing Group
http://nothung.umds.ac.uk/

Harvard - Ctr. for Imaging and Pharmaceutical Research Home Page
http://cipr-diva.mgh.harvard.edu/

Harvard Univ. Robotics Laboratory
http://hrl.harvard.edu

HIPS Image Processing Software
http://www.cns.nyu.edu/home/msl/
hipsdescr.cgi

Hi-Vision Promotion Ctr. (HDTV)
http://www.sfc.keio.ac.jp/~ishitake/KAWA/
hvc1.html

Hologramas de Mexico
www.holomex.com

Hughes STX
http://info.stx.com/

Human Factors and Ergonomics Society
http://vered.rose.utoronto.ca/HFESVE_dir/
HFES.html

Illuminating Engineering Society of North
America
http://www.aecnet.com/IES/ieshome.html

Image Processing With Live Video Sources
http://tns-www.lcs.mit.edu/cgi-bin/vs/vvdemo

Image Science Research Group
http://isg-www.mse.kyutech.ac.jp/ISG/home-
e.html

ImageNation
http://www.ImageNation.com

Indiana Univ Display Technology
http://www.cs.indiana.edu/csg/display.html

INRIA Sophia Antipolis RobotVis Project
http://www.inria.fr/robotvis/personnel/vthierry/
acvis-demo/demo2/main.html

Institute of Computer Science, Computer Vision, Robotics Laboratory in Greece
http://www.ics.forth.gr/proj/cvrl

IPR - Mobile Robotics - Institute for Real Time Computer Systems and Robotics
http://i60s30.ira.ulka.de/areas/
mobilerobots.html

IS&T — Society for Imaging Science & Technology
http://www.imaging.org

JHM
http://jhm.ccs.neu.edu:7043/

John Cowie's video engineering information (w/ SCART)
http://www.bbc.co.uk/aberdeen/tech.htm

Joint Research Program on Digital Video Broadcasting
http://www.tele.unit.no:8080/signal/hdtv.html

Key Centre of Design Computing
http://www.arch.su.edu.au/

Khoros and Khoral Research
http://www.khoros.unm.edu:80/

Kodak
http://www.kodak.com

KU Leuven, Computational Neuroscience & Artificial Intelligence in Vision
http://simone.neuro.kuleuven.ac.be

Lab for Scientific Visual Analysis, Virginia Tech
http://gopher.vt.edu:10021/vizlab/index.html

Laser Focus World
http://www.lfw.com

LBL Imaging and Distributed Computing Group
http://george.lbl.gov:80/ITG.html

Leeds Univ. Medical Imaging
http://agora.leeds.ac.uk/comir/resources/
links.html

LIFIA-IMAG
http://cosmos.imag.fr/PRIMA/prima.html

Light Measurement Handbook
http://www.intl-light.com/handbook.html

Machine Vision Related Research Papers
http://www.mbvlab.wpafb.af.mil/paper.html

Magnetic Resonance Imaging Group
http://www-mri.uta.edu/

Malin Space Science Systems
http://barsoom.msss.com/

Martin Marietta Energy Systems
http://www.ornl.gov/mmes.html

Massachusetts Institute of Technology
http://www.ai.mit.edu/projects/vision-machine/
vm.html

MIT Media Lab - Spatial Imaging Group
http://www.media.mit.edu/

Mathematics Experiences Through Image Processing (METIP)
http://www.cs.washington.edu/research/
metip/metip.html

McDonnell Douglas Corp.
http://pat.mdc.com/

Medical Image Processing Lab - SUNY at Stony Brook
http://clio.rad.sunysb.edu

Medical Imaging
http://agora.leeds.ac.uk/comir/resources/
links.html

Meta Virtual Environments
http://www.gatech.edu/gvu/people/Masters/
Rob.Kooper/Meta.VR.html

Microcosm, Inc.
http://www.softaid.net/spark

Mid-Southwest Data Systems
http://www.webcom.com/~msds/

Molecular Optoelectronics Corp.
http://www.automatrix.com/moec/

Montreal Neurological Institute
http://www.mni.mcgill.ca

Movie Samples from the Open Virtual Reality Testbed
http://nemo.ncsl.nist.gov/~sressler/
OVRTmovies.html

MPEG FAQ
http://www.crs4.it/HTML/LUIGI/MPEG/
mpegfaq.html

NASA Annotated Scientific Visualization URL Bibliography
http://www.nas.nasa.gov/RNR/Visualization/
annotatedURLs.html

NASA Colorless Polyimide Thin Film Technology
http://www.larc.nasa.gov/tops/Exhibits/Ex_W-619/Ex_W-619.html

NASA Helmet Mounted Displays
http://www.larc.nasa.gov/tops/Exhibits/Ex_D-142e.4/Ex_D-142e.4.html

NASA PRISM-3 Johnson Space Ctr.
http://tommy.jsc.nasa.gov/er/er6/mrl/projects/vision/

NASA/JPL Imaging Radar
http://southport.jpl.nasa.gov/

NASA Vision Science
http://vision.arc.nasa.gov/VisionScience

NAVE Navigating and Acting in Virtual Environments
http://www.cs.colorado.edu/homes/cboyd/public_html/Home.html

Navy Ctr. for Applied Research in Artificial Intelligence
http://www.aic.nrl.navy.mil

NIH Imaging Software
zippy.nimh.nih.gov

NII Workshop - Advanced Digital Video
http://www.eeel.nist.gov/advnii/

NIST Intelligent Systems Division
http://isd.cme.nist.gov

NIST Visual Image Processing
http://dsys.ncsl.nist.gov/asd/divsum95/hmisumm.html#Visual

Northeastern Univ. Robotics and Vision Systems Laboratory
http://r2d2.coe.neu.edu

OOPIC Project - George Mason Univ.
http://gui.gmu.edu:80/OOPIC/oopic_home.html

Open Virtual Reality Testbed
http://nemo.ncsl.nist.gov/~sressler/OVRThome.html

Optical Research Associates
http://www.opticalres.com

Optical Society of America
http://www.osa.org

OPTICS.ORG - The Photonics Resource Center
http://optics.org/

Oregon Graduate Institute - Flat Panel Display Research
http://www.eeap.ogi.edu/~barbero/Flat/FPD.html

Osaka Univ. Dept. of Mechanical Engineering for Computer Controlled Machinery
http://www_cv.ccm.eng.osaka-u.ac.jp/research/panther.html

Pattern Recognition Group
http://galaxy.ph.tn.tudelft.nl:2000/pr-intro.html

Pattern Recognition Information
http://www.ph.tn.tudelft.nl/PRInfo.html

Paul Scherrer Institute, PET Programm
http://pss023.psi.ch/

Penn State Multidimensional Image Processing Lab
http://cobb.ece.psu.edu/

Perceptics
http://www.perceptics.com/info

PERCH NMR Software
http://www.uku.fi/perch.html

Pilot European Image Processing Archive
http://peipa.essex.ac.uk/

Poynton's Video Engineering Page
http://www.inforamp.net/~poynton/Poynton-video-eng.html

Precision Digital Images
http://www.precisionimages.com/HOME.HTM

Radiology Imaging Ctr.
http://visual-ra.swmed.edu/

Rochester Institute of Technology— Carlson Center for Imaging Science
http://www.cis.rit.edu

Rochester Institute of Technology, Imaging and Photographic Technology
http://www.rit.edu/~andpph/ipt.html

Royal Institute of Technology Computational Vision and Active Perception Lab (CVAP)
http://www.bion.kth.se/whatis.html

Ruhr Univ. Bochum Institute for Neuroinformatics
http://www.neuroinformatik.ruhr-uni-bochum.de/ini/PROJECTS/NAMOS/NAMOS.html

Rutgers Lab. for Visiometrics and Modelling
http://vizlab.rutgers.edu/

Scientific Visualization of Plasma MHD Behavior
http://www.ornl.gov:80/fed/mhd/mhd.html

SHARE PROJECT CDR Page
http://gummo.stanford.edu/html/SHARE/share.html

SIGGRAPH (ACM Graphics)
http://www.siggraph.org

Signal Processing Information Base (SPIB)
http://spib.rice.edu/spib.html

Signal Processing, Josip Juric, Croatia
http://tjev.tel.etf.hr/josip/DSP/sigproc.html

Signal Processing, Lutz Falkenhagen, Hannover
http://www.tnt.uni-hannover.de/data/info/www/tnt/subj/sci/sig/overview.html

Sliicon Graphics
http://www.sgi.com/

SMPTE - Society of Motion Picture and Television Engineers
http://www.smpte.org

Society for Information Display
http://www.display.org/sid/

Software Spectra (optical thin films design)
http://www.teleport.com/~sspectra/

Sony
http://www.sony.com/~sspectra/

South Bank Univ. - Imaging and Radiotherapy
http://www.sbu.ac.uk/SAS/dirt/

Space Science and Engineering Ctr. Visualization Project at Univ. of Wisconsin-Madison
http://www.ssec.wisc.edu/~billh/vis.html

SPIE - The International Society for Optical Engineering
http://www.spie.org/

Stanford Univ. Vision and Imaging Science and Technology
http://white.stanford.edu/

Subtechnique, Inc.
http://www.subtechnique.com

Swales and Associates Optics Group
http://www.swales.com/optics.html

Synopsys
http://www.synopsys.com/

Technical Reports Index
http://www.cs.indiana.edu/cstr/search

Tecnet
http://www.tecnet.com

Teledyne Brown Electro-Optical Products Group
http://www.tbe.com/tech-pubs/products/optics/optics.html

Teleos Research
http://www.teleos.com

3D Graphic file formats
http://www.tnt.uni-hannover.de/data/info/www/tnt/soft/sci/vis/compgraph/fileformats/overview.html

TrekMUSE
http://grimmy.cnidr.org/trek.html

Triangle Virtual Reality Group (TRIVR)
http://www.trinet.com/trivr.html

UMDS Medical Image Processing Group
http://nothung.umds.ac.uk/

United Medical & Dental Schools Image Processing Group
http://www-ipg.umds.ac.uk/

Univ. of Bergen - Section for Medical Image Analysis and Pattern Recognition
http://www.uib.no/med/avd/miapr/homepage.html

Univ. of British Columbia Laboratory for Computational Intelligence
http://www.cs.ubc.ca/nest/lci/home

UCLA Computer Aided Design
http://cad.ucla.edu/Welcome

Univ. of California, Los Angeles - Crump Institute for Biological Imaging
http://www.nuc.ucla.edu/html_docs/crump/crump.html

Univ. of Coimbra Institute of Systems and Robotics
http://info-isr.dee.uc.pt/~jorge/varma.html

Univ. of Connecticut - Ctr. for Biomedical Imaging Technology
http://panda.uchc.edu/htbit/

Univ. of Derby (UK) Colour Research Group
http://ziggy.derby.ac.uk/colour/

Univ. of Genova Laboratory for Integrated Advanced Robotics
http://afrodite.lira.dist.unige.it:81/LIRA/expsetup/binocul.html

Univ. of Illinois Robotics/Computer Vision Laboratory
http://www.beckman.uiuc.edu/Facilities/BIRCVLab.html

Univ. of Iowa College of Medicine - Physiological Imaging
http://everest.radiology.uiowa.edu/

Univ. of Karlsruhe Institute for Real-Time Computer Systems and Robotics (IPR)
http://wwwipr.ira.uka.de/~priamos/projects/kastor/

Univ. of Kiel Cognitive Systems Group
http://www.informatik.uni-kiel.de/inf/Sommer

Univ. of Leeds - Centre of Medical Imaging Research
http://agora.leeds.ac.uk/comir/comir.html

Univ. of Maryland Computer Vision Laboratory
http://www.cfar.umd.edu/cvl

Univ. of Massachusetts Laboratory for Perceptual Robotics
http://piglet.cs.umass.edu:4321/lpr.html#Facilities

Univ. of Minnesota AHPCRC
http://www.arc.umn.edu/html/Ahpcrc.html

Univ. of Oxford Robotics Research Group
http://www.robots.ox.ac.uk:5000/~lav

Univ. of Pennsylvania GRASP Lab
http://www.cis.upenn.edu/~grasp/head/PennEyes/PennEyes.html

Univ. of Pennsylvania Medical Image Processing
http://mipgsun.mipg.upenn.edu/

Univ. of Rochester Vision and Robotics Lab
http://www.cs.rochester.edu/users/faculty/brown/lab.html

Univ. of Sheffield Artificial Intelligence and Vision Research Unit
http://www2.shef.ac.uk/uni/academic/A-C/aivru

Univ. of Strathclyde Anthropomorphic Robot Head
http://www.strath.ac.uk/Strath.html

Univ. of Surrey Mechatronic Systems and Robotics Research Group
http://robots.surrey.ac.uk/Activities/ActiveVision/activevis.html

Univ. of Surrey Vision, Speech and Signal Processing Group
http://www.ee.surrey.ac.uk/EE/VSSP/intro/node18.html

Univ. of Tennessee Computer Vision and Robotics Research Laboratory
http://kiwi.engr.utk.edu

Univ. of Texas at Arlington Magnetic Resonance Imaging Group
http://www-mri.uta.edu/

Univ. of Tokyo-Fasol Laboratory - Blue Light Emitters
http://kappa.iis.u-tokyo.ac.jp/~fasol/blueledslides.html

Univ. of Toronto Artificial Intelligence Group
http://www.cdf.toronto.edu:80/DCS/Faculty/AI-Faculty.html

Univ. of Utah Vision/Robotics Research Group
http://www.cs.utah.edu:80/projects/robot

Univ. of Washington Virtual Retinal Display
http://www.hitl.washington.edu/projects/vrd/sid-vrd.html

Univ. of Western Australia Robotics and Vision Research Group
http://www.cs.uwa.edu.au/robvis/projects/StereoVerging.html

Univeristy of Waikato Vision
http://www.waikato.ac.nz/

Utah Raster Toolkit
http://www.arc.umn.edu/GVL/Software/urt.html

Vanderbilt Univ. Intelligent Robotics Laboratory
http://www.vuse.vanderbilt.edu/~isac/pantilt.html

Video Webalog
http://figment.fastman.com/vweb/html/vidmain.html

Virginia Tech Laboratory for Scientific
Visual Analysis
http://www.sv.vt.edu

Virgo Optics, Division of II-VI
http://innet.com/~virgo/vhome2.html

Virtual Medical Imaging Ctr.
http://www-sci.lib.uci.edu/HSG/
MedicalImage.html

Virtual Reality Forum Mailing List
http://galaxy.einet.net/e-periodicals/virtual-
reality-forum.txt

Vision1 Image Database List
http://www.vision1.com/imagedb.html

Vision and Imaging Technology Resource
http://www.vision1.com/

Vision Science WWW Virtual Library
http://vision.arc.nasa.gov/VisionScience/
VisionScience.html

Vision Systems International (VSI)
vsi.html

Visioneering Research Lab. - New Mexico
State Univ.
http://vitoria.nmsu.edu/

Visual Systems Lab., Institute for Simulation
http://www.vsl.ist.ucf.edu/about.html

Visualization at the Cornell Theory Ctr.
http://www.tc.cornell.edu/Visualization/

Visualization at TNT
http://www.tnt.uni-hannover.de:80/data/info/
www/tnt/subj/sci/vis/overview.html

Visualization file formats
http://web.msi.umn.edu/WWW/SciVis/
Formats/formats.html

Washington Univ. - MIR Image Processing
Laboratory
http://imacx.wustl.edu/

Waxweb Mosaic MOO
http://bug.village.virginia.edu:7777/

Yale Univ. Image Processing and Analysis
Group
http://noodle.med.yale.edu/

York Univ. Vision, Graphics and Robotics
Lab
http://www.cs.yorku.ca/labs/vgrlab/
Welcome.html

Zentrum fuer Graphische
Datenverarbeitung e.V., Computer
Graphics Ctr.
http://zgdv.igd.fhg.de/

Linguistics & Natural Language

See also Artificial Intelligence, Computer Science, Virtual Reality

Aboriginal Studies Electronic Data
Archive
http://coombs.anu.edu.au/SpecialProj/
ASEDA/ASEDA.html

ACM SIGIR - Information Retrieval
http://info.sigir.acm.org/sigir/

American Dialect Society
http://www.msstate.edu/Archives/ADS

Annual Review of Applied Linguistics
http://www.cup.cam.ac.uk/Journals/
JNLSCAT95/apl.html

Applied Linguistics Association of New
Zealand
http://www.massey.ac.nz/~NZSRDA/
nzssorgs/alanz/alanz.htm

Applied Linguistics WWW Virtual Library
http://alt.venus.co.uk/VL/AppLingBBK/

Applied Science and Engineering Laboratories, U. of Delaware
http://www.asel.udel.edu/

Association for Computational Linguistics
http://www.cs.columbia.edu/~acl/home.html

Association for Computational Phonology
http://www.cogsci.ed.ac.uk/phonology/
CompPhon.html

Association for Linguistic Typology
http://www.ling.lancs.ac.uk/alt

Association for Persian Logic, Language &
Computing
http://www.cogsci.ed.ac.uk/~apl2c

Association for the History of Language
http://adhocalypse.arts.unimelb.edu.au/Dept/
Linguistics/nsn/Work/ahl.html

Austrian Research Institute for Artificial
Intelligence (OFAI)
http://www.ai.univie.ac.at/

Birkbeck College
http://144.82.22.3/Dept.s/AppliedLinguistics/

home.html

British Association for Applied Linguistics
http://www.swan.ac.uk/cals/baal.htm

Brown Univ.
http://www.cog.brown.edu/pointers/
cognitive.html

California State Univ. at Northridge
Program in Linguistics and ESL
http://www.csun.edu/~hflin001/linguist.html

Carnegie Mellon Computational Linguistics Program
http://hss.cmu.edu/HTML/Dept.s/philosophy/
computational_linguistics/
research_comp_ling.html

Carnegie Mellon Univ.- Center for
Machine Translation
http://www.mt.cs.cmu.edu/cmt/CMT-
home.html

Carnegie Mellon Univ. - Human-Com-
puter Interaction Inst.
http://www.cs.cmu.edu/afs/cs.cmu.edu/user/
hcii/www/hcii-home.html

Center for Applied Linguistics (Wash.,
DC)
http://www.cal.org

Center for Cognitive Science, SUNY
Buffalo
http://www.c3.lanl.gov/~rutvik/buffalo.html

Center for the Study of Lang. and Information - Stanford Univ.
http://kanpai.stanford.edu/

Centre for Cognitive Science, Univ.of
Edinburgh
http://www.cogsci.ed.ac.uk/ccs/home.html

Computation and Language E-Print
Archive
http://xxx.lanl.gov/cmp-lg/

Computational Epistemology Lab, U. of Waterloo, Canada
http://beowulf.uwaterloo.ca/

Computational Linguistics and Information Processing Lab, U. of Maryland
http://www.umiacs.umd.edu/labs/CLIP

Computational Linguistics Group, Univ. of Zurich
http://www.ifi.unizh.ch/groups/hess/CLpage.html

Computational Linguistics Journal
http://www-mitpress.mit.edu/jrnls-catalog/comp-ling.html

Computational Linguistics Laboratory, Nara University
http://cactus.aist-nara.ac.jp/lab-english/home-e.html

Computational Linguistics, Univ. of Erlangen
http://uranus.linguistik.uni-erlangen.de/Welcome.html

Consortium for Lexical Research
http://crl.nmsu.edu/clr/CLR.html

DFKI - Kaiserslautern
http://www.dfki.uni-kl.de/

ELSNET - European Network in Lang. and Speech
http://www.cogsci.ed.ac.uk/elsnet/home.html

European Association for Logic, Lang., and Information
http://www.fwi.uva.nl/fwi/research/vg2/folli/

European Lingua Project
http://www.loria.fr/exterieur/equipe/dialogue/lingua/lingua.html

European Speech Communication Association
http://ophale.icp.grenet.fr/esca/esca.html

Georgia Tech - Natural Lang. and Reasoning Research
http://www.cc.gatech.edu/cogsci/nlr.html

German Research Center for AI Computational Linguistics
http://cl-www.dfki.uni-sb.de/

GMD-KONTEXT, Darmstadt
http://www.darmstadt.gmd.de/KONTEXT/kontext.html

Haskins Laboratories, Yale University
http://www.haskins.yale.edu/

Head-Driven Phase Structure Grammar
http://ling.ohio-state.edu/HPSG/Hpsg.html

Hitaka Lab., Kyushu Univ.
http://lang.ai.kyushu-u.ac.jp:8080/nlp.html

Hong Kong Univ.of Science and Technology
http://www.cs.ust.hk

Humboldt Universitat Berlin - Computational Linguistics
http://www.compling.hu-berlin.de/

IJCAI - International Joint Conference on AI
http://ijcai.org

Indonesian Multilingual Machine Translation System
http://nataya.aia.bppt.go.id/immts/immts.html

Inst. for Computational Linguistics, Univ. of Koblenz
http://www.uni-koblenz.de/~compling

Inst. for Logic, Lang. and Computation, Univ. of Amsterdam
http://www.fwi.uva.nl/research/illc/

Inst. for Research in Cognitive Science
http://www.cis.upenn.edu/~ircs/homepage.html

Inst. for Semantic Information Processing
http://hal.cl-ki.uni-osnabrueck.de

Inst. for the Learning Sciences, Northwestern University
http://www.ils.nwu.edu/

Institut d'Informatique de l'Universite de Fribourg
http://www.unifr.ch

Institute of Speech Communication - Stendhal Univ.
http://cristal.icp.grenet.fr:8080/ICP/index.uk.html

Interactive Systems Lab, Univ.of Karlsruhe, Germany
http://werner.ira.uka.de/nnspeech_homepage.html

International Quantitative Linguistics Association
http://www.ldv.uni-trier.de:8080/~iqla/

Intl. Clinical Linguistics and Phonetics Association (ICPLA)
http://tpowel.comdis.lsumc.edu/icpla/icpla.htm

Istituto di Linguistica Computazionale
http://www.ilc.pi.cnr.it

Johns Hopkins University
http://www.cog.jhu.edu/index.html

Journal of Artificial Intelligence Research
http://www.cs.washington.edu/research/jair/home.html

Lancaster Univ.
http://eisv01.lancs.ac.uk/

Lang. & Information Lab - IFI Univ.of Basel
http://www.ifi.unibas.ch/grudo/grudo.html

Language Engineering, UMIST, Manchester
http://www.ccl.umist.ac.uk/

Lexical-Functional Grammar
http://clwww.essex.ac.uk/LFG/

Linguistic Society of America
http://www.lsadc.org

Linguistics Association of Great Britain
http://clwww.essex.ac.uk/LAGB/

Linguistics WWW Virtual Library
http://www.emich.edu/~linguist/www-vl.html

Lund Univ.
http://www.ling.lu.se/

Massachusetts Inst. of Technology - Spoken Lang. Systems Group
http://sls-www.lcs.mit.edu/ec-nsf/mit-sls.html

MENELAS PROJECT, Univ.of Rennes
http://www.med.univ-rennes1.fr/menelas.html

Middle East Technical University
http://www.lcsl.metu.edu.tr

MOL - The Association for Mathematics of Language
http://www-cse.ucsd.edu/users/savitch/MOL/intro.html

National Univ.of Singapore Linguistics Program
http://www.nus.sg/NUSinfo/FASS/linguist.html

Natural Lang. Processing at Columbia Univ.
http://www.cs.columbia.edu:80/~radev/nlp/

Natural Lang. Processing Lab at IRST
http://ecate.itc.it:1024/

New Mexico State Univ.Computing Research Lab
http://crl.nmsu.edu/Home.html

New York Univ.Linguistics Dept.
http://www.nyu.edu/pages/linguistics

NLP in Ireland
http://itdsrv1.ul.ie/NLP/nlp_directory.html

Northwestern Univ.
http://www.ling.nwu.edu/

Oregon Graduate Inst. - Center for Spoken Lang. Understanding
http://www.cse.ogi.edu/CSLU/

Parlevink Linguistic Engineering Project - Univ. of Twente
http://wwwseti.cs.utwente.nl/Docs/parlevink/parlevink.html

Psycoloquy — Psychology electronic journal
http://info.cern.ch/hypertext/DataSources/bySubject/Psychology/Psycoloquy.html

Research in the Lang., Information and Computation Laboratory
http://www.cis.upenn.edu/~cliff-group/94/cliffnotes.html

Simon Fraser University Natural Lang. Laboratory
http://fas.sfu.ca/0/cs/research/groups/NLL/toc.html

SNePS Research Group, SUNY Buffalo
http://www.cs.buffalo.edu/pub/sneps/WWW/index.html

Southern Illinois Univ.at Carbondale.
http://www.siu.edu/Dept.s/cola/ling01

Speech Communication and Music Acoustics, KTH, Sweden
http://www.speech.kth.se/

SRI AI Center Natural Lang. Program
http://www.ai.sri.com/aic/natural-Lang./

SRI International Speech Technology and Research Laboratory
http://www-speech.sri.com/

Stanford HPSG Project
http://hpsg.stanford.edu/

Stanford Univ.- CSLI
http://www-csli.stanford.edu/

Technical Univ.of Berlin, Project Group
KIT
http://flp.cs.tu-berlin.de/kit.html

Technion-Laboratory for Computational
Linguistics
http://www.cs.technion.ac.il/~lcl

Tilburg Univ. - Inst. for Lang. Technology
and Artifical Intelligence
http://itkwww.kub.nl:2080/itk/

Turkish Natural Lang. Processing Project,
Bilkent Univ.
http://www.cs.bilkent.edu.tr/~ko/Turklang.html

UC Davis Multilingual Lab
http://escher.cs.ucdavis.edu:1024/

UCREL - Unit for Computer Research on
the English Language
http://www.comp.lancs.ac.uk/computing/
research/ucrel/

UFRL - Linguistics, Jussieu, Paris
http://www.linguist.jussieu.fr/

Umea Univ.Inst. of Linguistics Umea
Univ.Phonetics Lab
http://jean.ling.umu.se/

Unit for Computer Research on the
English Language
http://www.comp.lancs.ac.uk/computing/
research/ucrel/

Univ. Cal. Irvine Dept. of Linguistics
http://www.socsci.uci.edu/ling/index.html

Univ. Cal. San Diego Center for Research
in Language
http://crl.ucsd.edu/

Univ. de Lausanne
http://www.unil.ch/ling/Bienvenue.html

Univ. of Geneva Dalle Molle Inst. for
Studies on Semantics and Cognition
http://issco-www.unige.ch/

Univ. of Goteborg
http://www.cling.gu.se/index-eng.html

Univ. of London
http://www.phon.ucl.ac.uk/

Univ. of Munich
http://www.phonetik.uni-muenchen.de/

Univ. of Reading
http://midwich.reading.ac.uk

Univ. Regensburg
http://rsls8.sprachlit.uni-regensburg.de/

Univ. Sains Malaysia
http://www.cs.usm.my/utmk/utmkhome.html

Univ. of Amsterdam - Inst. for Logic, Lang.
and Computation
http://www.fwi.uva.nl/fwi/research/vg2/illc/

Univ. of Amsterdam - Inst. of Phonetic
Sciences
http://fonsg3.let.uva.nl/

Univ. of Bielefeld
http://peel.lili.uni-bielefeld.de/

Univ. of Birmingham, Corpus Linguistics
Group
http://clg1.bham.ac.uk/

Univ. of Bochum
http://www.linguistics.ruhr-uni-bochum.de/

Univ. of Calgary
http://www.ucalgary.ca/~southerl/ling/ling.html

Univ. of California, Santa Cruz
http://ling.ucsc.edu

Univ. of Cambridge - NLP group
http://www.cl.cam.ac.uk/Research/NL/
index.html

Univ. of Chicago
http://ap-www.uchicago.edu/AcaPubs/
GradAnno/HumDiv/Lingf.html

Univ. of Copenhagen
http://www.cphling.dk/

Univ. of Delaware - Natural Lang. Interface Group
http://www.asel.udel.edu/natlang/nli.html

Univ.of Durham
http://www.dur.ac.uk/~dcs0rjc/lnle/
lnlehome.html

Univ. of Edinburgh Human Communication Research Center
http://www.cogsci.ed.ac.uk/hcrc/home.html

Univ .of Essen, Germany
http://www.uni-essen.de/fb3/linse/home.htm

Univ. of Essex CL/MT Research Group
http://www.essex.ac.uk/clmt

Univ. of Frankfurt
http://www.rz.uni-frankfurt.de/home/ftp/pub/
titus/public_html

Univ. of Freiburg - Computational
Linguistics
http://www.coling.uni-freiburg.de

Univ. of Groningen, BCN Linguistics
http://www.let.rug.nl/Linguistics/www/

Univ. of Hamburg
http://www.informatik.uni-hamburg.de/
Arbeitsbereiche/NATS/home.html

Univ. of Illinois Speech Lab
http://hawaii.cogsci.uiuc.edu/Speech.html

Univ. of Leeds, Speech Lab
http://lethe.leeds.ac.uk/research/cogn/
speechlab/

Univ. of Liverpool
http://www.liv.ac.uk/~tony1/linguistics.html

Univ. of Manitoba
http://www.umanitoba.ca/linguistics/local.html

Univ. of Maryland Information Filtering
Project
http://www.glue.umd.edu/enee/medlab/filter/
filter_project.html

Univ. of Massachusetts - Information
Extraction
http://ciir.cs.umass.edu/info/ie.html

Univ. of Melbourne
http://adhocalypse.arts.unimelb.edu.au/Dept/
Linguistics/home.html

Univ. of New Mexico
http://www.unm.edu/~bvanb/lingdept.html

Univ. of Nijmegen: Affix Grammars over a
Finite Lattice
http://www.cs.kun.nl/agfl/

Univ. of Oregon
http://babel.uoregon.edu/ling.html

Univ. of Ottawa Knowledge Acquisition
and Machine Learning Group
http://www.csi.uottawa.ca/dept/kaml/
KAML.html

Univ. of Passau
http://www.fmi.uni-passau.de/philf/
lehrstuehle/felix/uebersicht.html

Univ. of Pittsburgh Intelligent Systems
Program
http://www.isp.pitt.edu

Univ. of Reading Speech Lab
http://midwich.reading.ac.uk/research/
speechlab/index.html

Univ. of Rochester - Speech Lab
http://www.cs.rochester.edu/research/speech/
speechlab.html

Univ. of Sheffield - NLP
http://www.dcs.shef.ac.uk/research/groups/
nlp/nlp.html

Univ. of Stuttgart Inst. for Natural Lang.
Processing
http://www.ims.uni-stuttgart.de/IMS.html

Univ. of Sussex Computational Linguistics
http://www.cogs.susx.ac.uk/lab/nlp/index.html

Univ. of the Saarland
http://coli.uni-sb.de/

Univ. of Uppsala, Sweden
http://www.ling.uu.se/

USC - Information Sciences Inst.
http://www.isi.edu/

UT Arlington Linguistics
http://ling.uta.edu/

Victoria Univ.of Wellington, New Zealand
http://www.vuw.ac.nz/ling

Xerox Lexical Technology
http://www.xerox.com/lexdemo/

Yahoo Linguistics Index
http://www.yahoo.com/Social_Science/
Linguistics_and_Human_Languages/

Materials

See also Chemistry, Electronics & Electrical Engineering, Engineering, Optics, Physics

Alloy Tech
http://www.alloytech.com

Aluminium Industry World Wide Web Server
http://www.euro.net/concepts/industry.html

American Chemical Society
http://www.acs.org/

American Crystallographic Association
http://www.hwi.buffalo.edu/ACA/

American Crystallographic Institutes
http://www.hwi.buffalo.edu/ACA/institutes.html

American Geophysical Union
http://pubs.acs.org/

American Hydrogen Association
http://www.getnet.com/charity/aha/index.html

American Institute of Physics
http://aip.org/

American Iron and Steel Institute
http://www.steel.org/

American Iron and Steel Institute Automotive
http://www.autosteel.org/

American Physical Society
http://aps.org/

American Vacuum Society
http://www.vacuum.org/

Ames Lab Materials Preparation Center
http://www.ameslab.gov/mat_ref/mpc.html

Analytical Spectral Devices, Inc. (ASD)
http://www.csn.net/asd/

Anodizers' Plaza
http://www.cc.shibaura-it.ac.jp/~sato/

Arizona State Univ.
http://www.eas.asu.edu/~cbme/

Association of Vacuum Equipment Manufacturers
http://www.avem.org

Battelle
http://www.battelle.org

British Library
http://portico.bl.uk/

Building Industry Exchange (BIX)
http://www.building.com/bix/

Cal Poly Materials Engineering Department
http://www.calpoly.edu/~mate/

Cambridge Scientific Abstracts
http://www.csa.com

Carbon/Carbon Composites
http://www.isc.tamu.edu/~clint/html/CCcomposite.html

Carnegie Mellon Univ.
http://neon.mems.cmu.edu/Home_Page.html

CenBASE Materials on WWW
http://www.castech.fi/

Center for Advanced Materials
http://www.ems.psu.edu/CAM/cama.htm

Center for Advanced Materials Processing - Clarkson Univ.
http://www.clarkson.edu/~dcamp/

Center for Composite Materials - Univ. of Delaware (UDCCM)
http://www.ccm.udel.edu/

Center for Crystallographic Studies
http://weissenberg.ki.ku.dk/

Center for Nondestructive Evaluation at Iowa State Univ.
http://www.cnde.iastate.edu/

Ceramics and Industrial Minerals
http://www.ceramics.com

China Lake Research and Technology
http://peewee.chinalake.navy.mil:80/

China Materials Electronic Bulletin
http://www.chimeb.edu.cn

Colorado School of Mines
http://acsel.mines.edu

Columbus Metallurgical Services
http://www.pobox.com/~chaudhari

Composites Corner
http://www.advmat.com/links.html

Cornell Univ. Materials Science Center
http://www.msc.cornell.edu/

Corrosion Information Server
http://www.cp.umist.ac.uk/

Corrosion and Materials Technology Web
Site
http://www.clihouston.com

Copper Data Center
http://cdc.copper.org

Copper Page
http://www.copper.org/

Coppers Properties for Electrical Energy
Efficiency
http://energy.copper.org

Cornell Univ. - Materials Science and
Engineering
http://www.mse.cornell.edu

Corrosion Materials
http://www.corrmatls.com

Dresden - Ceramic Technologies and
Sintered Materials
http://www.ikts.fhg.de/ikts.engl.html

Drexel Univ. - Department of Materials
Engineering
http://arvind.coe.drexel.edu

Edison Welding Institute
http://www.ewi.org/

Electrochemical Society
http://www.electrochem.org/

Electronic Materials Laboratory at Seoul
National Univ.
http://gong.snu.ac.kr/~emlab/eml.htm

Energy Efficiency and Renewable Energy
Network
http://www.eren.doe.gov

ETHZ - Department of Materials Science
http://lomer.ethz.ch/

European Physical Society
http://aps.org/eps/

European Ceramic Society
http://www.chem.tue.nl/ecers/

Fibrous Monolithic Ceramics and
Stereolithography / Free Form Fabrication
http://www-personal.engin.umich.edu/
~usama

Florida State Univ. - Advanced Mechanics
and Materials Laboratory (AMML)
http://ammlsgi.magnet.fsu.edu/

Fraunhofer Institut fuer Werkstoffphysik
und Schichttechnologie Dresden
http://www.iws.fhg.de/ext/iwseng.htm

GE Plastics Home Page
http://www.ge.com/gep/homepage.html

Georgia Institute of Technology
http://www.prism.gatech.edu/~ph279sw/
group/group.html

Government Contractor Resource Institute
http://www.govcon.com/

Hauptman-Woodward Institute
http://www.hwi.buffalo.edu/

High Temperature Materials Information
Analysis Center
http://cindas.www.ecn.purdue.edu:80/htmiac/

Howard J. Foster Center for Irradiation of
Materials
http://cim.aamu.edu/

HUT / Materials Physics Laboratory
http://waist.hut.fi/

Hydrogen and Fuel Cell Letter
http://www.ttcorp.com/nha/thl/index.htm

Hydrometallurgy at Univ. of British
Columbia
http://www.interchg.ubc.ca/hydromet/
index.html

Hypervelocity Impact Test Facility
http://www-hitf.jsc.nasa.gov/

IKZ Institute of Crystal Growth
http://www.ikz.fta-berlin.de/en/e_info.html

The Institute of Metal Finishing
http://www.finishing.com/IMF/index.html

Institute for Materials Research, SUNY Binghamton
http://imr.chem.binghamton.edu/

International Union of Materials
http://mrcemis.ms.nwu.edu/iumrs/index.html

The Institute of Materials
http://www.instmat.co.uk/

International School of Technology, Krakow
http://www.ist.agh.edu.pl

International Society of Hybrid Microelectronics
http://weber.u.washington.edu/~andyw/ISHM/index.html

International Union of Crystallography
http://www.iucr.ac.uk/

Istituto Giordano
http://www.nettuno.it/fiera/ig/igpres.htm

Italian Institute of Copper
http://www.iir.it

Japan Information Center for Science and Technology
http://www.jicst.go.jp/

KTH Materials Science and Engineering
http://www.met.kth.se/

Kwangju Institute of Science and Technology
http://matla.kjist.ac.kr/

Laboratoire de MinÈralogie-Cristallographie Paris
http://www.lmcp.jussieu.fr/

Laboratoire de MÈcanique des Solides
http://xela.polytechnique.fr/

Laboratoire Des Verres
http://www.ldv.univ-montp2.fr

Laboratory for Solid Freeform Fabrication of Advanced Ceramics
http://www.caip.rutgers.edu/sff/

Materials Algorithms Project (MAP)
http://www.msm.cam.ac.uk/map/mapmain.html

Materials Preparation Center
http://www.ameslab.gov/mat_ref/mpc.html

Materials and Manufacturing Technology
http://picard.ml.wpafb.af.mil:80/

Materials Research Society (MRS)
http://www.mrs.org

Materials Science Education
http://msewww.engin.umich.edu/people/darcyc/default.html

Max-Planck-Institut fuer Eisenforschung
http://www.mpie-duesseldorf.mpg.de/

METAL Machining and Fabrication
http://www.mmf.com/metal/index.html

Metal Organic Chemical Vapor Deposition
http://mocvd.com

Metals Information Analysis Center (MIAC)
http://cindas.ecn.purdue.edu/miac/

Michigan State Univ.
http://web.egr.msu.edu/MSM/index.html

MineNet
http://www.microserve.net:80/~doug/

Minerals Metals and Materials Society (TMS)
http://www.tms.org/

MIT - Electroceramics Group
http://pyrochlore.mit.edu

MIT - Materials Systems Laboratory
http://web.mit.edu/org/c/ctpid/www/msl/index.html

Monash Univ. - Department of Materials Engineering
http://www.monash.edu.au/mateng/index.htm

Monsanto Web
http://www.monsanto.com/

MTIR - Materials Testing Internet Resources
http://www.geocities.com/SiliconValley/3300/

NACE International
http://www.nace.org/

NASA Technical Report Server (NTRS)
http://techreports.larc.nasa.gov/cgi-bin/NTRS

NASA Scientific and Technical Information Server
http://www.sti.nasa.gov/STI-homepage.html

National Hydrogen Association
http://www.ttcorp.com/nha/

National Center for Excellence in Metalworking Technology (NCEMT)
http://www.ncemt.ctc.com/index.html

National Excellence in Materials Joining
http://ewi.ewi.org/nemj/home.html

NIST Ceramics Division
http://www.ceramics.nist.gov

NIST Physics Laboratory Physical
Reference Data
http://physics.nist.gov/PhysRefData/
contents.htm

National Technical Univ. of Athens
http://www.metal.ntua.gr/

National Research Council of Canada
Non-Destructive Evaluation (NDE)
group
http://www.nrc.ca/iar/smp_nde-e.html

National Technical Univ. of Athens
http://www.metal.ntua.gr/

National Technology Transfer Center
http://www.nttc.edu/

The Navy Joining Center
http://ewi.ewi.org/njc/home.html

Nondestructive Tesing Information
Analysis Center
http://www.dtic.dla.mil/iac/ntiac/
ntiachome.html

Northwestern Univ. - Materials Research
Center
http://mrcemis.ms.nwu.edu/

Oak Ridge Centers for Manufacturing
Technology
http://www.ornl.gov/orcmt/

Ohio State Univ. Material and Science
Engineering
http://kcgl1.eng.ohio-state.edu/mse/

Optical Properties and Electronic Structure
http://www.lrsm.upenn.edu/~frenchrh/
opes.htm

OPTICS.ORG - The Photonics Resource
Center
http://optics.org

Oxygen Chemistry
http://wwwchem.tamu.edu./rgroup/sawyer/
sawyer.html/

Oxygen Club of California
http://radicals.berkeley.edu/

Oxygen Compatibility Page
http://l12id.jsc.nasa.gov/

Oxygen Society
http://www.biophysics.mcw.edu/oxsoc/

Particle-Surface Resources on the Internet
http://chaos.fullerton.edu/mhslinks.html

Pohang Univ. of Science and Technology
http://luv.postech.ac.kr/

PolySort
http://www.polysort.com/

Princeton Materials Institute
http://pmi.princeton.edu/

Protein Crystallography Links
http://www-mslmb.niddk.nih.gov/procryst.html

Purdue Univ. - High Temperature Materials Information Analysis Center
http://cindas.www.ecn.purdue.edu/htmiac/

Reynolds Metals World Wide Web Server
http://www.rmc.com/

Rockwell Science Center Materials Science
http://www.risc.rockwell.com:80/209/

Royal Institute of Technology Solid
Mechanics
http://www.hallf.kth.se/

Scientific Intrument Services
http://www.sisweb.com/

Seoul National Univ. - School of Materials
Science and Engineering
http://gong.snu.ac.kr/~smse_www

Smart Materials
http://www.sciam.com/explorations/
050596explorations.html

Society for the Advancement of Material
and Process Engineering (SAMPE)
http://www.et.byu.edu/~sampe/

Society of Plastics Engineers
http://www.4spe.org/

Society of Vacuum Coaters
http://www.svc.org

South East Asia Iron & Steel Institute
http://www.jaring.my/seaisi/

SRI International
http://www.sri.com/

Stanford Univ. - Material Sciences &
Engineering
http://www-mse.stanford.edu/

Steel Manufacturers Association Steelnet
http://www.steelnet.org/

Technical Univ. of Nova Scotia
http://www.tuns.ca/~brydenrh/ceramics.html

Technical Univ. of Denmark
http://www.fam.dtu.dk/

TRW, Inc.
http://www.trw.com/

TU Chemnitz - Materials Science
http://www.tu-chemnitz.de/~hkl/
info_2ls_e.html

TU Delft - Chemical Technology and
Materials Science
http://dutsh7.tudelft.nl/

Univ. of Alberta - Advanced Minerals &
Processing Laboratory
http://www.ualberta.ca/~mete/ampl/ampl.htm

Univ. of California, Santa Barbara -
Materials
http://www.materials.ucsb.edu/

Univ. of Cambridge - Materials Science
and Metallurgy
http://www.msm.cam.ac.uk/

Univ. of Cincinnati - Materials Engineering
http://www.eng.uc.edu/mse/index.html

Univ. of Connecticut - Institute of Materials Science
http://www.ims.uconn.edu

Univ.e Federal de Sao Carlos
http://www.nit.ufscar.br/dema.html

Univ. of Florida - Materials Science
http://zirconia.mse.ufl.edu

Univ. of Illinois Center for Microanalysis
of Materials
http://www.mrl.uiuc.edu/~www/mrl/cmm/

UIUC - Materials Research Laboratory
http://www.mrl.uiuc.edu/

Univ. of Maryland at College Park - Center
For Microanalysis
http://www.glue.umd.edu/~junhui/lab/

Univ. of Liverpool (UK) Materials Science
And Engineering
http://www.liv.ac.uk/mateng/home.html

Univ. of Manchester - Materials Science
Centre
http://www.man.ac.uk/MatSci/

Univ. of Massachusetts Lowell
http://ipi.eng.uml.edu/

Univ. of Michigan - Department of
Material Science
http://www.engin.umich.edu/~jfmjfm/
mse_folder/mse_home_page.html

Univ. of Mississippi - Composite Materials
Research Group
http://cypress.mcsr.olemiss.edu/~melackey/

Univ. of Missouri-Rolla
http://www.umr.edu/~meteng/wmeteng.html

Univ. Nacional Autonoma de Mexico -
Instituto de Investigaciones en
Materiales
http://serpiente.dgsca.unam.mx/iim/

Univ. of New South Wales
http://www.materials.unsw.edu.au/

Univ. of Pennsylvania - Laboratory for
Research on the Structure of Matter
http://www.lrsm.upenn.edu/

Univ. of Pretoria Material Science &
Metallurgical Engineering
http://www.ee.up.ac.za/mmi/intro.html

Univ. of Southern California
http://www.usc.edu/dept/materials_science/
materials_science.html

Univ. of Stuttgart State Material Testing
Laboratory
http://www.mpa.uni-stuttgart.de/index-
english.html

Univ. of Surrey - Materials Science and
Engineering
http://www.surrey.ac.uk/MSE.html

Univ. of Tennessee - Knoxville
http://www.engr.utk.edu/dept/mse/

Univ. of Toronto - Electronic Materials
Group
http://www.toronto.edu/~emg/

Univ. of Utah - Material Science and
Engineering
http://www.matsci.utah.edu/

Univ. of Utah - Metallurgical Engineering
http://www.mines.utah.edu/~wmmete/

Univ. of Virginia
http://bohr.ms.virginia.edu/

Univ. of Wisconsin, Madison - Materials Research Group
http://mrgcvd.engr.wisc.edu/

US National Committee for Crystallography
http://www.sdsc.edu/Xtal/USNCCr/USNCCr.html

Virginia Tech - Materials Science and Engineering
http://www.eng.vt.edu/eng/materials/mse.html

Visualizing Material Science
http://vims.ncsu.edu

Wakefield Corp.
http://www.tiac.net/users/twc/

Welding Information Network
http://www.vnetsys.com

Wright-Patterson Air Force Base Materials and Manufacturing Technology Directorates
http://picard.ml.wpafb.af.mil/

WWW Virtual Library for Technical Ceramics -
http://www.ikts.fhg.de/ceramics.html

X-ray Microscope for Solidification Studies
http://wwwssl.msfc.nasa.gov/ssl/msad/xray/

Mathematics

See also Computer Science, Physics

Acta Mathematica Universitatis Comenianae
http://www.emis.de/journals/AMUC/_amuc.html

Acta Numerica
http://www.cup.cam.ac.uk/Journals/JNLSCAT95/anu.html

Acta Scientiarum Mathematicarum
http://www.math.u-szeged.hu/publikac/acta/acta.htm

Advances in Computational Mathematics
http://www.math.psu.edu/dna/contents/aicm.html

Advances in Systems Science and Applications
http://assa.math.swt.edu

Algebraic Topology
http://hopf.math.purdue.edu/pub/hopf.html

Algebraic-Number-Theory
http://www.math.uiuc.edu/Algebraic-Number-Theory/

American Journal of Mathematics
http://muse.jhu.edu/journals/american_journal_of_mathematics/

American Mathematical Society
http://e-math.ams.org/

Annales Academiae Scientiarum Fennicae
http://geom.helsinki.fi/Annales/Anna.html

Application-oriented Algorithmic Mathematics

Applied Mathematics and Theoretical Physics (DAMTP)
http://www.damtp.cam.ac.uk/
http://elib.zib-berlin.de/

Argonne National Lab
http://www.mcs.anl.gov/index.html

Association for Computing Machinery (ACM)
http://info.acm.org/

Association for Women in Mathematics
http://xerxes.nas.edu:70/1/cwse/AWM.html

Australian CSIRO Math/Stat
http://www.dms.csiro.au/

Australian Mathematical Society
http://solution.maths.unsw.edu.au/htdocs.ams/amswelcome.html

Australian National Univ.
http://pell.anu.edu.au/index.html

Banach Spaces and Functional Analysis
http://math.okstate.edu/cgi-bin/wais.pl/banach

Basic Research Institute in the Mathematical Sciences
http://www-uk.hpl.hp.com/brims/

Biomathematics and Statistics Scotland
http://www.bioss.sari.ac.uk

Bulletin Board for Librarians, Mathematics
http://www.bubl.bath.ac.uk/BUBL/Mathematics.html

Bulletin of the London Mathematical Society
http://www.cup.cam.ac.uk/Journals/JNLSCAT95/blm.html

Calculus of Variations and the Geometry of Nature
http://www.sns.it/html/IPS/Main.html

California Institute of Technology
http://www.ama.caltech.edu/

California State Univ., Hayward
http://www.mcs.csuhayward.edu/mcs.html

Canadian Mathematical Electronic Web
http://camel.cecm.sfu.ca/

Canadian Mathematical Society
http://camel.cecm.sfu.ca/home.html

Catalogue of Algebraic Systems
http://www.math.usf.edu/algctlg/INDEX.html

Category Theory Home Page
http://www.mta.ca/~cat-dist/categories.html

Center for Advanced Studies, Sardinia
Applied Math Group
http://www.crs4.it/~valde/
group_homepage.html

Center for Applied Mathematics and
Theoretical Physics
http://www.uni-mb.si/robnik.html

Center for Complex Systems Research
http://www.ccsr.uiuc.edu/

Center for Dynamical Systems and
Nonlinear Studies
http://www.math.gatech.edu/CDSNS/info.html

Center for Geometry Analysis Numerics
and Graphics at UMass Amherst
http://www.gang.umass.edu/

Center for Gravitational Physics and
Geometry
http://vishnu.nirvana.phys.psu.edu/

Center for Statistical and Mathematical
Computing
http://www.indiana.edu/~statmath/

Center for Statistical Consultation and
Research
http://www.umich.edu:80/~cscar

Centre for Engineering and Industrial
Mathematics
http://www.uow.edu.au/public/faculties/
informatics/ceim.html#ceim_top

Centre for Experimental & Constructive
Mathematics
http://mosaic.cecm.sfu.ca/

Centre for Industrial and Applied Mathematics
http://phoenix.levels.unisa.edu.au/ciam/
index.html

Centrum voor Wiskunde en Informatica
http://www.cwi.nl/

Chalmers Tekniska Högskola/Göteborgs
Universitet
http://math.chalmers.se/Public/

CHANCE: Probability or Statistics course
information
http://www.geom.umn.edu/docs/snell/chance/
welcome.html

Chaos at Univ. of Maryland
http://www-chaos.umd.edu/

CIRM library
http://cirm.univ-mrs.fr/

CMU Center for Nonlinear Analysis
http://www.cmu.edu/mcs/math/cna.html

Coalition of Automated Mathematics and
Science Education Databases
http://www.enc.org/camsed/

Combinatorial and Geometric Group
Theory
http://zebra.sci.ccny.cuny.edu/web/html/
magnus.html

Combinatorics
http://www.c3.lanl.gov/laces

Communications in Analysis and Geometry
http://testweb.acs.uci.edu/mathweb/
commin.html

Communications in Numerical Methods in
Engineering
http://www.ep.cs.nott.ac.uk/wiley/
numeng.html

Complex Dynamics and Hyperbolic
Geometry
http://www.msri.org/preprints/cd-hg.html

Computational Fluid Dynamics
http://www.tfd.chalmers.se/CFD_Online/

Computer Algebra Information Network
http://cand.can.nl/

Constructive Approximation
http://www.math.usf.edu/CA

Cornell Center for Applied Mathematics
http://cam.cornell.edu/

Courant Institute of NYU
http://www.cims.nyu.edu/

Cryptography Archive
http://www.quadralay.com/www/Crypt/
Crypt.html

CTI Centre for Mathematics and Statistics
http://www.bham.ac.uk/ctimath/

Databases on Mathematics (in German)
http://www.zblmath.fiz-karlsruhe.de/

De Montfort Univ.
http://www.cms.dmu.ac.uk/People/maths-people.html

Delft Univ. of Technology
http://www.twi.tudelft.nl/TWI/Overview.html

Deutsche Mathematiker-Vereinigung
http://www_dmv.math.tu-berlin.de

Differential Geometry and Global Analysis
http://www.msri.org/preprints/dg-ga.html

DIMACS
http://dimacs.rutgers.edu/

Documenta Mathematica
http://www.mathematik.uni-bielefeld.de/DMV-J/

Dynamical Systems
http://math.sunysb.edu/preprints.html

Dynamics and Stability of Systems
http://www.amsta.leeds.ac.uk/Applied/news.dir/dss.dirvol10.html

Dynamics of Continuous, Discrete and Impulsive Systems
http://jeeves.uwaterloo.ca/AM_Dept/dcdis/dcdis.html

École Normale Supérieure - Paris
http://www.ens.fr/

Edinburgh Mathematical Society
http://www.maths.heriot-watt.ac.uk/ems/

Eindhoven Univ. of Technology
http://www.win.tue.nl/

Eisenhower National Clearinghouse
http://www.enc.org/

Electronic Colloquium on Computational Complexity
http://www.eccc.uni-trier.de/eccc/

Electronic Communications in Probability
http://math.washington.edu/~ejpecp/

Electronic Transactions in Numerical Analysis
http://etna.mcs.kent.edu/

EPF Lausanne
http://dmawww.epfl.ch/

Erdos Numbers
http://www.acs.oakland.edu/~grossman/erdoshp.html

Erwin Schrodinger Institute of Mathematical Physics
http://www.esi.ac.at/ESI-home.html

ETH Zürich
http://www.math.ethz.ch/

Euler Institute fot Discrete Mathematics and its Applications
http://www.win.tue.nl/win/math/eidma/index.html

EURHomogenization
http://www.informatik.unibw-muenchen.de/informatik/Institute/inst1/eurohom.html

Euromath Bulletin
http://sophie.helsinki.fi/~emb/

Euromath Center
http://dan-emir.euromath.dk/emc-www/euromath.html

European Mathematical Society
http://www.emis.de/

European Research Consortium for Informatics and Mathematics
http://www-ercim.inria.fr/

Exp(Pi*Sqrt(n)) Page
http://www.ccsf.caltech.edu/~roy/episqrtn.html

Experimental Mathematics
http://www.geom.umn.edu/locate/expmath

Fibonacci Numbers
http://math.holycross.edu/~davids/fibonacci/fibonacci.html

Flanders Mathematics Olympiad
http://www.kulak.ac.be/vwo/vwowww.html

Florida State Univ. Numerical Analysis
http://euclid.math.fsu.edu/Science/num.html

FORTWIHR
http://hpzenger2.informatik.tu-muenchen.de/forschung/fortwihr/fortwihr_e.html

Fractals
http://spanky.triumf.ca/

Freie Univ.Berlin
http://www.math.fu-berlin.de/

Functional Analysis
http://mentor.lanl.gov/eprints/mkheader/funct-an

Furman Univ. Electronic Journal of
Undergraduate Mathematics
http://math.furman.edu/~mwoodard/fuejum/
welcome.html

Fuzzy Logic Lab. Linz
http://www.flll.uni-linz.ac.at

Center for Geometry, Analysis, Numerics
and Graphics
http://www.gang.umass.edu/

Geometry Ctr.
http://www.geom.umn.edu/

Geometry Forum
http://forum.swarthmore.edu/

Geometry in Action-Applications of
Discrete and Computational Geometry
http://www.ics.uci.edu/~eppstein/geom.html

Georgia Tech's Applied Chaos Lab.
http://nextworld.cc.gatech.edu:8001/Matt/acl/
aclhome.html

Graphics and Analysis Software
http://www-ocean.tamu.edu/~baum/
ocean_graphics.html

Groupe Fractales
http://www-syntim.inria.fr/fractales/

Harmonic Maps Bibliography
http://www.bath.ac.uk/~masfeb/harmonic.html

Homogenization and Optimal Design
http://www.informatik.unibw-muenchen.de/
informatik/Institute/inst1/preprints.html

Hong Kong Mathematical Society
http://euler.math.cuhk.hk/hkms/hkms.html

Hub Resources for Mathematics Education
http://hub.terc.edu:70/hub/math/

Hypermedia Lab.
http://matwww.ee.tut.fi/hmlab/homepage.html

IMA Journal of Numerical Analysis
http://www.math.psu.edu/dna/contents/
imajna.html

Indiana Univ. Ctr. for Statistical and
Mathematical Computing
http://www.statmath.indiana.edu/

Industrial Mathematics Institute
http://www.indmath.uni-linz.ac.at/

INFORMS Online
http://www.informs.org/

Institut de Recherche Mathematique de
Rennes
http://www.univ-rennes1.fr/labos/IRMAR/
IRMAR.html

Institute for Advanced Study
http://www.math.ias.edu/

Institute for Applied Mathematics
http://www.num.uni-sb.de/

Institute for Computer Applications in
Science and Engineering
http://www.icase.edu/

Institute for Mathematics and its Applications
http://www.ima.umn.edu/

Institute of Applied and Computational
Mathematics
http://www.iacm.forth.gr/

Institute of Cybernetics, Applied Mathematics
http://www.ioc.ee/matem/maths.html

Institute of Information Theory and
Automation
http://www.utia.cas.cz/

Institute of Mathematical Modelling
(IMM) at The Technical Univ. of
Denmark (DTU)
http://snake1.imsor.dth.dk/homepage.html

Institute of Mathematical Sciences
http://www.imsc.ernet.in/

Institute of Mathematics and Computer
Science in Medicine
http://www.uni-hamburg.de/~medizin/imdm

Institute of Mathematics and its Applications
http://www-chel.anglia.ac.uk/~imacrh/
index.html

Institute of Mathematics, Physics and
Mechanics
http://www.mat.uni-lj.si/bin/counter/
webcount.exe?imfm

Institute of Numerical Mathematics
http://www.ac.msk.su/local.docs/inm/inm.html

Instituto de Matematicas y Estadistica
http://www.fing.edu.uy/imerl.html

Instituto Nacional de Pesquisas Espaciais
Brazil
http://www.inpe.br/lac/home

Interesting Places for Numerical
Analysists
http://aspin.asu.edu/provider/l.lu/num_anal/
index.html

International Centre for Mathematical
Sciences, Edinburgh
http://www.ma.hw.ac.uk/icms/

International Clifford Algebra Society
http://century22.martin.org/~clf-alg/

International Congress of Mathematicians
Berlin 1998
http://elib.zib-berlin.de/ICM98

International Federation of Nonlinear
Analysts
http://www.fit.edu/math/ifna.html

International Journal for Numerical
Methods in Engineering
http://www.ep.cs.nott.ac.uk/wiley/
numeng.html

International Linear Algebra Society
http://gauss.technion.ac.il/iic

International Mathematical Union
http://elib.zib-berlin.de/IMU

Internet Center for Mathematics Problems
http://www.mathpro.com:80/math/
mathCenter.html

Interval Computations Homepage
http://cs.utep.edu/interval-comp/main.html

Inverse Symbolic Calculator
http://www.cecm.sfu.ca/projects/ISC.html

Iowa State Univ.
http://www.public.iastate.edu/~math/
homepage.html

Isaac Newton Institute for Mathematical
Sciences
http://www.newton.cam.ac.uk/

Jobs in Mathematics
http://www.cs.dartmouth.edu:80/~gdavis/
policy/jobmarket.html

Jyväskylä Univ.
http://www.math.jyu.fi/

K-theory
http://www.math.uiuc.edu/K-theory/

Kent State Univ.
http://www.mcs.kent.edu/home.html

Konrad-Zuse-Zentrum
http://www.zib-berlin.de/

Lab. for Computer Aided Mathematics
http://sophie.helsinki.fi/

Lajos Kossuth Univ.
http://www.math.klte.hu/

Lancaster Univ.
http://mathssun5.lancs.ac.uk:2080/

Largest Known Primes
http://www.utm.edu/departments/math/
largest.html

Le Journal de maths
http://www.ens-lyon.fr/JME/JME.html

Linear Algebra and its Applications
http://gauss.technion.ac.il/iic/LAA.INDEX

Logic and Set Theory
http://www.math.ufl.edu:80/~logic/

Logic Eprints
http://www.math.ufl.edu/~logic/

London Mathematical Society
http://www.qmw.ac.uk/~lms/lms.html

Los Alamos Combinatorics E-print Server
http://www.c3.lanl.gov/laces

Louisiana Tech Univ.
http://www.math.latech.edu/math/
mathematics.html

Loyola Univ., Chicago
http://www.math.luc.edu/

Luleå Univ.
http://www.sm.luth.se/math/

Lund Univ. / Lund Institute of Technology
http://www.maths.lth.se/

Manchester Centre for Computational
Mathematics
http://www.ma.man.ac.uk/MCCM/MCCM.html

Massey Univ.
http://smis-www.massey.ac.nz/maths/
Math_htmls/maths.html

MATCH
http://btm2xd.mat.uni-bayreuth.de/match

Math-Net at Konrad-Zuse-Zentrum
http://elib.zib-berlin.de:88/Math-Net/Links/
math.html

Mathematica Militaris
http://euler.math.usma.edu:80/militaris.html

Mathematica Related URLs
http://smc.vnet.net/mathsite.html

Mathematica World
http://www.vut.edu.au/MW/

Mathematical Association of America
http://www.maa.org/

Mathematical BBS Ferrara
http://felix.unife.it/

Mathematical Branch of Russian Academy
of Sciences (RAS)
http://www.ras.ru/

Mathematical Institute of the Hungarian
Academy of Sciences
http://www.math-inst.hu/

Mathematical Logic
http://www.math.ufl.edu:80/~logic/

Mathematical Optimization TU
Braunschweig
http://moa.math.nat.tu-bs.de/welcome.html

Mathematical Physics
http://henri.ma.utexas.edu/mp_arc/mp_arc-
home.html

Mathematical Psychology
http://www.uniovi.es/UniOvi/Apartados/
Departamento/Psicologia/metodos/

Mathematical Quotations
http://math.furman.edu/~mwoodard/
mquot.html

Mathematical Resources on the Web
http://www.math.ufl.edu/math/math-web.html

Mathematical Sciences Education Board
http://xerxes.nas.edu:70/0/mseb/mseb.html

Mathematical Sciences Research Institute
http://www.msri.org/

Mathematics of Control, Signals, and
Systems
http://www.cwi.nl/cwi/departments/BS3/
mcss.html

Mathematics On-Line Bookshelf
http://mathbookshelf.fullerton.edu/

Mathematics-related LISTSERV lists
http://www.clark.net/pub/listserv/lsmath1.html

Mathematics WWW Virtual Library
http://euclid.math.fsu.edu/Science/math.html

Mathematische Gesellschaft in Hamburg
http://www.math.uni-hamburg.de/math/
mathges/

Mathematisches Forschungsinstitut
Oberwolfach
http://www.mfo.de/

MathSearch
http://ms.maths.usyd.edu.au:8000/
MathSearch.html

MathWorks Home Page
http://www.mathworks.com/homepage.html

MATLAB Gallery
http://www.mathworks.com/gallery.html

McMaster Univ.
http://www.science.mcmaster.ca/MathStat/
Dept.html

MegaMath
http://www.c3.lanl.gov/mega-math/index.html

Michael Trick's Operations Research Page
http://mat.gsia.cmu.edu/

Mittag-Leffler Institute
http://www.ml.kva.se/

Monash Univ.
http://www.maths.monash.edu.au/

Mount Allison Univ.
http://www.mta.ca/faculty/science/math/

MSRI E-Print Archive
http://www.msri.org/preprints/archive.html

Multidimensional Analysis
http://www.ctr.columbia.edu/~hart/
multanal.html

NA-Digest
http://www.netlib.org/na-digest/html/
index.html

National Academy of Science
http://www.nas.edu/

National Council of Teachers of Mathematics
http://www.pbs.org/learning/mathline/
nctmhome.html

Netlib Conferences Database
http://www.netlib.org/confdb/
Conferences.html

New Zealand Mathematical Society
http://www.math.auckland.ac.nz/~conder/
NZMS/

NIST's Guide to Available Mathematics
Software
http://gams.nist.gov/

Nonlinear Dynamics and Topological Time Series Analysis Archive
http://t13.lanl.gov/~nxt/intro.html

Nonlinear Dynamics and Topological Time Series Analysis Archive
http://cnls-www.lanl.gov/nbt/intro.html

Nonlinear Programming FAQ
http://www.skypoint.com/subscribers/ashbury/nonlinear-programming-faq.html

Nonlinear Science
http://xyz.lanl.gov/

Nonlinear Science Today
http://www.springer-ny.com/nst

Nonlinearity and Complexity
http://www.cc.duth.gr/~mboudour/nonlin.html

North Carolina State Univ.
http://www2.ncsu.edu/ncsu/pams/math/

Northwestern Univ.
http://www.math.nwu.edu/

NSF Science and Technology Information System
http://stis.nsf.gov/

Number Theory Web
http://www.maths.uq.oz.au/~krm/web.html

Numerical Algorithms
http://www.math.psu.edu/dna/contents/na.html

Numerical Algorithms Group Limited
http://www.nag.co.uk:70/

Numerical Analysis
http://www.na.ms.osakafu-u.ac.jp/

Numerical Harmonic Analysis Group
http://tyche.mat.univie.ac.at/

Oak Ridge National Lab. Mathematical Sciences
http://www.epm.ornl.gov/msr

Odense Univ. preprint archive
http://www.imada.ou.dk/Research/preprints.html

Operations Research and Management Science
http://www.maths.mu.oz.au/~worms/

Operator Algebra Resources
http://darkwing.uoregon.edu/~ncp/opalg.html

Paradoxes
http://neptune.corp.harris.com/paradox.html

pLab Project
http://random.mat.sbg.ac.at/home.html

Planet Earth Mathematics Node
http://white.nosc.mil/math.html

Probability Abstract Service
http://math.washington.edu/~prob

Probability Web
http://www.maths.uq.oz.au/~pkp/probweb/probweb.html

Pure Mathematics Preprints
http://www.mth.uea.ac.uk/maths/maths-preprints-pure.html

Quantum Algebra and Knot Theory
http://www.msri.org/preprints/q-alg.html

Queen's Univ. of Belfast
http://www.am.qub.ac.uk/

Random Number Generation and Stochastic Simulation
http://random.mat.sbg.ac.at/others/

REDUCE Computer Algebra system
http://www.rrz.uni-koeln.de/REDUCE/

Representations and Cohomology of Groups
http://www.math.uga.edu/~djb/archive.html

Research Centre of Applied Mathematics CIRAM
http://eulero.cineca.it/

Results in Mathematics/Resultate der Mathematik
http://www.uni-duisburg.de/FB11/PUBL/RiM/ResMath.html

Revista Colombiana de Matematicas
http://157.253.147.9/~olezama/

Royal Institute of Technology
http://www.nada.kth.se/

Russian Academy of Sciences
http://www.ras.ru/RAS/om.html

Russian Mathematicians Directory
http://www.ac.msk.su/cgi-bin/wld

SAD
http://www.sad.uci.edu

SASIAM
http://fourier.csata.it/

Science Television
http://www.service.com/stv/

Semigroup Forum
http://bach.math.tulane.edu/SF.html

Semigroup Theory
http://www.maths.soton.ac.uk/semigroups/
homepage.html

Shell Centre for Mathematical Education
http://acorn.educ.nottingham.ac.uk/ShellCent/

Society for Industrial and Applied
Mathematics
http://www.siam.org/

Southwest Journal of Pure and Applied
Mathematics
http://rattler.cameron.edu/swjpam.html

Spanky Fractal Database
http://spanky.triumf.ca/

SPIE-The Intl. Society for Optical Engineering
http://www.spie.org/

Statistical Lab., Univ. of Cambridge
http://www.statslab.cam.ac.uk/

Steklov Mathematical Institute
http://www.ac.msk.su/local.docs/mian/
mian.html

Stevens Institute of Technology
http://www.stevens-tech.edu/stevens/math/
math.html

Stochastic Finite Elements: A Spectral
Approach
http://venus.ce.jhu.edu/book/book.html

Stockholm Univ.
http://www.matematik.su.se/

Student Mathematical Societies in the UK
http://info.ox.ac.uk:80/~invar/home.html

SunSITE Mathematical Art Gallery
http://sunsite.unc.edu/pics/mathgif.html

Surveys on Mathematics for Industry
http://www.indmath.uni-linz.ac.at/

Swarthmore Geometry Forum
http://forum.swarthmore.edu/index.html

Systems and Control Archive at Dallas
http://www.utdallas.edu/research/scad/

TANGENTS - The Harvard Mathematics
Bulletin
http://www.digitas.org/tangents

Technical Univ. of Budapest, Hungary
http://www.vma.bme.hu/0h/html/
home_eng.html

Technical Univ. of Chemnitz-Zwickau
http://www.tu-chemnitz.de/2/mathe/
Mathe_E.html

Technische Univ.at München
http://www.mathematik.tu-muenchen.de/

Technische Univ.Berlin
http://www.math.tu-berlin.de/

TeX Archive Network
http://jasper.ora.com

TeX Information
http:/www.dante.de

Texas A&M Univ.
http://mosaic.math.tamu.edu/math-home-
page.html

Theory and Applications of Categories
http://www.tac.mta.ca/tac/

Transactions of Operations Research and
Management Science
http://catt.bus.okstate.edu/itorms/

Transactions on Mathematical Software
http://gams.nist.gov/toms/Overview.html

Transitional Mathematics Project
http://othello.ma.ic.ac.uk/

Trinity College Dublin
http://www.maths.tcd.ie/

Tulane Univ.
http://bach.math.tulane.edu/

Turkish Mathematical Society
http://gopher.bilkent.edu.tr:7001/1s/inet-hotel/
tmd/

UK Nonlinear News
http://www.amsta.leeds.ac.uk/Applied/
news.dir/index.html

Union Matematica de America Latina y el
Caribe
http://umalca.fing.edu.uy/

Unione Matematica Italiana
http://www.dm.unibo.it/~umi

United States Military Academy
http://euler.math.usma.edu/MathSci.html

Univ. de Coimbra
http://www.mat.uc.pt/

Univ. de Sao Paulo
http://www.ime.usp.br/

Univ. do Minho
http://alfa.di.uminho.pt/~mesamr/mosaic/mat/index.html

Univ. of Alaska
http://saturn.uaamath.alaska.edu/home.html

Univ. of Bath
http://www.bath.ac.uk/Departments/maths.html

Univ. Bayreuth
http://btm2xd.mat.uni-bayreuth.de/

Univ. Bern
http://iamwww.unibe.ch/index.html

Univ. of Birmingham
http://sun1.bham.ac.uk/ctimath/home_page.html

Univ. Bonn
http://rhein.iam.uni-bonn.de:1025/

Univ. of California Davis
http://math.ucdavis.edu/

Univ. of California Los Angeles
http://www.math.ucla.edu/

Univ. of Delaware
http://www.math.udel.edu/

Univ. of Durham
http://fourier.dur.ac.uk:8000/

Univ. of East Anglia
http://www.mth.uea.ac.uk/welcome.html

Univ. of Edinburgh
http://www.maths.ed.ac.uk/

Univ. of Florida
http://www.math.ufl.edu/

Univ. Frankfurt
http://www.math.uni-frankfurt.de/

Univ. of Glasgow Preprints archive
http://www.maths.gla.ac.uk/pre-prints.html

Univ. Göttingen
http://namu19.gwdg.de/

Univ. Halle
http://www.mathematik.uni-halle.de/

Univ. Hamburg
http://www.math.uni-hamburg.de/

Univ. of Helsinki
http://sophie.helsinki.fi/

Univ. of Illinois Urbana-Champaign
http://www.math.uiuc.edu/

Univ. Jena
http://www.uni-jena.de/fsu/math.html

Univ. Karlsruhe
http://www.rz.uni-karlsruhe.de/Uni/Fakultaeten/Mathematik/

Univ. Kiel
http://www.informatik.uni-kiel.de/

Univ. Mainz
http://www.Uni-Mainz.DE/UniInfo/Fachbereiche/mathematik.html

Univ. Marburg
http://www.mathematik.uni-marburg.de/

Univ. of Maryland Baltimore County
http://math.umbc.edu/

Univ. of Massachusetts Ctr. for Geometry Analysis Numerics and Graphics
http://www.gang.umass.edu/

Univ. of Massachusetts, Amherst
http://www.math.umass.edu/

Univ. of Melbourne
http://www.maths.mu.oz.au/

Univ. of Michigan, Ann Arbor
http://www.math.lsa.umich.edu/

Univ. of Minnesota Geometry Center
http://www.geom.umn.edu/

Univ. München
http://www.informatik.uni-muenchen.de/lmu/info/fakultaet.html

Univ. Münster
http://www.uni-muenster.de/

Univ. of Nevada, Reno Mathematics Center
http://www.scs.unr.edu:80/unr/arts-n-science/math-center/mathctr.html

Univ. of New England
http://fermat.une.edu.au/

Univ. of Nottingham
http://www.maths.nott.ac.uk/

Univ. of Oslo
http://math-www.uio.no/

Univ. Osnabrück
http://esther.mathematik.uni-osnabrueck.de/

Univ. Paderborn GH
http://math-www.uni-paderborn.de/

Univ. Passau
http://www.fmi.uni-passau.de/fmi/
uebersicht.html

Univ. Salzburg
http://www.mat.sbg.ac.at/home.html

Univ. of Sheffield
http://www2.shef.ac.uk/maths/maths.html

Univ. of Sydney
http://www.maths.usyd.edu.au:8000/

Univ. of Tennessee, Knoxville
http://mathsun1.math.utk.edu/

Univ. of Texas, Austin
http://henri.ma.utexas.edu/

Univ. of Toronto
http://www.cdf.utoronto.ca/math/math-
OverView.html

Univ. of Trondheim
http://www.imf.unit.no/

Univ. of Tsukuba
http://newton.math.tsukuba.ac.jp/

Univ. of Wales College of Cardiff COMMA
http://www.cm.cf.ac.uk/

Univ. of Warwick
http://www.maths.warwick.ac.uk/

Univ. Wuppertal
http://wmwap1.math.uni-wuppertal.de/pub/
Mosaic/Mathematics_WWW.html

Univ. of Zagreb
http://www.math.hr/index.html

Univ. Politecnica de Catalunya - Barcelona
http://maite120.upc.es/

Unsolved Mathematics Problems
http://www.mathsoft.com/asolve/index.html

UTK Mathematical Life Sciences Archives
http://archives.math.utk.edu/mathbio

Victoria Univ. of Wellington
http://www.vuw.ac.nz/directories/depart-
ments/maths/

Visual Math Institute
http://www.vismath.org/

Visual Software Support Lab
http://sslab.colorado.edu:2222/sw_list.html

Vrije Universiteit
http://www.cs.vu.nl/welcome.html

Wake Forest Univ.
http://www.wfu.edu/
Academic%20departments/

Warsaw Univ.
http://hydra.mimuw.edu.pl/

Wavelet Digest
http://www.math.scarolina.edu/~wavelet/
index.html

Wavelets
http://www.mat.sbg.ac.at/~uhl/wav.html

Week's Finds in Mathematical Physics
http://math.ucr.edu/home/baez/
README.html#TWF

Weizmann Institute of Science
http://eris.wisdom.weizmann.ac.il/

Wesleyan Univ.
http://www.cs.wesleyan.edu/

World Mathematical Year 2000 Newsletter
http://www.mathp6.jussieu.fr/~jarraud/
ma200.html

WWW Virtual Library Mathematics
http://euclid.math.fsu.edu/Science/math.html

Yahoo Mathematics Index
http://www.yahoo.com/Science/Mathematics/

Yale Univ.
http://www.yale.edu/HTML/YaleMath-
Info.html

Mathematics Journals

Electronic Journal of Combinatorics
http://ejc.math.gatech.edu:8080/Journal/
journalhome.html

Electronic Journal of Differential Equations
http://ejde.math.swt.edu/

Electronic Journal of Linear Algebra
http://gauss.technion.ac.il/iic/ela

Electronic Journal of Probability
http://math.washington.edu/~ejpecp/

Journal of Approximation Theory
http://www.math.ohio-state.edu/Groups/JAT/
index.html

Journal of Combinatorial Mathematics and
Combinatorial Computing
http://www.math.mtu.edu/home/math/
JCMCC/JCMCC.html

Journal of Lie Theory
http://www.EMIS.de/

Journal of Mathematics of Kyoto Univ.
http://neptune.kusm.kyoto-u.ac.jp:8080/
journal_e.html

Journal of Number Theory
http://www.math.ohio-state.edu/Groups/JNT/
index.html

Journal of the London Mathematical
Society
http://www.cup.cam.ac.uk/Journals/
JNLSCAT95/jlm.html

Mathematica Militaris
http://euler.math.usma.edu/militaris.html

Mathematical Physics Electronic Journal
http://www.ma.utexas.edu/mpej/MPEJ.html

Mathematical Proceedings of the Cambridge Philosophical Society
http://www.cup.cam.ac.uk/Journals/
JNLSCAT95/psp.html

Missouri Journal of Mathematical Sciences
http://www.mathpro.com/math/mjmsJournal/
mjms.html

New York Journal of Mathematics
http://nyjm.albany.edu:8000/

Medicine

See also Aeronautics & Aerospace, Biology & Biotechnology, Chemistry, Engineering, Imaging Technologies, Optics, Physics

Actinomycetes
http://www.bdt.org.br/bioline/bin/ac.cgi

Acute Pain Mgmt.: Operative or Medical Procedures and Trauma
http://text.nlm.nih.gov/ahcpr/apm/www/apmccvr.html

Alces
http://alces.med.umn.edu/start.html

American Association for the Advancement of Science
http://www.aaas.org/

American Association of Immunologists
http://glamdring.ucsd.edu/others/aai

American Association of Physicists in Medicine
http://www.aapm.org/

American Dental Association
http://www.ada.org/

American Journal of Nursing
http://www.ajn.org:80/ajn/page1.html

American Medical Association
http://www.ama.org/

American Medical Informatics Association
http://www.amia.org/

American Society for Microbiology
http://www.asmusa.org

Amyloid, The International Journal of Clinical and Experimental Investigation
http://med-med1.bu.edu/amyloid/amyloid.html

Annals of Saudi Medicine
http://www.kfshrc.edu.sa/annals/annals.html

Annual Reviews Inc. (series)
http://www.annurev.org/

Antimicrobial Agents and Chemotherapy
http://www.asmusa.org/jnlsrc/aac1.htm

Artificial Life
http://www-mitpress.mit.edu/jrnls-catalog/artificial.html

Auburn Domestic Animal Endocrinology
http://www.ag.auburn.edu/dae/dae.html

Auburn Univ. College of Veterinary Medicine
http://www.vetmed.auburn.edu/

Australian National University
http://life.anu.edu.au/

Avicenna
http://www.avicenna.com/

Base de Dados Tropical
http://www.ftpt.br/

Baylor College of Medicine
http://www.bcm.tmc.edu/

Biochemistry and Biotechnology
http://kiev.physchem.kth.se/

Biocomputation Ctr., NASA Ames
http://biocomp.arc.nasa.gov/

Biocomputing, Biozentrum der Universitaet Basel
http://beta.embnet.unibas.ch

BioInformatics
http://www.gdb.org/hopkins.html

Biomedical Conferences
http://id.wing.net/~chi/upcoming.html

Biomedical Engineering Society (BMES)
http://nsr.bioeng.washington.edu/ABME/bmes.html

Biomedical Resource List
http://www.nlm.nih.gov/current_news.dir/biomed.html

Biomedical WWW Sites
http://golgi.harvard.edu/biopages/all.html

bionet.software.www archives
http://www.ch.embnet.org/bio-www/info.html

Biophysical Journal
http://biosci.cbs.umn.edu/biophys/bj/bj.html

Biophysical Society
http://biosci.cbs.umn.edu/biophys/
biophys.html

Bioscene - Journal of College Biology
Teaching
http://papa.indstate.edu/0h/amcbt/
bioscene.html

BIOSCI (Bionet) News Group Archives &
Index to Biologists
gopher://net.bio.net

BioSciences (en Espaniol)
http://fiss.org.ec/BioBanco/BioCuentas/
BioSciences.html

Biospheres
http://biology.uoregon.edu/Biology_WWW/
Biospheres/index.html

BiOS—The Biomedical Optics Society
http://www.spie.org/web/working_groups/
biomedical_optics/bios_desc.html

BMES Bulletin
http://www.mecca.org/BME/BMES/
bmeshome.html

Breast Cancer Information Clearinghouse
http://nysernet.org/bcic/

British Medical Journal
http://www.bmj.com/bmj/

CABIOS: Computer Applications in the
Biological Sciences
http://www.oup.co.uk/oup/smj/journals/ed/
titles/cabios/

Cambridge Healthtech Institute
http://id.wing.net/~chi/homepg.html

Canadian Medical Research Council
http://hpb1.hwc.ca:8100/

CancerNet
http://biomed.nus.sg/Cancer/welcome.html

CareerPath
http://www.careerpath.com/

Center for Advanced Medical Informatics
http://camis.Stanford.edu

Centers for Disease Control and Prevention (CDC)
http://www.cdc.gov/

Chemistry and Biology Journal
http://www.cursci.co.uk/BioMedNet/cmb/
cmbinf.html

Cholesterol, Genetics, And Heart Disease
Institute
http://www.heartdisease.org/

Clinical and Diagnostic Laboratory
Immunology
http://www.asmusa.org/jnlsrc/cdli1.htm

Clinical Microbiology Reviews
http://www.asmusa.org/jnlsrc/cmr1.htm

Cold Spring Harbor Laboratory
http://www.cshl.org

College Nursing
http://indy.radiology.uiowa.edu/Nursing/
Nursing.Renal.html

Columbia-Presbyterian Medical Ctr.
http://www.cpmc.columbia.edu/

Computers in Medicine, Denver Medical
Library,
http://www.csn.net/~dorothys

Ctr. for Biomedical and Biophysical
Technologies
http://citbb.unige.it/

Ctr. for Imaging and Pharmaceutical
Research
http://cipr-diva.mgh.harvard.edu/

Ctr. for Medical Informatics
http://paella.med.yale.edu/

Current Clinical Strategies Publishing
http://www.ccspublishing.com/

Current Opinion in Biotechnology Journal
http://www.cursci.co.uk/BioMedNet/bio/
bioinf.html

Current Opinion in Cell Biology Journal
http://www.cursci.co.uk/BioMedNet/cel/
celinf.html

Current Opinion in Genetics and Development Journal
http://www.cursci.co.uk/BioMedNet/gen/
geninf.html

Current Opinion in Immunology Journal
http://www.cursci.co.uk/BioMedNet/imm/
imminf.html

Current Opinion in Neurobiology Journal
http://www.cursci.co.uk/BioMedNet/nrb/
nrbinf.html

Current Opinion in Structural Biology
http://www.cursci.co.uk/BioMedNet/stb/
stbinf.html

Cyberspace Telemedical Office
http://www.telemedical.com/~drcarr

De Montfort Univ. Pharmacy
http://www.dmu.ac.uk/0/www/departments/
pharm.html

DELTA Project - Biological Sciences,
CalPoly
http://www.calpoly.edu/delta.html

Den-Tel-Net
http://www.onramp.net:80/Den-Tel-Net/

DENTalTRAUMA
http://www.unige.ch/smd/orthotr.html

Diseases of Aquatic Organisms
http://www.int-res.com/int-res/dao/dao.html

Domestic Animal Endocrinology
http://www.ag.auburn.edu/dae/dae.html

Duke Medical Ctr.
http://www.mc.duke.edu/

Duke Univ. Medical Informatics
http://dmi-www.mc.duke.edu/

EIGalaxyNet Medicine Resources
http://galaxy.einet.net/galaxy/Medicine.html

EMBO Journal
http://www.informatik.uni-rostock.de/HUM-
MOLGEN/journals/EMBO-J/

Emerging Infectious Diseases
http://www.cdc.gov/ncidod/EID/eid.htm

EMF-Link
http://archive.xrt.upenn.edu:1000/emf/top/
emf-link.html

Encyclopedia Radiologica
http://www.xray.hmc.psu.edu/
EncyclopediaRadiologica.html

Entrez
http://atlas.nlm.nih.gov:5700/Entrez/
index.html

European Biophysics Journal
http://npbsn41.nimr.mrc.ac.uk/ebj1.html

European Molecular Biology Network
http://beta.embnet.unibas.ch/embnet/
info.html

Evolutionary Computation
http://www-mitpress.mit.edu/jrnls-catalog/
evolution.html

Experimental Searchable Index for the
WWW VL Biosciences
http://golgi.harvard.edu/htbin/biopages

Eye Research Network
http://lib1.biochem.vt.edu/eye

Fachbereich Biologie
http://www.uni-kl.de/FB-Biologie/AG-Nagl/
AG-Nagl.html

Federation of American Societies for
Experimental Biology (FASEB)
http://www.faseb.org/

Fred Hutchinson Cancer Research Ctr.
http://www.fhcrc.org/

French Genomics Server, Moulon
http://moulon.inra.fr/

Frontiers in Bioscience
http://bayanet.com/bioscience/

Fujita Health Univ.
http://pathy.fujita-hu.ac.jp/pathy.html

Ganglion - Medical Ctr.
http://ganglion.anes.med.umich.edu/

GASNet Anesthesiology Home Page
http://gasnet.med.nyu.edu/HomePage.html

GenBank — National Center for Biotechnology Information
http://www.ncbi.nlm.nih.gov

General Practice On-Line
http://www.cityscape.co.uk/users/ad88/
gp.htm

Genes & Development
http://www.cshl.org/journals/gnd/

Genome Database
http://gdbwww.gdb.org/

Genome Research
http://www.cshl.org/journals/gr/

Georgia Tech Medical Informatics
http://www.cc.gatech.edu/gvu/
medical_informatics/
medinfo_home_page.html

Good Medicine Magazine
http://none.coolware.com/health/good_med/
ThisIssue.html

Gordon Conference Information
http://hackberry.chem.niu.edu:70/1/
ConferenceListings/GordonConferences

Graduate Programs in the Biological/
Biomedical Sciences
http://www.faseb.org/graduate.html

Guide to Public Health
http://128.196.106.42/ph-hp.html

Guidelines for Cancer Pain
http://www.stat.washington.edu/TALARIA/
TALARIA.html

GUIs in Bioinformatics Workshop
http://nimsn41.nimr.mrc.ac.uk/mathbio/t-
flores/GUI-Bioinform/meeting.html

Guy's and St. Thomas' Hospitals Medical
Image Processing Group
http://nothung.umds.ac.uk/

Harvard Biolabs
http://golgi.harvard.edu/biopages/
medicine.html

Harvard Biological Journals
http://golgi.harvard.edu/journals.html

Harvard Biostatistics
http://biosun1.harvard.edu/

Harvard College of Pharmacy
http://golgi.harvard.edu/biopages/
kerouac.pharm.uky.edu/Default.html

Harvard Medical Ctr.
http://golgi.harvard.edu/www-
med.stanford.edu/MedCenter/welcome.html

Harvard Medical School
http://www.med.harvard.edu/

Health & Medicine
http://nearnet.gnn.com/wic/med.toc.html

Health Communication Network of
Australia
http://www.hcn.net.au/

Health in Perspective
http://www.perspective.com/health

Health Resources
http://alpha.acast.nova.edu/medicine.html

HealthNet
http://debra.dgbt.doc.ca/~mike/home.html

Henderson Newsletters
http://www.holonet.net/homepage/
samples.htm

Herb, Spice, and Medicinal Plant Digest
http://www-unix.oit.umass.edu/~herbdig/
index.html

Historical Ctr. for the Health Sciences
http://http2.sils.umich.edu/HCHS/

History of Medicine Exhibits
http://www.nlm.nih.gov/hmd.dir/hmd.html

HIV/AIDS information
http://vector.casti.com/QRD/.html/AIDS.html

Hospital News
http://www.gate.net/hospital-news/

HUM-MOLGEN - Internet Communication Forum in Human Molecular
Genetics
http://www.informatik.uni-rostock.de/HUM-
MOLGEN/

Human Genome News
http://www.ornl.gov/TechResources/
Human_Genome/home.html

Human Life
http://www.cen.uiuc.edu/~jj9544/4.html

Human Molecular Genetics
http://www.oup.co.uk/oup/smj/journals/ed/
titles/hmg/

Human Reproduction Update
http://www.oup.co.uk/oup/smj/journals/ed/
titles/hru/

Idaho State Univ. College of Pharmacy
http://pharmacy.isu.edu/welcome.html

Image Processing and Analysis Group
http://noodle.med.yale.edu/

Immunity Journal
http://www.cell.com/immunity

Infection and Immunity
http://www.asmusa.org/jnlsrc/ii1.htm

Institut fuer Pharmazeutische Technologie
http://www.tu-bs.de/pharmtech/pht.html

Institute for Genomic Research
http://www.tigr.org/

Institute for Health Informatics
http://www.ihi.aber.ac.uk/index.html

Inter-Research Science Journal
http://www.int-res.com/int-res/

Interconnection of Molecular Biology
Databases Workshop Summary
http://www.ai.sri.com/people/pkarp/
mimbd.html

InterJournal
http://dynamics.bu.edu/InterJournal

International Antiviral News
http://www.meditech.co.uk/iavn.htm

International Journal of Systematic
Bacteriology
http://www.asmusa.org/jnlsrc/ijsb1.htm

Internet/Bitnet Health Science Resources
http://kufacts.cc.ukans.edu/cwis/units/
medcntr/menu.html

Iowa State College of Veterinary Medicine
http://www.iastate.edu/colleges/vetmed/
index.html

Knowledge Finder (with MEDLINE
access)
http://www.ariessys.com/

Joel's Hierarchical Subject Index
http://www.cen.uiuc.edu/~jj9544/index.html

Journal of Bacteriology
http://www.asmusa.org/jnlsrc/jb1.htm

Journal of Biological Chemistry
http://www-jbc.stanford.edu/jbc/

Journal of Cell Science
http://www.gold.net/users/ag64/jcsindex.htm

Journal of Clinical Microbiology
http://www.asmusa.org/jnlsrc/jcm1.htm

Journal of Cognitive Rehabilitation
http://www.inetdirect.net/nsp/

Journal of Computer-Aided Molecular
Design
http://wucmd.wustl.edu/jcamd/jcamd.html

Journal of Experimental Biology
http://www.gold.net/users/ag64/jebindex.htm

Journal of Image Guided Surgery
http://www.igs.wiley.com/

Journal of Immunology
http://199.170.0.125/JI/

Journal of Medical Imaging
http://jmi.gdb.org/JMI/ejourn.html

Journal of Quantitative Trait Loci
http://probe.nalusda.gov:8000/

Journal of the Biological Inorganic
Chemistry Society
http://risc3.lrm.fi.cnr.it:8001/~jbic/

Journal of Therapeutic Botulinum Neuro-
toxin: Basic and Clinical Sciences
http://med-amsa.bu.edu/pharmacology/
neuropharm/journal.htm

Journal of Virology
http://www.asmusa.org/jnlsrc/jv1.htm

Journal Previews
http://www.informatik.uni-rostock.de/HUM-
MOLGEN/journals/

Journals of the Biomedical Engineering
Society
http://isdl.ee.washington.edu/ABME/
annals.html

JTCA Reference database
http://www.wdcm.riken.go.jp/htbin/
JTCA_ref.pl

Korean Journal of Parasitology
http://sun.hallym.ac.kr/~shuh/kjp.html

La Jolla Cancer Research Foundation
http://192.231.106.66/

Lab. for Biological Informatics and
Theoretical Medicine
http://bitmed.ucsd.edu/

Lab. of Mathematical Biology
http://www.ncifcrf.gov:2001/

LANL Medical Data Analysis Projects
http://www.c3.lanl.gov/cic3/projects/Medical/
main.html

Larg*net
http://johns.largnet.uwo.ca/

Learning & Memory
http://www.cshl.org/journals/lnm/

Les Sources D'Information En Medecine
Veterinaire
http://brise.ere.umontreal.ca/~jettejp

M.D. Anderson Cancer Center
http://utmdacc.uth.tmc.edu/

M.D. Anderson ONcolog
http://utmdacc.mda.uth.tmc.edu:5009/
homepage.html

Macromolecular Structures
http://www.cursci.co.uk/BioMedNet/mms/
mmsinf.htm

Magnetic Resonance Imaging Group
http://www-mri.uta.edu/

Mallinckrodt Institute of Radiology
http://ibc.wustl.edu:70/1/mir

Marine Ecology Progress Series
http://www.int-res.com/int-res/meps/
meps.html

Mayo Foundation Biomedical Imaging
Resource
http://autobahn.mayo.edu/BIR_Welcome.html

Medical Imaging
http://agora.leeds.ac.uk/comir/resources/
links.html

Medical Matrix - Guide to Internet
Medical Resources
http://kuhttp.cc.ukans.edu/cwis/units/medcntr/
Lee/HOMEPAGE.HTML

Medical Physics
http://info.biomed.abdn.ac.uk/

Medical Radiography Home Page
http://users.aol.com/RICTER/

Medical Reporter
http://www.dash.com/netro/nwx/tmr/tmr.html

Medicine and Global Survival
http://www.bmj.com/bmj/mgs/index.html

Medicine WWW Virtual Library
http://www.ohsu.edu/cliniweb/wwwvl/

MEDLINE
http://www.healthworks.co.uk/hw/medline/
medline.html

MedLink
http://www.ls.se/medlink/

MedScape (with MEDLINE access)
http://www.medscape.com/

MedSearch America
http://www.medsearch.com:9001/

Microbiological Reviews
http://www.asmusa.org/jnlsrc/mr1.htm

Mississippi State Univ. College of Veterinary Medicine
http://pegasus.cvm.msstate.edu/

Molecular and Cellular Biology
http://www.asmusa.org/jnlsrc/mcb1.htm

Molecular Medicine
http://www.informatik.uni-rostock.de/HUM-
MOLGEN/journals/MM/

Monash Univ. Medical Informatics
http://adrian.med.monash.edu.au/

Morbidity and Mortality Weekly Report
(MMWR)
http://www.crawford.com/cdc/mmwr/
mmwr.html

MultiMedia Medical Biochemistry Server
http://ubu.hahnemann.edu/

Multimedia Medical Textbooks
http://indy.radiology.uiowa.edu/
MultimediaTextbooks.html

Murdoch Univ. - Respiratory Images
http://http://134.115.224.48/vetscINTRO.html

MycDB
http://kiev.physchem.kth.se/MycDB.html

Nagoya Univ. School of Medicine
http://www.med.nagoya-u.ac.jp/

NAS Symposium on Biology of Developmental Transcription Control
http://mirsky.caltech.edu/nas_meeting.html

National Academy of Sciences
http://www.nas.edu/

National Cancer Ctr.
http://www.ncc.go.jp/

National Cancer Institute
http://www.nci.edu/

National Institutes of Health
http://www.nih.gov/

National Library of Medicine
http://www.nlm.nih.gov/

National Science Foundation
http://stis.nsf.gov/

NetVet — Veterinary Medicine
http://netvet.wustl.edu/

Neuro-Implant Program
http://he1.uns.tju.edu/~doctorb/bppp.html

Neurological Surgery
http://www.med.nyu.edu/NeuroSurgery/
HomePage.html

Neurology
http://132.183.145.103/

Neuron Journal
http://www.cell.com/neuron

Neuroscience Internet Resource Guide
http://http2.sils.umich.edu/Public/nirg/
nirg1.html

Neurotrophin
http://mab.physiol.washington.edu/nrotrphn/
nthompag.htm

New York Univ. Medical Ctr.
http://www.med.nyu.edu/HomePage.html

NIH Guide to Grants and Contracts
http://www.med.nyu.edu/nih-guide.html

North Carolina State Univ. College of
Veterinary Medicine
http://www2.ncsu.edu/ncsu/cvm/
cvmhome.html

Nova-Links
http://alpha.acast.nova.edu/start.html

Nucleic Acids Research
http://www.oup.co.uk:80/oup/smj/journals/ed/
titles/nar/

NYU Anesthesiology (Medicine)
http://gasnet.med.nyu.edu/index.html

Oak Ridge National Laboratory Review
http://www.ornl.gov/ORNL/EINS_Reports/
Review/text/home.html

Oklahoma State Univ. College of Veterinary Medicine
http://www.cvm.okstate.edu/

On-Line Mendelian Inheritance in Man
http://gdbwww.gdb.org/omimdoc/
omimtop.html

OncoLink
http://cancer.med.upenn.edu/

OPTICS.ORG - The Photonics Resource
Center
http://optics.org/

Oregon Health Sciences University
http://www.ohsu.edu/

Oxford University Press
http://www.oup.co.uk/

Pabst Science Publishers
http://www.hsp.de/pabst/

Palo Alto Medical Foundation
http://www.service.com/PAMF/home.html

PaperChase (with MEDLINE access)
http://www.paperchase.com/

Pathy for Medical Information
http://www.med.nagoya-u.ac.jp/pathy/
pathy.html

PCR Methods and Applications
http://www.cshl.org/journals/pcr/

Penn State Dept. of Radiology
http://www.xray.hmc.psu.edu/home.html

Pharmacy Case Review
http://pharmacy.isu.edu/pcr/pcr.html

Pharmacy Related Conferences
http://www.cpb.uokhsc.edu/pkin/conf.html

Pharmacy Server
http://157.142.72.77/

Physiological Society
http://physiology.cup.cam.ac.uk/

Physiology and Biophysics
http://www.physiol.washington.edu/pbio/
homepage.htm

Plymouth Area Communities Medical
Access Network (MEDLINE access)
http://www.pacman.org

Poisons Information Database
http://biomed.nus.sg/PID/PID.html

Polio and Post-Polio Resources
http://www.eskimo.com/~dempt/polio.html

Pollen Data
http://www.unlv.edu/CCHD/pollen/

Positron Emission Tomography
http://pss023.psi.ch/

Protein Science (peer-reviewed journal)
http://www.prosci.uci.edu/

Proyecto BioBanco
http://fiss.org.ec/

Psychiatry On-Line and the International
Journal of Psychiatry
http://www.cityscape.co.uk/users/ad88/
psych.htm

Radiation Research
http://www.whitlock.com/kcj/science/radres/
default.htm

Radiological Society of North America
http://www.rsna.org/

Radiology Imaging Ctr.
http://visual-ra.swmed.edu/

Radiology Webserver
http://www.rad.washington.edu/

Raven Press, Medical Publishers
http://www.ravenpress.com/raven/

RNA Journal
http://www.cup.cam.ac.uk/Journals/RNA/
RNAHomePage.html

Royal (Dick) School of Veterinary Studies
http://www.vet.ed.ac.uk/

Royal Free Hospital of Medicine
http://www.rfhsm.ac.uk/

Royal Postgraduate Medical School
http://mpcc3.rpms.ac.uk/rpms_home.html

SeqAnalRef
http://expasy.hcuge.ch/sprot/seqanalr.html

Simon Fraser University
http://mendel.mbb.sfu.ca/

SPIE-The Intl. Society for Optical Engineering
http://www.spie.org/

St. Francis Journal of Medicine
http://www.pitt.edu/~leff2/journal/journal.html

Swiss-Shop
http://expasy.hcuge.ch/swisshop/
SwissShopReq.html

TALARIA: Clinical Practice Guidelines for
Cancer Pain
http://www.stat.washington.edu/

Technical Conference on Plant Genetic
Resources
http://web.icppgr.fao.org/

The Scientist
http://ds.internic.net/11/pub/the-scientist

Thomas Jefferson Univ.
http://www.tju.edu/

Threatened Fauna in Australia
http://mac-ra26.sci.deakin.edu.au/fauna.html

TraumAID
http://www.cis.upenn.edu/~traumaid/
home.html

Tulane Medical Ctr.
http://www.mcl.tulane.edu/

U.S. Dept. of Health and Human Services
http://www.os.dhhs.gov/

UC Davis College of Veterinary Medicine
http://vmgopher.ucdavis.edu/

UCLA Dept. of Anesthesiology
http://hypnos.anes.ucla.edu/index.html

UniScience News
http://199.44.59.40/unisci/

Univ. of Bonn Medical Ctr.
http://imsdd.meb.uni-bonn.de/

Univ. of Delaware
http://www.udel.edu/

Univ. of Florida College of Veterinary
Medicine
http://www.vetmed.ufl.edu/

Univ. of Florida, Dept. of Anesthesiology
http://www.anest.ufl.edu/

Univ. of Geneva (ExPASy)
http://expasy.hcuge.ch/

Univ. of Illinois College of Medicine
http://www.med.uiuc.edu/

Univ. of Iowa College of Pharmacy
http://indy.radiology.uiowa.edu/Pharmacy.html

Univ. of Iowa Medical Ctr. (The Virtual
Hospital)
http://indy.radiology.uiowa.edu/
VirtualHospital.html

Univ. of Iowa Virtual Hospital
http://vh.radiology.uiowa.edu/

Univ. of Iowa, College of Medicine, Div. of
Physiologic Imaging
http://everest.radiology.uiowa.edu:8080/
home.html

Univ. of Kansas Medical Ctr.
http://kufacts.cc.ukans.edu/cwis/units/
medcntr/library.html

Univ. of Michigan Dept. of Anesthesiology
http://ganglion.anes.med.umich.edu/

Univ. of Michigan Neurosciences Internet
Resource Guide
http://http2.sils.umich.edu/Public/nirg/
nirg1.html

Univ. of Minnesota Dept. of Food Science
and Nutrition
http://fscn1.fsci.umn.edu/

Univ. of Oregon
http://biology.uoregon.edu/

Univ. of Pennsylvania
http://www.penn.edu/

Univ. of Pennsylvania Medical Image
   Processing Group
   http://mipgsun.mipg.upenn.edu/

Univ. of Pisa Dept. of Radiology
   http://www.rad.unipi.it:7080/
   IRMosaicHome.html

Univ. of Pittsburg Medical Centers
   http://www.pitt.edu/

Univ. of Queensland Anaesthesiology
   http://www.uq.oz.au/anaesth/home.html

Univ. of Southampton Biomedical server
   http://medstats.soton.ac.uk/

Univ. of Texas/Houston
   http://www.uthouston.edu/

Univ. of Vermont
   http://www.uvm.edu/

Univ. of Washington Center for Biomedical
   Engineering
   http://weber.u.washington.edu/d32/bioewww/

Univ. of Washington Health Sciences
   Center
   http://www.hslib.washington.edu/

Univ. of Washington School of Medicine
   http://www.washington.edu:1181/medical/
   som/index.html

Victorian (Australia) Institute of Forensic
   Pathology
   http://www.vifp.monash.edu.au/

Virginia Tech/Univ. of Maryland College
   of Veterinary Medicine
   http://www.vetmed.vt.edu/

Weizmann Institute Bioinformatics
   http://bioinformatics.weizmann.ac.il:70

Welch Medical Library
   http://www.welch.jhu.edu/

Whitehead Institute for Biomedical
   Research
   http://www.wi.mit.edu/

World Health Organization (WHO)
   http://www.who.ch/

Yale Univ.
   http://www.yale.edu

Meteorology

See also Geology & Geophysics, Oceanography

Alfred Wegener Institute
http://www.awi-bremerhaven.de/

Arizona State Univ.
http://aspin.asu.edu/provider/geography/climate/

Arkansas Basin River Forecast Ctr. (NOAA/NWS)
http://gopherpc.abrfc.noaa.gov/abrfc.html

Atmospheric and Oceanic Science at NCSA
http://redrock.ncsa.uiuc.edu/AOS/home.html

Australian Meteorological and Oceanographic Society
http://atmos.es.mq.edu.au/AMOS/

Australian National Univ.
http://life.anu.edu.au/weather.html

BLUE-SKIES for Java
http://cirrus.sprl.umich.edu/javaweather/

Boreal Ecosystem-Atmosphere Study (BOREAS)
http://boreas.gsfc.nasa.gov/

Centre for Atmospheric Science, Cambridge Univ.
http://www.atm.ch.cam.ac.uk/MiscMet.html

Center for Ocean-Land-Atmosphere Studies (COLA)
http://grads.iges.org/home.html

Center for Sea and Atmosphere Research of Argentina (CIMA)
http://www-cima.at.fcen.uba.ar

Clima, Satellite Images
http://www.dkrz.de/forschung/forschung.html

Climate Diagnostics Ctr. (CDC)
http://noaacdc.colorado.edu/cdc/cdc_home.html

Climate Modelling Laboratory
http://www.scar.utoronto.ca/homes/envsci/gough/

Climate Prediction Ctr.
http://nic.fb4.noaa.gov/

Climatic Research Unit
http://www.cru.uea.ac.uk/

Cloud Physics Modelling
http://www.op.dlr.de/~pa1u/

Colorado State Univ. - Atmospheric Science
http://www.atmos.colostate.edu/

Cooperative Institute for Meteorological Satellite Studies
http://cloud.ssec.wisc.edu/

Creighton Univ. - Atmospheric Sciences
http://sundog.creighton.edu/cuhome.html

Ctr. for Air Sea Technology of Mississippi Univ.
http://www.cast.msstate.edu/

Center for Ocean-Atmospheric Prediction Studies
http://www.coaps.fsu.edu/

Ctr. for the Study of Terrestrial and Extraterrestrial Atmospheres (CSTEA)
http://www.cstea.howard.edu/

Current Weather Maps/Movies
http://clunix.cl.msu.edu/weather/

Current Weather, Climate and Forecast Maps
http://grads.iges.org/pix/head.html

Daily Planet & Weather World
http://www.atmos.uiuc.edu/

Defense Meteorological Satellite Program (DMSP)
http://www.ngdc.noaa.gov/dmsp/dmsp.html

Deutsche Meteorologische Gesellschaft
http://www.met.fu-berlin.de/deutsch/DMG/index.html

Deutsches Klimarechenzentrum
http://www.dkrz.de/

Eindhoven Univ. of Technology (NOS Teletext)
http://www.win.tue.nl/teletext/index.en.html

EISCAT Scientific Association
http://seldon.eiscat.no/homepage.html

Environment Canada WWW Server
http://www.ns.doe.ca/how.html

European Space Agency - ESA/ESRIN
http://shark1.esrin.esa.it/

FAQ - Weather
http://www.cis.ohio-state.edu/hypertext/faq/usenet/weather/top.html

Finnish Meteorological Institute - Geophysics
http://www.geo.fmi.fi/

Florida Institute of Technology
http://sci-ed.fit.edu/wx.html

Florida State Univ. - Meteorology
http://thunder.met.fsu.edu/

Freien Universität Berlin Institut für Meteorologie
http://www.met.fu-berlin.de/

Geophysical Data of Norway
http://www.service.uit.no/geofysisk/geofysisk.html

Georgia Tech
http://www.gatech.edu/eas/eas.html

Global Atmospheric Modeling
http://rossby.larc.nasa.gov/

Global Energy and Water Cycle Experiment (GEWEX)
http://www.cais.com/gewex/gewex.html

Global Warming Update
http://www.ncdc.noaa.gov/gblwrmupd/global.html

Gold Coast Weather Ocean Chart Access
http://www.vcnet.com/goldcoastwx/home.html

Great Lakes Forecasting System
http://glfs.eng.ohio-state.edu/

GSI Hamburg
http://www.gsi.de/misc/misc.html

HAPEX SAHEL Information System
http://www.orstom.fr/hapex/

Idaho's Weather Station
http://www.mrc.uidaho.edu/weather/weather.html

INPE — Brasilian Space Agency
http://www.inpe.br/

Institut für Meteorologie FU-Berlin
http://www.met.fu-berlin.de/index.html

Institut für Meteorologie und Klimaforschung Karlsruhe
http://imkhp3.physik.uni-karlsruhe.de/index.html

Institute of Aviation Weather Information Server
http://www.aviation.uiuc.edu/institute/avilinks/weather/weather.html

Institute for Global Change Research and Education (IGCRE)
http://space.hsv.usra.edu/

Institute for Global Environment and Society, Inc.
http://grads.iges.org/home.html

Institute for Meteorology and Climate Research (Germany)
http://imkhp3.physik.uni-karlsruhe.de/

INTELLiCast
http://www.intellicast.com/

Interactive Marine Observations
http://thunder.met.fsu.edu/~nws/buoy/

Interactive Weather Browser
http://rs560.cl.msu.edu/weather/interactive.html

Interactive Weather Information Ctr.
http://thunder.atms.purdue.edu/interact.html

Intl. HIRLAM Project
http://www.knmi.nl/hirlam/

Intl. Severe Storms Interceptors
http://www.indirect.com/www/storm5/issi.html

Intl. Society of Biometeorology
http://www.acru.uq.oz.au/~isb

Intl. Weather Watchers
http://groundhog.sprl.umich.edu/IWW/

Lawrence Livermore National Laboratory Atmospheric Research
http://www-ep.es.llnl.gov/www-ep/atm.html

LDEO Climate Data Catalog
http://rainbow.ldgo.columbia.edu/datacatalog.html

Lyndon State College's New England Weather Server
http://apollo.lsc.vsc.edu/

Macquarie Univ. - Atmospheric Science
http://atmos.es.mq.edu.au/

Maryland Earthcast
http://www.metolab3.umd.edu/EARTHCAST/earthcast.html

Maui Weather Today
http://weather.satlab.hawaii.edu/

McGill - Centre for Climate and Global Change Research
http://www.meteo.mcgill.ca/

Meteo France
http://www.meteo.fr/

Meteofax Wetterdienste GmbH
http://www.meteocon.nl/meteofax/index.html

Meteorology Virtual Library
http://www.met.fu-berlin.de/DataSources/MetIndex.html

Meteorology: Mother of all Bulletin Boards
http://www.cs.colorado.edu/homes/mcbryan/public_html/bb/41/summary.html

Meteosat
http://www.crs4.it/~luigi/METEO/meteo.html

Meteosat 3 (South America)
http://www.inpe.br/grid/meteosat

Michigan State Univ.
http://rs560.cl.msu.edu/weather/textindex.html

MIT Ctr. for Meteorology and Physical Oceanography
http://www-cmpo.mit.edu/CMPOhome.html

MIT Lincoln Laboratory Weather Sensing Group
http://jaquenetta.wx.ll.mit.edu/

MIT Radar Lab
http://graupel.mit.edu/Radar_Lab.html

MIT Weather Gateway
http://www.mit.edu:8001/weather

MITSA - Weather Page
http://acro.harvard.edu/GA/weather.html

Monthly Temperature Anomalies
http://www.ncdc.noaa.gov/onlineprod/ghcnmcdwmonth/form.html

Nansen Environmental and Remote Sensing Ctr. (NERSC)
http://www.nrsc.no:8001/

NASA Ames Mars Global Circulation Modeling Group
http://www-mgcm.arc.nasa.gov/MGCM.html

National Climatic Data Ctr. (NCDC)
http://www.ncdc.noaa.gov/

National Ctr. for Atmospheric Research
http://www.ucar.edu/

National Data Buoy Center (NDBC)
http://seaboard.ndbc.noaa.gov/

National Institute of Space Research - INPE Environmental Geochemistry
http://www.met.inpe.br/geochem/home

National Institute of Water and Atmosphere - NIWA
http://www.niwa.cri.nz/

National Oceanic and Atmospheric Administration (NOAA)
http://www.hpcc.noaa.gov/biglist.html

National Severe Storms Laboratory
http://www.nssl.uoknor.edu/

National Weather Service (NWS)
http://www.nws.noaa.gov/

Nationwide School Weather Network
http://www.aws.com/index.html

Nationwide Weather Links
http://www.icon.net/users/tornado/tornado.html

Naval Environmental Operational Nowcasting System (NEONS)
http://helium.nrlmry.navy.mil/neons_home.html

NCSU Meteorology
http://meawx1.nrrc.ncsu.edu/

NERC Satellite Station, Dundee Univ.
http://www.sat.dundee.ac.uk/

New Jersey Forecast (WOI)
http://woi.com/woi/weather.html

NEXOR
http://web.nexor.co.uk/places/satelite.html

NOAA Weather Page
http://www.esdim.noaa.gov/weather_page.html

NOAA Weather Venues
http://www.nnic.noaa.gov/weather.html

NOAA-11/12 (Europe)
http://www.sat.dundee.ac.uk/

NOS TeleText
http://www.win.tue.nl/cgi/tt2www/nos/gpage/
701-1.html

Ohio State Univ. Dept.
http://www.cis.ohio-state.edu/hypertext/faq/
usenet/weather/top.html

Perilous Times
http://www.teleport.com/~jstar/

Pine, Colorado Weathercam
http://www.igc.apc.org/mushroom/pine.html

Planteforsk (The Norwegian Crop
Research Institute)
http://norpre.nlh.no/weather/

Plymouth State College Meteorology
http://vortex.plymouth.edu/

POLES
http://psc.apl.washington.edu/poles/

Potsdam Institute for Climate Impact
Research
http://www.pik-potsdam.de/

Princeton - Department of
Hydroclimatology
http://earth.princeton.edu/

Program for Climate Model Diagnosis and
Intercomparison
http://www-pcmdi.llnl.gov/

Purdue Weather Processor
http://thunder.atms.purdue.edu/

Royal Meteorological Society (RMS)
http://typhoon.rdg.ac.uk/rms/rms.html

Rutgers Univ. Meteorology
http://snowfall.rutgers.edu/meteorology/

Sandia Geosciences Center
http://www.sandia.gov/eesector/gs/
center.html

SILMU, The Finnish Research Programme
on Climate Change
http://www.etla.fi/Silmu/silmu.html

South Carolina Drought Information Ctr.
http://sercc.dnr.state.sc.us/sc/drought.html

SPAM: Schools of the Pacific Atmosperic
Monitoring
http://aaron.gcn.uoknor.edu/spam/index.html

Space Science and Engineering Center
(SSEC)
http://www.ssec.wisc.edu/

Texas A&M Meteorology
http://www.met.tamu.edu/

Today's Space Weather
http://www.sel.bldrdoc.gov/today.html

Todd Gross' (of Ch. 7, Boston) Weather &
Astronomy Page
http://www.weatherman.com/

UC Davis, Atmospheric Science Group
http://www-atm.ucdavis.edu/home.html

UCLA Atmospheric Sciences
http://www.atmos.ucla.edu/

UNAVCO, Univ. NAVSTAR Consortium
http://www.unavco.ucar.edu/

UNIDATA — University Corporation for
Atmospheric Research
http://www.unidata.ucar.edu/

Univ. at Albany, SUNY
http://www.atmos.albany.edu/

Univ. Berlin Meteorology
http://www.met.fu-berlin.de/DataSources/
MetIndex.html

UIUC Weather Machine
gopher://wx.atmos.uiuc.edu/1

Univ. of Hawaii
http://lumahai.soest.hawaii.edu/

Univ. of Maryland at College Park
http://metolab3.umd.edu/meteorology.html

Univ. of Missouri - Columbia
http://www.phlab.missouri.edu/~wxcat/

Univ. of New Jersey
http://aristarchus.rutgers.edu/

Univ. of North Carolina at Asheville
http://vortex.atms.unca.edu/

Univ. of North Dakota
http://www.aero.und.nodak.edu/

Univ. of Oklahoma - Ctr. for Analysis and
Prediction of Storms
http://wwwcaps.uoknor.edu/

Univ. of Oklahoma - Weather Radar
Laboratory
http://aaron.gcn.uoknor.edu/index.html

Univ. of Utah
http://www.met.utah.edu/

Univ. of Washington
http://www.atmos.washington.edu/

USGS Global Change and Climate History
http://geochange.er.usgs.gov/gch.html

Utah Climate Ctr. Network Resources
http://tsunami.agsci.usu.edu/

Virginia State Climatology Office
http://faraday.clas.virginia.edu/~climate

Water Resources
http://www.wco.com/~rteeter/waterlib.html

Weather & Global Monitoring
http://life.anu.edu.au/weather.html

Weather Channel
http://www.weather.com

Weather Links
http://dana.ucc.nau.edu/~jdd/weather.html

Weather Report
http://www.best.com/~piraeus/cookies/
weathrep.shtml

Weather Station IDs
http://rs560.cl.msu.edu/weather/wids.html

Weather Underground of Hong Kong
http://www.underground.org.hk/

Weather Unit
http://faldo.atmos.uiuc.edu/WEATHER/
weather.html

Weatherboy Online! Weather Information
http://www.cybercom.com/~weather/

WeatherLinks USA
http://ngwwmall.com/frontier/vortex/

Weatherman
http://www.pixi.com/~gattoga/index.html

WeatherNet
http://cirrus.sprl.umich.edu/wxnet/

WeatherNet4
http://wxnet4.nbc4.com/

WebWeather
http://www.princeton.edu/Webweather/
ww.html

World Climate Report
http://www.nhes.com/

World Meteorological Organization
http://www.wmo.ch/

World Wide Weather on the Internet
http://www.weather.net/fn/
submitit.weather.html

Yankee Weather Index
http://www.tiac.net/users/macgyver/wea.html

Oceanography

See also Geology & Geophysics, Meteorology

Acoustical Society of America
http://asa.aip.org/

Acoustic Thermometry of Ocean Climate
http://atoc.ucsd.edu/

Air Project
http://www-rocq.inria.fr/air/

Alfred Wegener Institute
http://www.awi-bremerhaven.de/

Algalita Marine Research Foundation
http://www.vandelay.com/surfrider/algalita

American Geophysical Union
http://earth.agu.org/kosmos/homepage.html

American Society of Limnology and
Oceanography
http://aslo.org/

AquaNet
http://www.aquanet.com/aquanet/

Atlantic Oceanographic and Meteorological Laboratory - AOML
http://www.aoml.noaa.gov/

Atmospheric & Oceanic Science Group,
NCSA
http://redrock.ncsa.uiuc.edu/AOS/home.html

Australian Oceanographic Data Ctr.
http://www.aodc.gov.au/AODC.html

AWI Polar and Marine Research Database
http://www.awi-Bremerhaven.de/Index/

Baltic Sea Resources
http://biomac.io-warnemuende.de/baltic

Bedford Institute of Oceanography
http://biome.bio.ns.ca/

Bermuda Biological Station for Research,
Inc.
http://www.bbsr.edu/

BODC: The British Oceanographic Data
Ctr.
http://biudc.nbi.ac.uk/bodc/bodcmain.html

British Antarctic Survey
http://www.nerc-bas.ac.uk/

Brookhaven National Laboratory
http://bnloc7.das.bnl.gov/ocean/oasd.html

Canadian Coast Guard College
http://www.cgc.ns.ca/

Centre for Climate and Global Change,
McGill Univ.
http://www.meteo.mcgill.ca/

CME
http://www.ucar.edu/oceanmodel.html

Coastal Ocean Modeling at the USGS
http://crusty.er.usgs.gov/

Common Heritage Corp
http://www.aloha.com/~craven/

Consortium for Oceanographic Research
and Education
http://core.cast.msstate.edu

Coral Reef Alliance
http://www.coral.org/

Coral Reefs and Mangroves: Modelling
and Management
http://ibm590.aims.gov.au/

CSIRO Marine Laboratories
http://www.ml.csiro.au

Ctr. for BioAcoustics
http://www.unipv.it/~webcib/cib.html

Ctr. for Climate and Global Change,
McGill Univ.
http://www.meteo.mcgill.ca

Ctr. for Coastal Physical Oceanography
http://www.ccpo.odu.edu/

Ctr. for Coastal Studies
http://www-ccs.ucsd.edu/

Ctr. for Earth and Ocean Research, Univ. of
Victoria
http://wikyonos.seaoar.uvic.ca/

Ctr. for Earth Observation - Coastal Zone
http://acri.cica.fr/Coastal.html

Ctr. for Marine Science Research
http://www.uncwil.edu/sys$disk1/cmsr/cmsr.html

Ctr. of Biological Research, La Paz
http://www.cibnor.conacyt.mx

Ctr. of Excellence for Research in Ocean Sciences
http://www.ceros.org

Ctr. of Scientific Research and Superior Education, Ensenada
http://www.cicese.mx

Dalhousie Univ.
http://www.phys.ocean.dal.ca

Dartmouth Gulf of Maine Project
http://fundy.dartmouth.edu/

Data Zoo
http://www-ccs.ucsd.edu/ccs/about_datazoo.html

Davidson Laboratory — Hydrodynamic and Ocean Engineering Reseach Center
http://www.dl.stevens-tech.edu/

Deep Submergence Laboratory
http://www.dsl.whoi.edu/

Deep-Sea Research, Univ. of Victoria
http://darwin.ceh.uvic.ca/deepsea/deepsea.html

Delft Univ. of Technology
http://dutlru8.lr.tudelft.nl

Digital Information Analysis Laboratory
http://tone.whoi.edu/

Distributed Ocean Data System
http://lake.mit.edu/dods.html

DOE Survey of CO2 in the Oceans
http://www.oasdpo.bnl.gov/~oasdpo/mosaic/DOECO2/

DSI: Information processing System Development
http://www.ifremer.fr:80/ditidsiw3/

Earth Sciences Virtual Library
http://www.geo.ucalgary.ca/VL-EarthSciences.html

El Nino and climate-related information
http://rainbow.ldeo.columbia.edu/

El Nino Theme Page
http://www.pmel.noaa.gov/toga-tao/el-nino/home.html

Electronic Journals
http://www.mth.uea.ac.uk/ocean/oceanography.html#electronicjournals

Electronic preprint archive
http://www.gfdl.gov/~smg/pointers/announcement.html

Environment Virtual Library
http://ecosys.drdr.virginia.edu/Environment.html

Environmental and Engineering Geophysical Society (EEGS)
http://www.esd.ornl.gov:80/EEGS/

Environmental Information Services
http://www.esdim.noaa.gov/

Environmental Research Laboratories
http://www.erl.gov/

ESA/ESRIN Ionia Global AVHRR Data Set Browser
http://shark1.esrin.esa.it/

Estuarine and Coastal Oceanography Laboratory, Univ. of South Carolina
http://coast.geol.scarolina.edu/office.html

European Geophysical Society (EGS)
http://www.mpae.gwdg.de/EGS/EGS.html

Fachbereich Geowissenschaften der Universität Bremen
http://www.palmod.uni-bremen.de/

Finnish Institute of Marine Research
http://www.fimr.fi/

Five-College Marine Science WWW Guide
http://geology.smith.edu/marine/marine.html

Flinders Institute for Atmospheric and Marine Sciences, Adelaide
http://www.es.flinders.edu.au/FIAMS/

Florida State Univ.
http://ocean.fsu.edu/

FRAM
http://www.mth.uea.ac.uk/ocean/fram.html

Geophysical Fluid Dynamics Lab.
http://www.gfdl.gov/gfdl.html

Geophysical Institute, Univ. of Bergen
http://www.gfi.uib.no/

Geophysics Virtual Library
http://www-crewes.geo.ucalgary.ca/VL-Geophysics.html

German Climate Computer Ctr.
http://www.dkrz.de/

German Virtual Library - Geosciences
http://www.rz.uni-karlsruhe.de/Outerspace/VirtualLibrary/55.html

GFDL Modular Ocean Model
http://www.gfdl.gov/MOM/MOMWWW.html

GLOBEC Georges Bank Information
http://lake.mit.edu/globec.html

Great Lakes Forecasting System, Ohio State Univ.
http://glfs.eng.ohio-state.edu

Gulf of Maine Project, Dartmouth
http://fundy.dartmouth.edu/

Habitat Ecology Div., Bedford Institute of Oceanography
http://biome.bio.ns.ca/

Hadley Ctr.
http://www.meto.govt.uk/sec5/sec5pg1.html

Helium Isotope Laboratory
http://kopernik.whoi.edu/

Hopkins Marine Station, Stanford Univ.
http://www-marine.stanford.edu/

Hydrographic Atlas of the Southern Ocean
http://www.awi-bremerhaven.de/Atlas/SO/Deckblatt.html

Icelandic Fisheries Laboratories
http://www.rfisk.is/

IFREMER
http://www.ifremer.fr/

Indian National Institute of Ocean Technology
http://www.niot.ernet.in/

Institut Pierre Simon Laplace-Numerical Modelling Group
http://www-ipsl.lodyc.jussieu.fr

Institute for Marine and Atmospheric Research Utrecht
http://ruund3.fys.ruu.nl

Institute of Geophysics and Planetary Physics
http://igpp.ucsd.edu/

Institute of Marine and Coastal Sciences, Rutgers Univ.
http://marine.rutgers.edu

Institute of Marine Research, Bergen
http://www.imr.no/0N/IMR.html

Institute of Ocean Sciences Canada
http://www.ios.bc.ca/

Institute of Oceanographic Sciences
http://www.nerc.ac.uk/ios/

Institute of Oceanology PAS, Sopot, Poland
http://www.iopan.gda.pl/

International Arctic Buoy Program
http://iabp.apl.washington.edu/

International Council for the Exploration of the Sea, ICES
http://www.ices.inst.dk/

InterRidge
http://www.dur.ac.uk/~dgl0zz1/

James Rennell Centre
http://www.nso.ac.uk/

JAMSTEC: Japan Marine Science & Technology Ctr.
http://www.jamstec.go.jp/

Joint Research Ctr.
http://me-www.jrc.it/home.html

KK Tech International, Hong Kong
http://www.hk.linkage.net/~kkt/

Lamont-Doherty Earth Observatory
http://www.ldeo.columbia.edu

LDEO Climate Data Catalog
http://rainbow.ldgo.columbia.edu/datacatalog.html

Live DMS Ocean Biological Model
http://me-www.jrc.it/dms/dms.html

LLNL Climate Model Diagnosis and Intercomparison
http://www-pcmdi.llnl.gov

Marine Biological Laboratory
http://www.mbl.edu/

Marine Geology and Geophysics Servers
http://www.ngdc.noaa.gov/mgg/othermarine/othermarine.html

Marine Minerals Bibliography and Database
http://www.ngdc.noaa.gov/mgg/geology/mmdb.html

Marine Research Institute - Iceland
http://www.hafro.is/

Marine Sciences Research Ctr., Stony Brook
http://www.msrc.sunysb.edu/

Mediterranean Oceanic Data Base
http://modb.oce.ulg.ac.be

Meteorology Virtual Library
http://www.met.fu-berlin.de/DataSources/MetIndex.html

Miami Isopycnic Coordinate Model
http://www.rsmas.miami.edu/groups/micom.html

Mississippi State Univ. Ctr. for Air Sea Technology
http://www.cast.msstate.edu/

MIT Ctr. for Meteorology and Physical Oceanography
http://www-cmpo.mit.edu/CMPOhome.html

MMarie, Application of High Performance Computing Techniques for the Modeling of Marine Ecosystems
http://www.kuleuven.ac.be/mmarie/

Mother of all Bulletin Boards: Meteorology
http://www.cs.colorado.edu/homes/mcbryan/public_html/bb/41/summary.html

Nansen Environmental and Remote Sensing Ctr., Bergen
http://www.nrsc.no:8001/

NASA Earth Observing System (EOS) Project
http://spso2.gsfc.nasa.gov/spso_homepage.html

NASA Global Change Master Directory
http://gcmd.gsfc.nasa.gov/

NASA Goddard Physical Oceanography Group
http://oraac.gsfc.nasa.gov/~rienecke/phys_o_home_page.html

NASA Goddard Space Flight Ctr.
http://hypatia.gsfc.nasa.gov/NASA_homepage.html

NASA Jet Propulsion Lab
http://podaac-www.jpl.nasa.gov/

NASA SeaWiFS Project
http://seawifs.gsfc.nasa.gov/seawifs.html

NASA TOPEX/POSEIDON
http://topex-www.jpl.nasa.gov/

NASA/NOAA AVHRR Oceans Pathfinder
http://podaac-www.jpl.nasa.gov/sst/

National Estaurine Research Reserve Centralized Data Management
http://inlet.geol.scarolina.edu/nerrscdmo.html

National Geophysical Data Center
http://www.ngdc.noaa.gov/

National Marine Fisheries Service
http://kingfish.ssp.nmfs.gov/home-page.html

National Ocean Service
http://www.nos.noaa.gov/

National Oceanographic and Atmospheric Administration (NOAA)
http://www.noaa.gov

National Oceanographic Data Ctr. (NODC)
http://www.nodc.noaa.gov/index.html

National Weather Service (NWS)
http://www.nws.noaa.gov/

NATO SACLANT Undersea Research Ctr.
http://www.saclantc.nato.int/

Naval Architecture and Ocean Engineering Virtual Library
http://arioch.gsfc.nasa.gov/wwwvl/engineering.html#naval

Naval Command, Control & Ocean Surveillance Ctr..
http://trout.nosc.mil/NCCOSCMosaicHome.html

Naval Oceanographic Office
http://www.navo.navy.mil/

Naval Research Laboratory
http://www.nrl.navy.mil/

NCAR
http://www.ucar.edu/metapage.html

Near-Earth Navigation & Geodesy Section ESOC
http://nng.esoc.esa.de/

NEMO - Oceanographic Data Server (SIO)
http://nemo.ucsd.edu/

Newcastle Univ.
http://www.ncl.ac.uk/~nmscmweb/mscm/index.html

New Zealand Limnological Society
http://webtwo.rsnz.govt.nz/limsoc/limsoc.html

NOAA Web Servers (many)
http://www.noaa.gov

North Atlantic Fisheries College
http://www.zetnet.co.uk/nafc/

Northeast Fisheries Science Ctr.
http://www.wh.whoi.edu/noaa.html

NRaD
http://trout.nosc.mil/NRaDMosaicHome.html

OCCAM
http://www.mth.uea.ac.uk/ocean/occam.html

Ocean Acoustics Laboratory
http://www.oal.whoi.edu/

Ocean Awareness
http://www.cs.fsu.edu/projects/sp95ug/
group1.7/ocean1.html

Ocean Drilling Program, Texas A&M
http://www-odp.tamu.edu

Ocean Information Center (OCEANIC)
http://diu.cms.udel.edu/

Ocean Information Technology Showcase
http://www.summit.halifax.ns.ca/oceans/

Ocean Research Institute, Univ. of Tokyo,
Japan
http://www.ori.u-tokyo.ac.jp/

Ocean Systems Laboratory, Heriot Watt,
Edinburgh
http://anchovy.cee.hw.ac.uk

Ocean Voice International
http://www.conveyor.com/oceanvoice.html

Ocean-Science Related Acronyms
http://www.pmel.noaa.gov/pubs/
acromain.html

Oceanographic & Earth Science Institutions Directory
http://orpheus.ucsd.edu/sio/inst/

Oceanographic USENET News groups
http://www.mth.uea.ac.uk/ocean/
oceanography.html#usenet

Oceanography and Atmospheric Science
Hotlist
http://bnloc7.das.bnl.gov/ocean/

Oceanography Society
http://www.tos.org/

Oceanography Virtual Library
http://www.mth.uea.ac.uk/ocean/
oceanography.html

Oceanography WWW servers
http://www.whoi.edu/html/www-servers/
oceanography.html

Oceanor, Trondheim
http://www.oceanor.no/

Oceans and Ice Branch
http://biggles.gsfc.nasa.gov/~adamec/
971.home_page

Old Dominion Univ.
http://www.ocean.odu.edu/

Oregon Sea Grant Home Page
http://seagrant.orst.edu

Oregon State Univ.
http://www.oce.orst.edu

Our Living Oceans Annual Report
http://kingfish.ssp.nmfs.gov/olo.html

Oxford Univ.
http://www-atm.atm.ox.ac.uk/index.html

Pacific Knowledge Research Foundation
http://pk.org/pkrf

Pacific Marine Environmental Lab.
(PMEL)
http://www.pmel.noaa.gov/pmelhome.html

Pacific Sea Surface Temperature Images
http://satftp.soest.hawaii.edu/avhrr.html

Parallel Ocean Program (POP) Model
http://dubhe.cc.nps.navy.mil/~braccio/

Patagonian Shelf - Falkland Islands
Models
http://biudc.nbi.ac.uk/gslc/glorioso.html

Pathfinder Cafe: AVHRR SST Image
Archive
http://satori.gso.uri.edu/archive/images.html

Pelagic Fisheries Research Program
http://www.soest.hawaii.edu/rbailey/
pfrp1.html

Physical Oceanography Distributed Active
Archive Ctr.
http://seazar.jpl.nasa.gov/

Physical Oceanography Research Div.
http://jedac2.ucsd.edu/

Planetary Coral Reef Foundation
http://pk.org/pcrf

Plymouth Marine Laboratory
http://www.npm.ac.uk/

Princeton Univ. Geophysical Fluid
Dynamics Laboratory
http://www.gfdl.gov/

Proudman Oceanographic Laboratory
http://biudc.nbi.ac.uk/

Radio Expeditions' Ocean of Life
http://www.npr.org/RE/

Reef Ball Development Group Ltd
http://www.america.net/~reefball/

REINAS Project
http://sapphire.cse.ucsc.edu/MosaicMet/top-
view.html

Remote Sensing Virtual Library
http://www.vtt.fi/aut/ava/rs/virtual/

RIDGE Multibeam Synthesis Project
http://imager.ldeo.columbia.edu/

Ridge Inter Disciplinary Global Experiment
http://copper.whoi.edu/RIDGE

Rosenstiel School of Marine and Atmospheric Science
http://www.rsmas.miami.edu/

SALMON: Sea Air Land Modeling
Operational Network
http://modb.oce.ulg.ac.be/SALMON/
Welcome.html/

San Diego's Ocean
http://orpheus.ucsd.edu/sio/ocean/

Satellite and Ocean Dynamics Branch
http://www.grdl.noaa.gov/SAT/SAT.html

Satellite Observing Systems
http://www.satobsys.co.uk

Save Our Seas
http://www.hotspots.hawaii.com/sos.html

School of Ocean and Earth Science
Technology
http://www.soest.hawaii.edu/

School of Ocean Sciences
http://www.sos.bangor.ac.uk/

sci.geo.meteorology FAQ
http://www.cis.ohio-state.edu/hypertext/faq/
usenet/weather/top.html

Scripps Institution of Oceanography
http://sio.ucsd.edu/

Sea Surface Temperature Satellite Images
http://dcz.gso.uri.edu/avhrr-archive/
archive.html

SeaWiFS Project
http://seawifs.gsfc.nasa.gov/SEAWIFS.html

SISMER: Marine Scientific Information
Systems
http://www.ifremer.fr/sismer/

Skidaway Institute of Oceanography
http://minnow.skio.peachnet.edu/

South African Data Ctr. for Oceanography
http://fred.csir.co.za/ematek/sadco/
sadco.html

Southampton Oceanography Ctr.
http://www.soc.soton.ac.uk/

Southern California Sea Grant Program
http://www.usc.edu/dept/seagrant/
seagrant.html

Space Research and Technology, Delft
Univ. of Technology
http://dutlru8.lr.tudelft.nl/

Stable Isotope Laboratory, Univ. of East
Anglia, Norwich
http://www2.env.uea.ac.uk/sil/ocean.html

Stellwagen Bank National Marine Sanctu-
ary
http://vineyard.er.usgs.gov/

Stephen Birch Aquarium-Museum
http://aqua.ucsd.edu/

Supplements to Atmospheric & Oceanic
Publications
http://www-cmpo.mit.edu/met_links/
index.html

Technical Univ. of Denmark
http://www.ish.dtu.dk/

Technology Review
http://www.mit.edu:8001/afs/athena/org/t/
techreview/www/tr.html

Texas A&M Univ.
http://www-ocean.tamu.edu/

Tidal Modelling, Applied Mathematics,
Univ. of Adelaide
http://michell.maths.adelaide.edu.au/
UA_DAM_FLUIDS/TIDAL/tidalhome.html

TOGA COARE International Project Office
http://www.coare.ucar.edu/

Topex/Poseidon - The Ocean Topography Experiment
http://topex-www.jpl.nasa.gov/

U.K. Ocean Drilling Program
http://www.dur.ac.uk/~dgl0zz3/

U.S. Coast Guard Navigation Ctr.
http://www.navcen.uscg.mil

USGS Oceanography Resources
http://www.usgs.gov/network/science/earth/oceanography.html

U.S. JGOFS Information
http://lake.mit.edu/jgofs.html

U.S. Joint Global Ocean Flux Study (JGOFS)
http://www1.whoi.edu/jgofs.html

US Navy Advanced Arctic Ocean model with sea ice
http://vislab-www.nps.navy.mil/~braccio/maslowski/arctic.html

US Navy Fleet Numerical Meteorology and Oceanography Ctr.
http://www.fnoc.navy.mil/

US Navy Parallel Ocean Climate Model
http://vislab-www.nps.navy.mil/~rtt/

US WOCE
http://www-ocean.tamu.edu/WOCE/uswoce.htm

UNAVCO
http://www.unavco.ucar.edu/

Under Waterworld, Deep Sea Submersibles off Oregon
http://www.teleport.com/~samc/seas/deep1.html

Underwater Technology
http://www.u-net.com/scotweb/rov/home.htm

Univ. of Alaska, Fairbanks
http://www.ims.alaska.edu:8000/

Univ. of British Columbia
http://www.ocgy.ubc.ca/

Univ. of California at Davis
http://www-wfb.ucdavis.edu/

UC Santa Cruz
http://scilibx.ucsc.edu/iamslic/ucsc/ucsc.html

Univ. of Cape Town, South Africa
http://emma.sea.uct.ac.za/

Univ. of Colorado Astrodynamics Research
http://shaman.colorado.edu

Univ. of Colorado, Boulder
http://marigold.colorado.edu/

Univ. of Delaware
http://triton.cms.udel.edu/

Univ. of East Anglia, Norwich
http://www.mth.uea.ac.uk/climateinfo.html

Univ. of Guelph
http://www.uoguelph.ca/zoology/ocean/indexg.htm

Univ. of Hawaii
http://www.soest.hawaii.edu/

Univ. of Massachusetts/Boston
http://www.es.umb.edu/

Univ. of North Carolina at Wilmington
http://www.uncwil.edu/sys$disk1/cmsr/welcome.html

Univ. of Rhode Island
http://www.gso.uri.edu/

Univ. of Southern Mississippi/Stennis Space Ctr.
http://www.coam.usm.edu/

Univ. of Tokyo Underwater Robotics and Application Lab.
http://manta.iis.u-tokyo.ac.jp/Welcome-e.html

Univ. of Tokyo, Ocean Research Institute
http://www.ori.u-tokyo.ac.jp/

Univ. of Trieste
http://oce715a.ogs.trieste.it/

Univ. of Washington
http://www.ocean.washington.edu/

Univ. of Washington Fisheries
http://www.fish.washington.edu/

UNSW Mathematics Fluid Dynamics Group, Sydney
http://solution.maths.unsw.edu.au/WWW.fluids/homepage/

Wave Vectors from APL Processor, John Hopkins Univ.
ftp://fermi.jhuapl.edu/sirc/sirc.html

Woods Hole Oceanographic Institute (WHOI)
http://www.whoi.edu/

WHOI Deep Submergence Lab.
  http://www.dsl.whoi.edu/

WHOI Helium Isotope Lab.
  http://kopernik.whoi.edu/

WHOI Marine Biology Lab.
  http://alopias.mbl.edu/Default.html

WHOI Ocean Acoustics Lab.
  http://www.oal.whoi.edu/

World Data Center-A (WDC-A) for Marine
  Geology & Geophysics
  http://www.ngdc.noaa.gov/mgg/aboutmgg/
  wdcamgg.html

Optics

See also Aeronautics & Aerospace, Astronomy & Astrophysics, Biology
& Biotechnology, Computer Science, Engineering, Imaging Technologies,
Medicine, Physics, Virtual Reality

Advanced Research Projects Agency
(ARPA)
http://ftp.arpa.mil/

Alabama A & M University, Center for
Applied Optical Sciences
http://caos.aamu.edu/

American Astronomical Society
http://blackhole.aas.org/AAS-homepage.html

American Institute of Physics
http://aip.org/

American Mathematical Society
http://www.ams.org

American Physical Society
http://aps.org/

American Society for Engineering Education
http://www.asee.org/

American Society for Nondestructive
Testing
http://www.asnt.org/

Amerinex Artificial Intelligence, Inc.
http://www.aai.com/

Ansel Adams photographs
http://bookweb.cwis.uci.edu:8042/
SlicedExhibit/oru.html

Association for Computing Machinery
http://www.acm.org

Association of Vacuum Equipment
Manufacturers (AVEM)
http://www.avem.org/

Astronomy and Astrophysics Virtual
Library
http://www10.w3.org/hypertext/DataSources/
bySubject/astro/astro.html

Astronomy Group, Univ. of Manchester
http://axp2.ast.man.ac.uk:8000/

AT&T Bell Laboratories
http://www.research.att.com/

Australian Optical Society
http://www.dap.csiro.au/OPTECH/Optics-
Radiometry/aoshome.htm

Biomedical Optics Society
http://www.spie.org/web/working_groups/
biomedical_optics/bios_desc.html

Boston Univ. Center for Photonics Research
http://eng.bu.edu/Photonics_Center/

California Institute of Technology
http://www.caltech.edu/

Canada-France-Hawaii Telescope
http://www.cfht.hawaii.edu/

Capovani New and Used Optical Equipment
http://www.capovani.com/

Carnegie Mellon Univ. Computer Vision
http://www.cs.cmu.edu:8001/afs/cs/project/cil/
ftp/html/vision.html

CASIX
http://www.newsight.com/newsight/casix.htm

Center for Electromagnetic Materials and
Optics Systems
http://www.uml.edu/Dept/EE/RCs/CEMOS

Center for Extreme Ultraviolet Astrophysics
http://cea-ftp.cea.berkeley.edu/
HomePage.html

Center for Nondestructive Evaluation
(Iowa State University)
http://www.cnde.iastate.edu/cnde.html

Center for Particle Astrophysics
http://physics7.berkeley.edu/home.html

Center for Research and Education in
Optics and Lasers (CREOL at UCF)
http://www.creol.ucf.edu/

Charged Particle Optics Software
http://wwwdo.tn.tudelft.nl/bbs/cposis.htm

Chromophore, Inc.
http://www.chromophore.com/

CIDTECH (CID cameras)
http://www.cidtec.com/info/cid/index.html

CIE - International Commission on
Illumination
http://www.hike.te.chiba-u.ac.jp/ikeda/CIE/
home.html

COBRA InterUniv. Research Institute on
Communication Technology
http://www.cobra.tue.nl/

Coherent Laser Instrument Div.
http://cid.cohr.com/

Colorado State Univ.
http://www.lance.colostate.edu/optical/
index.html

Colorado Video
http://www.colorado-video.com

Conferences, Workshops, etc.
http://www.automatrix.com/conferences/

CONNECT - New England Alliance of
Photonics Technology Deployment
http://www.eotc.tufts.edu/CONNECT.html

Consortium for Optical and Optoelectric
Technologies in Computing
http://co-op.gmu.edu

COSMIC Information Services
http://www.cosmic.uga.edu/

Curt Deckert Associates
http://www.deltanet.com/cda

Cygnus Support
http://www.cygnus.com

Defense Research and Engineering
http://www.acq.osd.mil/ddre

Defense Technology Information Ctr.
http://www.dtic.dla.mil/defenselink

Delft Univ. of Technology Electronic
Instrumentation Laboratory
http://guernsey.et.tudelft.nl/

Delft Univ. of Technology Optics Research
Group
http://www.tn.tudelft.nl/optica/optica.html

Delft Univ. of Technology Pattern Recognition Group
http://galaxy.ph.tn.tudelft.nl:2000/pr-intro.html

Department of Energy (U.S.)
http://apollo.osti.gov/home.html

DLR Particle Image Velocimetry course
http://www.dlr.de/dlr_calendar_PIV.html

Duisburg Univ., Optoelectronic Department
http://optorisc.uni-duisburg.de/

DVC Company
http://www.optics.org/dvc/dvc.htm

Early Instruments of the Institute of
Physics of Naples: Optics Instruments
http://hpl33.na.infn.it/Museum/Optics.html

Electro-Optics Technology Ctr. (EOTC)
http://www.eotc.tufts.edu/

Electron Microscope Images
http://www.uq.oz.au/nanoworld/
images_1.html

Ellipsometry Site
http://www.afep.cornell.edu/ellipsometry.html

Ellipsometry on the Web
http://www.vuw.ac.nz/~db/bes/bes.html

EULF
http://luce.iesl.forth.gr/~ulf/ulfhome.htm

European Optical Society
http://www-eos.unine.ch

European Physical Society
http://www.nikhef.nl/www/pub/eps/eps.html

European Southern Observatory
http://http.hq.eso.org/eso-homepage.html

European Space Agency
http://www.esrin.esa.it/

European Space Research and Technology
Centre
http://www.estec.esa.nl/

European Ultraviolet Laser Facility
http://luce.iesl.forth.gr/~ulf/ulfhome.htm

Federal Laboratory Consortium for Technology Transfer
http://ixc.net/zyn/trpa.html

FedWorld Information Network
http://www.fedworld.gov/

Fiber Optic Marketplace
http://fiberoptic.com/

Fraunhofer Resource Center for Laser Technology
http://www.ilt.fhg.de/

Friedrich-Schiller-Univ. Jena, Physics and Astronomy
http://einstein.physik.uni-jena.de/

General Imaging Corporation
http://www.gicorp.com

German Aerospace Research Establishment (DLR)
http://www.dlr.de/

Harvard Univ. Experimental and Optical Physics
http://em-office.harvard.edu/MazurPhysWWW.html

Harvest search software from Univ. of Colorado
http://harvest.cs.colorado.edu/

High Energy Physics Automated E-print Archives
http://xxx.lanl.gov/

High Energy Physics Information Server
http://www.hep.net/

High Performance Computing Article Archive
http://www.lpac.qmw.ac.uk/SEL-HPC/Articles/index.html

Hologramas de Mexico
www.holomex.com

Hughes STX Corporation
http://info.stx.com/

Human Computer Interaction Article Archive
http://www.lpac.qmw.ac.uk/SEL-HPC/Articles/HciArchive.html

Human Computer Interaction Bibliography
http://www.tu-graz.ac.at/CHClbib

Human Interface Technology Laboratory
http://www.hitl.washington.edu/

Icarus — The International Journal of Solar System Studies
http://astrosun.tn.cornell.edu/Icarus/Icarus.html

IEE — The Institution of Electrical Engineers
http://www.iee.org.uk

IEEE
http://www.ieee.org

Image Processing and Analysis Group
http://noodle.med.yale.edu/

Imperial College Applied Optics Group, Blackett Lab
http://op.ph.ic.ac.uk/

Institute of Computer Science, Hebrew Univ. of Jerusalem
http://www.cs.huji.ac.il/

Institute of Physics
http://www.iop.org

Institute of Physics Publishing
http://www.ioppublishing.com/IOPP/ioppwelcome.html

Instituto de Astrofisica de Canarias
http://www.iac.es/

Intl. Commission on Illumination
http://www.hike.te.chiba-u.ac.jp/ikeda/CIE/home.html

Intl. Standards Organization (ISO)
http://www.hike.te.chiba-u.ac.jp/ikeda/ISO/home.html

IRIA Infrared Information Analysis Center, ERIM
http://www.erim.org/IRIA/iria.html

IS&T — Society for Imaging Science & Technology
http://www.imaging.org

ISPRS Congress 1996
http://www.ipf.tuwien.ac.at/isprs.html

Jet Propulsion Laboratory
http://www.jpl.nasa.gov/

KAOS Advanced Optoelectronic Systems Research Group
http://drip.colorado.edu/

Laboratory for Materials, Device and Circuit Simulation
http://nida.eng.wayne.edu/

Lambda Research Corporation
http://www.lambdares.com/

Large Binocular Telescope Information System
http://euterpe.arcetri.astro.it/

Laser Focus World
http://www.lfw.com

Laser Stars
http://www.achilles.net/~jtalbot

Laser WWW Information Server
http://www.law.indiana.edu/misc/laser.html

Lasers & Electro-Optics Society (IEEE)
http://msrc.wvu.edu/leos/

Lattice High Energy Physics
http://info.desy.de/user/projects/Lattice.html

Laval Univ.
http://www.ulaval.ca/texte.anglais.html

Lawrence Berkeley Lab.
http://www.lbl.gov/LBL.html

Lawrence Livermore National Lab.
http://www-lasers.llnl.gov

Lebedev Physical Institute
http://www.lpi.msk.su/

Lighting SuperFAQ
http://www.cco.caltech.edu/~aquaria/Krib/Lights/faq.html

Lightwave Communications Research Laboratory
http://optics.genie.uottawa.ca:8080/LtComResLab.html

Liquid Mirror Telescope, University of British Columbia
http://www.geop.ubc.ca/~cabanac/lmt.html

loQtus: Quotations Resources on the Internet
http://pubweb.ucdavis.edu/Documents/Quotations/homepage.html

Los Alamos National Lab.
http://www.lanl.gov/

Lunar and Planetary Institute
http://cass.jsc.nasa.gov/lpi.html

Martin Marietta Energy Systems
http://www.ornl.gov/mmes.html

Materials Research Society
http://dns.mrs.org/

Matlin Space Science Systems
http://barsoom.msss.com/

Maui High Performance Computing Center
http://www.mhpcc.edu/mhpcc.html

McDonnell Douglas Corporation
http://pat.mdc.com/

McGill Univ., Photonic Systems Group
http://www.photonics.ee.mcgill.ca/

McGill Univ. - Physics Servers around the World
http://www.physics.mcgill.ca/deptdocs/physics_services.html

Medical Radiography Home Page
http://web.wn.net/user1/ricter/web/medradhome.html

Mercury Project: Remote Robotic Tele-excavation via WWW
http://www.usc.edu/dept/raiders/

Micro-Electromechanical Systems Information Clearinghouse
http://esto.sysplan.com/ESTO/MEMS/

Microcosm, Inc.
http://www.softaid.net/spark

MIT Media Lab
http://www.media.mit.edu/

MIT Microsystems Technology Laboratories
http://www-mtl.mit.edu/

Molecular Manufacturing Shortcut Group
http://www.gpl.net/mmsg/mmsg.html

Molecular Optoelectronics Corp.
http://www.automatrix.com/moec/

Moscow State Univ.
http://www.msu.ru/

Mossberg Optical Physics Laboratory
http://opticb.uoregon.edu/~mosswww/Home.html

Motion Analysis FAQ
http://www.redlake.com/imaging/faq.htm

Mount Wilson Observatory
http://www.mtwilson.edu/

NASA
http://hypatia.gsfc.nasa.gov/
NASA_homepage.html

NASA Astrophysics Data System Abstract
Service
http://adswww.harvard.edu/abs_doc/
abstract_service.html

NASA Cool Site of the Week
http://www.jsc.nasa.gov/~mccoy/nasa/
Cool.html

NASA EOS IDS Volcanology Team
http://www.geo.mtu.edu/eos/

NASA Goddard Space Flight Ctr.
http://hypatia.gsfc.nasa.gov/
NASA_homepage.html

NASA, Guide to Online Resources
http://naic.nasa.gov/naic/guide/

NASA/JPL Imaging Radar Home Page
http://southport.jpl.nasa.gov/

NASA/JSC Digital Image Collection
http://images.jsc.nasa.gov/html/home.htm

NASA Langley Research Center
http://mosaic.larc.nasa.gov/larc.html

NASA Solar Data Analysis Center
http://umbra.gsfc.nasa.gov/sdac.html

NASA Technical Report Server
http://techreports.larc.nasa.gov/cgi-bin/NTRS

National Institute of Standards and
Technology (NIST)
http://www.nist.gov/welcome.html

National Optical Astronomy Observatories
http://www.noao.edu/

National Optics Institute of Canada
http://www.ino.qc.ca/

National Research Council Canada,
Photonic Systems Group
http://alpha.ps.iit.nrc.ca/

National Technological University
http://www.ntu.edu/

NCSA Virtual Reality Lab
http://www.ncsa.uiuc.edu/Viz/VR/
vr_homepage.html

Neural Networks Article Archive
http://www.lpac.qmw.ac.uk/SEL-HPC/Articles/
NeuralArchive.html

New England Fiber Optics Council
http://www.eotc.tufts.edu/nefc.html

New Mexico State University, Applied
Optics Laboratory
http://gauss.nmsu.edu:8000/optics/
optics.html

Nonlinear Optics Resource
http://marv.eng.uiowa.edu/

Nonliner Optical Spectroscopy at the Univ.
of Pennsylvania
http://www.lrsm.upenn.edu/~angerer/

Northwestern Univ. EE/CS
http://www.eecs.nwu.edu/eecs-home.html

NSF Microelectronics Research Center (U.
of Idaho)
http://www.mrc.uidaho.edu/

NSF Optoelectronic Computing Systems
Ctr. (Colorado State Univ.)
http://www.lance.colostate.edu/optical/
index.html

NSFNET Backbone Statistics
http://www.cc.gatech.edu/gvu/stats/NSF/
merit.html

Oak Ridge National Lab.
http://www.ornl.gov/

Office of Technology Assessment
http://www.ota.gov/

Office of the Secretary of Defense (U.S.)
http://enterprise.osd.mil/

Opkor
http://www.opkor.com

Optical Computing Systems Center at the
NSF
http://www.lance.colostate.edu/optical/
index.html

Optical Research Associates
http://www.opticalres.com

Optical Science and Engineering WWW
Virtual Library
http://www.spie.org/wwwvl_optics.html

Optical Society of America
http://www.osa.org/

OptiComp Corporation
http://www.opticomp.com

Optics and Machine Vision Applications
http://www.iti.org/eoe/index.htm

OPTICS 1
http://www.optics1.com

OPTICS.ORG — The Photonics Resource Center
http://optics.org/

OptikWerk
http://www.optikwerk.com

Optolectronic Research Centre
http://www.orc.soton.ac.uk/

Optoelectronics Technology Center
http://www.ece.ucsb.edu/OTC/

OptoSigma Corporation
http://www.optosigma.com

Oregon Univ.
http://opticb.uoregon.edu/

Oriel Instruments
http://www.oriel.com/WWW/adv/oriel.html

Particle Optics Research, Technical Univ. of Delft
http://wwwdo.tn.tudelft.nl/

Patent Search System
http://sunsite.unc.edu/patents/intropat.html

Perceptics
http://www.perceptics.com/info

Phillips Laboratory, Kirtland AFB
http://www.plk.af.mil/

Photek Ltd.
http://www.spie.org/photek/photek.html

Photonics Switching and Integrated Optoelectronics Lab, Univ. of Maryland
http://www.ee.umd.edu/photonics/

Portland State Univ.
http://www.ee.pdx.edu/

Precision Digital Images
http://www.precisionimages.com/gateway.htm

Prentiss Group, Harvard Univ.
http://atomsun.harvard.edu/

Radiology Imaging Ctr.
http://visual-ra.swmed.edu/

Radiology Webserver
http://www.rad.washington.edu/

Redlake Camera
HTTP://www.redlake.com/imaging/

Remote Sensing Virtual Library
http://www.vtt.fi/aut/ava/rs/virtual/

RLE - Research Laboratory of Electronics
http://rleweb.mit.edu

Rochester Institute of Technology, Imaging and Photographic Technology
http://www.rit.edu/~andpph/ipt.html

Rockwell Laser Industries LASERNET
http://iac.net/~rli/

Rose Hulman Institute - Center for Applied Optics Studies
http://www.rose-hulman.edu/Class/phao/html/caos.html

Sandia National Laboratories
http://www.cs.sandia.gov/Sandia_home_page.html

Semiconductor Corporations
http://mtmis1.mis.semi.harris.com/semi.html

Semiconductor Subway
http://www-mtl.mit.edu/cgi-bin/Mapgen/subway/

SemiWeb
http://www.semiweb.com

SensorPhysics
http://www.sensorphysics.com

Shoemaker-Levy Comet impact
http://alfred1.u.washington.edu:8080/~roland/sl/sl.html

Sloan Digital Sky Survey
http://www-sdss.fnal.gov:8000/

Smithsonian Astrophysical Observatory
http://sao-www.harvard.edu/home.html

Society for Applied Spectroscopy
http://esther.la.asu.edu/sas/

Society for Industrial and Applied Mathematics
http://www.siam.org/

Society for Information Display
http://www.display.org/sid/

Society of Manufacturing Engineers
http://www.sme.org

Society of Vacuum Coaters
http://www.svc.org/

Software Spectra (optical thin films design)
http://www.teleport.com/~sspectra/

Space Activism Home Page
http://muon.qrc.com/space/start.html

Space Telescope Science Institute
http://stsci.edu/top.html

Spacecraft Planetary Imaging Facility (SPIF) at Cornell Univ.
http://astrosun.tn.cornell.edu/SPIF.html

SPIE — The International Society for Optical Engineering
http://www.spie.org/

SRI International's Visual Sciences Program
http://os.sri.com/vision

Stanford Univ.
http://www.stanford.edu/stanford.html

Stanford Univ., Holography and Optical Data Storage Group
http://www-leland.stanford.edu:80/group/holography/

Stereoscopic Volume Visualization
http://www.dataspace.com/WWW/documents/stereoscopic.html

Swales and Associates Optics Group
http://www.swales.com/optics.html

Swedish Optical Society
http://www.optics.kth.se/sos/

Technological Institute of Costa Rica
http://www.cic.itcr.ac.cr/cic.html

Technology Review magazine
http://web.mit.edu/afs/athena/org/t/techreview/www/tr.html

Tecnet
http://www.tecnet.com

Teledyne Brown Electro-Optical Products Group
http://www.tbe.com/tech-pubs/products/optics/optics.html

Tufts Univ. Electro-Optics Technology Center
http://www.eotc.tufts.edu/

U.S. Dept. of Energy
http://apollo.osti.gov/home.html

U.S. Patent and Trademark Office
http://www.uspto.gov/

UCSD Science & Engineering Library
http://scilib.ucsd.edu

UIUC Photonic Systems Group
http://www.phs.uiuc.edu/

UMASS Astronomy
http://donald.phast.umass.edu/umasshome.html

UMASS Lowell, Ctr. for Electromagnetic Materials and Optical Systems (CEMOS)
http://web.uml.edu/Dept/EE/RCs/CEMOS/

Univ. of Alabama in Huntsville Center for Applied Optics
http://www.uah.edu/cao/

Univ. of Arizona Optical Sciences Center
http://www.opt-sci.arizona.edu/

Univ. of Calgary Micronet Multidimensional Signal Processing Research Group
http://www-mddsp.enel.ucalgary.ca/

Univ. of California/San Diego Optoelectronic Computing Group
http://soliton.ucsd.edu/

Univ. of California/Santa Barbara, Optoelectronics Technology Center
http://www.ece.ucsb.edu/department/centers/otc.html

Univ. of Central Florida - CREOL — Center for Research and Education in Optics and Lasers
http://www.creol.ucf.edu/

Univ. of Colorado, Boulder
http://ocswebhost.colorado.edu/

Univ. of Connecticut Photonics Research Center
http://www.eng2.uconn.edu/prc/index.html

Univ. of Delaware EE/CIS
http://www.eecis.udel.edu/

Univ. of Edinburgh Applied Optics Group
http://prism.ph.ed.ac.uk/

Univ. of Florida EE
http://www.eel.ufl.edu/

Univ. of Illinois: Center for Compound Semiconductor Microelectronics
http://www.ccsm.uiuc.edu/micro

Univ. of Iowa College of Medicine Div. of Physiologic Imaging
http://everest.radiology.uiowa.edu:8080/home.html

Univ. Laval
http://www.ulaval.ca/

Univ. of Limburg Dept. of Medical Informatics
http://www.mi.rulimburg.nl/

Univ. of Maryland Baltimore County (UMBC) Physics Department
http://umbc7.umbc.edu/~dguyke1/dept/home.html

Univ. of Melbourne Photonics Research Lab
http://www.ee.mu.oz.au/papers/prl/PhotonicsPage.html

Univ. de Murcia, Spain, Lab. Optica
http://iriso.fcu.um.es

Univ. of New Hampshire Robotics
http://www.ece.unh.edu/robots/rbt_home.htm

Univ. of Oregon Center for Optics in Science and Technology
http://opticb.uoregon.edu/

Univ. of Ottawa, Broadband Communications Research Lab
http://optics.genie.uottawa.ca:8080/LtComResLab.html

Univ. of Pennsylvania Medical Image Processing Group
http://mipgsun.mipg.upenn.edu/

Univ. of Queensland Centre for Microscopy and Microanalysis
http://www.uq.oz.au/nanoworld/images_1.html

Univ. of Rochester, Institute of Optics
http://www.optics.rochester.edu:8080/

Univ. of Southampton (UK), Optolectronic Research Centre
http://www.orc.soton.ac.uk/

Univ. of Southern California
http://www.usc.edu/

Univ. of Sydney Mathematics and Statistics
http://www.maths.usyd.edu.au:8000/

Univ. of Virginia Laboratory for Optics and Quantum Electronics
http://www.ee.virginia.edu/AEPL/labs/loqe

Univ. of Wales College of Cardiff, Dept. of Computing Mathematics
http://www.cm.cf.ac.uk/

Univ. of Washington High Energy Physics
http://squark.phys.washington.edu/

Univ. of Waterloo Electronic Library
http://www.lib.uwaterloo.ca/

Virginia Tech Robotics and Machine Intelligence Laboratories
http://armyant.ee.vt.edu/

Virgo Optics, Division of II-VI
http://innet.com/~virgo/vhome2.html

Virtual Reality Lab, Johnson Space Center
http://www.jsc.nasa.gov/~mle/vr.html

Virtual Reality Society
http://web.dcs.hull.ac.uk/VRS/

Vision and Image Processing Article Archive
http://www.lpac.ac.uk/SEL-HPC/Articles/VisionArchive.html

Vision and Imaging Technology Resource
http://www.vision1.com/

Visioneering Research Lab.
http://vitoria.nmsu.edu/

Western Washington Univ.
http://www.wwu.edu

Wilkes Univ. School of Science & Engineering
http://www.wilkes.edu/WilkesDocs/SSEHome.html#101

X-Ray Interactions with Matter (LBL)
http://www-cxro.lbl.gov/optical_constants/

X-Ray WWW Server
http://xray.uu.se/

Yale Univ. Image Processing and Analysis Group
http://noodle.med.yale.edu/

Yale Univ. Mathematics
http://www.yale.edu/HTML/YALE/MATH/FrontDoor.html

Zory Laser Lab, Univ. of Florida
http://nervm.nerdc.ufl.edu/~largent/

Physics

See also Aeronautics & Aerospace, Astronomy & Astrophysics, Biology & Biotechnology, Chemistry, Computer Science, Electronics & Electrical Engineering, Energy, Engineering, Imaging Technologies, Mathematics, Medicine, Optics, Virtual Reality

Advanced Photon Source
http://epics.aps.anl.gov/welcome.html

AMANDA- Antarctic Muon And Neutrino Detector Array
http://dilbert.lbl.gov/www/amanda.html

American Center for Physics
http://acp.org/

American Institute of Physics
http://aip.org/

American Nuclear Society
http://www.ans.org

American Physical Society
http://aps.org/

American Vacuum Society
http://www.vacuum.org/

Argonne National Lab
http://axp1.hep.anl.gov/

Aston Univ. - Electronic Engineering and Applied Physics
http://www.eeap.aston.ac.uk/home.html

Astro, VR, Space, & Infosystems News-groups
http://guinan.gsfc.nasa.gov/WebStars/NEWS.html

ATLAS-Japan
http://arkhp1.kek.jp/

Atomic and Molecular Physics Servers Links {Europe}
http://www.sc.ucl.ac.be:80/~stoop/links/europe.html

Atomic and Plasma Physics Databases
http://plasma-gate.weizmann.ac.il/DBfAPP.html

Atomic and Solid State Physics, Cornell Univ.
http://www.lassp.cornell.edu/

Atomic, Molecular and Optical Physics
http://gomez.physics.lsa.umich.edu/~denison/

Atomic Physics Resources
http://plasma-gate.weizmann.ac.il/API.html

Biophysical Society
http://molbio.cbs.umn.edu/biophys/biophys.html

Biophysical Society of Hong Kong
http://biosci.cbs.umn.edu/biophys/FBS/HK-BS.html

BNL
http://suntid.bnl.gov:8080/bnl.html

Boston Univ. - Center for Polymer Studies
http://cps-www.bu.edu/

Bradley Univ.
http://www.bradley.edu/las/phy/

Bristol Univ.
http://gaia.phy.bris.ac.uk/research/pppages/particle_physics_94.html

Brookhaven National Lab Accelerator Facility
http://www.tvdg.bnl.gov/~tvdg/tvdg.html

Brown Bag Preprint List - Caltech
http://chaos.fullerton.edu/brownbag.html

Brown Univ. - High Energy Physics
http://www.het.brown.edu/

Brown Univ. Physics
http://www.physics.brown.edu/

Caltech
http://www.theory.caltech.edu/

Caltech GEM Information
http://www.cithep.caltech.edu/gem/gem.html

Caltech High Energy Physics
http://www.cithep.caltech.edu/

Canadian Association of Physics
http://www.inrs-ener.uquebec.ca/surfsci/index.html

CAP/CIC - Surface Science Index
http://www.inrs-ener.uquebec.ca/surfsci/
index.html

CASS: Univ. of California - San Diego Ctr.
for Astrophysics and Space Sciences
http://cassfos01.ucsd.edu:8080/

CBPF Laboratorio de Cosmologia e Fisica
Experimental de Altas Energias
http://www.lafex.cbpf.br/

Centre for Industrial Bulk Solids Handling
— Glasgow-Caledonian Univ.
http://plean.gcal.ac.uk

Center for Theoretical Studies of Physical
Systems
http://galaxy.cau.auc.edu/

Centre de Physique des Particules de
Marseille
http://marcpl1.in2p3.fr/

CERN
http://www.cern.ch/

CERN High Energy Physics
http://www.cern.ch/Physics/HEP.html

CERN Theoretical Physics
http://nxth21.cern.ch/

CfA High Energy Astrophysics Division
http://hea-www.harvard.edu/

Charged Particle Optics Software
http://wwwdo.tn.tudelft.nl/bbs/cposis.htm

Chungbuk National Univ. Theoretical
Physics
http://bohr.chungbuk.ac.kr/welcome.html

CITHEP
http://www.cithep.caltech.edu/

CLEO-II SVX Images
http://charm.physics.ucsb.edu/people/hnn/
svx_images.html

Collisions: When Two Tennis Balls Collide
and a Bowling Ball Flies Out
http://fnnews.fnal.gov/collisions.html

Complex systems
http://life.anu.edu.au/complex_systems/
complex.html

Contemporary Physics Education Project
(CPEP)
http://pdg.lbl.gov/cpep.html

Cornell University - Laboratory of Atomic
and Solid State Physics
http://www.lassp.cornell.edu/

Cornell Univ. Wilson Lab/CLEO
http://w4.lns.cornell.edu/

CPT
http://fourier.dur.ac.uk:8000/

Crystallography Virtual Library
http://www.unige.ch/crystal/crystal_index.html

DACcess - The Diamond Anvil Cell Forum
http://DACcess.phy.cam.ac.uk/

Daresbury Laboratory home page
http://www.dl.ac.uk/

DESY - Deutsches Electronen-Synchrotron
http://info.desy.de/

DESY Lattice Field Theory
http://info.desy.de/user/projects/Lattice.html

Durham/RAL HEP Databases
http://cpt1.dur.ac.uk/HEPDATA/

E-Print archive at babbage.sissa.it physics
(SISSA - ISAS)
http://babbage.sissa.it/

East Michigan Univ.
http://www.emich.edu/public/art_sci/phy_ast/
p&ahome.htm

Einstein Archive Service
http://adswww.harvard.edu/
einstein_service.html

Electromagnetics Library
http://emlib.jpl.nasa.gov/

Electrophysics
http://www.icis.on.ca/homepages/london/
electrophysics/

Elementary Particle Physics, Univ. of
Arizona
http://www.physics.arizona.edu/physics/
research.html#particle

ENSLAPP Laboratory for Theoretical
Physics
http://enslapp.ens-lyon.fr/

ESRS - Synchrotron Radiation Users in
Europe
http://www.fy.chalmers.se/esrs/welcome.html

European Physical Society
http://www.nikhef.nl/www/pub/eps/eps.html

Fermilab
http://fnnews.fnal.gov/

Fermilab Library
http://www-lib.fnal.gov/library/welcome.html

FreeHEP software guide
http://heplibw3.slac.stanford.edu/FIND/
FHMAIN.HTML

Fundamental Physics Section, ETL
http://www.etl.go.jp/Organization/Bussei-kiso/

GAMS - Guide to Available Mathematical
Software
http://gams.nist.gov/

Gen. Relativity and Quantum Cosmology
http://xxx.lanl.gov/gr-qc

Geomagnetic Index Kp
http://www.gwdg.de/~rhennin/

George Smoot Astrophysics Research
Group
http://spectrum.lbl.gov

Glasgow HEP
http://d1.ph.gla.ac.uk/

Harvard Univ. Physics
http://string.harvard.edu/

Health Physics Society
http://www.umich.edu/~bbusby/hps.htm

HEPIC - High Energy Physics Information
Center
http://www.hep.net/

HEP-Phenomenology
http://xxx.lanl.gov/hep-ph

HEP Physics Newsletters
http://www.hep.net/documents/newsletters/
newsletters.html

HEP preprint index
http://slacvm.slac.stanford.edu/find/hep

HEP-Theory
http://xxx.lanl.gov/hep-th

HEP Theory Software
http://heplibw3.slac.stanford.edu/FIND/
FREEHEP/SECTION/heptheory/INDEX

HEPIX
http://info.cern.ch/hepix/Overview.html

High-Energy Physics Virtual Library
http://www.cern.ch/Physics/HEP.html

HEPLIB info
http://heplibw3.slac.stanford.edu/FIND/
HLMAIN.HTML

HEPnet
http://www.hep.net/

HERMES
http://dxhra1.desy.de/

Hi-Tech Commerce
http://guinan.gsfc.nasa.gov/WebStars/
Commerce.html

High Energy Group, Institute of Physics,
Academia Sinica, Taiwan
http://hep3.phys.sinica.edu.tw/

Homeokinetics
http://www.trincoll.edu/psyc/Homeokinetics/

HUT/Materials Physics Lab
http://waist.hut.fi/

I. Physikalisches Institut
http://www.physik.rwth-aachen.de/group/
ibphys/ibphys.html

IAPS Home Page
http://www.tn.tudelft.nl/iaps/iaps.html

ICTP
http://euclid.tp.ph.ic.ac.uk/

IEE - Institution of Electrical Engineers
(UK)
http://www.iee.org.uk/

IEEE - Institute of Electrical and Electronics Engineers
http://www.ieee.org/

Institut de Física d'Altes Energies, Univ.
Autònoma de Barcelona
http://u1.ifae.es/

IFIC Valencia Univ.
http://evalu0.ific.uv.es/

IHEP in Heidelberg
http://hp01.ihep.uni-heidelberg.de/

Imperial College - Theoretical Physics
http://euclid.tp.ph.ic.ac.uk/

Imperial College Mathematical Physics
http://telemachus.ma.ic.ac.uk/~psswain/
mathphys.html

Imperial College Theory
http://euclid.tp.ph.ic.ac.uk/

IN2P3 - Institut National de Physique
Nucèaire et de Physiques des Particules
http://info.in2p3.fr

Indiana Univ. - Experimental HEP
http://needmore.physics.indiana.edu/
iuhep.html

Indiana Univ. - High Energy Astrophysics
http://mimosa.astro.indiana.edu/

Institut Laue-Langevin
http://jade.ill.fr/

Institute for Materials Research
http://imr.chem.binghamton.edu/

Institute for Theoretical Atomic and
Molecular Physics (ITAMP)
http://cfa-www.harvard.edu/cfa/itamp.html

Institute of High Energy Physics,
Academia Sinica
http://solar.rtd.utk.edu/~china/ins/IHEP/
ihep.html

Institute of High Energy Physics, Beijing
http://www.ihep.ac.cn:3000/ihep.html

Institute of Physics
http://www.iop.org/

Instituto de Astrofisica de Canarias
http://www.iac.es/home.html

Instituto de Fisica, Uruguay
http://fisica.uy/fisica2/WWW/fisica.html

Instituto Nacional de Pesquisas Espaciais
(INPE) Astrophysics Div. (DAS)
http://www.inpe.br/astro/home/

Istituto Ricerca Onde Elettromagnetiche
(IROE)
http://www.iroe.fi.cnr.it

Institut de Physique Nucléaire de Lyon
http://lyoinfo.in2p3.fr/

ISA - The International Society for
Measurement and Control
http://www.isa.org/

Kansas State Univ.
http://www.engg.ksu.edu/MEDEPT/

Keith Burnett Group Home Page
http://eve.physics.ox.ac.uk/KBGhome.html

KEK - National Laboratory for High
Energy Physics
http://www.kek.jp/

KEK Theory Physics Group
http://theory.kek.jp/

KVI
http://kviexp.kvi.nl/

Laboratorio de Instrumentacao e Fisica
Experimental de Particulas
http://www.lip.pt/

Laboratory for Materials, Device and
Circuit Simulation
http://nida.eng.wayne.edu/

Laser Stars
http://www.achilles.net/~jtalbot

LASSP
http://www.lassp.cornell.edu/

Lattice Archives
http://info.desy.de/user/projects/Lattice.html

Lawrence Berkeley Lab.
http://www.lbl.gov/LBL.html

Lawrence Livermore National Lab.
http://babar1.llnl.gov/

Los Alamos National Lab.
http://www.strauss.lanl.gov/

LANL Physics e-Print archive
http://xxx.lanl.gov/

LANL Physics Information Service
http://mentor.lanl.gov/Welcome.html

Low Temperature Lab.
http://www.hut.fi/Erill/kylma/

Manchester Univ.
http://h2.ph.man.ac.uk/home.html

Materials Research Society
http://dns.mrs.org/

MAX-lab
http://www.maxlab.lu.se/

Max-Planck-Institut fuer Physik, Munich,
Germany
http://iws132a.mppmu.mpg.de/

McGill Univ.
http://www.physics.mcgill.ca/physics-
services/

McMaster Univ.
http://www.physics.mcmaster.ca/

Metaphysics, Metamath
http://www.xnet.com/~raydbias/
metamath.htm

Middlesex Univ., Advanced Manufacturing and Mechatronics Centre
http://www.mdx.ac.uk/www/ammc/ammc.html

Mike Wetherley's Home Page
http://www.tcel.com/~mike/

MIT Center for Theoretical Physics
http://ctpa02.mit.edu/

MIT-LNS
http://marie.mit.edu/

Moscow State Univ. - Skobeltsyn Institute of Nuclear Physics
http://www.npi.msu.su/

Mossberg Optical Physics Laboratory
http://opticb.uoregon.edu/~mosswww/Home.html

MPI
http://www.mppmu.mpg.de/welcome.html/

MPI-K
http://www.mpi-hd.mpg.de/

Nanotechnology Index
http://erie.csis.gvsu.edu/~vanoflej/NanoTech/

Nanotechnology Resources
http://nano.xerox.com/nano/

NASA - National Aeronautics and Space Administration
http://hypatia.gsfc.nasa.gov/NASA_homepage.html

National Hydrogen Association
http://www.paltech.com/ttc/nha/index.htm

National Univ. of Singapore
http://www.physics.nus.sg

ND HEP
http://undhe6.hep.nd.edu/

Niels Bohr Institute
http://www.nbi.dk/

Nijmegen High Energy Physics Institute
http://thef-nym.sci.kun.nl/

NIKHEF
http://www.nikhef.nl/www/pub/default/NikhefGuide.html

NORDITA - Nordic Institute for Theoretical Physics
http://www.nordita.dk/

Northwestern High Energy Physics Group
http://nuhepz.phys.nwu.edu/welcome.html

Notre Dame HEP
http://undhe6.hep.nd.edu/

Nuclear Physics for Software Resources
http://www.scri.fsu.edu/~drago/srin.html

Nuclear Physics, Netherlands
http://www.nucphys.nl/www/pub/nucphys/npe.html

Ohio State Univ.
http://www-physics.mps.ohio-state.edu/~cleo/home.html

OPAL group - Bonn Univ.
http://opalr2.physik.uni-bonn.de/

OPTICS.ORG - The Photonics Resource Center
http://optics.org/

ORNL Physics Division
http://www.phy.ornl.gov/

Oxford Univ. Astrophysics Server
http://www-astro.physics.ox.ac.uk/

Particle Data Group (PDG)
http://www-pdg.lbl.gov/

Particle Optics Research, Technical Univ. of Delft
http://wwwdo.tn.tudelft.nl/

Particle Surface Resources
http://chaos.fullerton.edu/mhslinks.html

PASA - Physics and Astronomy Students Association
http://www.ucalgary.ca/~physastr

Penn State - Gravitational Physics and Geometry
http://vishnu.nirvana.phys.psu.edu/

Physical Societies
http://www.cern.ch/Physics/PhysSoc.html

Physics at the Australian Defence Force Academy
http://www.adfa.oz.au/physics/

Physics Department - Saga Univ., Japan
http://www.cc.saga-u.ac.jp/saga-u/riko/physics/physics.html

Physics Hypertext
http://web.phys.washington.edu/

Physics Servers Around the World - European Server
http://tph.tuwien.ac.at/physics-services/physics_services2.html

Physics Servers Around the World - North American Server
http://www.physics.mcgill.ca/physics-services/physics_services.html

Physics Servers Around the World - Scandinavian Server
http://www.tp.umu.se/physics-services/

Physics World Digest
http://info.desy.de/pub/faq/physics/PhysicsWorld

Physics-Uspekhi On-Line
http://ufn.ioc.ac.ru/

Plasma Gate
http://plasma-gate.weizmann.ac.il/

Plasma Science and Technology
http://www-plasma.umd.edu/

Pohang Univ., Korea
http://sol.postech.ac.kr

Prarie View HEP
http://hp73.pvamu.edu/

PSI
http://www.psi.ch/

PSI F1 Theory Group
http://pss058.psi.ch/

Queen's Univ. of Belfast
http://www.am.qub.ac.uk/

RAL
http://www.rl.ac.uk/home.html

Rechenzentrum der Max-Planck-Gesellschaft in Garching
http://www.ipp-garching.mpg.de/rzg.html

Remote Sensing Virtual Library
http://www.vtt.fi/aut/ava/rs/virtual/

Rensselaer Polytechnic Institute
http://www.rpi.edu/dept/phys/physics.html

Rensselaer Polytechnic Institute - Nuclear and Particle Physics
http://www.rpi.edu/dept/phys/nuclear.html

RIKEN
http://www.riken.go.jp/

Royal Holloway
http://www.ph.rhbnc.ac.uk/research/hep/hep_home.html

RPI - Plasma Dynamics Lab
http://hibp.ecse.rpi.edu/

Saga Univ.
http://www.cc.saga-u.ac.jp/saga-u/riko/physics/physics.html

SCRI at Florida State Univ.
http://dirac.scri.fsu.edu/

Sezione di Trieste
http://www.ts.infn.it/

SHEP
http://wwwhep.phys.soton.ac.uk/

SISSA, Italy
http://babbage.sissa.it/

Society for Applied Spectroscopy
http://esther.la.asu.edu/sas/

Society for Nonlinear Dynamics and Econometrics
http://www.interactive.net:80/~mizrach/SNDE/snde.html

Society of Exploration Geophysicists
http://sepwww.stanford.edu/seg/

Space Research Unit
http://www.puk.ac.za/fskdocs/

Space Science Web Group
http://enemy.gsfc.nasa.gov/sswg/SSWG.html

SPIE - The International Society for Optical Engineering
http://www.spie.org/

SPIRES Databases
http://heplibw3.slac.stanford.edu/FIND/default.html

SRRC : Synchrotron Radiation Reseach Center
http://www.srrc.gov.tw/

SSCL
http://www.ssc.gov/SSC.html

St. Petersburg Nuclear Physics Institute
ftp://rec03.pnpi.spb.ru/web/home.html

Stanford Lattice Field Theory
http://heplibw3.slac.stanford.edu/FIND/FREEHEP/SECTION/lattice_field_theory/INDEX

Stanford Linear Accelerator Center (SLAC)
http://heplibw3.slac.stanford.edu/FIND/SLAC.html

SLAC BaBar Detector Home Page
http://www.slac.stanford.edu/BF/doc/www/bfHome.html

SLAC SPIRES
http://www-spires.slac.stanford.edu/FIND/hep/

SLAC Top-40 Cited Papers
http://www-slac.slac.stanford.edu/find/top40.html

Stanford Univ. Experiments Online
http://slacvm.slac.stanford.edu/find/explist.html

String Theory Group, Queen Mary and Westfield College (Univ. London)
http://stringswww.ph.qmw.ac.uk/

Sudbury Neutrino Observatory (Queens Univ., CA)
http://snodaq.phy.queensu.ca/sno/sno.html

SUNY Stony Brook Xray
http://xray1.physics.sunysb.edu/

Suomen Fyysikkoseura
http://www.physics.helsinki.fi/~sfs/

Super-Kamiokande at UCI
http://www.ps.uci.edu/sk/

Superconducting Super Collider (SSC)
http://www.het.brown.edu/news/ssc/index.html

Swiss Federal Institute of Technology - Institute for Particle Physics
http://wwwphys.ethz.ch/IPP/

Tata Institute of Fundamental Research (TIFR) - Theoretical Physics
http://theory.tifr.res.in/

Tel Aviv Univ. - High Energy Physics
http://proton.tau.ac.il/

Theoretical Physics Group, Tata Insitute of Fundamental Research, Bombay, India
http://theory.tifr.res.in/

Timing, Trigger and Control (TTC) Systems for LHC Experiments
http://www.cern.ch/TTC/intro.html

TIPTOP, The Internet Pilot to Physics
http://www.tp.umu.se/TIPTOP/

TRIUMF
http://www.triumf.ca/

TU Vienna - Institute for Theoretical Physics
http://tph.tuwien.ac.at/

UK Solar Energy Society
http://sun1.bham.ac.uk/thorntme/

UNICAN — Instituto de Física de Cantabria
http://www.gae.unican.es/

Univ. of Alberta, Dept. of Physics
http://www.phys.ualberta.ca/

Univ. of Bayreuth - Theoretical Phsyics
http://btp4x2.phy.uni-bayreuth.de/

Univ. of Boston
http://cbsgi2.bu.edu/cb/cb.html

Univ. of British Columbia Theoretical Physics Web
http://axion.physics.ubc.ca/

Univ. of Calgary Geophysics
http://www-crewes.geo.ucalgary.ca/VL-Geophysics.html

Univ. of Calgary Micronet Multidimensional Signal Processing Research Group
http://www-mddsp.enel.ucalgary.ca/

Univ. of California/Berkeley Center for Particle Astrophysics
http://physics7.berkeley.edu/home.html

Univ. of California/Irvine High Energy Physics
http://www.ps.uci.edu/physics/heexpt.html

Univ. of California/LA Particle Beam Physics Lab
http://pbpl.physics.ucla.edu/

Univ. of California/LA Theoretical Elementary Particles Group
http://spike.physics.ucla.edu/

Univ. of California/Santa Barbara High Energy Physics
http://charm.physics.ucsb.edu/

Univ. of California/San Diego Science & Engineering Library
http://scilib.ucsd.edu

Univ. of Colorado Condensed Matter Lab
http://bly.colorado.edu/cml/cml.html

Univ. of Colorado Plasma and Accelerator Physics Group
http://jove.colorado.edu/homepage.html

Univ. Dortmund, Fachbereich Physik
http://www.Physik.Uni-Dortmund.De/

Univ. Erlangen-Nürnberg - Theoretische Physik II
http://theorie2.physik.uni-erlangen.de/

Univ. of Erlangen-Nürnberg, Institut für Theoretische Physik III
http://theorie3.physik.uni-erlangen.de/

Univ. of Freiburg
http://hpfrs6.physik.uni-freiburg.de/

Univ. of Illinois - High Energy Physics
http://www.hep.uiuc.edu/

Univ. of Indiana Cyclotron
http://www.iucf.indiana.edu

Univ. of Iowa
http://marv.eng.uiowa.edu/

Univ. of Karlsruhe - Institut für theoretische Physik
http://itpaxp1.physik.uni-karlsruhe.de/

Univ. of Liverpool
http://www.cern.ch/Liverpool/welcome.html

Univ. of Manitoba - Physics
http://www.umanitoba.ca/physics/

Univ. of Maryland Plasma Science and Technology
http://www-plasma.umd.edu/

Univ. of Mississippi High Energy Physics Group
http://beauty1.phy.olemiss.edu/homepage.html

Univ. Montreal Departement de physique
http://ftp.astro.umontreal.ca/physique/index.html

Univ. of Napoli, Italy
http://www.na.infn.it/htbin/bib

Univ. of Nevada, Las Vegas
http://pauli.lv-physics.nevada.edu/

Univ. of New Mexico - HEP
http://wwwhep.unm.edu/

Univ. of Newcastle-u-Tyne - Relativity and Quantum Fields Group
http://matmos.ncl.ac.uk/

Univ. of Oldenburg Physics
http://marvin.physik.uni-oldenburg.de/Docs/home/phys-links.html

Univ. of Oregon - High Energy Physics
http://zebu.uoregon.edu/~dmason/uohep.html

Univ. of Otago, Dunedin, New Zealand
http://newton.otago.ac.nz:808/homepage.html

Univ. of Oulu - Theoretical Physics
http://jussi.oulu.fi/

Universitaet des Saarlandes - Theoretische Physik
http://www.uni-sb.de/matfak/fb10/ph10ml/lusi.html

Univ. of Stockholm - Theoretical Physics
http://vanosf.physto.se/

Univ. at Stony Brook, Institute for Theoretical Physics
http://insti.physics.sunysb.edu/itp/

Univ. of Tasmania - Theoretical Physics Group
http://info.utas.edu.au/docs/njones/TGHome.html

Univ. of Tennessee
http://enigma.phys.utk.edu/

Univ. of Tokyo
http://hep1.c2.u-tokyo.ac.jp/

Univ. of Victoria Physics & Astronomy
http://info.phys.uvic.ca/

Univ. of Virginia Engineering Physics
http://bohr.ms.virginia.edu/ep/

Univ. of Washington Applied Physics Lab
http://www.apl.washington.edu/

Univ. of Washington Cosmic Ray Lab
http://marge.phys.washington.edu/

Univ. of Washington High Energy Physics
http://squark.phys.washington.edu/

Univ. of Washington Nuclear Physics Lab
http://mist.npl.washington.edu/home_npl.html

Univ. of Winnipeg - Theoretical Physics
http://theory.uwinnipeg.ca/

Univ. Zaragoza - Dept Fisica Teorica (DFTUZ)
http://dftuz.unizar.es/

Vacuum Technology
http://nyquist.ee.ualberta.ca/~schmaus/vac.html

Vector Particle Physics
http://www.best.com/~lockyer/

Visual Techniques Lab.
http://geb.phys.washington.edu/

Warsaw High Energy Physics Group
http://info.fuw.edu.pl/HEP/

Warsaw Univ.
http://info.fuw.edu.pl/

Wayne State High Energy Physics
http://gluon.physics.wayne.edu/

WebStars
http://guinan.gsfc.nasa.gov/WebStars/
About.html

Weizmann Institute
http://wissgi.weizmann.ac.il/physics/
physics.html

Weizmann Institute - Plasma Laboratory
http://plasma-gate.weizmann.ac.il/

Wilson Lab/CLEO/CESR
http://w4.lns.cornell.edu/hypertext/public/
README.html

ZEUS
http://zow00.desy.de:8000/

Security

See also Computer Science

Alt.Security FAQ
http://www.cis.ohio-state.edu/hypertext/faq/
bngusenet/alt/security/top.html

American Bar Association Guidelines on Digital Signatures
http://www.intermarket.com/ecl/

Ames Research Center
http://ccf.arc.nasa.gov/security

Anti-Virus Resource Center
http://www.symantec.com/avcenter/
index.html

Anti-Virus Resources
http://www.primenet.com/~mwest/av.htm

ARL Information Server
http://info.arl.army.mil/

Association for Computing Machinery
http://info.acm.org/

Australian Computer Emergency Response Team
http://www.auscert.org.au/

bsy's Security Related Net-pointers
http://www-cse.ucsd.edu/users/bsy/sec.html

CADD Homepage
http://cadd.cern.ch/welcome.html

CERT — Computer Emergency Response Team
http://www.cert.org

Christopher L. Menegay's Security page.
http://tamsun.tamu.edu/~clm3840/
security.html

CNLS General Information
http://cnls-www.lanl.gov/generalinfo.html

COAST Laboratory/Spaf's Hotlist
http://www.cs.purdue.edu/homes/spaf/
hotlists/csec.html

Computer and Network Security Reference Index
http://www.telstra.com.au/info/security.html

Computer Incident Advisory Capability
http://ciac.llnl.gov/

Comp.Security FAQ
http://www.cis.ohio-state.edu/hypertext/faq/
bngusenet/comp/security/top.html

Computer Security Information
http://www.alw.nih.gov/Security/security.html

Computer Security at SAIC
http://mls.saic.com/mls.security.html

Computer Security Research Laboratory at UC Davis
http://seclab.cs.ucdavis.edu/

Computer Virus Information
http://business.yorku.ca/mgts4710/rizello/
viruses.htm

Computer Virus Research Lab (CVRL)
http://www.spidernet.net/web/~cvrl/

CRIMELAB.COM
http://crimelab.com/crimelab.html

Cryptography Archive
http://www.quadralay.com/www/Crypt/
Crypt.html

Cryptography FAQ
http://www.intac.com/man/faq/cryptography-
faq/

Crytography FAQ from RSA
http://www.rsa.com/faq/faq_toc.html

Cryptography, PGP, and Your Privacy - WWW Virtual Library
http://world.std.com/~franl/crypto.html

Ctr. for Social Science Computation and Research
http://augustus.csscr.washington.edu/

Dartmouth College
http://www.dartmouth.edu/

Digital Money & Transactions Archive
http://www.eff.org/pub/Privacy/Digital_money/

Electronic Privacy Information Center
http://epic.org/

FAQ: Computer Security Frequently
Asked Questions
http://www.cis.ohio-state.edu/hypertext/faq/
usenet/security-faq/faq.html

FIRST — Forum of Incident Response and
Security Teams
http://www.first.org/

Information about RIPEM
http://cs.indiana.edu/ripem/dir.html

Information Retrieval Resource Page
http://camis.stanford.edu/people/felciano/ir/

International PGP Homepage
http://www.ifi.uio.no/~staalesc/PGP/

Internet Network Security
http://www.saturn.net/~halflife/security.html

LANL ACL Home Page
http://www.acl.lanl.gov/Home.html

Lewis Research Center
http://gumby.lerc.nasa.gov

MetaCenter Home Page
http://www.ncsa.uiuc.edu/General/
MetaCenter/MetaCenterHome.html

Morning Star Technologies
http://www.morningstar.com/

NASA Information Technology Security
http://www.larc.nasa.gov/org/isd/security

NASIRC
http://nasirc.nasa.gov

National Inst. of Standards and Technologies
http://www.nist.gov/

National Computer Security Association
(NCSA)
http://www.ncsa.com/

No More Secrets! Comprehensive Guide
to Security and Hacking
http://underground.org/

Pretty Good Privacy - PGP
http://www.mantis.co.uk/pgp/pgp.html

Privacy WWW Virtual Library
http://draco.centerline.com:8080/~franl/
privacy/privacy.html

Purdue COAST project
http://www.cs.purdue.edu/coast/coast.html

RSA Data Security, Inc.
http://www.rsa.com/

SCRI Home Page
http://www.scri.fsu.edu/

Secure HTTP
http://www.eit.com/creations/s-http/

Secure Sockets Layer Protocol (SSL)
http://www.netscape.com/newsref/std/
SSL.html

Security - CSC Security Items.
http://spy.org:70/1s/System/bbs/BBS/SIGS/
SECURITY

Security Issues in Embedded Networking
http://www.mit.edu:8001/people/eichin/
embedded-kerberos.html

Security Reference Index
http://www.tansu.com.au/Info/security.html

Shen: A Security Scheme for the World
Wide Web
http://www.w3.org/hypertext/WWW/Shen/ref/
shen.html

SPYBBS Security
http://spy.org:70/1s/System/bbs/BBS/SIGS/
SECURITY

Sunrise project
http://www.acl.lanl.gov/sunrise/sunrise.html

T4 Computer Security Profile
http://www.nuance.com/~fcp/t4.html

Telecom Australia
http://www.telstra.com.au/info/security.html

Telnet URL Problem
http://south.ncsa.uiuc.edu/telnet-details.html

Trusted Information Systems Home Page
http://www.tis.com/

Unix Security Primer
http://hea-www.harvard.edu/~wendy/
security.html

Using the Web to Provide Private Information

http://ursaminor.scs.carleton.ca/Papers/
www94-paper.html

Virus FAQ

http://www.cis.ohio-state.edu/hypertext/faq/
bngusenet/comp/virus/top.html

Virus Information - from the Computer
Security Resource Clearinghouse

http://csrc.ncsl.nist.gov/virus/

WWW-Security Index

http://www-ns.rutgers.edu/www-security/
index.html

WWW Security Mailing list archive

http://www-ns.rutgers.edu/www-security/
archives/index.html

WWW Virtual Library: Cryptography,
PGP, and Your Privacy

http://draco.centerline.com:8080/~franl/
crypto.html

Yahoo Security & Encryption

http://www.yahoo.com/
Computers_and_Internet/
Security_and_Encryption/

Virtual Reality

See also Artificial Intelligence, Computer Science, Imaging Technologies, Optics, Physics

Atlantis Cyberspace
http://vr-atlantis.com/

Buyer's Guide to VR Equipment
http://www.cs.jhu.edu/~feldberg/vr/vrbg.html

Cardiff Univ. VR Page
http://www.cm.cf.ac.uk/User/Andrew.Wilson/
VR/index.html

Chris Hand's VR Page
http://www.cms.dmu.ac.uk:9999/People/cph/
vrstuff.html

Cyberspace Report
http://www.ics.uci.edu/~ejw/csr/cyber.html

Delft Univ. of Technology
http://www.twi.tudelft.nl/welcome.html

DesignSpace
http://gummo.stanford.edu/html/
DesignSpace/home.html.

Digital Equipment Corporation
ftp://gatekeeper.dec.com/pub/DEC/DECinfo/
html/home.html

Electronic Visualization Lab., Univ. of
Illinois, Urbana Champaign
http://www.ncsa.uiuc.edu/EVL/docs/
Welcome.html

EVE - The Encyclopedia of Virtual
Environments
http://www.cs.umd.edu/projects/eve/eve-
main.html

Graphics, Visualization and Usability Ctr.,
Georgia Tech
http://www.cc.gatech.edu/gvu/virtual/

HCI Bibliography Project by Gary Perlman
archive.cis.ohio-state.edu/pub/hcibib

HCI Launching Pad
http://www.twi.tudelft.nl/Local/HCI/HCI-
Index.html

Human Interface Technology Lab at Univ.
of Washington (HIT LAB)
http://www.hitl.washington.edu/

Index to Multimedia Information Resources
http://cui_www.unige.ch/OSG/MultimediaInfo

Johnson Space Center Virtual Reality Lab
http://www.jsc.nasa.gov/~mle/vr.html

Lateiner Dataspace
http://www.dataspace.com/WWW/
welcome.html

LTRS - Langley Technical Report Server
http://techreports.larc.nasa.gov/ltrs/ltrs.html

LUTCHI Research Centre
http://pipkin.lut.ac.uk

McDonnell Douglas Aerospace-Houston
Div.
http://pat.mdc.com/

MediaFusion
http://www.mfusion.com

Mississippi State Virtual Environment/
Interactive Systems Program
http://www.erc.msstate.edu/vr

M.I.T. - Virtual Environment Technology
for Training
http://mimsy.mit.edu/

MR Toolkit Software Tools and Library
http://web.cs.ualberta.ca/~graphics/
MRToolkit.html

NASA/JSC - Virtual Reality Lab
http://www.jsc.nasa.gov/cssb/vr/vr.html

Naval Postgraduate School, Monterey
Calif.
ftp://taurus.cs.nps.navy.mil/pub/
NPSNET_MOSAIC/npsnet_mosaic.html

NCSA Virtual Reality Lab
http://www.ncsa.uiuc.edu/Viz/VR/
vr_homepage.html

NPSNET Research Group
http://www-npsnet.cs.nps.navy.mil/npsnet

NTT - Nippon Telegraph and Telephone Corporation.
http://www.ntt.jp/index.html

Open Virtual Reality Testbed Home Page
http://www.nist.gov/itl/div894/ovrt/OVRThome.html

Principia Cybernetica Web
http://pespmc1.vub.ac.be/Default.html

Project GeoSim Information Server
http://geosim.cs.vt.edu/index.html

QuickTime VR Web Site
http://qtvr.quicktime.apple.com

Rapid Development Lab (RDL)
http://ollie.jsc.nasa.gov/~wood/RDL/RDL_Home.html

Rutgers CAIP Virtual Reality Lab
http://www.caip.rutgers.edu/vrlab

Sandia Virtual Reality Lab
http://www.sandia.gov/2121/vr/vr.html

SIGGRAPH On-line Bibliography Project
http://iicm.tu-graz.ac.at/CSIGGRAPHbib

Silicon Graphics, Inc. - Silicon Surf
http://www.sgi.com/

Sun Microsystems
http://sunsite.unc.edu/sun/inform/sun-info.html

Top Ten VRML Worlds
http://www.virtpark.com/theme/proteinman/

TRIVR - The Triangle Virtual Reality Group
http://www.trinet.com/trivr.html

UK VR-SIG
http://pipkin.lut.ac.uk/WWWdocs/LUTCHI/people/sean/vr-sig.html

Univ. College of Cape Breton Virtual Reality Lab
http://vrpc2.uccb.ns.ca/

Univ. of Hull - Virtual Environments, Graphics and Applications
http://www.enc.hull.ac.uk/CS/VEGA/

Univ. of Kansas - VR On-Stage Project
http://ukanaix.cc.ukans.edu/~mreaney/

Univ. of Toronto - Augmented and Virtual Reality Research
http://vered.rose.utoronto.ca/

Univ. of Maryland
http://gimble.cs.umd.edu/vrtp/vrtp.html

Univ. of Michigan Virtual Reality Laboratory (VRL)
http://www-VRL.umich.edu

Univ. of North Carolina at Chapel Hill
http://www.cs.unc.edu/cs.unc.edu.html

University of Washington - Human Interface Technology Lab (HIT)
http://www.hitl.washington.edu/

VENUS — Virtual Environment Navigation in the Underground Sites
http://sgvenus.cern.ch/VENUS/

Virtual Legos
http://trailhead.mit.edu/~lego/

Virtual Reality Society
http://www.vrs.org.uk/

Visual Systems Laboratory, Univ. of Central Florida
http://www.vsl.ist.ucf.edu/

VRASP - Virtual Reality Alliance of Students and Professionals
http://www.vrasp.org/vrasp/

VRML FAQ
http://vag.vrml.org/VRML_FAQ.html

VRML for Rocket Scientists, Astronomers, and Truck Drivers
http://WWW.Stars.com/Authoring/VRML/

VRML Repository at SDSC
http://sdsc.edu/vrml/

VRML Review CyberZine
http://www.imaginative.com/VResources/vrml/

VRMLSite Magazine
http://www.vrmlsite.com/

VRML — Virtual Reality Modeling Language — Specifications
http://www.eit.com/vrml/

VR Resources
http://www.ncsa.uiuc.edu/Viz/VR/vr_other_ftp.html

Xerox Palo Alto Research Ctr. (Pub Web)
http://pubweb.parc.xerox.com/

Appendix

SEARCH ENGINE
COMPARISON CHART

Most search engine comparison charts are made for search engine users. The search engine features chart below is designed primarily for webmasters and anyone else who cares about how search engines index their sites. It provides a summary of important factors and features that can affect how a site is indexed. Search engine users will also find portions of the comparison chart useful in determining how fresh and complete the different search engines are.

Full explanations can be found in the section immediately after the chart. Please note that in a few places on the chart, a hyphen (-) is used to denote unknown or unresearched answers.

Search Engine	AltaVista	Excite	HotBot	InfoSeek	Lycos
Size (pages in mills)	Big (100)	Big (55)	Big (80)	Medium (30)	Medium (30)
Pages crawled per day	10 million	3 million	Up to 10 million	-	6 to 10 million
Freshness	1 day to 3 months	1 to 3 weeks	1 day to 2 weeks	Minutes to 2 months	1 to 2 weeks
Date	Yes	No	File Date	No	Yes (via detailed display)

Crawling
—Factors that affect if and when a page is indexed—

Search Engine	AltaVista	Excite	HotBot	InfoSeek	Lycos
Submitted Pages	1 day	3 weeks	1 to 2 days	Within minutes	1 to 2 weeks
Non-submitted pages	1 to 3 months	3weeks	2 weeks	1-2 months	1 to 2 weeks
Depth	No limit	No limit	No limit	Sample	Sample
Frames Support	No	No	No	Yes	Yes
Image Maps	Yes	No	No	Yes	No
Password Protected Sites	No	Yes	No	Yes	Yes
Link Popularity	No	No	Yes	No	Yes
Learns Frequency	Yes	No	Yes	Yes	No
Keep Out	robots.txt	robots.txt, both in future	Both	robots.txt	robots.txt
Redirection	Redirected URL used	Redirected URL used	-	Redirected URL used	-

Ranking
—Factors that affect how a page is ranked—

Search Engine	AltaVista	Excite	HotBot	InfoSeek	Lycos
Stop Words	Yes	Yes	Yes	No	Yes
Relevancy Boosters	None	3 or 4 star review	Keywords in meta tag	Keywords in meta tag	None
Spam Penalty	Yes	Yes	Yes	Yes	Yes

Display
—Factors that affect how a page is listed—

Search Engine	AltaVista	Excite	HotBot	InfoSeek	Lycos
Meta Tag Support	Yes	No	Yes	Yes	Partial
Title	Page title, otherwise, "No title"	Page title, otherwise, "Untitled"	Page title, otherwise, URL	Page title, otherwise, first line on page	Page title otherwise, first line on page
Description	Meta tag, or first few lines on page	Sentences grouped by concept; most dominant sentences extracted	Meta tag, or first few lines on page	Meta tag, or first 200 characters after <body> tag	Created based on content
Results at a time	10	**10**, 20, 30, 40, 50	**10** ,25, 50, 75, 100	**10**,20 (titles only)	**5**, 10, 15 20, 30, 40, 50
Display Options	Standard, Compact, Text-Only	Summaries, Titles only, Sort by site	Full (4 lines), Brief (1 line), Titles only	Summaries, Titles Only	Standard Summary, Details

Other

Search Engine	AltaVista	Excite	HotBot	InfoSeek	Lycos
URL Status Check	Displays listing	None	Semi-displays listing	Displays listing	Reports if indexed
Site Removal	Remove pages and resubmit	Remove site or install robots.txt	Install robots.txt	Remove and resubmit site or install robots.txt	
Crawler Name	Scooter	Architext Spider	Slurp the Web Hound	Side winder	T-Rex
Indexes ALT text	Yes	No	No	Yes	Yes
Indexes comments	No	No	Yes	Yes	No
Stemming	No	No	No	Yes	Yes

Size

The larger a search engine is, in terms of pages indexed, the more likely pages from your Web site will be included. Actual numbers can be misleading, as explained below. So, search engines are categorized as big, medium, or small. Expect to find most of your pages in a big search engine, some to many of your pages in a medium search engine, and few or none of your pages in a small search engine. Why might a page not be included? See the section about Depth, below.

The figures shown are the last reported prior to publication of this book. Take them with a grain of salt. Some search engines may accidentally keep two copies of a Web page but not take duplication into account when quoting numbers. There are also other factors that make comparisons difficult.

Pages Crawled per Day

This shows how many pages a search engine can index per day. The more it can crawl, the more likely it can maintain a fresh index. However, this is not the only way to measure freshness. Search engines may learn how frequently pages change or use other methods to improve freshness to maximize a smaller crawling capacity.

Freshness

The Web is constantly changing, so it's easy for search engine listings to become out-of-date. However, some listings may only be days old, while others may be months old—or longer. There are various reasons why this occurs. Some search engines "instantly" index any page submitted to them, as explained below. It takes longer for them to return and gather non-submitted pages. Search engines also may crawl the "popular" parts of the Web more frequently than other portions. Freshness shows the age of listings, from best to worst case scenarios for each search engine.

Date

Some search engines show the date when a Web page was added. This provides a clue as to how fresh or stale the search engine's listings may be. Kudos to these search engines. The others leave you guessing about freshness. File date means that the date of the file is shown, rather than the date it was added to the index. For example, imagine you created a file on Aug. 1, 1997, and it was spidered on Sept. 1, 1997. A search engine showing file date would list the Aug. 1 date, not the Sept. 1 date.

Submitted Pages

Ideally, a search engine will find your pages as it follows links while crawling the Web. Realistically, your pages will appear much faster if you submit them directly to the engine. This shows how soon to expect a page you submitted to appear in the search engine's listings.

Non-Submitted Pages

Once a page has been submitted, a search engine will usually find other pages from the site by following links from the submitted page. However, some engines take longer to gather these "non-submitted" pages. In particular, this is because some search engines "instantly" index a page that is submitted, then add the site to the schedule for future crawling.

The chart shows how soon to expect other pages from your site to appear once you've submitted a single page—and assuming there are no problems preventing the engine from finding these pages, such as frames or image maps, as explained below.

Depth

This is closely related to non-submitted pages. It indicates how many pages beyond the submitted page a search engine will gather. Search engines are operating in two manners:

No Limit

These search engines will diligently try to gather everything they find at a Web site. They may not get every page, but that remains the general goal.

Sample

These search engines gather a sample of Web pages from a site. Some gather a bigger sample than others. Use the size listed as a guide to how large a sample you can expect each search engine to have gathered. Usually, the more popular a site is, the more likely it will be better represented in the search engine. Keep in mind that part of the Web remains unindexed due to physical hurdles. Frames, image maps, and dynamically generated pages can all cause information to be missed.

Frames Support

Can the search engine follow frame links? If it can't, the search engine is probably missing much of your site.

Image Maps

Can the search engine follow client-side image maps? As with frames, if the search engine cannot follow image maps, it is probably missing much of your site.

Password Protected Sites

Some search engines can enter a password protected site, if you arrange for them to have a user name and password. Why do this? You may want people to discover you have content that matches their query. They'll still need to fill out the appropriate registration information at your site to access it, but at least they'll know it exists.

Link Popularity

All search engines can determine the popularity of a page by analyzing how many links there are to it from other pages. Some engines use this as a means to determine which pages they will include in the index.

Learns Frequency

A number of search engines can learn how often your pages change. A site that changes often will be visited more often. Those that change infrequently get infrequent visits.

Keep Out

This indicates you to tell the search engines to keep out of your site. All of the major engines respect the ROBOTS.TXT exclusion standard, which tells them not to index a site or parts of a site. Some also support the robot's meta-tag, where a crawler can be told "noindex" on a particular page. For more information about ROBOTS.TXT, see the Getting Found on the Web portion of the Advanced Web Publishing chapter.

Redirection

Some sites redirect visitors from one Web address to another. For example, someone going to **http://maxonline.com/Webmasters/** gets redirected to: **http://searchenginewatch.com.** The chart shows which URL is associated with your listing, if your server performs a redirection. This is important, because if the search engine indexes the redirected page, you could have a problem with visitors locating it should it be moved or changed at a later date.

Stop Words

Some search engines either leave out words when they index a page or may not search for these words during a query. These "stop words" are excluded as a way to save storage space or to speed searches. For the webmaster, it's important to consider stop words when crafting your pages. For example, AltaVista will ignore the word *web* in a search for *web developer*, so there's little sense in trying to improve your ranking under those keywords. Stop words are an excellent reason why search engine users should surround keywords with quotes or use other power tips to ensure that words are not ignored in their search.

Relevancy Boosters

All the search engines use the location of keywords and frequency in a Web page as the basis for ranking pages in response to a query. The exact mechanism is slightly different for each engine. In addition to location/frequency, some engines may give a page a relevancy boost based on link popularity or other factors. These help a little, but they don't guarantee a boost to the top. It's quite possible that the most linked-to page on the Web will still perform poorly if there's another page that's more relevant to the particular query.

Spam Penalty

All major search engines penalize sites that attempt to "spam" the engines in order to improve their position. One common technique is "stacking" or "stuffing" words on a page. This is where a word is repeated many times in a row. There are a number of other techniques. In general, they don't work well, and they often make a page look stupid and unprofessional. If the search engines spot a spamming technique, they may downgrade a page's ranking or exclude it from listings altogether. One easy way search engines discover pages are through "spam narking," when people complain about pages using spam.

Meta-Tag Support

Many believe all search engines acknowledge keywords and descriptions placed in meta-tags. In reality, only some do. A rating of "partial" indicates that the search engine will index the text of the tags, but they don't control descriptions nor have any special meaning attached to them.

Titles

This shows how the search engines generate a page title for your listing.

Descriptions

This shows how the search engines generate a description for your listing.

Results at a Time

How many results you can display at one time. Defaults are shown in bold. Sometimes you may need to use a special power search page to change the default, but in most cases, you do not.

Display Options

Shows the different ways you can display results, with the default listed first.

URL Status Check

This shows whether you can determine if a Web page has been indexed by the search engine. "Displays listing" means that you can easily search for a particular page and see exactly how it appears in the index. This is marked as "semi" for HotBot, as it is not so easy to specific a particular URL. "Reports if indexed" means that there is a URL status check form that will tell you if the page is in the index. However, you can't see the actual listing easily.

Site Removal

Sometimes Web pages are removed or sites shifted to a new domain. Some search engines may continue to find the "old" pages unless certain measures are taken. These are noted on the chart for each search engine and include:

Removal

Removing the old pages from the server. The engine will revisit and try to reindex the pages using the addresses in its database. When it discovers they no longer exist, they will be removed from the database.

ROBOTS.TXT

Creates a *robots.txt* file listing the site or pages. The engine will note the new restriction and remove the pages from the index.

Crawler Name

Each search engine uses a "crawler" or "spider" agent to gather Web pages. Most have nicknames. These names are often part of the crawler's host name. Web site administrators can tell if you've been visited by a crawler by checking their access logs and looking for the various names. In addition, spiders often report an agent name. Instead of saying "Mozilla," as the Netscape browser does, a spider reports its own name. For example, Excite will say "Architext" spider.

Indexes ALT Text/Comment Text

Shows if the search engine indexes ALT text associated with images or text in comment tags. Stemming shows whether the search engine will also search for variations of a word based on its stem. For example, entering *swim* might also find *swims* and *swimming*.

GLOSSARY

address   A specific location on the Internet, such as a person (e-mail address) or computer (e.g., nasa.gov), defined by a discrete numerical Internet address. Also called *URL*.

alias   A software placeholder that allows one thing, such as a file, to be referenced from another location; or, a convenience feature found in many e-mail software interfaces that allows the user to assign a short and easy-to-remember name for a longer one, such as an e-mail address or list of addresses.

animated GIF   See *GIF89a*.

anonymous FTP (File Transfer Protocol)   A standard Internet protocol for transferring data from one computer to the other using the TCP/IP transmission protocol. Conceptually, open and public access to a computer archive on the Internet for the purpose of uploading or downloading files.

applet   Small executable used with Java-type client-server interactions. Allows for more efficient use of Web bandwidth by making the client work more.

application   A software program designed to perform a task or function. Also called an executable.

ASCII (American Standard Code for Information Interchange)   An important standard for describing computer-readable text, including alphabetic, numeric, and control characters, all coded in hexadecimal notation. The first 128 values are sometimes called "low ASCII," and the last 128 "high ASCII."

attachment   A document or other digital entity (picture, application, etc.) that is appended to an e-mail message, usually using an "attach" feature of the e-mail software. Since Internet e-mail does not recognize non-ASCII characters, binary files are usually encoded before attaching and sending.

auto-load   Feature supported by most Web browsers allowing the user to choose to have all Web-page graphics load automatically. If you have a slow or modem-type connection, you should not choose auto-load.

bandwidth   Term used to quantify the amount of digital information a circuit or network can carry in a given amount of time. Usually measured in bytes, so "a 56K line" is a circuit capable of carrying 56 kilobytes per second.

baud   A unit of measurement for describing the number of change states per second in telecommunications processes. The "baud rate" is usually used to describe modem speed. The term is often misused to mean bits per second (bps), which is only true in some situations.

BBS (bulletin board system)   A computer system that typically provides such services as e-mail, file storage, and transfer, and special interest groups that exchange messages by posting them to the BBS's computer for others to read online.

binhex   The de facto standard for encoding non-ASCII Macintosh files and applications for transmission over the Internet.

bit   Unit of measurement used in computer systems, short for "binary element." It's the smallest unit of data—either a 1 or a 0.

BITNET (Because It's Time Network)   An e-mail and file-sharing network used by a large number of academic and research institutions. Origination point for listserv software still used widely for automated management of discussion groups. BITNET now has many gateways to the Internet. See the chapter on Discussion Lists.

body   That portion of an e-mail message where you type your message. See also *header*.

bookmark   A feature of some software interfaces that allows you to "save your place" for future access, usually another computer connected to the Internet. Sometimes called a "hotlist" or "favorite places."

Boolean operators   Words used to connect and construct words to be queried in a database search. Typical operators include the words *and, or, near,* and *not.*

bounce   Slang for an e-mail message that is returned to the sender as undeliverable, usually for reasons such as incorrect or erroneous addressing. See also *daemon.*

browser   Software interface for accessing certain services such as the World Wide Web. See also *graphical browser* and *line browser.*

BTW   Common abbreviation in e-mail and news postings meaning "by the way."

bulletin board   See *BBS.*

byte   A unit for measuring data consisting of eight bits.

cascade menu   A computer menu that extends more than one level in a hierarchical fashion.

caching   In Internet software, a term used to describe the process of storing in computer memory previously displayed information for quick retrieval. For example, most Web browsers cache some number of pages you have recently viewed, so that if you return to view those pages, the images are displayed immediately instead of re-downloading them to the browser software. The term "cache" in general denotes any kind of temporary data storage technique used to enhance computer performance.

Cascading Style Sheets (CSS)   A new feature proposed for HTML 4.0 that will allow HTML authors to specify styles that can be reused across multiple pages instead of having to write those specifications on every single page.

CGI (Common Gateway Interface)   A software application used to communicate information between a browser and a Web server. Usually written in a programming language such as Perl, C, or Java.

character-based   See command-line interface.

CLI   See command-line interface.

client   A computer or process that relies on the resources of another computer (a server) for operations. When you connect to the Internet, in most cases your computer is a client retrieving information from a server computer such as an FTP archive, database, or Web site.

client-side   Usually refers to a function that is handled by a Web browser, such as a client-side image map, as opposed to the Web server. Generally preferred over server-side implementations for performance reasons.

command-line interface   A non-graphical or non-windowing interface to a computer system. All commands are entered as text from a keyboard, and all information output by the computer is displayed as text.

command prompt   See *prompt*.

commercial online service   Generic term used to describe a handful of large online service providers with multiple transnational or transcontinental access points. Most originated as discrete online environments with no Internet access, but most are now creating gateways to change this.

compression   Software-based algorithms used to reduce the amount of storage or bandwidth that information occupies without permanently altering the content. Much of the information stored in anonymous FTP archives is in a compressed format. See also *binhex, uuencode*.

cookies   Originally developed by Netscape as "Magic Cookies" and now widely incorporated into most browsers, cookies are small text files generated by Web servers that can be stored in a browser to help the server recognize that specific browser whenever it visits the server's site. Often used by shopping sites or advertising vendors to track customers' visits.

country code   A two-letter extension added to some Internet domain names denoting the country in which that address resides, such as ulaval.ca (Canada) or cosy.sbg.ac.at (Austria). Not common for U.S.-based addresses but almost universal for non-U.S. addresses.

CSS   See *Cascading Style Sheets*.

cybercafe   Common term for a store or cafe generally found in larger cities where anyone can rent a computer to access the Internet, to do e-mail, browse the Web, etc.

daemon   A software program that intercepts information that is unusable due to errors. For example, a mail daemon intercepts incoming e-mail messages and sends back any addressed to invalid usernames at that location.

decoding   See *encoding*.

dedicated line   A telephone line directly connecting two Internet domains, providing a continuous connection for Internet access (as opposed to temporary connections, such as over a modem). Many organizations that use the Internet subscribe to this kind of connection for uninterruptable (in theory) and high-bandwidth (fast) connections. Some typical dedicated line bandwidths are 56K (kilobytes per second) and T1 (1.54 megabytes per second). See also *ISDN*.

demoware   Software applications released publicly by commercial software companies to demonstrate their products' features.

deprecate   Term used in the official HTML standards and specifications written by the W3 Consortium to denote a particular HTML element (such as a tag set) that will eventually become obsolete. They do this to warn HTML authors that they should stop using the deprecated element as soon as possible.

dial-up   Slang for connecting to another computer using a modem, such as "I have dial-up access to the university's library computer."

direct connection   Internet access through a non-modem connection, such as a computer on a local area network, where that network has a dedicated line to the Internet.

directory   A software structure used for storing data (files, applications, etc.). Sometimes called a folder.

discussion list   Generic term used in this book to describe any type of e-mail-based group communications method, such as listservs and mailing lists, where individuals join or "subscribe" to a group and share a common e-mail address. This address is used as a central forum for posting questions, answers, and commentaries, usually in a particular (and narrow) topical area. Anyone with an Internet e-mail address can participate. See also *lurking*.

DNS (domain name system)   The online distributed database that translates domain names into numerical IP addresses. DNS servers are located throughout the Internet, and no one DNS server contains information for all Internet hosts; rather, they work as a system. Many large Internet sites operate their own domain name servers or resolvers (which do the translation work).

domain name   An Internet convention for constructing an address by using the syntax userID@domain.name, where everything to the right of the @ symbol is the domain name. A domain name is not an actual physical description of a location, but rather a sort of alias for the location's Internet IP address, which is numerical. Domain names exist as a convenience, since numerical addresses are more difficult to remember. See also *domain name system*.

dot files   Slang for Unix files that begin with a period (.) or "dot," usually found at the top of some FTP directories on the Web.

download   To move a file from a remote computer to your local computer. When you retrieve a file from another computer, you are downloading it.

dropped   Slang for having a connection terminated, such as when you are connected to another computer via modem and for some reason your connection is severed, as in, "My connection dropped and I lost the whole file!"

e-journal   An electronic journal, usually available online. Sometimes these journals are supplementary to paper journals, but there are also e-journals starting up that are digital-only.

e-mail   Any electronic mail messaging system.

e-mail address   From the Internet perspective, a user ID + domain name (e.g., president@whitehouse.gov) that designates a person or service at a particular computer or network host connected to the Internet.

e-mail server   See *mail server*.

emoticon   See *smileys*.

encoding   The process of converting data (usually non-ASCII data) for transmission over the Internet. If not encoded, many types of files will lose attributes during transmission and be unusable by the recipient. Encoding is a common practice on the Internet. See also *binhex*, *uuencode*.

EPS (Encapsulated PostScript)   A common standard for importing and exporting PostScript language files in all environments. Most commonly used to "describe" an illustration for the purpose of including it with a PostScript data file for printing. See also *PostScript*.

ethernet   A popular local area network system allowing relatively high transmission speeds.

Eudora   A popular Macintosh and Windows e-mail management program with both freeware and commercial versions. From Qualcomm.

executables   See *applications*.

extension   Technical jargon for a feature built into a Web browser that is not actually part of the current HTML standards definition. See also *file extension*.

FAQ (Frequently Asked Questions)   Documents created by Internet users all over the world who are often experts in the particular topic area. FAQs are usually associated with and posted regularly to one or more applicable Usenet newsgroups. The term FAQ can also refer to one of the questions that is in fact frequently asked in a newsgroup, as in, "That's an FAQ from the comp.graphics newsgroup."

favorite places   See *bookmark*.

file server   See *mail server*.

file extension   Usually a two- to four-letter suffix, preceded by a period (.) and appended to the name of a file or other data entity. Sometimes it serves no other purpose than to identify the type of file, such as .hqx to indicate that a file is binhex encoded.

fixed font   A user-definable setting in most Web browsers defining which typeface on the user's computer system is used to display preformatted text. "Fixed" means the user should choose a monospace typeface such as Courier. See also *proportional font*.

flame   Virulent and often juvenile response to a message posted to a Usenet newsgroup or discussion list. "Flame wars" are not uncommon in some newsgroups. The term "flame bait" is slang for a message posted by someone designed specifically to incite readers. Flames are best dealt with by just ignoring them.

flavor   Slang term for variation, as in, "Ultrix is one of many flavors of Unix."

folder   See *directory*.

follow-up   A response to a message posted to a Usenet newsgroup where the response is posted to the newsgroup, not just to the person who posted the message.

forms   A feature supported now by most Web browsers that allows the user to type into available fields to send information to a Web server.

frames   A Web browser feature that allows specially prepared Web pages to be divided into multiple "zones" that can function independently of other elements displayed on the Web browser.

freeware   Software typically available at FTP or Web archives that is free.

FTP (File Transfer Protocol)   An Internet tool that allows you to move a file from one place to another. The word "file" is used to include any type of digital entity—documents, images, artwork, movies, sounds, and software. Anything you can store on a computer can be moved with FTP.

gateway   Can mean a number of things, but usually describes a computer or computer system that connects networks that use different communications protocols, such as the Internet and BITNET, often so users on both networks can exchange e-mail, files, and other information.

GIF (Graphics Interchange Format)   An image storage type developed originally by CompuServe and used widely on the Internet and Web.

GIF89a   A specific GIF standard that allows for other features such as transparency and animation.

gopher   An online archiving system that allows information from all over the Internet to be presented to a user in a hierarchically organized interface. For the most part, the Web has replaced the need for gopher, and so the gopher system is slowly dying.

graphical browser   A windowing interface with display capabilities beyond those of a command-line (character cell) environment, usually including the ability to display color graphics and utilize mouse-driven commands via pull-down menus, icons, and buttons. Graphical browsers are designed to access specific Internet services such as the World Wide Web.

header   Usually refers to that portion of an e-mail message that contains information about the message's origin, destination, and route. Can also refer to the same information attached to Usenet articles and even individual packets of information sent over the Internet.

helper application   An application resident on a user's computer that is designated, via a Web browser, to launch whenever a particular file type is encountered that the Web browser cannot execute.

hexadecimal   A notational system used to describe a specific color that is part of the HTML specification used to designate colors such as backgrounds, links, and table cells. See also *RGB*.

hierarchical menu   A computer menu that extends more than one level in a hierarchical fashion.

high ASCII   See *ASCII*.

home page   Generally describes the first "page" displayed when you access a Web site.

host   See *server*.

hotlist   See *bookmark*.

HTML (Hypertext Markup Language)   A text tagging language developed for formatting information available on the World Wide Web.

HTML tag   A text-based coding system used to mark text to be displayed in a particular manner (bold, italic, headline, etc.) in a Web browser. The browser program interprets the tag or tag set and converts it to the corresponding formatting in the browser window.

HTML 3.2 and 4.0   Refers to standards definitions for HTML features and encoding language governed by the W3 Consortium.

HTTP (Hypertext Transport Protocol)   Communications protocol used for transmitting information between Web servers and clients (browsers).

hypertext   A system of "point-and-click" connections between information that allow the user to jump from one information source to another on the Internet.

image map   Feature supported by most Web browsers that allows the user to click (with a mouse) on various areas of a displayed image in order to be linked to various points on the Web server. In other words, areas or zones on the image are hypertext linked to other locations.

IMHO   Common shorthand for "in my humble/honest opinion."

Internet address   See *IP address*.

Internet service provider   See *service provider*.

inline viewer   A feature of some Web browsers that allows another application to be launched and used as part of the Web browser, as opposed to being launched separately, as with helper applications. Usually requires a plug-in.

InterNIC (Internet Network Information Center)   The place where you register domain names, databases, and information services.

IP The Internet Protocol, an integral protocol used by the Internet for data transfer. See also *TCP/IP*.

IP address A domain name or numerical address identifying a computer location on the Internet. Examples: spie.org or 192.149.147.1

ISDN (Integrated Services Digital Network)   Digital (as opposed to analog) telephone service becoming increasingly available and offering relatively high bandwidths for reasonable rates.

Java   Complex programming language developed by Sun Microsystems that can be used to write applets for creating enhanced or multimedia features on a Web browser, as well as full-scale applications that will run on a variety of computer operating systems.

JavaScript A scripting language developed by Netscape that can be used within HTML and the browser to create enhanced functionality, such as on-the-fly forms calculations. Its relationship to the Java programming language is minimal.

JPEG (Joint Photographic Experts Group)   A standard for image compression and storage.

line browser   Client interface with only text-based commands and display. You can access the Web from a line browser (such as Lynx), but you cannot view any graphics, etc.

link   A connection between two documents or locations on the Internet, usually used to describe a hypertext link.

list address   In e-mail discussion lists, the place you send messages you wish to be read by the entire group (cf. *listserv address*).

listserv   Software that originated in the BITNET network of computers and is still widely used for managing discussion lists. See also *discussion list*.

listserv address   In listserv-based discussion lists, the place you send command messages (subscribe, signoff, etc.).

lossy or lossless compression   Defines whether a data compression algorithm, such as JPEG or GIF, causes the item being compressed to lose a portion of its composition during the compression process, usually resulting in a reduction in image quality.

lurking   Slang for someone who joins a discussion list but never sends messages. This is perfectly acceptable behavior.

Lynx   Popular line browser for accessing the Internet.

mail daemon   See *daemon*.

mail server   Generic term for a computer that accepts commands via e-mail and acts according to the commands, such as "send filename_x".

mailing lists   See *discussion lists*.

meta-search site   One of the publically accessible search sites on the Web that allows users to search multiple search sites at the same time.

META tags   An HTML tag specification that lets HTML authors provide keywords and descriptions to be used by some robot crawlers.

MIME (Multipurpose Internet Mail Extensions)   De facto standard for encoding e-mail to allow transmission of non-ASCII data (takes the place of old-style encoding).

mirror   FTP or Web site that contains an exact replication of files and directories of another site, usually updated regularly. Designed to distribute the load away from popular servers.

moderated   Usually refers to a newsgroup or discussion list that is monitored for propriety, relevance, length of postings, or for any number of other reasons.

Mosaic   The original Web browser from the National Center for Supercomputing Applications at the University of Illinois, Urbana/Champaign. Now obsolete.

MPEG   Multimedia Photographic Experts Group standard for encoding and compressing video signals.

MUD (Multi-User Dungeon)   Loosely used term to describe a variety of role-playing games. Usage is now expanding into experimental work done in distance education and teleconferencing development.

net   Slang meaning the Internet, as in, "I was on the net last night but didn't check my mail."

netiquette   "Net etiquette," a set of generally agreed upon rules of conduct for Internet users.

Netscape   Popular Web browser software application developed by Netscape Communications. Available for almost all current computer operating systems and platforms. Currently accounts for over half of all Web browsers in use.

newsfeed   A computer that provides another computer with regular updates of Usenet news postings. The entire Usenet system is a large "store and forward" system that relies on many computers handing off postings to other subscribing computers.

newsgroup   Any one of thousands of Usenet topical groups.

newsgroup newsreader   Any software interface that allows you to read and post to newsgroups on Usenet.

nickname   See *alias*.

NNTP (Network News Transport Protocol)   The networking protocol used by the Internet to transmit Usenet news.

node   Generally used to mean a place (computer) on the Internet with its own address.

numerical address   An Internet address described as a unique set of numerals divided by three periods, such as 149.156.221.2 See also *domain name system and IP address*.

online forms   See *forms*.

Perl   A rich programming language widely used on the Web for a variety of applications, especially the creation of CGIs.

Pine   Popular freeware e-mail management software for Unix, VMS, and other computers available from the University of Washington.

pixel   A unit of measure that describes the smallest possible value of computer display systems.

plug-in   A software file commonly used by Netscape and other browsers to add capabilities to that browser, often developed by other software vendors. For example, if you install the free Shockwave plug-in, you can then view Shockwave animations directly from your browser.

point of presence   Term sometimes used to describe a service provider's physical Internet access location, such as "CTSNet has numerous points of presence on the Internet."

POP mailbox   E-mail receiving software that uses the Post Office Protocol. Provides user with their own Internet address to receive e-mail even when their computer is not turned on or on the Internet. POP software must reside and run on a computer with a dedicated connection to the Internet.

port   A number assigned to a computer that allows access only when that number is included with the address to that computer. Also, a physical input or output connection on a computer, such as a serial or parallel port for a modem or printer.

PNG (Portable Network Graphic)   A new graphic file type currently proposed to eventually replace the widely used GIF format.

post   To add a new message to a Usenet newsgroup. See also *follow-up*.

PostScript   Page description language developed by Adobe Systems to describe pages of text and images with ASCII-based coding. Arguably the most versatile and universal language for communicating with printers. Capable of drawing to computer screens and any kind of drawing device.

preformatted text   HTML tag set <pre> and </pre> that tells a Web browser to display text exactly as it appears in the original document, including line breaks. Can be used to create vertical white space also.

PPP (Point to Point Protocol)   Increasingly common method connecting TCP/IP-based computers to each other using modem (serial) connections.

prompt   A symbol, such as % or $, used in a command-line interface to show where the user can type commands.

proportional font   A user-definable setting in most Web browsers defining which typeface on the user's computer system is used to display fully tagged text. "Proportional" means the user should choose a scalable typeface such as Times Roman or Helvetica. See also *fixed font*.

protocol   A language that computers or networks use to transmit and exchange data.

public-access Internet hosts   See *service provider*.

readme file   Generic term for any document that accompanies any software file or executable for the purpose of documenting it. Often the filename will be something like readme!, readme.txt, etc.

relevance ranking   A system of searching used by some Web sites that searches for user-provided keywords and reports back the most likely files to be of interest based on the number of "hits" of keywords found in each file. The files are usually listed in descending order in direct relation to the percentage of hits found in each.

RGB   Short for "red green blue," RGB is a notational system used by most graphics software applications to describe a specific color value. For designating colors in HTML, RGB values must be converted to hexadecimal notation.

Rich Text Format (RTF)   A common format for saving word processor documents for the purpose of reading them in another word processor while maintaining typesetting elements such as fonts, styles, tables, and similar formatting. Most word processors allow you to save a document in RTF.

robot crawler   An automated software routine used to sample and catalog a Web site's contents for the purpose of including in a searchable index, usually by one of the Internet's major search sites. Also called a spider.

robot.txt   File name of a simple text file that can be placed in the root directory of a Web server to help guide some robot crawlers so that they don't index certain files or directories. Not supported by all search sites.

root directory   The top-level directory in any hierarchical computer directory structure.

router   See *gateway*.

search site   Any of the major public servers on the World Wide Web that offer free searchable indexes of the Internet's contents (e.g., AltaVista, Excite, Yahoo, etc.).

server   Generically, refers to a computer you log into and either use or retrieve data from (cf. *client*).

server-side   Usually refers to a function that is handled by a Web server, such as a server-side image map, as opposed to the Web browser. Generally only used if a comparable client-side functionality is not available, because it places a heavier load on the Web server.

service provider   Term used in this book and elsewhere to define any organization that provides access to the Internet for a fee.

SGML (Standard Generalized Markup Language)   The de facto standard for tagging and encoding of complex information (e.g., scientific journals) for redistribution or other uses.

shareware   Publicly archived commercial software released with a "try before you buy" type of licensing agreement, usually described with accompanying documentation.

shell account   A user account on a Unix-based computer.

Shockwave   Software plug-in developed by Macromedia to create multimedia applications that can be viewed from the Web.

signature   Several lines of text many people append to their outgoing e-mail messages that provide contact information such as affiliation, address, and telephone number. Often e-mail software can be set to append this information automatically.

site   Generic term for a computer or server on the Web, as in, "I found a great site yesterday while looking for some stat software."

smileys   Use of ASCII characters to create facial expressions that suggest tone of voice and avoid miscommunications. Most common is the :-) smiley.

SMTP (Simple Mail Transport Protocol)   The protocol standard used on the Internet to support transport of e-mail.

snail mail   Slang for regular postal (paper) mail service.

spider   See *robot crawler*.

Sprint   One of the major Internet backbone providers.

streaming   Technology being developed to bring real-time audio and video to Web browsers using compression and Java-type applets. Allows the video or audio clip to be sent to the browser/applet and, after front-loading a small portion, begin streaming the signal continuously to the applet, where it is played for the user.

style sheets   See *Cascading Style Sheets*.

surfing   Slang for browsing computers on the Internet.

tables   Feature supported by most Web browsers that allows properly tagged text to be displayed in word processor style tables format. Good for displaying data best viewed in a row-and-column format, such as financial documents.

tag   See *HTML tag*.

tag set   Term used to describe an HTML tag that requires an opening and closing tag, such as <strong> and </strong>.

TCP/IP (Transmission Control Protocol/Internet Protocol)   The underlying protocol used by the Internet that makes telnet, FTP, electronic mail, and other services possible among the many different computer types on the Internet.

telnet   Standard protocol allowing one computer to access and utilize another computer.

terminal emulation   A software process by which one computer type can emulate another, thus allowing each to communicate. For example, DEC developed the VT series of terminals (VT100, VT200, etc.) for their mainframes, so any terminal emulation software that emulates a VT terminal can operate in that computer's environment.   Most telecommunications (modem) software will emulate a variety of terminal types.

text-based   See *command-line interface*.

thread   A topic that is being discussed in a successive series of messages from two or more participants within a newsgroup or discussion lists.

transparency   Usually refers to a GIF image file that has one or more colors designated as transparent when displayed in a browser window, meaning that the page background pattern or color will show through.

Unix   A multiuser, multitasking operating system that includes many utilities for Internet access. Most Web sites on the Internet are still Unix-based, although this predominance is slowly changing.

unmoderated   See *moderated*.

upload   To move a file from your (local) computer to another (remote) computer. See *download*.

URL (Uniform Resource Locator)   The standard syntax for Internet resource addresses, such as **http://www.spie.org** or **ftp://www.nasa.gov**.

Usenet   A global bulletin board service that uses the Internet as an access point. It is composed of thousands of topical groupings that you can read to keep current on the discussions in those groups. Usenet is not a physical entity like the Internet, but rather a software-based structure accessible to Internet hosts.

user ID   The name by which someone can access a computer system. Synonymous with username.

username   See *user ID*.

UUCP (Unix-to-Unix Copy)   (a) A method of sending files and e-mail via modem telecommunications that was originally developed for use between Unix computers; or (b) a network that currently uses the UUCP software for transmitting Usenet news and e-mail.

uuencode   Standard for encoding non-ASCII files and applications for transmission over the Internet. See also *attachment*.

VGA   Short for "Video Graphics Adaptor," which is the original Windows video standard limited to only 256 color values.

Virtual Library   See *W3 Virtual Library*.

Web   See *World Wide Web*.

Web server   Any computer on the Web that offers HTML-encoded files that can be read by a Web browser.

World Wide Web   A client-server software interaction that uses HTTP and HTML (hypertext protocol and tagging conventions) to organize and present information and services throughout the Internet.

W3 Consortium   The group of industry representatives that govern and publish HTML specifications.

W3 Virtual Library   A large collection of subject-specific indexes on the Web. **http://www.w3.org/hypertext/DataSources/bySubject/Overview.html**.

WYSIWYG   Acronym for "what you see is what you get," generally used to describe software or interfaces that are graphics based as opposed to text based. A "WYSIWYG editor" therefore usually refers to HTML editing software that lets you compose Web pages without having to type in or see the actual HTML tags.

BIBLIOGRAPHY

Books about the Internet and World Wide Web have quickly become a highly profitable niche for publishers. This means that a glut of books have hit the shelves in the race to capitalize on this topic's popularity. So, if you find yourself at the local bookstore and feel the urge to buy something, there are a few publishers that I would recommend as consistently good bets. That is, they generally sign high-quality authors who get good reviews. These are, in no particular order, O'Reilly & Associates, Hayden Books, Sams Publishing, and Peachpit Press. Of course, this is not meant to imply that books from other publishers are not equally good or better; there are certainly some great books out there (like this one!) from smaller or less well known publishers.

Nearly every book referenced in this bibliography is there because I have either read it, heard good things about it, or read positive reviews from others who have read it. You can often find reviews and real reader comments on these books at online booksellers such as Amazon (**http://www.amazon.com**).

Creating Great Web Graphics, Laurie McCanna, MIS Press (1997). ISBN: 1558285504.

Creating Killer Web Sites, Second Edition, David S. Siegel, Hayden Books (1997). ISBN: 1568304331

Designing with JavaScript : Creating Dynamic Web Pages, Nick Heinle, O'Reilly & Associates (1997). ISBN: 1565923006.

Designing Web Graphics 2, Lynda Weinman, New Riders Publishing (1997). ISBN: 1562057154.

Directory of Electronic Journals, Newsletters, and Academic Discussion Lists, Lisabeth A. King, Diane Kovacs, Ann Okerson, Office of Scientific & Academic Publishing (1996). ISBN: 9995288850.

Dynamic HTML: A Primer, Simon St. Laurent, MIS Press (1997). ISBN: 1558285695

Finding It on the Internet, Paul Gilster, John Wiley & Sons, Inc. (1996). ISBN: 0471126950.

FrontPage '97 Web Designer's Guide: Supercharging World Wide Web Sites With the FrontPage Visual Publishing System, Gary L. Allman, Jason Ledtke, Michael C. Stinson, Waite Group Pr. (1997). ISBN: 157169045X

The Guide to Internet Job Searching, Margaret Riley et al. and Public Library Association, Vgm Career Horizons (1996). ISBN: 0844281972.

How to Set Up and Maintain a Web Site, Lincoln D. Stein, Addison-Wesley Publishing Co. (1997). ISBN: 0201634627.

HTML Unleashed, Rick Darnell, Michael Larson, Dmitry Kirsanov, Sams (1997). ISBN: 1575212994.

HTML Sourcebook: A Complete Guide to HTML 3.2 and HTML Extensions, Ian S. Graham, John Wiley & Sons (1997). ISBN: 0471175757.

Internet Audio Sourcebook, Lee Purcell, Jordan Hemphill, John Wiley & Sons (1997). ISBN: 0471191507.

The Internet Power Toolkit : Cutting-Edge Tools & Techniques for Power Users, Sean Carton and Gareth Branwyn, Ventana (1996). ISBN: 1566043298.

Internet Research Companion, Geoffrey W. McKim, Que Corp. (1997). ISBN: 1575760509.

The Internet Searcher's Handbook : Locating Information, People & Software, Peter Morville et al., Neal Schuman Publishers (1996). ISBN: 1555702368.

The Internet Science, Research, and Technology Yellow Pages, Rick Stout and Morgan Davis, Osborne McGraw-Hill (1996). ISBN: 0078821878.

Internet Starter Kit for Macintosh, Fourth Edition, Adam C. Engst and William Dickson, Hayden Books (1996). ISBN: 1-56830-294-0. Includes software on CD-ROM.

Internet Starter Kit for Windows 95, Adam C. Engst, Corwin S. Low, Stanley K. Orchard, Hayden Books (1996). ISBN: 1568302606.

Java in a Nutshell: A Desktop Quick Reference (The Java Series), David Flanagan, O'Reilly & Associates (1997). ISBN: 156592262X.

Javascript: The Definitive Guide (Nutshell Handbook), David Flanagan, O'Reilly & Associates (1997). ISBN: 1565922344.

Manufacturing and the Internet, Richard G. Mathieu, Inst. of Industrial Engineers (1996). ISBN: 0898061644.

Medicine and the Internet: Introducing Online Resources and Terminology, Bruce C. McKenzie, Oxford Univ. Press (1996). ISBN: 0192627058.

Neal Schuman Complete Internet Companion for Librarians, Allen C. Benson, Neal Schuman Publications (1997). ISBN: 1555703178.

NetResearch: Finding Information Online, Daniel J. Barrett, O'Reilly & Assoc. (1997). ISBN: 1-56592-245-X.

Netscape ONE Developer's Guide, William Robert Stanek, Blake Benet Hall, Sams (1997). ISBN: 1575210940.

The New Internet Business Book, Jill H. Ellsworth, Matthew V. Ellsworth, John Wiley & Sons (1996). ISBN: 0471141607.

The Non-Designer's Web Book: An Easy Guide to Creating, Designing, and Posting Your Own Web Site, Robin Williams, John Tollett, Peachpit Press (1997). ISBN: 020168859X.

Official Netscape Javascript 1.2 Book: The Nonprogrammer's Guide to Creating Interactive Web Pages, Peter Kent, John Kent, Ventana Communications (1997). ISBN: 1566046750.

Official Netscape Guide to Internet Research: For Windows & Macintosh, Tara Calishain, Ventana Communications (1996). ISBN: 1566046041

The Online Deskbook: Online Magazine's Essential Desk Reference for Online and Internet Searchers, Mary Ellen Bates, Reva Basch (Editor), Independent Pub Group (1996). ISBN: 0910965196

Practical Unix and Internet Security, Simson Garfinkel and Gene Spafford, O'Reilly & Assoc. (1996). ISBN: 1565921488.

Rittner's Field Guide to Usenet, Don Rittner, Mns (1997). ISBN: 0937666505.

Science and Technology on the Internet : An Instructional Guide (Internet Workshop Series, No. 4), Gail P. Clement, Library Solutions Inst. (1996). ISBN: 1882208129.

Secrets of Successful Web Sites: Project Management on the World Wide Web, David S. Siegel, Hayden Books (1997).ISBN: 1568303823

Teach Yourself Web Publishing with HTML 3.2 in 14 Days: Premier Edition, Laura Lemay, Sams Publishing (1996). ISBN: 1575210967.

Virtual Reality: Strategies for Intranet and World Wide Web Applications, John Vacca, Computer Technology Research (1996). ISBN: 1566079713.

The VRML 2.0 Handbook: Building Moving Worlds on the Web, Jed Hartman, Josie Wernecke, Addison-Wesley (1996). ISBN: 0201479443.

Web Authoring Desk Reference, Aaron Weiss, Rebecca Tapley, Robert C., Benedict, Kim Daniels, Hayden Books (1997). ISBN: 1568303521

Web Designer's Guide to Style Sheets, Steven Mulder, Hayden Books (1997). ISBN: 1568303068

Web Search Strategies, Bryan Pfaffenberger, M&T Books (1996). ISBN: 1558284702.

Web Security & Commerce, Simson Garfinkel, Gene Spafford, O'Reilly & Associates (1997). ISBN: 1565922697.

Web Server Technology: The Advanced Guide for World Wide Web Information Providers, Nancy J. Yeager, Robert E. McGrath, Morgan Kaufman Publishers (1996). ISBN: 155860376X.

Web Site Source Book 1997: A Guide to Major U.S. Businesses, Organizations, Agencies, Institutions, and Other Information Resources on the World Wide Web, Kay Gill, Darren L. Smith, Editors, Omnigraphics, Inc. (1997). ISBN: 0780801695.

The Whole Internet User's Guide & Catalog (Nutshell Handbook), Ed Krol, Bruce C. Klopfenstein, Wadsworth Publishing Co. (1996). ISBN: 0534506747.

The World Wide Web Unleashed, John December, Sams (1997). ISBN: 157521184X.

Windows 95 and NT 4.0 Registry & Customization Handbook, Jerry Honeycutt, Bernard Farrell, Rich Kennelly, Jerry Millsaps, Que Education & Training (1997). ISBN: 0789708426.

Windows 95 Communication and Online Secrets, David W. Boles, IDG Books (1996). ISBN: 1568848374.

INDEX